ALBION

About the author

Andy Ross is a philosopher, born in Britain. He earned four degrees in Oxford and London, did research in mathematical logic, and worked for 25 years in Germany in science and technology. He then returned to Britain and worked for five years as a UK parliamentary assistant. He blogs at:

www.andyross.net

By the same author

LIFEBALL
MINDWORLDS
G.O.D. IS GREAT
PHILOSOPHER
CORAL
BRITIZEN JON

ALBION

LOOKING FOR WISDOM
IN TORY ENGLAND

By Andy Ross

R**O**VER
BRITAIN

A Rover Book

An imprint of Ross Verlag Britain

Copyright © J. Andrew Ross 2022

Text build 20220228

ISBN 979-8-4171-3120-2

Contents

'We shall require a substantially new manner of thinking if mankind is to survive.'
Albert Einstein

'The best argument against democracy is a five-minute conversation with the average voter.'
Winston Churchill

The question

In Brussels, on 22 January 1972, British prime minister Edward Heath signs the treaty of accession to the European Communities. The UK duly becomes a member of the EC on 1 January 1973.

———

In Poole Civic Centre, in the early hours of 24 June 2016, I'm partying with MPs, MEPs, local councillors, television crews, and others. At 4:40 local time, our big screens show BBC news anchor David Dimbleby announcing: 'The British people have spoken, and the answer is: We're out.'

The electorate has ordered Brexit.

———

In my Poole flat, on the afternoon of 24 December 2020, I stand in front of my television as prime minister Boris Johnson makes a big announcement: 'We have taken back control of our laws and our destiny. We have taken back control of every jot and tittle of our regulation, in a way that is complete and unfettered.'

The government has delivered Brexit.

———

In London, exactly fifty years after Ted Heath signed the treaty of accession, Johnson's government is in its death throes. Its sins are many and vile, and behind them all looms Brexit. A Conservative government's casual disregard for its European and Irish partners has led to a meltdown of trust all round.

———

British Conservatives are commonly called Tories. The word 'Tory' originated in an old Irish word for an outlaw or robber. The name arose when Conservative rulers in London presided over grievous atrocities in Ireland.

———

I've seen how the last three Tory prime ministers have bungled Brexit. I've formed my own opinion as to what went wrong.

In this book, I tell the story as I experienced it. I hope to show just how lamentable the episode has been and how far Conservative responsibility for it extends.

I don't see myself as a political animal. I'm a philosopher who has enjoyed a good career in science and technology. All this Brexit nonsense has burst in like a mad killer on my inner peace.

Throughout the story, I explore a big question: What deeper forces led to Brexit, what horrors has it exposed, how can Britain and Europe move on from the mess, and by what right do I presume to pass judgement on it all?

The story is personal. It involves a deep dive into my psyche and into personal and philosophical issues surrounding the turmoil. No one can plough through a big book on politics without some redeeming narrative purpose, and my purpose is to achieve a wider and deeper understanding of things.

A personal story cannot be objective. For that reason, I've bagged the psychic stuff in a fictional thread. I hope this packaging makes the book read more like a novel than a political history.

In short, enjoy.

PART 1
EXASPERATION

January 2013 – July 2016

'The EU needs to change.'
David Cameron

1.   Back to Blighty

London, January 2013: Prime minister David Cameron gives a big speech on Britain's membership of the European Union:

'Seventy years ago, Europe was being torn apart by its second catastrophic conflict in a generation.'

After the two wars, the European project changed everything: 'What Churchill described as the twin marauders of war and tyranny have been almost entirely banished from our continent.'

Cameron says he'll never forget his visit to Berlin after the Wall came down. But now he speaks for Britain.

He cites three challenges: 'First, the problems in the eurozone are driving fundamental change in Europe. Second, there is a crisis of European competitiveness, as other nations across the world soar ahead. And third, there is a gap between the EU and its citizens, which has grown dramatically in recent years.'

His vision for revising the terms of UK membership of the EU adds a zinger: 'The next Conservative manifesto in 2015 will ask for a mandate from the British people for a Conservative government to negotiate a new settlement with our European partners in the next parliament. … And when we have negotiated that new settlement, we will give the British people a referendum with a very simple in or out choice: to stay in the EU on these new terms or come out altogether.'

———

Germany, June 2013: A row of about forty cardboard boxes forms a new parapet in my living room. Beside the walls, stacks of white planks lie where my IKEA bookcases stood a week ago.

The doorbell rings. I let my guests in.

'Wow,' says Angie, 'Are these all just books?' She's maybe a decade younger than me, English by birth, tall and athletic, with tangled straw hair and irregular front teeth. She's dressed in jeans, a baggy sweatshirt, and old sneakers.

'Mostly, yeah.' I'm ready for our dinner date in jeans and a polo shirt, still barefoot. 'I accumulated a ton of them in my quarter-century here. I've given away a lot already.'

'We would have this many boxes too,' says Rolf in his German accent. He's Angie's husband. He looks much like me, with average height and build and light colouring, except that his hair and beard are a few notches longer than my fierce buzz-cuts.

We go off to dine in downtown Schwetzingen. The restaurant faces onto the busy market square, and we sit outside to watch the people go by. The square is a paved hectare in front of a massive baroque palace to the southwest, framed now by golden light, where the Rhineland Palatinate princes lived long ago.

'Tell me again why you're moving back to England,' says Angie. She and I met decades ago in Heidelberg, editing physics books in the modern Springer publishing palace beside the river Neckar.

'My mother's getting old, and my sister is finding it hard work, so I agreed to help. Also, being there will refresh my English.'

'I get enough refreshment with my book series.' Angie manages a series on the frontiers of physics. She has a Cambridge doctorate in physics. I broke off my Oxford doctorate.

'Any new books I can help with?'

'Something on the discovery of the Higgs boson, of course, but that may be too technical for you. There's one coming up on con-sciousness and one on cosmology you might like.'

Scientists announced the Higgs discovery less than a year ago at the Large Hadron Collider just a few hours south of where we sit. Physics nerds worldwide shared my joy that day.

'Good. I'll need them to keep up my contacts here.'

Rolf speaks: 'What will you do in England?' He and Angie met at Springer too. He's an independent journalist and publisher.

I frown. 'British politics is getting interesting. I need to scope it out and see what I can do.'

———

Days before the summer solstice, I'm speeding along the final stretch of the E40 trunk road around Brussels and past Dunkirk to Calais. The fields around me are flat and open, and the sky above is blue and dotted with white clouds.

I'm on my way from Schwetzingen to Poole on the south coast of England. My luggage is packed in bags behind the rear seats. I'm alone with my thoughts.

I joined the E40 at Aachen, the city where Charlemagne was crowned emperor of most of central Europe in the year 800 of the Common Era. The First Reich endured for a thousand years until Napoleon dissolved it. The Second Reich began with Otto von Bismarck in 1871 and ended in defeat in 1918. After a doomed German republic ended in 1933, the reviled Third Reich ended in defeat in 1945. That German century was a bit of a bummer.

It takes a couple of hours to drive from Aachen through the little kingdom of Belgium and into France. A hundred years ago, Britain and France declared war on Germany for driving into Belgium. Twenty-five years later, the Germans did it again. They defeated the Brits, who fell back in disarray onto Dunkirk. I speed past Dunkirk in a minute.

The European Union is the outcome of a lot of grim history. And thanks to Anglo-French stubbornness, it isn't German or a Reich at all. I barely even notice crossing all those borders.

At the Calais passenger terminal for the Eurotunnel, I drive onto the Shuttle train that passes under the antitank ditch to Dover. There I sit patiently in the car, munching sandwiches, listening to music, and rocking to the rhythm of steel wheels rolling on steel rails, with only a brief excursion to apply a matched pair of white anti-dazzle stickers to my headlights.

I've taken this route back to England almost every year since the tunnel opened in 1994. My car is now a BMW hatchback built for speeding along the autobahn. Hard springs and abundant horsepower make short work of the dash to England and back.

I made my move to Germany in 1987. Prime minister Margaret Thatcher – victrix of the Falkland war – had just won her third election victory by a landslide, and I saw no profit in continuing to teach physics in London under her rule. The land of thinkers and poets was the place for a philosopher with big ideas.

My exodus was more of a homecoming. The new and improved Federal Republic felt far better than the rainswept midden occupied by Thatcherite Tories on the islands in the North Sea. Years of exile turned into decades of happiness until the call back to Blighty.

Once I've cleared Dover, I motor northward to the M25 ring road around London, take the M3 exit for the Southwest, and pause at Fleet to phone my mother Liz and warn her I'm on my way.

An hour or two later, I drive my white charger up a steep driveway onto a courtyard behind a big Edwardian house on a hilltop. The house is on a residential road in a quiet part of Poole, and Liz is in the ground-floor flat. I ease myself slowly out of my cockpit and stretch in the dappled evening sunlight under a pine tree. The row of four garages in front of me looks tatty and tumbledown.

Liz comes out of the back door to greet me. She's going on ninety years old, still fit but getting slower. Her nimbus of silver hair frames a crumpled face animated by good cheer and she glows with inner peace. She's pleased to see me back safe and well.

———

Weeks later, I drive back to the house on the hill and park beside a Volkswagen. I admire the row of garages behind the house. A few days ago, I helped a neighbour repair them. That's the young surfer dude who lives upstairs with a wife and baby son. Dude and I tar-papered the roof and sealed over the cracks to make it rainproof.

My next chore is to clear the junk in Liz's garage.

Today I'm clad in a linen suit with an open shirt and perforated white rubber shoes without socks. My hair is short and silvering, and my chin is lightly stubbled. I look a bit like Forrest Gump.

Liz's flat is spacious and airy, with big windows looking out all around over surrounding houses and trees. The back door, her main threshold, opens into a wide and cluttered kitchen. She's lived alone in the flat since Don had to be moved into a care home, and she's happy here. For me, used to a modern German apartment, it takes some getting used to.

I walk into the kitchen to find Liz with Helen, my sister. Helen is big and blonde, two years younger than me, recently retired from a career in the National Health Service. She has five grown kids and lives with her husband and a dog in a former council house.

'Well, I've done it now,' I say. 'Decided to crown my return to the Sceptred Isles by joining the Conservative and Unionist Party. I've just signed up and paid my dues at the little office where our member of parliament holds his weekly surgeries. The secretary has given me a list of party events to fill out my social calendar, and now I'm ready to go. A life in the party awaits me.'

While Liz fixes me with a sharp glare, Helen replies wearily: 'So, you've joined the Tories. Good luck with that. Why?'

'If it was good enough for Ma and Don, it's good enough for me. Seriously, it's a way to get reacquainted with British life and to develop a social network.'

'Sounds dire … By the way, did you fix your car issues?'

I take a deep sigh. 'Yes, after a nightmare of hassle and expense, but my German car is now street-legal for British roads, if you can call them that. Half the roads in Poole haven't been resurfaced for decades. Unbelievable negligence!'

'Thank austerity for that,' she says. 'And be grateful you don't work in a hospital. What did you have to do to the car?'

I sigh again. 'Basically, new headlights and new speedometer. But even that was expensive. Just because Brits are too stubborn to drive on the right side of the road.'

Helen looks unmoved. 'You could have sold it and bought a British car with the steering wheel on the right side.'

'But I like my car. It's my ticket back to Germany. All this fuss is too idiotic. We're in the EU, so why haven't we standardised?'

'Because this is Britain. Why standardise things when we can make life difficult for foreigners and immigrants?'

Liz joins in: 'Why should we adapt to the Europeans? Let them adapt to us if they want to drive over here. I'm sick and tired of bossy bureaucrats in Brussels telling us what we can and can't do.'

I look down at the *Daily Telegraph* newspaper on the table. Liz was quite liberal when she was young, but once she took up with Don after divorcing Bob – father of Helen and me – she soon joined the local Conservatives and turned into another Poole Tory.

I'm sure the *Telegraph* has slowly poisoned her mind with its daily doses of nationalist propaganda. Don was a lifelong Tory and read it too. But then he sank to the *Daily Express*, a demotic tabloid rag distinguished only by its vicious Europhobia.

'Careful, Ma,' I say. 'You're showing your age. If you were still as young and idealistic as me, you'd know joining the EU was one of the best things to happen in this country in my lifetime.'

———

I'm back, not only in the English corner of Europe but also in the urban landscape of my younger years.

A reminder pops up when I go to a theatre at the Poole Arts Centre with Helen and her husband David. He's a technical writer and a sports car buff, but he's also a member of the amateur choral and drama group that's staging the musical spectacle we've gone to see. After the show, we meet another group member, an old friend called Deborah, or Deb.

A spot of back story may help you here. As a teenager, I worked on Saturdays at a local Woolworths shop as a stockroom boy to pay for my motorbike. Deb worked there too as a Saturday girl at the toy counter. As I pushed my barrow past her toys, we'd exchange a few words. She was lovely, with long blonde hair and a face so fair it graced a pin-up picture in the local paper, but we were both very shy. Somehow, I found the courage to invite her to my eighteenth birthday party. To the sweet sounds of the Beatles' *Sergeant Pepper* album, we enjoyed a glorious snog.

We didn't date again and soon went our own ways. Decades passed. I met girls galore and forgot her.

Deb is now a dignified lady with a divorce behind her and a new man beside her. But meeting her again has revived old feelings. She could make life fun again.

Three men are dominating the British debate about relations with Europe: Nigel Farage, David Cameron, and Boris Johnson.

Nigel Farage has the air of a chap who enjoys downing pints with his mates in the pub. But he's a canny chap. At boarding school he traded in schoolboy treats, and then he followed his stockbroker father to work in the City as a commodity broker.

The young Farage joined the Conservative party but resigned in protest when Tory prime minister John Major signed the Maastricht treaty that formally founded the European Union.

Farage was a founder member of the United Kingdom Independence Party. He was then elected as a member of the European parliament for South East England and became the UKIP leader. Dismissed at first as a nonentity leading a fringe party of nutters and fruitcakes, he now basks in name recognition nationwide.

In the local elections in May, UKIP made big gains. From just eight councillors in total before the elections, the party now boasts almost a hundred and fifty. UKIP is on a roll.

Farage is leading a crusade to free the UK from the fatal decay he sees seeping from a bloated and corrupt EU bureaucracy. In early June, he had this to say: 'If you want real political corruption then you have to look to Brussels ... In Westminster, lobbyists are scrabbling for crumbs from the legislative cake. It is Brussels where the size and the ingredients of that cake are laid out.'

David Cameron is a quite different kind of politician. His father was a stockbroker, too, but young Dave was more of a swot and went to Eton and Oxford. As Tory prime minister leading a coalition government with the Liberal Democrats, he supports British membership of the EU. But he's now on the defensive against Tory right-wingers and UKIP.

He stated his policy in January. Now he says: 'All Conservative cabinet ministers agree that we should be spending the next period improving the EU and improving our relations with the EU and then putting that choice to the British public in a referendum. That is our policy.'

Boris Johnson is something else again. Born in New York, schooled for years in Brussels, and groomed like Dave at Eton and Oxford, where they were drinking pals, Boris spent years as a journalist in Brussels and gained fame for writing scurrilous nonsense about the EU. He was elected to parliament in 2001 but later stood down to become Mayor of London. His finest hour as mayor was in August 2012, when he got stuck on a zipwire while wearing a blue helmet and carrying two little union jacks, where he passed the time mugging for the cameras like a clown.

Johnson backs the prime minister. He says 'David Cameron is bang on' about renegotiating UK membership of the EU.

Russell Brand, a comedian whose own hipster politics are way out left, wrote after interviewing the clownish mayor: 'Eye-to-eye, the bumbling bonhomie appeared to be a lacquer of likability over a living obelisk of corporate power. Johnson is the most dangerous politician in Britain, precisely because of his charm. The members of the Conservative party that are rallying to install him as leader are those to the right of David Cameron.'

Johnson is a devoted fan of Winston Churchill. His view of Europe is saturated with stereotypes from the Second World War. For him, America is the shining city on a hill, the former British colony that became a beacon for mankind, whereas the continental power that Churchill fought in two world wars was a frightful beast, an evil empire, and anything that grows from its bloodied soil has a lingering taint.

This is the British bugaboo I'm facing back in Blighty.

2. The sound of victory

On the last Saturday of August, I go swimming off the wide beach of Poole Bay. Up to my neck in cooling water, I look up to see a Hawker Hunter doing a fast low pass over my head. The former RAF jet fighter is silent as it approaches at transonic speed, then as it passes overhead its tailwind bathes me in glorious thunder. I see 'Miss Demeanour' sports a snazzy yellow, red, white, and blue paint scheme. Nice job.

The Bournemouth Air Festival is a big attraction on the local tourist calendar, and an estimated four hundred thousand people pack the beaches as I swim. The mighty British Hunter is waving the flag for all the foreign visitors in the crowd.

The final day of the festival is Sunday. I go along with Liz, Helen, and her husband David to a hotel on the Bournemouth sea-front cliffs. We've booked a table for tea in the clifftop garden.

We sit around the table under a parasol to shade us from the hot solar rays. The location gives us a good view of the show and lets us enjoy a running commentary from a radio jock manning a booth in the garden. I've brought along my father's old wartime binoculars and stand up to spot the aircraft.

The supersonic Eurofighter Typhoon is a star of the show. It roars through blue sky over the seascape and along the crowded shoreline. It flies parallel to the clifftop, almost level with it, then flips upward and accelerates vertically. Its twin afterburners pour out hot thunder and glow like taillights as the image shrinks into the deepening blue of space. *Herrlich!*

I've been an aviation buff since my teenage years, when I biked with my mates to a sleepy airport near Bournemouth to see an earlier generation of aircraft take off and land. I recall fondly the Meteor and Vampire jets, the Dakotas, the Tiger Moths, the Doves and

Herons, and even the Superfreighters with their big nose doors and fat bellies that ferried cars over the Channel to France.

That English boyhood is now fifty years behind me. I've outgrown the curious ways of the proud people who live on the British archipelago I once called home. With the vintage binoculars around my neck, floppy sunhat on my head, and linen suit over a blue shirt on my body, I look English enough, but I still feel German.

Standing on the manicured hotel lawn, I admire the genteel crowd of local citizens at table, observing their bliss to be English, at tea, on Sunday. They're quietly enjoying the show over scones with jam and cream and pots of tea and coffee.

It's an idyllic scene. The Edwardian hotel looms over a terrace with maybe a dozen tables. Its guests live regally in a top-dog nation with a Conservative prime minister who can say with pride that all's quiet on the home front. The guests are clad in classic summer style, with light slacks and blazers and straw hats and airy frocks and sandals. Liz and Helen wear printed cotton, and tall, thin David sports a polo top and corduroys.

At the clifftop end of the garden, between big loudspeakers, the master of ceremonies continues his running commentary on the aerial spectacle. The sound is staccato and occasionally punctuated by blasts of stirring martial music I recall from patriotic British movies in years gone by, but his words come through.

'That, ladies and gentlemen, was the Typhoon, the Royal Air Force's top gun fighter, a worthy successor to the immortal Spitfire, the Hunter, and the Lightning of former years. And now, to warm the hearts of all of you who thrill to tales of our Finest Hour in 1940, we have the Battle of Britain Memorial Flight. Look to your left, and you can see them fly in. Today in the flight we have the Lancaster with a Spitfire and a Hurricane at the wings.'

I scan the flight line and see the trio approaching slowly. I raise my binoculars for a closer look. The black bulk of the Lancaster looms first, its glazed cockpit facets glinting in the sun and its four spinning propellers blurred against the blue sky.

'Here they come, a glorious sight. The mighty Avro Lancaster was the mainstay of the bombing war over Germany in the latter half of the war. With its four Merlin engines, it carried over twice the bomb load of the American heavies. Over seven thousand were built, and almost half of them were lost in action. Truly a legend.'

I recall the finer details all too well. Between 1943 and 1945, Lancaster heavy bombers dropped some six hundred thousand tons of bombs, at night and with lamentably poor aim, onto Germany. As well as high-explosive blockbusters, they dropped some fifty million fire-bombs to burn down buildings in crowded cities.

The morality of the British bombing war over Germany was hotly disputed even then. RAF Bomber Command chief Arthur 'Butcher' Harris took a lot of flak for his relentless policy of targeting civilian areas with his carpet-bombing raids.

Seventy years before this Lancaster flies by me, in Operation Gomorrah in July 1943, hundreds of these arson machines caused a big firestorm in Hamburg that in a single hellish night incinerated as many people as all those killed during the entire German bombing campaign over England in 1940 and 1941 that Brits call the Blitz.

In all, British and American bombing raids over Germany slaughtered between four and six hundred thousand civilians. Aerial bombing on all sides became a monstrous orgy of mass murder, a homicidal jamboree where aircrews were licenced to kill without any regard for the infernal horrors their bombs were causing on the ground.

I feel I know both sides of the human story. The British tale of heroic duty I know from boyhood. But now I also know the stories of those hapless German citizens, betrayed by a criminal government, who met their nightmarish deaths under merciless hailstorms of bombs. In human terms, the moral balance was a total bust.

Yet unbelievably, the patriotic master of ceremonies on the hotel lawn is praising this paragon of British aircraft, the Lancaster, this weapon of mass destruction, painted soot-black and sporting an array of raid checks below the cockpit, as if it were a dispenser of peace and happiness to all mankind.

Well, perhaps it was. Perhaps there's no beauty without pain. Perhaps millions of butchered and roasted corpses are the price we pay for a world worth living in. If so, someone had to be the first to harken to the call of nature and kick off the butchery. A maniac called Adolf Hitler caught the fateful scent. The final slaughter was epic, historic, and the beauty that bloomed from the bloodied soil was wondrous to behold.

Standing with my binoculars, I boggle at the moral idiocy of it all. My boyhood was showered with war comics and war toys that hammered home the doctrine of righteous anger. If you're at war, don't hold back. Kill your enemies, burn them to ashes, demolish their cities, root out their cultures, and reduce any survivors to gathering broken bricks in a hellscape.

I think it's time to move on. Nations need to do better than that. I feel relieved that the European Union now puts such murderous national hostilities, at least between Britain and Germany, firmly in the past, where they belong.

The radio jock continues: 'And here is the Hurricane, the workhorse of the Battle of Britain, a strong and stable gun platform for shooting down bombers. And above it, turning now to show off its elliptical wings, is the beautiful Spitfire, the greatest fighter of the war, a legend of its time and ever since, so good that even the German pilots envied it.'

I study the pair. The Hurricane is a later model with four cannons in the wings, painted to resemble the planes that flew in South East Asia Command against the Japanese. The Spitfire is a later model too, this one a Mark Nine, the variant that corrected the flaws in the earlier marks that made them easy prey for raiding Focke-Wulf fighters after the Blitz. But, hey, poetic licence.

The commentator rattles on: 'Feast your eyes, ladies and gentlemen, on this glorious and historic sight. The Spitfire was developed near here at Supermarine, in Southampton, from a purebred line of racing seaplanes. Just listen to that Rolls-Royce Merlin engine, to the six Merlin engines of the three planes in front of us, to that unforgettable purring sound – the sound of victory.'

It is a lovely sound, I admit. I recall the purring whoosh from the Merlin in the American Mustang fighter that flew a thrilling low pass in the Spielberg movie *Empire of the Sun*, set in wartime China, where the English schoolboy hero jumped and waved with excitement and shouted: 'Cadillac of the skies!'

Victory or not, I don't associate such sentiments with a noisy engine. I watch the warbirds fly away and lower my binoculars.

I turn from the flight line and sit back down at the table with my folks. Shaking my head in disbelief, I say: 'This commentary is shockingly bad. It's shameless jingoism.'

Helen smiles: 'But this is Britain. We're proud of our history. Don't you remember your model aircraft?'

'I remember.' In my childhood and early teens, I made dozens of plastic scale models of aircraft, almost all of warbirds from the Second World War. I pursued this obsession relentlessly, reading about arcane variants in hobby mags and taking extra trouble to craft my own replicas of them. I did the same for model tanks and military vehicles, where I built armies for all the opposed powers in the war. And I built a navy of little waterline models of warships.

For the English schoolboy growing up in postwar Britain, all this was more than a hobby. It was a hands-on education in modern engineering and technology, in world history and politics, and in the moral realities that lay behind the pious sermons of the philosophers. The lesson was a hard one.

What I learned is that the world is brutal. Get armed up and fight your corner. Let millions of corpses pave your path. Victory is all that counts. Churchill said so.

Despite the best efforts of my grammar school to civilise me, I almost drowned in a toxic swamp of war memorabilia. I learned science and maths and languages, but my priorities came from war studies. My first words of German were for Panzers, U-boats, Stukas, V-weapons, and other such tools of depravity.

It wasn't just me. Postwar Britain was a world of war-surplus shops, of Churchillian metaphors, of war movies and military parades, where Europe was flagged as ground zero for a nuclear war that would leave Germany a radioactive desert.

What saved me was physics. My studies forged ahead, the Apollo programme dramatized the dream of a human future in space, and my headmaster sent me as the school representative to an international congress of young scientists in London. A new world was revealed, and the schoolboy emerged from the swamp.

I snap back to the moment: 'But I grew out of it.'

Helen shrugs: 'Be charitable. Some people need more time.'

———

I've developed a casual interest in seeing the latest shows put on by the local amateur choral and drama group. Deb sings in the choir, so sometimes I see her up on stage singing her heart out. It's fun in a toe-curling kind of way.

Deb married her new man, Colin. They invite me, with Helen and David and others, to dinner at her place, which is a detached family house with a big garden. Greeting me at the door, she puts her arms around me for a big kiss, truly a snog.

I don't recall much of the rest. Colin is an admirably nice chap. He sings in the same choir as Deb and loves cooking and gardening. She reads the *Telegraph*.

———

Nigel Farage addresses the UKIP annual conference in September. He says he wants to turn the next European parliamentary elections, set for May 2014, into a national referendum on UK membership of the EU: 'Let us send an earthquake through Westminster politics and let's say we want our country back.'

Farage goes to Manchester to speak at the Conservative party conference. He plans to agitate again for more UKIP members in the European parliament. But his UKIP candidates will take votes from Conservative candidates, and the Tories are not about to help him. They deny him entry to their conference, and so he speaks at Manchester town hall instead.

There he tells a packed crowd why he'll never make a deal with Cameron: 'They regard us as members of the lower orders.'

Farage is wrong about this. Cameron faces pressure from his own right wing on Europe, and Tory hardliners have proposed making a deal with UKIP. But he's almost right: Cameron is too posh a patrician to bow to the hardliners, and so he appeases them with his promise of a national referendum.

Cameron has been lucky so far in his career. He's beaten the odds a few times on his meteoric rise to the top, and he seems sure he'll win a referendum on Europe too.

I'm no longer so sure. I feel uneasy about the whole thing. I've built my whole career on the EU freedom to live and work in another member state, and most of my state pension will come from Germany. If the UK leaves the EU, adapting my car will be the least of my worries.

I'm not the man to stop Farage. The strutting MEP, who seems so like the pre-war British fascists, is way beyond my comfort zone. But someone must arrest the arsonist. He's playing with fire.

3.   The ice-cream cone

David Cameron writes in November on how he'd restrict freedom of movement in the EU.

He sees a problem: 'Since 2004, we have witnessed the biggest migration in Europe outside wartime. In Britain's case, a million people from central and eastern Europe are now living here.'

Yet he fails to see the British failure that led to it: 'If it does not pay to work, or if British people lack skills, that creates a huge space in our labour market for people from overseas to fill.'

And he points the finger of blame elsewhere: 'It is time for a new settlement which recognises that free movement is a central principle of the EU, but it cannot be a completely unqualified one.'

He concludes: 'The EU needs to change.'

———

I read Russell Brand's latest spiritual guidance:

'We have … succumbed to an ideology that is totally corrupt and must be overthrown. … The reality is we have a spherical eco-system, suspended in infinite space … The only systems we can afford to employ are those that rationally serve the planet first, then all humanity. The Spiritual Revolution has come.'

I sympathise. I've independently decided much the same thing. We humans must learn to think of ourselves as Earthlings, offspring of a fertile planet. I back this up not only with facts and theories about ecosystems and global limits but also with grand ideas about expanding knowledge and moral horizons.

I'm a philosopher. I begin my time in post-cool Britannia haunted by old thoughts. I need to fix them in a souvenir snapshot. Then I can enter the political fray in a state of spiritual calm.

As an undergraduate at Oxford, I found a philosopher who caught my imagination. The thinker Immanuel Kant, who lived and worked in the Prussia of Frederick the Great (alias 'the old Fritz'), wrote a brilliant critique of pure reason. I was impressed.

But I learned caution. Modern Anglo-American analytic philosophers take pride in the technical precision of their work and look for guidance to logic, where in Bismarck's Germany an unknown mathematics professor called Gottlob Frege had quietly launched a revolution that led to set theory.

The old logic my Oxford teachers deplored topped out about when Napoleon lost at Waterloo, when the great philosopher Georg Wilhelm Friedrich Hegel lectured in Heidelberg and Berlin on his dialectical logic. My tutors detested his work. Karl Marx exploited its baffling contradictions to invent dialectical materialism, which Vladimir Lenin abused to build Soviet communism. Hegel is an embattled name in philosophy.

The first modern analytic philosopher, the man who introduced Frege's logic to the English-speaking world, was Bertrand Russell. As an aristocratic don at Cambridge, he had the credibility to launch a new style in British academia. This marked the parting of the ways for German philosophy and Anglo-American analytics. The whole history of the twentieth century branches out from that divide.

I was hooked. I hacked ever deeper into a jungle of big ideas. But I held onto logic and obsessed over how computer logic could ever reproduce the conscious thinking of a human mind.

Now, in December 2013, I write an essay I call *The Answer*. 'The answer to the meaning of life, the universe, and everything is 42, said Douglas Adams in *The Hitchhiker's Guide to the Galaxy*. ... I have a big answer of my own, which is about as practical as 42 and rather less amusing.'

I plunge in with my riff on how the brain works. I see it as a neural network that builds sense impressions and memories and so on into an evolving world-model in consciousness and keeps the model up and running for a lifetime. My big idea is to represent this mortal coil, as Shakespeare called it, in logic and set theory.

Set theory has flourished into a highly technical tale about an amazing structure. I don't plan to goof off with a lecture on maths, and the finer detail is strictly for its fans, but the theory starts from the empty set and builds up in ranks toward infinite sets beyond all reckoning, to form a universe we call V.

Mathematicians have a nickname for V. They imagine it as a cone, with the empty set at the point and the higher ranks as ever bigger slices through the cone. The cone tops out in a fuzzy cloud that rises into nirvana. This is the ice-cream cone universe.

I loved this ice-cream. An American logician I'd seen in action called Willard Van Orman Quine said we can model everything with sets, so the entire universe boils down to V. All you need is sets – cue for a riff of Beatles music.

This got me thinking. I imagined how sets were conjured up from nothing into the ice-cream paradise. I saw this magic trick as the key to the dialectical jargon Hegel used to conjure up stuff from nothing into what he called the Absolute. I found the key unlocked the door to a hidden world of truth behind Hegel's great dialectical histories of everything.

His first history traced phenomenology, which is the drama of personal cognition. That drama was Kant's main concern. But for us, cognitive science is part of neuroscience. This is what I explored in Germany. I went along to conferences in Copenhagen, Bremen, Tucson, Stockholm, New York, Prague, Oxford, and Berlin, and then wrote a book, *Mindworlds*, published in 2009.

In *The Answer*, I say we can see the brain as a kind of computer, with the same limits: 'This … applies to the Kantian software that generates a synthetic unity, to the Hegelian software that generates dialectics, and to the ultimate worldview of hard science itself.'

Here's my new psychology: 'The cumulative hierarchy of sets also known as V is our logical scaffold for everything. Logically speaking, our minds bring a mass of stuff represented by lots of odd sets to a unity represented by a mindset. We occupy a rising succession of mindsets that can be mapped to a rising series of ranked versions of V in a dialectic.'

Then I glimpse the mind of God: 'It turns out that the entire juggernaut of monotheism invites a clear logical reading.'

There we have it. My mind is made known, my ambition staked out. For now, *The Answer* is a snapshot for the thoughts in my head. It's the rational distillate of my decades of wandering among the snowy peaks of Anglo-German culture.

—

As soon as I finish my philosophical short story, I realise that the ice-cream cone solves nothing. It doesn't help me clean up the political mess I face in the Britain of UKIP and the Eurosceptic Tories. All it does is help me stand more confidently on the topmost icy tip of a cultural landscape riven with fault lines between Britain and its continental neighbours.

But that's already a useful start. Brits who recall only wars with Germany have no inkling of the glories in the sunlit uplands tipped with ice. I can make it my mission to spread the ice-cream gospel. I can unearth the fallen gems in the bloodstained lowland soil and offer them up as tokens of a new way forward for humanity.

Easier said than done. I need to explore the political mess in depth before I can offer my patent remedy. This will take time.

First, I recall two more big names. Kant and Hegel mean a lot to me for deep logical reasons. Two later German philosophers were more human. They expose an issue I need to confront.

Friedrich Nietzsche was a bright young professor in Bismarck's Germany. He wrote extraordinary books about the revaluation of all values, the death of God, and the coming of the superman. He was also a friend and disciple of the composer Richard Wagner. But they fell out over Jews. Wagner detested the influence of Jews in

German life and art, and he was bold in saying so. Continuing a dark Germanic tradition that went back at least to Martin Luther, he wallowed in antisemitic prejudice.

Nietzsche, by contrast, rather admired the Jews and detested the brute animosity of German racists. But sadly, after a brief and troubled career, he went mad. His final works are unsound.

My second big name takes us from the collapse of Bismarck's Reich to the collapse of Hitler's Reich.

While German physicists were forging ahead with Einstein's theories of relativity and the paradoxes of quantum mechanics, German philosophers were struggling with Martin Heidegger's new philosophy of being. It was hard work.

Heidegger was a strange figure, from a modest Catholic background in the Black Forest, but his philosophy was radical. The question of being, as he put it, was raised by the ancient Greeks only to be largely forgotten over centuries of Christian ascendancy.

For Heidegger, to be authentically human was to have *Dasein*, determinate being, located in space and time and set in the ways of a folk community. He repudiated what he called the inauthentic being of Christian identity in a rational society and accused Jews of leading Germans astray by promoting it. They were rootless cosmopolitans, whereas he preached the earthy virtues of a rooted existence.

Betraying both his wife and his own principles, he spent years in a secret affair with one of his students, Hannah Arendt, a Jewish girl. When in 1933 he joined the Nazi party and tried as rector of the University of Freiburg to impose Nazi authoritarianism on the student body, his reputation was ruined.

After the war, Arendt was kinder about him than he deserved. His sole recorded response to the tragedy of the Holocaust was to compare 'the manufacture of corpses in the gas chambers and the death camps' with the industrialised food industry.

Both Nietzsche and Heidegger fell under a dark shadow. Their followers boiled up their best ideas in a toxic stew that brought the Reich to grief. What to do about the Jews became a watershed issue for the concept of a racist Reich versus the more open approach to dominance of pragmatic Anglo-Americans. That opening to Jews led to the Anglo-American world hegemony.

—

When a local cinema screens a live performance from the Royal Opera House of Wagner's opera *Parsifal*, I go along and see the show. I once enjoyed *Parsifal* in Mannheim and found it helpful.

I'm not a fan of Wagner's ponderous art. Rock and pop music and American movies have updated Anglo culture beyond recognition since his day. I need to dig around to make sense of it.

Parsifal is a tale of the quest for the holy grail where a holy fool finds redemption. Wagner was updating the Christian myth with something more Germanic. He saw *Parsifal* as his masterpiece and used it to consecrate his opera house at Bayreuth.

But Wagner's Ring cycle was his defining work. One fan was King Ludwig the Second of Bavaria, who build Neuschwanstein Castle in honour of Wagner, and whose grandfather, Ludwig the First, had built a massive neoclassical temple of Valhalla beside the Danube. Another besotted fan was Adolf Hitler.

Wagner still inspires countless modern Germans. Even the chancellor, Angela Merkel, is a fan. She and her husband go along every year to the Bayreuth festival.

—

In her younger years, Liz loved playing Bach, Chopin, Mozart, and the like on our old piano. But although she'd learned German at school, she never warmed to Wagner.

She's ailing now. Helen and I buy a lightweight wheelchair to get her out of the house from time to time. I become adept at getting her in and out of my car and in and out of the wheelchair. I take her on brisk runs to local attractions before the winter closes in.

Over the Christmas holidays, I watch the *Lord of the Rings* movie trilogy based on the book by Oxford professor JRR Tolkien. That magical book recalls the timeless myths of ancient Europe, the same myths Wagner drew on, but in a gentler English setting.

For the 2013 viewing, I persuade Liz to share the treat. She's been trying to reread the tattered paperback copy of *Lord of the Rings* that I read in 1969, but she's only managed a few pages.

As I watch the movies, I think of Wagner, Jews, and UKIP. Is the evil eye of Sauron a metaphor for the all-seeing Jewish god? Are the Hobbits of the shires perhaps just English nationalists in disguise? Is all this ring nonsense a rebellion against power in all its forms – be it Sauron, the Old Testament god, or the Brussels bureaucracy?

———

The Holocaust – the Shoah – haunts me. I suspect the lingering stench of that atrocious achievement is the driver behind British mistrust of the European Union. The EU aims to restore civic virtue on the continent and to offer a safe space for German atonement, but its moral bubble looks fragile.

In January, I learn that Sam Harris, a young American neuroscientist who in the wake of 9/11 wrote a bestseller condemning Islam, is offering a prize for a brief essay on morality.

I guess Sam is doing this to gather ideas for how to rethink his recent book *The Moral Landscape*. That tome landed with a dull thud among philosophers, who politely panned it. I panned it too, but now I can help him out by explaining post-Nazi morality in two pages.

Sam says morality is about maximising the flourishing or the well-being of all conscious creatures within the scope of moral concern. He proposes a mathematical landscape to help us maximise pleasure and minimise pain. This is an update of the utilitarian morality advocated by the Victorian philosopher John Stuart Mill and caricatured by Charles Dickens with the Gradgrind character in his novel *Hard Times*.

I suggest a different approach: 'The self-proclaimed well-being of a supreme moral legislator may be a formally sufficient ground for a moral ruling. The balancing of the legislator's well-being against the pleasure or pain of others can be interpreted as a political question for creatures within the moral sphere.'

I dare an icy plunge: 'A ... rich state of consciousness may conceivably have a hierarchy of owners. In a hierarchy, well-being at the top may be ultimately all that counts. In the totalitarian limit, a godlike legislator may claim all moral rights.'

My message to Sam: 'A scientific morality will need a unified theory of consciousness. Until that theory exists, human beings can only make anthropocentric moral maxims to regulate their daily activities. And just as biological evolution is neutral with reference to human pleasure or pain, a scientific morality will surely be neutral on human flourishing.'

I don't hear from Sam again. Authoritarian morality may be a step too far for a Jewish neuroscientist in California. But it's the best I can do to explain the Nazi moral meltdown.

———

One Saturday in January, I go along to a symposium on mathematics and physics in Oxford. It's hosted by my student *alma mater*, Exeter College, to commemorate its first seven hundred years. I sit through talks by distinguished old boys and chat with college fellows.

That evening, I have a dinner date with Dr Daniel Isaacson. Dan is the Oxford University lecturer in the philosophy of mathematics. I used to hear him lecture decades ago when he was a young man fresh from Stanford.

In those days, I was a graduate student working on the foundations of maths in logic and set theory. My bible was a specialist

yellow-bound volume on set theory by a trio of Israeli mathematicians. My aim was to build a dialectical view of the ice-cream cone
as a confection prone to meltdown in paradox.

But my effort foundered on the rocks of reason. Dr Isaacson
was chosen as an examiner for my thesis, and for sensible reasons
he couldn't let it pass. After the crucifixion, I licked my wounds for
years and ended up in Germany.

In January 2014, Dan and I dine in a pub across the road from
his faculty office. I recall the pub from my student years. It's down
the road from St Anne's College, which was a ladies' college where
I cultivated a bevy of girlfriends.

Nearing retirement, Dan is still trim and alert, with his cheeky
grin and New York accent, but his hair is thin and grey now. He's
my closest faculty friend from the years of my wild ride in logic.

As we each select tasty dishes and sit with beers to wait for
them, Dan brings me up to date with Oxford news, and I sum up
my German years and stress how far Germans have moved on from
the war. Dan looks benignly agnostic and airs his optimism that the
EU is making progress in civilising European politics.

We then talk shop. I tell him: 'The basic lines of human thought
may conform to logic and reason, but the limits aren't far away.'

Dan replies carefully: 'Mathematics goes beyond those limits.
There's nothing psychological about mathematical objects. How we
grasp them is a matter of psychology, sure, but mathematical truth
is what it is, whether we like it or not.'

I smile. 'You're taking sides with Frege against Husserl, but
things have moved on since then.'

Let's not go there. Frege, who was bitterly antisemitic, debated
with the Jewish philosopher Edmund Husserl on the nature of
mathematical objects. Husserl was a phenomenologist. He was also
Heidegger's thesis supervisor, but Heidegger moved on and went
his own antisemitic way. There's a political quagmire beneath all this

academic chatter.

Dan raises an ironic eyebrow. 'Don't get me wrong. I'm sympathetic to looking at how we construct mathematical objects, but that's all about being methodical. We reveal more about them, but it's already there to be revealed.'

'Maybe. Like the Moon. Einstein thought it's there whether we look at it or not. Some of the quantum youngsters, like Heisenberg, were inclined to deny that.'

Werner Heisenberg also temporised awkwardly during the war about developing a German atom bomb. That quagmire again.

Dan shrugs. 'That approach might work in physics, but I don't see how it can apply to maths.'

'Well, it applies to human minds, and those are the instruments through which we see mathematical truths. We can't correct for any instrument bias unless we know the limits.'

'We prove mathematical truths by following rules in a formal language. Where's the psychology in that?'

I sit back and smile. 'Humans don't think very logically at all. Do you remember the work of Dan Kahneman?'

He frowns. 'Kahneman – no, I don't think I do.'

'Well, he won the Nobel prize in economics a few years ago for showing just how close in the limits of human rationality are. He wrote a bestseller a couple of years ago. *Thinking, fast and slow*, it's called. I read it in Germany. I can recommend it. Freeman Dyson said he thinks Kahneman is the first scientific psychologist.'

Dyson is an emeritus mathematician in Princeton. He proved the equivalence of three variant formulations of quantum electrodynamics, QED: one by Richard Feynman, one by another New York Jew, and one by a Japanese guy. The trio won a Nobel prize for their work. And Kahneman is an Israeli Jew.

I think the Nazis' Jewish problem arose from fear and shame that Jews often do so impressively well in the life of mind.

'Hmm.' Dan nods his head. 'I must look out for it.'

A waiter arrives with our chosen dishes. We attack our nosh with gusto, and our talk becomes more personal.

After dining with Dan, I stay overnight in St Hugh's College, another former ladies' college, which offers a basic but cheap bed and breakfast experience. I leave Oxford feeling that my German decades have saved me, thanks to the European Union.

———

Back in Poole on Sunday, I pick up Liz from her experimental overnight stay in a Jewish care home in Bournemouth. She doesn't like sleepovers, but she continues to enjoy regular afternoon visits there to make new friends.

Reflecting on Nazis, Jews, and the Holocaust, I ponder the roots of Christianity. I've read a lot about Jesus: He survived the crucifixion and retired with his wife to the south of France; he prepared for his messianic mission with years of training in the mystic arts in India; he recovered from the cross in Damascus and then worked his way through Persia to reach a ripe old age in Srinagar; he enacted the entire gospel drama among Essene monks in the Dead Sea retreat of Qumran; he was a Palestinian freedom fighter against a brutal Roman occupation; and his story was fabricated by later Romans to secure their rule over Jews with the new catholic ideology of Christianity.

I agree with Albert Schweitzer that the historical truth is lost and gone. I agree too with Leo Tolstoy that the Sermon on the Mount is about all that's worth keeping in the New Testament. That was how I left things in Germany.

At Dan's prompting, I now read three books on the history of early Christianity written by the Oxford professor of Jewish studies Geza Vermes. He tells me that Christianity drifted away from Jewish roots. By spurning those roots, antisemitic Christians betrayed their heritage – much like radical Islamists today.

Europe was built on a Christian heritage that accorded a special status to Jews. But the Nazi rebellion put an end to that thraldom. Modern Europe is a haven for secular humanism.

—

For many years, a big fixture on the calendar for global thought leaders has been the annual gathering at the ski resort of Davos in the Swiss Alps. The meetings are staged by the World Economic Forum, an organisation founded and chaired by Klaus Schwab.

At the 2014 Davos, David Cameron speaks out on a pet theme: 'The key challenge for politicians and business leaders in Europe is how we make a success of globalisation.'

He takes a pop at the EU: 'All of us here in Davos know what it is that businesses need if they are to choose to locate in Europe … an unashamedly pro-business regulatory environment.'

Professor Schwab ends the forum on a wiser note: 'Rising economic inequality [is] a serious challenge to policymakers.'

—

On Valentine's Day, a Friday, Liz has a stroke over lunch. I call 999, then Helen. We put her into her wheelchair and calm her down. The ambulance arrives and takes her off to Poole Hospital.

4. Three old boys

Liz died quietly at Poole Hospital in the early hours of Sunday morning. We hold the funeral at the end of the month in a small chapel at a woodland cemetery, where I deliver a eulogy to a packed audience. I stand at the podium in a black suit over a black pullover. My voice is sombre:

'Liz was my mother. She made me in 1949 and raised me until 1969 when I went off to university.'

The audience sits silent and respectful in the chilly room, no doubt musing on the coffin beside me.

I fill in some back story: 'Liz was a teenager during the Second World War, and Winston Churchill was like an ideal father figure to her. She was still fifteen when Winston's bulldog spirit helped her through the Battle of Britain.'

For Liz, as for so many of her generation, the war was a defining experience that cast its shadow over all the years that followed. I went to Germany in part to dispel the demons that haunted them.

I conclude: 'When in the fullness of time the dream faded and Don had to move to a care home, my sister and I stepped in to close off Liz's life in what we hope was contentment and finally peace. We shall always remember her with fondness and gratitude.'

After the ceremony, I mingle with the crowd as they stand up. I greet old friends and meet new wives and husbands. Among the friends are two old boys from my schooldays, with their wives.

Both men, now wrapped in winter coats, have distinguished careers behind them. The three of us stayed on at school to sit the Oxbridge entrance exams and then used the summer of '69 to hitch-hike together around Europe. That trip has bonded us for life.

I shake hands with Steve and catch his eyes. He's slightly bigger than me, with good proportions, and his short white hair frames a face carved into strong lines, accented with black-framed spectacles. He read history at Cambridge and is now a successful publishing director. At school, he led rugby and cricket teams and served as head boy.

I greet Steve's wife Anne with a brief kiss on either cheek. She's an elegant Scottish lady with a cheery face and friendly manners who loves country life. Together they've raised three sons, all now grown into young men.

'Well done,' says Steve. 'How are you feeling?'

'Okay, thanks. She had a good life and a quick and peaceful end, so no need to be sad. Glad to see you here.'

I look around and see Graham standing nearby. He read physics at Oxford, like me, and then, again like me, dropped physics to graduate in philosophy, politics, and economics (PPE) – the degree that many British parliamentarians, cabinet ministers, and prime ministers have read at Oxford since the war.

Unlike me, Graham went on to pursue an academic career at a new London university, where he became a professor and vice-chancellor and is now nearing retirement. He looks academic too, with an abstracted air and a halo of curly hair, now gone silver-grey, around a long face whose lower half sports silver stubble.

'Graham!' We shake hands. 'Great to see you again. Must be – what – twenty years?'

Graham smiles broadly. 'Great to see you too. Pity about the occasion – our condolences.'

'Thanks. She was old and happy, and she died peacefully. A good example for us all, you might say.'

'Yes – how are you, anyway? I see you're back from Germany.'

I nod. 'Been back nine months now. Finding it hard to get used to the old place. Poole seems to have suffered under austerity.'

He glances around. 'I don't get back much since my mother died. London is much more interesting – when I'm not in France or boating in Greece.'

'Oh, I see. The only boat I've been on recently is a river cruiser in Heidelberg. Driving back and forth to Germany is travel enough for me.'

'Jules is here too.' He turns in her direction. She's still sitting, waiting for the crowd to disperse.

'Ah, must say hello,' I stride toward her. Although she's raised two sons, she looks small and frail in her dark winter wrap. 'Hi, Jules, great to see you again.'

She sits up straight as I lean over a row of chairs to shake her hand. She's as bright as a button and replies chirpily: 'Great to see you too. You're still looking good – you must be doing something right.'

'How nice of you to say so. You're looking good too. I trust life is treating you well.'

'Yes – weren't you in Germany?'

'Back a while now. I came back to look after mother, to share the load with Helen, who was finding it too much like hard work.'

'Oh, God, how selfless! Are you going to stay now?'

I raise an eyebrow. 'Maybe. I'm getting old and lazy, but I liked it there. Are you coming to the reception at mother's place?'

'Yes, of course, as soon as we can get out of here.'

———

A small crowd gathers in the lounge at Liz's flat for the wake.

Wintry sunlight fills the room. The cabinets and shelves are laden with cards, flowers, plates of finger food, and glasses and bottles. The best cabinet is topped with a silver-framed black-and-white portrait of Liz as a young lady, taken soon after the war, about when she married Bob.

I talk with Steve and Graham. I visited Steve and Anne a few weeks ago, and I often used to see Steve at the annual Frankfurt Book Fair. But in Germany I largely lost touch with Graham.

I still feel at ease with them both, but I'm the odd one out. In the years before and after graduating, I lived together with a fellow student from St Anne's called Judy, who also read PPE. We parted when my career stalled between my third and fourth degrees. She was working in a trade union by then – and went on to become a Labour member of parliament – whereas I struggled to find a practical use for my degrees for years, until I realised that mathematical logic and German philosophy were just right for a decent career in computer science in Germany.

Unlike Steve and Graham, I never married and have no children. My years with Judy and their dramatic end put me off settling until my career looked more secure, and that seemed to take forever. But slowly I got over all that – and even learned to like celibacy.

As we chat over glasses of fruit punch, I hold forth on politics: 'Did you catch Angela Merkel addressing the British parliament yesterday? I was quite impressed by the case she made for Britain staying in the European Union.'

'I saw an extract on the evening news,' says Graham.

'I was convinced. I've been listening to her for years, and her line on Europe makes sense to me.'

Steve fiddles with his glasses. 'I don't think it makes sense to David Cameron. His ideas for changing the British relationship would put a coach and horses through the Merkel vision.'

Graham chips in: 'True, but I think he's scared of UKIP and the radical right. He understands Merkel but he doesn't dare agree with her.'

Steve and Graham share my disquiet about the rise of UKIP. We agree that British membership of the EU is a good thing.

'Nigel Farage is pulling the Conservatives to the right and wrecking the coalition,' says Steve. 'And Labour is no help at all. Jeremy Corbyn is a Marxist who wants to nationalise everything, so voters have to choose between two absurd extremes.'

Graham demurs. 'Labour has become more extreme since the Blair years, agreed, but I don't think they're unelectable. I just don't think they can get a big enough swing to win an election, or at least not unless Cameron really screws up on Europe.'

I sigh. 'It's first-past-the-post again. We really need to get over the idea that a simple majority qualifies a government to do what it likes. British politics zigzags back and forth like a yo-yo.'

Graham replies: 'We had a referendum here two years ago on proportional representation. Two thirds voted against it.'

I sigh again. 'I know. I still think we need a consensus government, like they have in Germany and Japan.'

I like Japan. I lived there for a year during Thatcher's first term. It was a great adventure. I prepared by building a Japanese model of a Japanese motorcycle and reading a few books on Japan, and by listening to John and Yoko (Lennon had died just months earlier). I came back with new friends, a love of the culture, and a beginner's feel for the language. Japan set me up for Germany by making it feel like home by comparison.

Steve disagrees. 'But Japan suffered a lost decade of stagnation because of its consensus. I don't see any real political debate there. At least British democracy is still alive.'

'I agree we need proportional representation,' says Graham. 'But the two main parties have no reason to vote for it. I don't see how we can change that.'

I try a new tack: 'I think we need to get the monarchy out of politics. If anything is stifling political debate in Britain, it's the idea that the prime minister answers to the Queen. I think we should become a republic, like France and Germany.'

Steve shakes his head. 'Won't work. The great British public loves their monarchy. They love all that pomp and circumstance. Ask any expat in Mumbai or Singapore. They say the royal magic lets us punch above our weight on the global stage.'

'Royal magic?' I grimace. 'That's more likely to make them pity us. America doesn't have royals, and they punch pretty well.'

'True. But they have lots of nukes … Okay, it's the British nuclear deterrent that lets us punch above our weight.'

I spent a year working in the Ministry of Defence, so I know about nukes. 'As we used to say in the ministry, we have a nuclear deterrent to keep the Americans in, the Russians out, and the Germans down.'

Steve frowns: 'I thought that was NATO.'

'Maybe so,' I concede, miffed at muffing my line. 'But we need our own nuclear deterrent to keep NATO credible in Europe. Otherwise, we'd need much bigger armies in Germany.'

Steve smiles impishly. 'We need the deterrent to keep up with the French. And to keep our place at the top table. We can't let the colonial upstarts in America have a deterrent if we don't have one.'

'It's much simpler than that,' I say. 'We buy American nuclear missiles because we love America. I think you'll find your average Brit would rather go to hell with the Americans than go to heaven with the Europeans.'

Anne and Jules move into our little old-boy huddle. 'Are you talking politics?' Jules asks. 'I'd rather go to heaven in America. At least they speak English there.'

Anne changes the subject. 'That's a lovely portrait of your mother, Andy. Do you have any more like that?'

'No. In those days, you'd get one good portrait at the local photographers and that was it. We live in a different age.'

Anne nods. 'What did she do during the war?'

'She worked as a secretary in a factory that made tank parts. And my father was a senior aircraft engineer who worked with the RAF in India. They met in Huddersfield a few years after the war.'

Helen joins in: 'Our father never got used to life in postwar Britain. He was always hankering after the privileged life he'd lived in India, with humble servants and obedient workers and garden parties with his fellow colonial overlords. British austerity was too demeaning for him. Liz needed the patience of a saint to put up with him.'

I frown. 'Let's not get too negative. He did the best he could.' She was right, I admit, but I never quite understood my father. Bob founded two engineering companies during my childhood, but neither did very well, and so he divorced Liz, moved up north, remarried, and died there some years later.

Jules pulls Graham's arm playfully. 'I need the patience of a saint to put up with you sometimes.'

———

What do Brits want? Europe or America – heaven or hell? That seems to be the crux of this ugly agitation against the EU that's spreading like a plague in the kingdom I once called home.

That night, alone in front of my Mac screen, I brood on heaven and hell, on marriage and celibacy. America certainly looks more fun than Europe – like marriage is more fun than celibacy.

Out of idle curiosity, I google a name from my troubled past and study the results. I find a small, pixelated image of a female face. Both the sharp character in the face and the uneasy feeling in my depths are still there. I search further and find she's into yoga.

Embarrassed to confront such truth, I close the browser and go to bed. The bed is narrow, and I lie awake awhile. Above my head, the surfer dude and his wife in the upstairs flat are emitting the grunts and groans of extravagantly orgasmic sex.

———

I've lost interest in amateur dramatics. It's all vanity.

I need a new life.

5.   Windows of opportunity

I start dropping by regularly at the Poole Conservative Association office. The secretary Pam always seems happy to see me, and I'm glad to bask in her cheery company.

I still live alone in the flat that Helen and I have inherited. We're still sorting out Liz's estate before selling the flat and moving on. Dropping into the office lifts my mood.

Pam is slightly younger than me and keeps fit with regular dance classes. She must have cut a charming and elfin figure when young. I guess that went down well with the local member of parliament, Robert Syms, back at the end of the previous century when he was a glamorous new boy and she started working for him.

Pam is fast and efficient and does her job well. She keeps her blonde hair in a youthful style and always looks smart, usually with a miniskirt over black tights and ballet slippers. She answers the phone in a brisk and professional tone, with a high note of barely controlled indignation that brooks no opposition, making clear to all that she's in charge.

The office is a small ground-floor unit in a block owned by a firm of accountants, who fill the shared parking spaces on the street frontage with new and expensive saloons that outshine my modest BMW. My car stands out mainly for the iron-cross decal on the back surrounded by German words saying I support the German lifeboat rescue service.

I'm bemused by the office. A conversion from a former garage, it's divided into a front room, a back room, and between them a tiny toilet cubicle beside a narrow space with a broom cupboard and some shelves for files, a kettle, and the like.

The front door, with wood frames around glazed panels like a Dickensian shopfront, opens directly into the office, where Pam sits at a big desk piled high with papers around a small, old flat-screen computer monitor. Behind her, along the side wall, is a snake-pit of dusty cables, coiled and tangled together, beside a cabinet, a printer, and a copier. Next is another big desk with another small monitor, set by the toilet corner.

Pam speaks with a strong Dorset accent, which reminds me of my schooldays. She shows me around the office and invites me to sit at the vacant desk.

'That's where the agent sits, when we hire one for elections,' she says, pointing at a plastic swivel chair on castors. 'You can sit there, if you like, and try out the computer.'

'Okay, let me see what you have here … you know this version of Windows is going out of service soon. You need to update it.'

From my time in Germany, I'm used to state-of-the art desktop computer setups, with hardware replaced every three years and software maintained centrally for peak performance. I'm also used to spacious modern offices in glass-and-steel palaces with coffee corners and armchairs. I expect fresh coffee from shiny machines, and pot plants and wall art to ease the soul.

But Germany is another world. Here in England, the lowlier minions are expected to be grateful for what they get. Mend and make do, keep calm and carry on, stiff upper lip and all that.

'The monitor's rather old too,' I say. 'The screen is too small, and you need more resolution.'

'If you're going to keep complaining,' she replies in a shrill tone, 'you can leave now and let me work in peace.'

'Just giving you the benefit of my professional advice. Good equipment is the prerequisite for good work, and modern equipment gives you new ways of working that increase workplace productivity and enhance team capability. Do more, better – what's wrong with that?'

'I'm quite happy with what I've got.'

'Well, I strongly recommend new hardware and software.'

'I shall forward your recommendation to the chairman. Would you like a cup of coffee?'

'Now you mention it, yes, thanks.'

'There's the kettle,' she points. 'You can make it yourself – and make me one too, please. Black, no sugar.'

I go and study the narrow kitchen shelf over the fridge. I turn on the kettle. Beside it is a jar of cheap instant coffee.

'Paper cups? That's not good for the environment. Why not pottery mugs?'

'Because I'd have to do all the washing up. Besides, the sink is too small, and I don't trust the tap water.'

I look through the doorway to the toilet cubicle. Before the toilet door, a closet-sized lobby frames a tiny sink for washing hands. The sink is grubby and stained, and I recoil in disgust. Then I see a few plastic flagons of mineral water under a baby fridge just big enough for milk cartons.

'Plastic water bottles too. This is no good at all for the environment. Can't you get the chairman to upgrade all this?'

'We don't have the money for that sort of thing,' Pam keeps her eyes fixed on her screen. 'We put all our donations in the fighting fund.'

'Okay, I understand.' I decide to say no more until I've figured all this out more fully. I make two instant coffees.

I step into the ill-lit back room. This is where the MP holds his surgery meetings with constituents during his regular Friday visits down from Westminster. It's crowded with a huge conference table and a clutter of office chairs, and the walls are covered with framed portraits of past and present Tory grandees.

The portraits are revealing. The biggest two show Winston Churchill. One is a painted panorama of the crowded Tory benches in the Commons, with Harold Macmillan at the dispatch box and

Sir Winston in dignified repose on the front bench. The other is a black-and-white portrait of the warlord looking sombre in a formal civvie outfit.

The next portrait is a fine photographic study of Margaret Thatcher, taken at the height of her power and glory. Below it, looking small, is a standard mugshot of the present party leader and prime minister, David Cameron. The rest are artless snaps of past and present Poole MPs schmoozing with various locals.

I give Pam her coffee and start exploring my desktop.

————

Robert Syms, member of parliament for Poole, sits in the back room below Churchill the warlord. He's a big man, aged about sixty, beginning to run to fat, with a full head of unkempt grey hair, a broken nose, heavy jowls, and a morose expression. He wears a creased navy suit jacket with grey trousers and scuffed brown shoes. His necktie is parliamentary green with a portcullis motif.

I sit facing him, in a dark suit recently purchased from a chain store over a white shirt with a blue necktie. A few days ago, I sent Syms an email complaining about the poor state of the roads in Poole and explaining, with facts and figures from the *Financial Times*, how all the roads nationwide could be fixed for an estimated ten billion pounds, a sum we could easily find by scrapping HS2.

Syms responded by inviting me to come to his next surgery, which is here and now.

'I wanted to thank you for your mail,' he begins. 'I'm not convinced the government should change its transport policy yet, but I'm glad to know there are good alternatives available if we ever wish to explore them.' His voice is smooth and mellifluous, with a posh accent overlaid with an occasional twang of local dialect, and I'm sure it goes down well among his Westminster colleagues.

I put on an Oxford accent: 'I don't expect instant improvement in the roads, but the potholes will only get worse if the council continues to ignore them. And making life difficult for motorists is counterproductive. Business drivers waste paid time in traffic jams, pump out more exhaust gases, get angry and stressed, increase wear and tear on their vehicles, and clog the roads for everyone.'

Syms is listening. He commutes weekly on the motorway between Westminster and Poole in his Mercedes saloon, and I'm sure he's as frustrated by the roads as I am. But he sticks to the party line: 'I don't get many complaints about the state of the roads, and I also get people complaining that we're not doing enough to get more traffic onto the railways, so I guess we're getting our policy about right.'

I pull a sour face. 'The people who would complain are likely to be richer, and they can always replace their cars with big SUVs that just ride over all the bumps. Then the rest of us have even less room on the roads and have to breath the exhaust from their bigger engines.'

Syms pauses. 'Actually, I called you in for something else. Our local chairman, Tony Reeves, says you studied politics at Oxford. Is that right?'

I sigh. 'Yes. I graduated in Philosophy, Politics and Economics, and then went on to do three more degrees, one from London and two more from Oxford, in more technical subjects.'

Syms blinks slowly as he rallies his thoughts. 'Where did you go to school? And what did you do after Oxford?'

I begin the familiar recitation: 'The grammar school here in Poole. I took my A-levels in physics and maths. Between school and university, I spent six months working on the buses in Poole as a bus conductor. After my degrees, I worked for a year as an administrator in the Ministry of Defence, but it wasn't really my style, so I taught physics and maths for a while before moving to Germany.'

Six months on the buses – I'm proud of that. It gave me street cred at Oxford. As a fully paid-up member of the Transport and

General Workers' Union, I earned enough money to buy my first car and to finance my summer tour of Europe with Steve and Graham.

The Ministry of Defence was something else. There I picked up a few office skills and joined another union, the First Division Association, with a much more elitist view of the world. My past life with Judy turned out to be a chewy morsel for the security team that had to vet me before letting me read secret files. And the stuff I then learned about the British armed forces in Germany and NATO is with me still.

Syms looked up, alert. 'Germany – what did you do there?'

'First, I worked for a decade or so for a science publisher in Heidelberg, editing books in physics and computer science. Then I worked for another decade at a nearby global software company, in the development team for a database engine. That was fun. Then I retired and wrote a few books, then I returned to England to look after my old mother – who died in February.'

Heidelberg was as magical for me as Oxford. It was one of the very few German cities to have survived the war largely intact, and its medieval heart offers a sense of the German soul that's hard to find elsewhere. The publisher, Springer, founded in 1842, had deep links with the scientific community across Europe.

The software company, SAP, is extraordinary on an altogether different scale. Founded in 1972 and a global leader in business software, it's in a space of its own, where the petty concerns of nation states look like small beer.

Syms nods slowly. 'Yes, we read your eulogy for your mother. She did some work for us, many years ago now, and her partner Don Barr was the chairman here for several years.'

'Yes, that's right. They were both committed Conservatives.'

Syms takes a deep breath. 'Well, after all that, I have an offer to make. We're looking for an agent to prepare for the elections next spring, and I could use some extra help for my parliamentary work. Between us, we can offer you four days a week of work, two for the local association as an election agent and two for me as a parliamentary assistant. How does that sound to you?'

I smile. 'That's an interesting offer. I'm not too short of money and I still have books to write, but it would certainly be interesting.'

'As you say, interesting work. And it would pay the bills.'

I nod. 'Yes, I like it. Okay, I accept the offer, thank you.'

———

The European elections are held before I join the payroll in June. I dutifully vote Conservative. The results come a few days later.

For South West England, the EU proportional voting system assigns two of six places to candidates from the UKIP list, two to the Conservatives, one to Labour, and one to the Greens. The turnout was barely over a third of the electorate.

The leading Conservative MEP is the former solicitor Ashley Fox, twenty years younger than me, whom I like because he has an unusually tall egghead that makes him look wise. Reflecting on the weak result for the Tories and the poor turnout, Fox says: 'Voters have sent a message that the EU has to change.'

David Cameron uses the results to push on with his ambitions for reform in Europe: 'We need an approach that recognises that Brussels has got too big, too bossy, too interfering.'

———

One of my first acts in post is to attend a big public meeting on a government proposal to build a wind farm in Poole Bay. The plan, called Navitus Bay, is to erect a few hundred wind turbines, enough for a gigawatt of power, a few miles offshore from the celebrated beaches of Poole and Bournemouth, where they'd be visible on the horizon. Residents are incensed, and local activists have leveraged their outrage to make a fuss.

The meeting is held in the main theatre in the Bournemouth

International Centre. This prestigious venue sits on a clifftop site overlooking the beach, the pier, and the central gardens. It offers ample space for leisure and conference facilities of all kinds, yet its theatre overflows with the protesters.

Here I sit and absorb the public mood. The MP for Bournemouth West seeks to channel the public anger and champions the cause of scrapping the plan. He says he'd prefer more oil drilling in Dorset, climate change be damned.

I report back to my new boss that he'd better get on the bandwagon too. Let the wind farm go elsewhere.

The summer soon grows hot, and I put in time on the beach.

In July, the new Mayor of Poole, a wily old Tory called Peter Adams, holds a charity beach festival at Sandbanks.

Isaac, as I choose to call him, is a former businessman and now an investor in the international world of machine tools, and he did a lot of his business in Germany. He's proud of his background as a barrow boy in London, where he picked up a Cockney accent and a cheerful disdain for higher literacy. He's short and thin, but wiry and agile, even sporty, and he has a bulbous head fringed with hair and a long face sprouting a little silver goatee beard.

The site of the charity festival is the millionaire beach peninsula of Sandbanks, with the world's fourth most expensive real estate. The rich residents there are angry this season about party houses, which young outsiders rent for a weekend to hold loud parties, causing neighbours to dread Friday nights when carloads of revellers show up next door. They've provoked our MP to make a speech in parliament on the outrage. This is the sort of action that keeps up his safe-seat majority in Poole.

The festival is fun. Held in a marquee on boards over the sand, it attracts dozens of stalls run by local businesses and draws a good crowd. A reporter's photo shows me with Robert Syms, Peter Adams, and a former paratrooper I call Buzz because he's like Buzz

Lightyear. I'm in my linen suit with a blue shirt, Syms is in a similar outfit, Mayor Adams is laden with his chain of office, and Buzz sports a summer shirt. The beach vibe prompts me to park my shoes and enjoy the event barefoot.

As the summer heat goes on, I zone out again from local politics to read the latest novel by Martin Amis, *The Zone of Interest*. This is billed as a vaguely comic novel about the Holocaust.

Martin and I were undergraduate friends at Exeter College in Oxford. We shared a few joints and talked about novels and so on, as students do, and then lost touch.

But I still read his books as they appear. Some I like and some I don't. I don't like his new Holocaust comedy. With a strange plot and a scattering of cod German to carry it along, it leaves me cold. I write a review:

'Within the ugly context of an industrialized total war … some six million Jewish corpses were manufactured in a scattering of factories … The rationale for this action was a racist ideology that seems in retrospect like a perverse and demonic caricature of the ethnocentric ideology of the Jewish people.'

I have a better idea for Martin: 'A more fully conceived novel about the Nazi genocide would delve with forensic imagination into the mad science of racial types and the military acceptance of slaughter in the line of duty.'

I'm not amused that he's fanned the stink of death around the topic for a dud.

———

At the end of August, Bournemouth holds its annual air show again. I meet up with Helen and David on the same hotel terrace again. We recall Liz's absence but carry on.

One old bird grabs my attention. It's the wartime US Flying Fortress bomber called 'Sally B' that featured in the movie *Memphis Belle*. The radio commentary is just as jingoistic as last year.

What gets me is the lingering sentiment of the Anglo-American bond in the war years. Fortress and Lancaster bombers shared the load of killing Germans. A joker once said Germans are good at killing Jews, and Brits are good at killing Germans.

My ruminations on Jews and history get a welcome boost when I read the new book *Sapiens: A Brief History of Humankind* by the Israeli historian Yuval Noah Harari. I write a happy review.

———

Days later, in the office, I'm sitting at my desk beside Pam at hers. We're both facing big new screens fed by new computers running the latest version of Windows.

Tony Reeves stands facing us, looking pleased. He's a stocky, punchy guy, a former senior manager in a company that made army vehicles, and he has an emphatic and decisive manner. Like Pam, he speaks with a strong local dialect, and he has the ruddy face of a man of action. He loves campaigning door to door, and today he sports a blue parka over a striped rugby shirt and jeans.

He looks at me: 'What do you think of the new machines, then?'

I nod. 'Just what we need. Now we can really get working for the elections.'

'Glad to hear it. They've blown a big hole in the budget, so they'd better be good. We can blame you now if we don't win a thumping majority.'

———

Days before Christmas, prime minister David Cameron visits Poole. I wait at a housing development on the Poole dockside and watch his motorcade sweep into view. The silver Jaguar containing the man himself speeds past, lights flashing, and stops around a corner for Cameron to get out and greet our local MP.

I wait with council officials and building contractors in the site office, where a scale model of the development sits on a table under a display case. I'm admiring the model when Cameron and Syms walk in, surrounded by staffers in hi-vis vests. They pause to admire it too.

Cameron addresses me: 'Hello, what do you do here?' He extends his hand politely and we shake hands.

'Hello, Andy Ross. I, ah, work for Dave – I work for Robert, as his election agent.'

Dave smiles for a second. His manner is tight, almost manic, and the pupils of his eyes are small. Whatever, he has a reply: 'Well, thanks for your help.' And that's it. He moves on.

Why did I say 'Dave'? A Freudian slip like that is telling. In truth, I'm working more for the centrist and coalition-minded brand of conservatism he represents than for the stale fogeyism that most party members seem content to accept.

I'm even on board with Dave's mission to renegotiate the terms of Britain's membership of the European Union. What could possibly go wrong?

6. Battling for Britain

Dave calls the next general election for 7 May 2015, to make a combined election for local councillors and for members of parliament. The long campaign kicks off in January and the short campaign, when parliament and councils dissolve and 'purdah' rules apply for campaign spending, begins in late March. I have two dozen councillor candidates to support as well as our parliamentary candidate, so these months are ridiculously busy for me.

My favourite councillor is the new mayor and hero of the Sandbanks festival 'Isaac' Adams, who likes to get involved in the office. Isaac writes campaign texts and slogans that, when corrected, make easy reading for the consumers of tabloid headlines. This, he says, is the only way for party leaflets to grab their reader in the moments between front door and waste bin. His philosophy of propaganda is to be light on facts and strong on spin.

One day in the office, I sit at my keyboard while Isaac hovers over me, reading my words.

He points at the screen: 'Don't say "More affordable housing". Give it more impact, personalise it – "We build more homes for you". Then give a number in the first sentence: "We listened to your concerns and we pledge to deliver five hundred new homes for young families." See the difference?'

'Really, five hundred? Is that a fact we can back up?'

'We projected the number in a recent council meeting. We're still fighting to find the sites for them, but that's our target.'

'Okay … Do you want to get the word "affordable" in there?'

Isaac smiles. 'Better not. They're not all affordable. Wait – add the sentence: "The Lib Dems blocked these homes for two years, but now you can give us the green light to push on without delay." Any chance to slag the Lib Dem record is worth taking.'

'Are you sure? I can't believe they blocked new housing.'

Isaac frowns: 'They voted against some of the infill sites and brown-field sites – that's good enough.'

'Slagging off the opposition can backfire. You give them name recognition.'

'We have to keep attacking them,' he growls. 'Paint them as evil. Remember the wise words of Joseph Goebbels: "A lie repeated often enough becomes the truth." They slag us off often enough. If they complain, we'll point them to the council records.'

This is how we do it. I craft the layouts on my new computer and have them printed by a local firm that turns them into elegant newsletters for hand delivery by party volunteers.

Thousands of leaflets pile up in boxes for each ward, and I have ten wards to supply, so the office is like a busy bus station as relays of volunteers come to collect their bundles of paper.

The party holds the data for all these wards in a central database. As a database expert, I could have sat and worked on it for the campaign, but I soon leave it to Pam. Only she has the patience to endure the infuriating interface the party has given its new toy. Vote Source is being rolled out with great fanfare to replace a medieval relic called Merlin. But Vote Source was developed in a hurry and on a tight budget. I see its rushed rollout as a textbook example of how not to do the job, and I try to avoid using the thing.

Pam looks over: 'I've just got another mail from central office with a set of slides on how to select and print out canvassing cards. I haven't got time for all this. Do you want to read them and show me later?'

I grimace. 'I haven't got time either. Central office needs to do better than this. Anyway, haven't you learnt that job already?'

'Well, yes, I've just been clicking around until I get what I want. But the screens keep changing. Today there are several new buttons on the tabs, and I don't know what they do yet.'

'You mean they're changing the interface without warning you in advance?'

'Yes, several times now. I've got hundreds of slides to explain the new features – but I haven't had time to go through them. You must have seen them. Haven't you got them too?'

I trot out my excuse: 'Yes, but I ignore them. The guys on the helpdesk still haven't given me a new password. I'm locked out.'

Party hacks had high hopes for Vote Source, but it's buggy and slow. If I could find the time, I'd write central office a professional critique of the system. I'd invoice them for it.

To escape from the office on sunny days, I go out on delivery walks around the wards. This also lets me get to know the other candidates. Isaac has talked me into standing as a candidate for the ward I lived in as a boy, so a chance to see the others in action is helpful.

My two Conservative running mates in the Old Town are new too. The ward harbours a nest of local populists. A former Conservative in the ward started his own tiny party – I call them the Poole Xenophobes – on a platform of proud independence from all outside associations, and the locals are loving it.

My two running mates are the former paratrooper I call Buzz and a son of Indian immigrants I call Ali. We start out in confusion, but soon Buzz is meeting and greeting locals in volume.

As for Ali, I can only admire his chutzpah. He's the scion of a family of traders and has a beautiful young wife from his local ethnic community. The pair of them once organised an impressive curry evening, where Ali did the jocking for the dance music, which raised a good sum for our fighting fund. But most ward locals will never vote for him.

One cold, sunny morning in February, the three of us go out for a photoshoot on the quayside. We're with Kevin, who's a quiet party man with a good camera.

We meet at the pilot house near the old bridge. I'm muffled up in a blue winter parka over a blue fleecy jacket and blue jeans. Buzz is in a padded red sleeveless body-warmer over a check shirt and jeans. He's a stocky guy with a military buzz-cut, now silvering, and a sharp and clipped but matey manner. Ali is shorter and slighter, but endowed with a friendly and gentle presence, as well as a neatly trimmed black beard. He has a sleeveless vest too, over a hoodie and blue jeans, plus a fat pair of gloves.

The quayside is good for snaps like this. The harbour's pilot boats are moored by the bridge alongside a floating jetty. Beside the pilot boats sit a police motor launch and a maintenance boat, and just along the quay is a tugboat. On the other bank of the waterway, a bridge away, is a row of sleek luxury motor yachts built in Poole for the global market. Young millionaires in Sandbanks buy them as babe magnets.

Kevin raises his camera as we pose in front of the old bridge. 'Ready? Three, two, one.' He takes a few snaps.

I squint aside at the solar radiance. 'Are you sure the lighting was good enough? Do we need any more shots here at the bridge?'

Kevin looks down at the camera. 'This is the best we can do with the bridge behind you.'

Buzz turns around and flexes his shoulders. 'Where shall we go next? Any other good backgrounds we can use while we're here?'

I knew this quayside as a boy. 'Sure, if we go along the quay at bit. Let's take a few in front of the old customs house.'

Buzz smiles. 'Sounds like a plan. Let's do it.'

We walk on to the customs house, an old brick building with a curved double staircase at the front rising to an upper doorway. A flagpole flying a union jack tops it off.

Kevin snaps us with full-frontal lighting.

I look eastward: 'How about a few a bit further along, with the statue of Lord Baden-Powell?'

Buzz waves a hand. 'You know the way, lead on.'

Lieutenant General Robert Baden-Powell, hero of the siege of Mafeking in 1900 and founder of the Boy Scouts, built his castle on an island in Poole Harbour, just a mile offshore from the quay. His quayside statue is life-sized and set at ground level, ideal for tourist photos. His story is a local legend, despite his early Nazi sympathies, and a photo here is just right for our propaganda.

We stand around the statue as if we're friends of the wiry old man in his broad-brimmed hat and baggy shorts, and Kevin snaps away. Behind us for the shots is a stormproof gazebo that neatly screens off a couple of notorious local pubs.

'I think we've got enough now,' I say. 'What do you think, Kevin?'

'I'm happy with that.'

Buzz flexes his arms. 'That's good because I'm getting chilly. How about we drop in at the Jolly Sailor for a jar before we go our separate ways? I know the manager there, and if we treat him well, he can put the word around and land us a few votes.'

Ali looks away. 'I have to go. My customers are waiting.'

'I'd better go, too,' I say. 'I have to finish off the next round of newsletters today. You go ahead and have a drink on us.'

'Okay, cheers, guys, catch you later!' Buzz strides off.

I know the pub – and a few like it – from my teenage years with Steve and Graham and others. We learned to avoid them. Since then, like the rest of the quay, they've been cleaned up for the tourist trade.

Days later, I'm out again campaigning door to door. Isaac said the best way to win is to say hi to just about every voter in the ward.

Isaac also warned me about Lib Dem tricks. True enough, they pull one. When the list of local candidates is published, I see a surprise Lib Dem candidate called Andrew Ross standing against me in the old town. I hastily make a leaflet to say I'm the true-blue candidate and the other chap is an imposter, but I fear the damage is done.

Toward the end of the action, I take a breather by helping in a neighbouring ward, where one of our candidates is a lady I briefed when she joined up.

Susan Lever, I'll call her, is a wife and mother with a career in marketing behind her. Her husband is a businessman who often travels abroad, and their kids are teenagers with lives of their own. She wants to serve the community as a councillor.

I enjoy her company. She has long dark hair in bouncy waves surrounding a Mediterranean face, and she dresses elegantly. After delivering leaflets in streets I know from childhood, we take a tea break at a nearby waterside clubhouse. It feels good.

———

April the twentieth this year is the seventieth anniversary of Adolf Hitler's last birthday before he shot himself in his Berlin bunker. A lot has happened since then, but for many Tory voters in Poole those wartime events are still in living memory.

On this day, I stand in for Robert Syms at an election hustings event at the Salvation Army Hall in my Old Town ward. The event features a panel session organised by the charity Mencap on the topic of helping people with learning difficulties to feel better about claiming welfare benefits. The other panellists are parliamentary candidates, but Syms doesn't want to give them delusions of grandeur by sitting beside them, so he lets me go instead.

Any association with the Salvation Army is fine by me. They did good work in the ward in my childhood, when their marching band visited our street on a Sunday morning to belt out uplifting tunes. I like their policy of soup, soap, and salvation, in that order.

I also like to be posing alongside parliamentary candidates. I think I could be a credible MP after a stint on the local council to get used to public life, and exposure here is good training.

Four other faces sit on the Mencap panel beside me. The Labour hopeful for Poole is a strident young lady with emphatic opinions, the Green candidate for Poole is a gentle young man with fuzzy views, the UKIP candidate for the seat of Mid Dorset and North Poole is a sharp young man with a shaved head, and the Lib Dem candidate for Mid Dorset and North Poole is a feisty lady called Vikki Slade.

The Salvation Army Hall is a modern edifice, standing free, with big windows opening into the sunlit street. Our audience consists mostly of Mencap protégés who need patience from everyone as they fight to have their say in words they find difficult. The minders around the edge choose not to embarrass them by butting in.

We've been asked to go easy and speak slowly, in short words and sentences. As a former teacher of English as a foreign language I can do this, but the other panellists struggle to throttle back their habitual campaigning style.

The event goes smoothly. As reported by the local paper, Vikki Slade says: 'Everyone needs to be treated with dignity and respect.'

I say: 'Benefits are a right in our society. Those who need them will get them, should get them.'

As I make my departure along a line of organisers, I reflect that Hitler would have had all these welfare dependants exterminated. Adolf used a eugenic excuse for mass murder to baptise his minions in blood. This put them beyond soup, soap, and salvation.

———

The Poole Arts Centre is lit up cheerily on the evening of election day. I climb up a grand stairway to a lobby with a bar. This lobby opens onto a big hall prepared for the count with an array of tables behind tape barriers where ranks of helpers sit ready. Officials buzz in all directions and an air of expectancy fills the hall.

I'm in my dark suit and blue tie set off by a big blue rosette on my lapel. I pause to pick up a pass and stride in. I'm there to help invigilate at the count by watching the counters, most of whom are young volunteers recruited to read, bundle, and count the ballot papers. I'm supposed to spot any errors.

On the stage at the front of the hall, the local election officer, a civic employee, presides over the event. Press and TV cameras will be there when he calls the results, but until then, he and his staff are busy just running the show.

I say hello to fellow candidates as I scope the scene. I meet a chap I call Percy Payne who's standing as an independent. He's an army vet, with a warty face over a pot belly and a peg leg, who trolls me on Facebook with his detestation of the EU.

A year ago, I infiltrated a local UKIP meeting as a spy. There I heard Payne and a series of sour old boys complain about the state of the nation and the need to get out of Europe and get rid of immigrants. At the end, as we all made our exit, I overheard Percy telling a mate a joke: 'I'm not racist – I drive a black Cherokee.'

I greet Percy, now wearing his red, white, and blue independent rosette: 'Hi, Percy, feeling optimistic?'

Percy smirks. 'At least I'm not selling out to Brussels. You need to open your eyes.'

I smile back: 'Eyes wide open, thanks. We're on course to win tonight, in my informed opinion.'

'You still haven't seen the truth about Europe, have you?' Percy fixes me with a baleful glare. 'It's the Fourth Reich. You're collaborating with the Germans, you and your Tory friends.'

I don't want to reply, but I can't help myself. 'The European Union is a lot bigger than Germany. Anyway, what's wrong with Germans? So long as they're not Nazis, it's not a problem.'

His eyes swivel. 'It's the Kalergi plan to commit white genocide in Europe by letting in black and Muslim immigrants to swamp us.'

'The – what? Is that supposed to be a joke?'

'Look it up – Count von Coudenhove-Kalergi – he was the

president of the Paneuropean Union, which was founded in 1923. Then look up the European *Wirtschaftsgemeinschaft*, founded in Berlin in 1942. This is all fact.'

I sigh sadly. Indulging Percy takes patience. 'Look, anyone who digs around can find old roots like that. But the postwar union has an obvious legitimacy that transcends all that.'

'The EU is a German plot to dominate Europe. The Germans are using the euro to keep their industries competitive, so they can swamp our car market.'

'Good for them,' I nod. 'But if the euro is supposed to keep their prices down, it hasn't worked. Anyway, so what? If we don't like it, we can join the euro too and get the same benefit. All this is free and fair competition on a level playing field.'

'But they want to dominate us! I don't want Germans parading around shouting *Sieg Heil* in London! I'd rather go down fighting.'

I smirk. 'Well, good for you, but I don't think that'll help. Modern Germans are quite capable of running Britain as well as we do, if it ever comes to that. Our royal family is German if you go back to Queen Victoria von Saxe-Coburg-Gotha. We're ruled by Germans already.'

'You Conservatives are going to sell us out to the Germans.'

'Bring it on!' I walk off.

Soon the ballot boxes arrive. The count begins.

The polls predict a squeaker. Thanks to the first-past-the-post system, even a small increase in the national vote for either main party can lead to a landslide parliamentary majority. But by the early hours of Friday, the national forecasts on the big TV screens in the foyer show the Conservatives on course to win a working majority. Cameron will be free to hold his promised referendum on Europe.

The count for the next MP for Poole is finished first. Long lines of colour-coded bundles of ballot papers are stacked on tables in front of the stage. The blue lines are way ahead.

When the presiding officer announces the results, I listen for the key line: 'Robert Syms, Conservative, 23,745.'

It's an absolute majority, with just over half of all votes cast. The runner-up is the UKIP candidate, with a sixth of the votes. Labour and the Lib Dems split most of the rest evenly. Payne gets fifty-odd votes.

A beady-eyed Syms talks with a local journalist. I catch a phrase: 'The whole campaign has been a joy.'

Next to come are the local election results. Again, the Conservatives are way ahead. In the ten wards I served, almost all our guys are in. We've won control of the council for the next four years.

Thanks to a recount, my ward is last to declare. Buzz and two of the Poole Xenophobe candidates are in. Ali and I are out. The only other Tory to fail is Susan in the ward across the bridge. Poole Xenophobes take all three seats we fail in.

I was sure I'd be swept in with the tide. But the Lib Dem joker split the vote. The two Ross names on the ballot confused voters. I'm stunned.

A victorious party colleague called Mohan buys me a beer and stands with me at the bar for a while. He's a big chap, tall and muscular, of Indian heritage, and he looks presidential in a smart suit and tie. His manner is friendly and bumbling, and he has a Brummie accent.

'That must have been hard. What you need is a stiff drink.'

'Yeah, that was quite a disappointment,' I admit. 'But I'm not going to let it get me down. I have a longer game plan to work on.'

Mohan and I sat in the same candidate class. Among the new recruits, he was the one most fancied by our MP and the local party grandees. They selected him to stand in the most prosperous ward, where I thought my Oxford degrees would trump his Harvard MBA, but I was wrong. Mohan is not only a respected business consultant in the Poole area but also has a beautiful redhead wife and three charming teenage daughters.

'Game plan?' he asks. 'What's the secret strategy, then?'

'Well, I'm a thinker. I'm not cut out for council business. I have bigger ideas. I'm collecting material for a strategic review of British politics. The whole British establishment needs an update, a refresh, a reset, a reboot. We need an overview of what to change. That's my job.'

'Aha, a philosopher. Well, I have a family to feed.'

When he goes off to talk with someone else, I sit down in front of a big TV screen to follow the national results. My old partner in propaganda, Isaac, sits down beside me.

'How are you feeling, my old mate?'

I pull a wan smile: 'Not so bad. I can take it. I'm too much of a philosopher to be bothered by losing a council seat. Now I'll have more time to work on my next book and reflect on bigger things.'

He nods: 'Glad you're not in the dumps about it. We should congratulate you anyway for organising a winning campaign. I'm sure we can run the council without you, but we're grateful.'

The Conservatives win a small national majority. On Friday, Labour leader Ed Miliband, Lib Dem leader Nick Clegg, and UKIP leader Nigel Farage all resign. Dave is the winner on the seventieth anniversary of VE Day, Victory in Europe day.

I'm angry to have failed. Letting a joker terminate my political career so easily is humiliating. Okay, I didn't really put my back into it, but most politicians go a bit further before they crash.

I soldier on. A week after the count, I chauffeur Syms to the harbourside clubhouse of the Poole Flying Boat Club for an event. A local author has published a book about the flying boats that used to fly in and out of Poole. He's sponsoring a plaque for them at the site, and Robert is unveiling it.

I recall the end of that history from my childhood, when the last of the big boats still flew local trips for tourists. Old and noisy as they were, they made a beautiful sight when they landed and took off in the harbour. Just a few years earlier, they flew scheduled runs for British Overseas Airways Corporation across the old empire, to Africa and India, to Singapore, and onward to Australia and New Zealand. And during the war, BOAC Clipper boats flew between Poole and America. Winston Churchill piloted one during a trip to parlay with President Franklin Roosevelt.

I take a few pictures of the clubhouse ceremony. The author gives Robert a printed placard with images from his book. Back at the office, I mount it in the portrait gallery beside the Churchills.

Cameron's former chief strategist Steve Hilton has published his memoirs in a book outlining his ideas. Over the weekend, I read a few extracts.

'Democracy is in crisis. Between Westminster, Whitehall, and the City, the same people are in power. It is a democracy in name only, operating on behalf of a tiny elite.'

I think the elite is safer than the people.

'The assumptions, the structures, the rules that govern our lives are not subject to anything as unpredictable as the will of the people.'

I'm glad they aren't.

'We need to make democracy work as a vehicle for real people power, not the plutocrat power we have today. We need to take power out of the hands of big donors and unions and business and put it back in the hands of the people.'

I prefer capitalism to mob rule.

I think Hilton's argument is overwrought. But perhaps it shows what happens to a chap after he's worked at the cutting edge of British politics for a few years. It's a sobering thought.

Cable Network News, CNN, cheers me up. My addiction began in Germany, in January 1991, when CNN live action reports from the Gulf War filled my TV screen with thrilling images of modern tanks and warplanes doing their stuff in earnest.

CNN keeps me focused on global issues. Its founder, media mogul Ted Turner, is a man who puts his money where his mouth is on green themes and thinks about the planet even when others don't.

At the end of the month, CNN applauds when Pope Francis issues a papal encyclical on the environment. The Holy Father says the global warming caused by huge consumption on the part of some rich countries has repercussions. The Earth, our home, he says, is looking more and more like an immense pile of filth.

Britain is ruled from a smaller pile.

7.   Government in the round

Soon after his victory, Robert Syms invites me to accompany him on a personal guided tour of the Palace of Westminster. As agreed, I take the train to Waterloo and walk over Westminster Bridge to Portcullis House. This is a plain modern building, filled with offices, across the street from Big Ben and the Houses of Parliament.

I show up an hour or so before lunch, in my dark suit and blue tie, on the street in front of Robert's workplace. A gaggle of security police with assault rifles at the ready is gathered around the main entrance, but they let me through.

In the foyer between the first and second row of doors, I'm told to remove anything metal from my pockets and person and put them, with my shoes and the belt from my trousers, into a tub for scanning. I then shuffle in and retrieve my stuff before seeking out an armchair in the atrium and waiting.

Robert walks up with a smile widening his pudgy cheeks, sporting a less crumpled jacket than usual. 'Hi, sorry I'm late, had a few calls to make. Did you have a good journey up here?'

'Pretty good, thanks, except that I took a slow train and it stopped at every station up to Winchester.'

'Still better than trying to park here in London. Let's go up to my office.'

We go upstairs and along a corridor to a small, bland office and talk about trivia for a while. Then Robert leads me down to a basement corridor linking Portcullis House to the Victorian palace across the street. Once we're back at ground level, I look around and see the place is so run down they'll need to spend several billion pounds to bring it up to scratch. The style is ornate and archaic, but I spot the damaged and worn detail – the rusty window frames, hollowed flagstones, dented doorways, and threadbare carpets.

Robert is used to all this and simply gives me his standard running commentary for visitors, who come regularly as guests from Poole to marvel at the historic centre of so much national endeavour and imperial glory. I let most of it wash over me. I'm just curious as to how a kingdom aspiring to fit into the modern world can possibly be run from such an antique pile.

After a tour of all the main tourist stations, including libraries and ancillary rooms, the two main debating chambers, and a Lords cloakroom offering space not only to hang cloaks and swords but also to don wigs and silk stockings for the day's proceedings in the upper house, Robert and I end up in the members' dining room overlooking the Thames, where we have lunch.

I choose stoically to drink only water, but Robert orders a bottle of wine from his bottle bank at the bar. The menu looks good. The waiter service is good, too.

Robert sips his wine. 'Well, this is my workplace. What do you think of it?'

I sip my water. 'I think it needs a very thorough renovation. It looks to me like a big and labyrinthine version of an Oxford college. All the details are depressingly familiar. I'm sure all the Oxbridge old boys feel completely at home here.'

Robert went to an elite boarding school but not to a university. He worked in the family company before getting into government. His career is proof that higher degrees aren't much use in politics. 'It works, and that's the main thing. It is being renovated, slowly, but we don't want to interrupt the daily business.'

'Something else bothers me. Why are the debating chambers still arranged as two banks of seats facing each other? All the modern parliaments in the world have semicircular chambers, so that speakers can stand at the centre and face everyone.'

'Tradition,' he says. 'It's always been like that, and it's worked so far, so why change it?'

'I'm not so sure that it has worked. The parallel rows make two sides, like a sporting contest, instead of a gathering of equals. When they renovated the German Reichstag building for the Bundestag, they made a semicircular chamber and it looks much better. It also works well, with proportional representation and so on.'

Robert answers like a history buff: 'The Reichstag building was almost demolished by RAF bombs and Red Army artillery, so they had a free hand to rebuild it any way they liked.'

'But they made a good job of it. They even hired a British architect, Sir Norman Foster, to redesign the central dome. I walked up the spiral ramp inside it once. The dome is glazed, and you get a glorious view of Berlin from the top.'

The main course arrives, and we start eating.

I speak up. 'What do you think about the euro? Are you glad Britain didn't join it?'

'Very glad,' he says after swallowing. 'You only have to look at what's happening in Greece. It's a nightmare. They're talking about Grexit. They should never have allowed Greece into the eurozone.'

'Maybe not. But the euro is a good idea. I was very grateful for it when I was driving around Europe. They just need centralised deposit insurance and harmonised fiscal rules to make the system work better.'

Our talk is technical for a while. The dessert arrives when we're onto immigration.

'My main issue with the EU is they don't seem to have a firm grip on immigration,' he says. 'Look at what the Germans are having to endure. A million immigrants, just streaming in, with no control at all. Angela Merkel will have to answer for that.'

'Maybe she will, but you have to see it in historical context.' I'm on home turf here. 'Millions of Germans were forced to flee from the Red Army in 1945, so most Germans understand the need to help the Syrians escaping from all the chaos around them.'

He shakes his head: 'They'll never integrate them properly. All those Muslims will be a security nightmare, as well as a burden on the welfare services.'

I know better: 'You forget that Germans have had a fairly good experience for decades with their Turkish immigrants. The Turks are working well for them. Inviting in Syrians too is a good business investment.'

Our table talk moves on to wider defence issues. Like his party colleagues, Robert is a staunch advocate of the British nuclear deterrent. The issue is in the news because it's time to issue contracts for the next generation of nuclear submarines to replace the navy's V-class subs, which carry the Trident missiles for the nukes.

I cite the facts: 'The replacement cost for the Trident submarines will be around twenty billion pounds, and the lifetime cost of the system is up in the region of a hundred billion. It's a colossal waste of money when we can't afford decent housing or properly funded schools or a health service that can keep going in winter.'

'We need it. Otherwise, the Russians could blackmail us. In effect, we're buying into the American nuclear deterrent. The missiles are American, and we're not likely to use them without American backing. Without the Americans, we'd be defenceless.'

'I see that. But the Americans have more than enough nukes already. By having them too, we only make ourselves a nuclear target. We'd do better to beef up our conventional capabilities.'

'We're a nuclear target anyway. We need to be able to hit back.'

Our policy debate continues.

———

Back in Poole, the new leader of the council is Janet Walton. She's slightly younger than me, and everyone agrees she has the right managerial talents. Her new personal problem is that she's a widow, yet she needs an escort for some of the social functions that come with being the leader.

I'm a natural candidate for the role. Ever since I started my job, single women of late middle age in the party have seen me as a prospect for a more personal relationship. A wealthy widow I call Lady Luck shows an obvious interest. But I still have enough animal spirits to lust after younger mates, so I just play along politely.

Janet is different. She's careful to respect my space and my dignity and has a clear need for a male escort from time to time. When she invites me to accompany her on a tour of a local art museum in the company of local dignitaries from across the conurbation, I say yes.

The Russell Cotes art gallery and museum is a treasure trove of erotic delights. Founded a century ago by a wealthy man who doted on his wife and wanted a permanent memorial to his love for her, the museum's fairy-tale mansion is sited superbly on the breast of a cliff overlooking the beach in central Bournemouth. So far as I'm aware, it houses the best art museum in the entire conurbation.

As Janet and I tour the museum in a loose crowd of dignitaries, we quietly discuss the various exhibits with the judicious and discerning eyes of a pair of art connoisseurs. Since many of the exhibits are statues or paintings of naked men and women in poses or scenes of clearly erotic intent, this becomes an amusing game of discussing sex without descending to vulgar banality. It's a fun date.

Our next date is a month later, and it's a totally different game. This time, we enjoy a guided tour, again with other civic dignitaries, of a Royal Navy frigate, HMS Iron Duke, anchored offshore from Bournemouth Pier. For me it's fascinating, and I take the time to interrogate the officers on board closely regarding their operational deployments, for example in defending merchant vessels as they ply the pirate-infested waters off Somalia.

———

This year's Bournemouth air show happens while I'm entertaining visitors from Germany. Rolf and Angie, the friends I last saw in

Schwetzingen, are visiting England – with the kids – to visit Angie's parents, and they stop by to see me.

I lead Rolf and Angie, plus their son and daughter, along the seafront. As we stride along in the baking solar flux, beside beaches crowded with thousands of holidaymakers, the aircraft fly low over the sea. The show includes the usual staccato commentary from loudspeakers on the lampposts standing sentry along the prom. At first, it's all harmless babble about aerobatic speedsters and their daring pilots. Then a bigger beast flies in.

'The next item in our show, flying in from the left, is the mighty Vulcan,' says the voice. 'This is the last flying example of this magnificent aircraft, the heavy bomber that was a mainstay of the British nuclear deterrent in the Fifties and Sixties, and this could be its last flight. Its airframe is old, and it has almost run out of flying hours.'

The delta-winged monster flies alongside the beach, low and slow, to give everyone a good look at it. The noise from its four Olympus turbojets is deafening, overwhelming all commentary until it passes and begins a long turn to fly back the other way.

'Just imagine,' the commentator says when he can, 'the team that designed this incredibly beautiful aircraft was the same team that only a few years earlier had designed the Lancaster, the most successful bomber of the Second World War, the mainstay of the RAF bombing campaign over Germany that did so much to win the war. Imagine – in one step from the Lancaster to this amazing delta-winged design, which was capable of dropping a nuclear bomb onto Moscow.'

The Vulcan flies by this time with its bomb doors open to show off its long and cavernous bomb bay. When the noise abates, the staccato voice resumes.

'The RAF kept over a hundred of these glorious aircraft poised and ready to scramble at a few minutes' notice to go and bomb targets all over Europe. Ladies and gentlemen – the Vulcan!'

Rolf isn't looking at the plane and not listening. He's spotted a computer exhibition in a marquee on the beach and headed off quickly with his son to explore it. He must think the Vulcan is a monstrous and infernal machine.

———

Weeks later, I move out of the old flat and into a small two-bedroom flat a few miles away. I'm still in Poole, but nearer the beach, in a big, secluded block with a manager and a security gate. My car is safe in a basement garage and my IKEA bookcases just about fit into the flat.

Since I live alone and still dream of returning to Germany, my housing needs are simple. I just want a quiet and secure base where I can read and write to my heart's content, with the pleasures of the seafront nearby and a natural paradise a hike away to the south. The flat is a few floors up, facing west, overlooking a big tree.

Soon after I move in, my old schoolfriends Steve and Graham with wives Anne and Jules visit me on a day trip. We chillax in my lounge before heading off to lunch.

I show them around my new digs. The lobby is big enough for a coat stand and a shoe rack. The spare bedroom is filled with two walls of bookcases and a foldaway bed disguised as a padded chair. The main bedroom has a single bed, more bookcases, a chest of drawers with a television on it for viewing movies, and a display cabinet for my collection of model tanks. The lounge features a wall of bookcases, an armchair, a big glass table for two Mac computers, a television for news, a few shelves for model aircraft, and a round table with three dining chairs. Apart from two tiny bathrooms and a kitchen alcove, that's it.

Steve gazes around the lounge. 'Looks good. Are you happy here?'

'Yes, it's fine. It precisely meets my needs as a solitary philosopher.'

Anne, the country girl who raised three sons in a marital home as big as a barn, sits down in the armchair. 'It looks quite cosy. I'm sure you'll be very happy here.'

Graham stands in the doorway. 'Yes, it looks – very cosy. Ah, I see you have a pair of Mac computers. I have a Mac network at home in London. Great machines.'

'Indeed,' I reply. 'I used Windows machines too in Germany, but then I decided to standardise.'

Jules looks at the wall of books. 'What a lot of books you have! Have you read them all?'

'Most of most of them, yes. Reading, writing, blogging, watching news and movies, and communing with nature in the great outdoors – that's my life.'

Jules looks across the lobby. 'Is that your bedroom?'

'Yes. That reminds me – let me show you my tank collection.'

Steve smiles: 'Ah, the tanks, I remember them from Germany.'

I collected a few little die-cast models of army vehicles after the sixtieth anniversary of D-Day prompted me to read Churchill's six-volume history of the Second World War. When I then visited a couple of local technical museums south of Heidelberg, the wartime German tanks there prompted me to buy souvenirs.

I show my guests the rows of little models parked in a glazed cabinet. On top of the shrine, a small faux bronze bust of Churchill reposes in splendour. I bought the bust a decade ago on a family outing to Churchill's country home in Chartwell in Kent.

'Well, here it is. My historic tank collection.'

Steve cracks a joke. 'I suppose we should call it Churchill's war cabinet.'

'Very good. In Germany, I called it my *Panzerschrank*.'

I treat my guests to a brief lecture on tanks. We soon agree to head out for lunch at a nearby restaurant.

Late that evening, alone again, I reflect on marriage. It would be good to have a wife to share the ups and downs of social life. I google again the name of my romantic nemesis, the Oxford girl who symbolises for me the end of my days with Judy. There's that little pixelated image again.

Quickly, before I can reflect on my folly, I grab the image, zoom it up to A4 size, and print it. Then I bury the printout in a stack of papers. Best to forget all that horror.

———

Later in the year, I drive to Oxford for a seminar on global security issues held at the university's Department of Politics and International Relations. The department is housed in a new building, and the seminar rooms are smart and fit for purpose. I learn a lot that day about terrorism and cyberwarfare.

During the break, where speakers and attendees mingle over canapes and drinks, I talk with a young German lady, Dr Annette Idler, about her talk on terrorism. Although she's perilously pretty and obviously of Nordic ethnic heritage, she travelled extensively in the Mideast region to do her research. She's an expert on Islamic terrorist groups in Syria and Iraq.

I ask her: 'Why did you go into this line of research? There must be easier ways to do useful work than travelling in war zones and talking to murderers.'

Dr Idler stares into her orange juice. 'I wanted to understand why they chose to fight the Americans when they knew they would die. They were very committed to their cause.'

'Does that mean the rest of us are not? Personally, I'm committed to better things than killing Americans.'

She frowns: 'They love the warrior code, the lifestyle, the weapons, the comradeship with each other. Their code of honour is to welcome martyrdom in order to redeem the holy places.'

'Sounds horrifying. What do you think of Angela Merkel's welcoming so many immigrants from Syria into Germany?'

She frowns again. 'Risky. But almost all of them will integrate peacefully. As refugees from war, they deserve our support.'

I also chat with a young Estonian man, Dr Lucas Kello, about his talk on cyberterrorism. The Baltic state of Estonia has a large fraction of its government services online, and Russian hackers hit it with a major cyberattack and inflicted serious damage. The attack was a wake-up call for Western governments.

I ask Dr Kello about the risk: 'Do you think Russian hackers will attack other Western countries? Why would they do that?'

'Why?' He's a tall man but looks boyish. 'Because they want to push NATO forces back. All NATO member states are targets.'

'In Britain we have strong cyber-defences, thanks to GCHQ, as you probably know, so why should we be concerned?'

'Because the Russians know it too,' he says. 'They have other weapons, as they showed in Ukraine. They will spread lies and propaganda on social media to disrupt democratic politics.'

I nodded sagely. He was right.

After the seminar, I walk around the new Radcliffe Observatory campus in the city and admire the new Blavatnik School of Government. It's a cylindrical structure, not yet open, and I guess it has a round central hall big enough for a parliament to meet.

If Britain ever suffers a revolution that takes out the Palace of Westminster, perhaps a provisional parliament will meet here. The city of Oxford is officially twinned with Bonn in Germany, and Bonn was the capital of the federal republic for decades before the government moved to Berlin in 1999.

In the event of a constitutional crisis, Oxford is well equipped to host a new government for the British Republic.

8.   A big collision

In February 2016, responding to new text from Brussels on the terms of British membership in the EU to meet his complaints, David Cameron makes a statement in the Commons:

'I have spent the last nine months setting out the four areas where we need reform and meeting ... to reach an agreement that delivers concrete reforms in all four areas.'

First: 'We wanted new protections for our economy to safeguard the pound, to promote our industries ..., to protect British taxpayers from the costs of problems in the eurozone, and to ensure we have a full say over the rules of the single market ... And we got all of those things.'

Second: 'We wanted commitments to make Europe more competitive ... Again, we got them.'

Third: 'We wanted to reduce the very high level of migration from within the EU by preventing the abuse of free movement ... We have also secured ... agreement for Britain to reduce the unnatural draw that our benefits system exerts across Europe.'

Fourth: 'We wanted ... to protect our country from further European political integration ... And now Britain will be permanently and legally excluded from it.'

He says he's satisfied: 'We will be in the parts of Europe that work for us, influencing the decisions that affect us ... But we will be out of the parts of Europe that do not work for us.'

Now he nails that zinger: 'I am today commencing the process ... to propose that the British people decide our future in Europe through in-out referendum on Thursday 23 June.'

———

On Ash Wednesday 2016, I drive to Oxford to show a visiting German couple the Penrose paving at the Mathematical Institute.

I respond to the news the next morning like a true science nerd. Scientists at an observatory called LIGO have detected gravitational waves from the collision and merger of two massive black holes over a billion light years away.

LIGO has two sites some three thousand kilometres apart, each with two long tunnels at right angles to each other. The scientists shot a laser beam along each tunnel and timed how long it took to bounce back, as gravitational waves rippled through both sites, making one arm shorter and the other longer, vibrating back and forth. They recorded changes in length equivalent to measuring the distance between the Earth and the nearest star down to the width of a human hair.

The two black holes that collided were big. They merged into a black hole of over sixty solar masses and turned three solar masses into energy as gravitational waves. For a moment, the power surge outdid all the other stars in the observable universe combined. The theory behind all this is Einstein's general theory of relativity.

Earthlings were rocked by a big noise a billion light years away. As a physics buff, I think that's really cool.

———

I meet a lady called Rachel (the name means mother of the lamb in Hebrew) on the Friday afternoon a fortnight later. Rachel leads the student union in Bournemouth University. She phoned Pam a week ago to make a surgery date to talk with Robert about how to get BU students more involved in politics.

Pam and I agree I should attend the meeting too, not only to add my views on student political activism but also to act as chaperone. When I check Rachel's profile online, I see she's a lovely young woman, and this means our MP needs insurance against malicious accusations of impropriety. Robert is a renowned ladies' man, and Isaac says I should be alert when ladies come to the surgery.

Rachel enters the office like a dream. As a recent graduate, she's in the first bloom of her womanhood, tall, slender, athletic, and fair of face. Her long, dark, wavy hair cascades over a tailored jacket and a dark dress that ends short to expose elegant legs in black tights. Forget Robert – she already needs protection from me.

The member for Poole is taking his time with previous surgery visitors, so I enact the welcome. I'm dressed sharply, as usual on Friday. Today I sport a black former suit jacket, cut in the style Helmut Kohl favoured during his years as German chancellor, over pressed grey trousers, polished wingtip shoes, clean white shirt, and an Italian silk tie patterned in fifty shades of grey. I offer Rachel a coffee and stand in front of her as the kettle boils.

Rachel sits with legs crossed and tells me: 'I graduated last summer in biology, but now I want to work in politics.'

I stand back from a raised foot. 'Giving up science for politics? Risky move. Have you considered graduate study in politics?'

'I'm not so into academic study. I prefer getting involved. How did you start?'

'Start?' I sigh. 'In physics at Oxford, but then I graduated in PPE and later worked in Whitehall.'

She reddens slightly: 'I was going to sit for Oxford, but then I fell ill and had to abandon it.'

I appraise her carefully and reply gently: 'Student politics is a good way to start, so long as you're not too radical. I did a master's at the London School of Economics – there were plenty of real radicals there, busy wrecking their careers.'

She smiles suddenly: 'I'm a Conservative.'

I serve coffee. Robert emerges from the back room with his surgery guests, and a scrum of awkward bodies forms and dissolves before Rachel and I are seated with Robert in the back room, all waiting for three coffees in paper cups to cool.

Robert doesn't look like a ladies' man today. There's something heavy and morose about his presence, but he rallies with smooth phrases: 'So, Rachel, how can we help you raise interest among the students in getting more involved in party politics?'

Rachel looks animated, turning on the charm, but I'm alert for this. She pulls a little smile as she answers: 'I thought we could hold a few events on political questions more generally, perhaps with debates or seminars on active themes.'

I cut in on Robert, who's too slow, with an idea: 'The most active theme right now is the EU referendum. How about holding a debate or a panel session on whether we should leave the EU or remain? That would surely animate the students.'

Rachel looks at me with big eyes and a smile: 'That's a good idea. We do sometimes hold debates like that on campus, and I agree Europe would be a good topic.'

Cameron's referendum on UK membership of the EU is still four months away, but the campaign rhetoric is already heating up. His proposed new deal with his European partners looks thin, and everyone in the country has their own opinion on what to do next. I'm eager to hear what students think we should do.

I reply: 'if you can do that, I'd be happy to get involved.'

The meeting continues. As always, the contents of our discussion are confidential, and I don't wish to break my oath of office, but as I lead her out, I sense a liveliness in her manner that shows she's glad she's sparked my interest in her. As we part with a handshake, she invites me to keep in touch and I repeat my offer to help with a Europe debate.

———

The Bournemouth University student debate on Europe takes place on Friday 15 April. For the Remain side, the speaker is Julie Girling, who's a Conservative member of the European parliament. For the Leave side, the speaker is Martin Houlden, a former UKIP parliamentary candidate for Bournemouth West.

I'm the chairman and moderator. The event is staged in the

union building on the university campus. The campus is modern, financed with generous new money, and the SUBU building is a smart cylindrical tower with open-plan floors around a central shaft of lifts and stairs. The debate venue is high up in the block.

As I wander around the site to get acquainted with it, I'm impressed by how well behaved the students are. It's an international campus, with visitors from all parts of the world, and the university teaches practical subjects like hotel management and digital media production to paying students. No hippies here!

I've dressed formally for the debate, in my dark suit with white shirt and a sober tie, and I pace around the debating area like a lost VIP. The students sit working on laptops or tablets, without books. I feel old as I read a poster for the event that features my mugshot plus a few words about me.

Rachel pops up and reviews the event planning with me. She blends in well among the students, and she greets and chats with them in such a smooth and practised way that I see why she might wish to be a politician. Her student friends all look up to her.

When Julie Girling MEP steps out from the lift, I'm there to greet her. She cuts a smart figure, of average height and build and in early middle age, with short fair hair and big glasses, a string of big plastic pearls, and a red jacket over a black top and skirt. I find her instantly sympathetic. We're on the same side.

By contrast, when Martin Houlden, the UKIP man, appears from the lift, I see he's an opponent straight from central casting for his party. He's friendly and soft-spoken in manner, but his bald head and robust presence suggest hard views. He's in a black V-neck pullover over an open white shirt, trying to fit in.

There's a reassuringly big audience for the event. The students fill the rows of seats, and plenty more stand around the edge, maybe to give it a go for a minute before drifting off. At least the central phalanx looks earnest and eager.

I open the proceedings and introduce the speakers.

'Julie Girling is a member of the European parliament and a member of the Conservative group within it, where she has been since 2009. She's one of the members representing our own southwest region of England, which also includes Gibraltar. She specialises in the issues around agriculture and fisheries, to which she brings a scientific perspective. Julie will be presenting the case for the Remain side of the debate.'

I stop there. If she wants to say more, she can.

'Martin Houlden will present the case for the Leave side of the story. As a member of the United Kingdom Independence Party, UKIP, Martin stood as a parliamentary candidate here in Bournemouth West in 2015. As a businessman, Martin knows how our EU membership impacts business and will doubtless explain how it affects all of us.'

I invite Julie Girling to make her case.

'Thank you, Andy,' she begins. 'As one of your representatives in the European parliament, I try to make sure that we in Britain have a fair say in the drafting of the legislation that governs all of Europe, ourselves included, and to make sure that reason and common sense prevail in the laws and regulations that come out of our work. Many people here seem to think that European parliamentarians don't always act in the British best interests, so I feel it's important for us to be there to make sure that our interests are properly represented.'

Calmly and smoothly, she reviews the issues the Conservative group has tackled over the years and how the parliament works.

'In summary,' she says, 'Britain needs a voice in Europe just as Europeans need to hear what we have to say on the issues that concern us all. If we were to leave the EU, we would lose that voice in the debates and run the risk that the rest of the union went on to make decisions we didn't like. The input we can have on the issues that concern us certainly makes our membership worthwhile. And that's my case for voting Remain on 23 June.'

The students clap politely. I invite Houlden to speak.

'Thanks,' he begins. 'Britain is a strong nation with a proud history. We can stand alone as an independent nation, as we did for hundreds of years when we built a global empire that was bigger than any other in human history. We don't need permission from Europeans to decide how we run our lives and our economy and our businesses.'

He continues. 'So, to sum up, the EU is tying us down with red tape and arbitrary rules that we really don't need. We can prosper as a sovereign nation, and we can make new trade deals with other sovereign nations around the world, starting with the United States and the Commonwealth countries. Europe is stagnating under its own bureaucracy. We need to break free while we still can. So, I say vote Leave on 23 June.'

More polite applause. I invite questions. Rachel raises a hand.

'I just wanted to add that the EU scheme for letting students live and work anywhere in Europe – and to cooperate internation-ally on shared projects – is really important for us as a university. My question is, how could all that continue if we left the EU?'

Martin replies: 'That's a very good question, and one with a very good answer. Europeans will be as eager as we are to minimise dis-ruption of these student exchange schemes after we leave. They have a strong interest in letting them continue, as we do. We have American students here in Britain, so why shouldn't France or Germany have British students in just the same way? With that sort of arrangement, I don't see this as a problem at all.'

I once worked as housemaster for some American students on an exchange programme in London, and I recall a host of problems EU students don't face. But I say silent.

When I hold a final vote to see who'd now vote Leave and who

Remain, I'm cheered to find a strong majority for Remain.

When the event ends, Rachel comes up and thanks me warmly. I quietly take the chance to admire again her fresh and radiant face. Then I usher Julie and Martin politely off the premises and drive back to base camp. I'm happy.

———

Two weeks later, I meet the home secretary, Theresa May, at a Conservative tea party in the Dorset village of Shaftesbury. She's visiting us on a meet-and-greet mission to fire us up for the campaign to support the government policy of ensuring that the UK remains in the EU. For me, it's a chance to size her up as a person. Her zealous attempts to restrict immigration are too controversial to ignore.

The tearoom is in a stone cottage that would seem old even in a Thomas Hardy novel, and the tea-drinking guests need to stoop for the doorways. But Theresa, who's tall even in her flat leopard-skin shoes, copes well as she takes the time to shake hands with all those present, uttering polite words as she does so. I'm impressed by her composure in face of this duty.

One of her duties is to answer assorted questions. I'm impressed again by her easy fluency in answering a tricky question about trade policy. I see a lady with the right stuff for high office.

———

I ask Rachel to be my date for a gala dinner to be held at an Italian villa in a formal garden in Poole on Friday 13 May. This is a bold move for an older man with a duty of care toward a recent student, but I'm confident enough in my ancient wisdom to go ahead anyway. She accepts my invitation with thanks.

The gala dinner is held by and in the name of the outgoing mayor of Poole, Cllr Ann Stribley, JP, MBE, a formidable lady who has dominated the council for years and earned her membership of the order of the British Empire for her work as an EU emissary in

Ukraine. The worshipful madam mayor is holding the dinner to raise funds for the charities she supports.

Rachel insists on meeting me at my flat, which is only a walk away from the Italian villa. I open my door to see her standing askew and awkward in the hallway but looking great. She's in a tailored jacket over a white blouse with black trousers. I wave her in.

It's a warm day and I'm still dithering over what to wear. I've settled on black cord jeans and an open white shirt, which I'll top with a black velvet tux I can take off again when we get there. I'm still barefoot. I've dusted and hoovered the flat, but I'm aware she'll be unimpressed by it.

She steps in cheerfully and kicks off her flat black shoes, leaving her barefoot too. I'm glad she didn't need prompting. Living in Japan has taught me to take off my shoes in someone's personal home. There they offer slippers to guests, but I think that's too much fuss.

She takes off her jacket. I wave an invitation to hang it up. Her white blouse is translucent and airy, and under it she has a white bralette. I feel the warm air from her body and resist an impulse to plant kisses on her cheeks. Instead, I lead her calmly into the work-room, where bright sunlight streams in through a big window. It's open for air, but the room temperature is at tropical heights.

'Can I offer you a drink before we go?'

Rachel smiles. 'Yes, thanks, water would be fine.'

'Fruit juice, maybe? A non-alcoholic grape cordial, perhaps.'

'Yes, I'll try that, thanks.'

I gesture at the armchair. 'Please take a seat.'

She remains standing as I pour the drinks. I hand her one and stay standing too. She's slightly taller than I am.

I drink as she silently checks my bookshelves. I ask: 'Did you get any follow-up from the big debate?'

She turns to me and nods slowly: 'Yes, a lot of people said how much they enjoyed it. Thank you again for chairing it.'

'You're welcome. I'm glad you accepted my invitation to come to this dinner. I wouldn't have gone otherwise. I needed a fascinating female escort to make it worth attending.'

She looks at me coolly. 'I understood that. I told my boyfriend I was out to have dinner with local politicians.'

'I assumed you'd have a boyfriend. But in your social media posts you said you were bisexual.'

She smiles suddenly and glances aside at the books: 'Not actively, but I am in principle. I support LGBT equality.'

'Don't we all? Sexuality is always an ambiguous thing. So is most human interaction, come to that.'

She ponders that idea for a moment, then asks: 'Have you really read all these books?'

'Most of them, yes. That's my thing, reading and writing. You can't be a philosopher without this much study, or at least not the sort of philosopher I try to be.'

'I haven't read any of your books,' she says. 'Which one should I start with?'

I smile. 'Let's take it slowly. I don't know what you know already and what your main interests are.'

'Not much. I'm not such a bookish person. Biology was more a matter of lab work and online resources.'

'Quite right too. Books are old-fashioned now. But they're what I'm used to, and I find them a good working tool.'

She slowly drains her glass. 'Shall we go?'

I drain mine quickly. 'Sure. Let's go.'

We move to the lobby for our shoes. I opt for a pair of black rubber water shoes with open mesh uppers that feel good without socks. We head out for dinner.

The Italian villa is enchanting in the early evening sunlight. It's set in an extended formal garden full of exotic flowers, and it's fronted by a rectangular pond with a fountain and a wide flight of marble steps up to the entrance. Trees and a stone wall separate us from the rest of the garden and gave us some privacy for our exclusive dinner.

The madam mayor of Poole stands beside the drinks table in her best evening gown, resplendently bedecked with her heavy golden chain of office. She's a quietly imposing lady, but friendly and charming in manner. She's not as tall as Rachel or me.

'Hi, Ann,' I say as I kiss her formally on one cheek. I introduce Rachel, and the two ladies exchange pleasantries. I look around and recognise maybe half of the guests. Next in the rope line is a married gay couple I like to joke with, now in matching black ties and tuxes. The younger one is John, a Conservative councillor, and the older one, balding and bearded, is Jon, a retired psychologist. I introduce them to Rachel.

Soon we climb the stairs and enter the banquet hall.

Hours pass in convivial company. Rachel and I sit at a round table with a gaggle of older ladies plus a wealthy old party patriarch. The other tables are out of reach as we eat. This is provincial Conservative social life at its best – civilised, respectable, and assured beyond doubt of its own fundamental decency and good taste.

For grass-roots Tories, functions like this are the essence of being English. For them, this exquisite blend of politeness and reserve is the great contribution of the island race to civilisation. For them, to be English is still somehow special.

Rachel and I talk about many things in politics and philosophy. She speaks in such a soft and gentle tone that I find it hard to place her voice or pin down her positions, so I just speak from the heart and trust she gets it. She pours her heart out too, I sense, and I feel warmth at the intimacy and trust she shows.

One personal thing she tells me, apart from her feelings about gender roles and leadership, is that she has family roots in Germany.

Her grandparents came to England just before the war. But I'm too lost in the moment to probe further.

After all that, we come down the stairs to the flagstones beside the pond and stand in the fresh night air, still warm from a hot day.

I pop the question: 'Would you like to come back to my place for a while?'

She demurs softly: 'No thanks, I must be getting back. Can I get a taxi here?'

'Yes, but I can offer you a lift back in my car.'

'Thanks, but I'd rather take a taxi.'

I relent. 'Okay, your call. Thank you for a delightful evening.'

She smiles widely: 'Thank you, I really enjoyed it. I've had a wonderful time.'

We go our separate ways. I'm old and wise enough to be grateful for the happy hours. I'm a philosopher.

9.   Bestowing the kiss

I make my next contribution to the national debate on UK membership of the EU a week later. I speak to a local audience at a Poole
tennis club and prepare my speech carefully.

The tennis club has a long history at its extensive site. The clubhouse resembles a merged row of wartime concrete prefab huts and
is set in a parking lot that might once have been a parade ground.
Many of the club members are staunch Tories.

I'm the main speaker for the Remain case, backed up by a
councillor I know well. John Rampton is an engineer, not a showman, and he takes an interest in the big questions councillors ignore.
I like his intelligence and common sense.

Our main opponent in the debate is the MP for the Bournemouth West constituency. Conor Burns is a tribal Conservative on
the right wing of the party with whom I'm wearily acquainted. He's
of middling height and build, with short greying hair and a ruddy
complexion over a bull neck. His manner is humble to the point of
grovelling toward superiors in the party hierarchy but arrogant to
the point of self-righteous grandstanding with those he regards as
his inferiors.

Conor's backup speaker in the debate is a former marine, who
held a junior rank and is still young.

The restaurant hall housing the event is well packed, and extra
chairs are brought in at the back to seat them. The median age of
the attendees is about fifty.

My speech is titled 'European Union: I Love EU' and I've
checked in advance that I can deliver it in three minutes.

I begin in what I hope is a disarmingly honest style: 'I come to
this debate as a scientist and a philosopher. For me the big picture
is essential. Get that right and the rest is clear.'

I then launch into my big idea that the European Union, the United States of America, and the People's Republic of China together form a triad of powers that set the tone for global politics. I got this idea from my software years in Germany, where SAP runs its global software empire on the 'Follow the Sun' principle between its centres in Walldorf, Palo Alto, and Shanghai.

Next, I recite facts about the architecture and benefits of the EU. I emphasise its role in curbing the excesses of global corporations and in advancing human rights and environmental causes. I add: 'Much of its structure and function is imperfect. There's a lot of work to do before we can say it's done.'

Then I roll out Cameron's claim in his case for Remain: 'Our recently clarified terms of membership give us the best deal possible within the framing principles of the European project.'

I say the EU complements NATO: 'Today security covers not only military threats but also threats from cybercrime and terrorists. … Without the EU, the nations of Europe could fall to them like dominoes.'

I also mention immigration and the temptation to retreat into Fortress UK: 'We are an open society that derives much of its strength from an open culture.'

The 'open' word is my nod to Sir Karl Popper, whom I liked enough to earn my Master's in his department at the LSE.

Economics is next: 'People who dislike the EU often cite the cost of membership. In fact, the cost to Britain last year of EU membership was barely one percent of GDP. This is a small price to pay for the economic benefits.'

I end on what I hope is a ringing note: 'This is not 1940. Our national existence is not at stake. Our neighbours in Europe respect and admire our national identity. We can stay in the club. We can all prosper together in a rapidly globalising world.'

With that, I mumble thanks and sit down to polite applause.

Conor Burns is next. He holds himself in a hunched pose that looks both obsequious and aggressive at once. He doesn't bother with notes. He's bursting with confidence and trusts in the power of his oratorical skills to smooth the way to his declamatory destination. He speaks in a rumbling monotone inflected only by spittle-spattering crescendos when the rumble increases in volume.

'Britain faces the most important decision for a generation in June,' he begins, with an air of parliamentary pomp. 'People of principle and patriotism on both sides should set out their reasons with positive conviction.'

This is not verbatim: 'A little over forty years ago, Britain voted to join the EEC, as the Common Market was then known. Now we find ourselves members of a European Union that has a flag, an anthem, a currency, a parliament, and a supreme court with power to veto UK laws.'

His killer line: 'The restoration of UK democracy is the fundamental reason for leaving the EU. Once the UK is outside the EU, we will again make our own laws in our Westminster parliament, elected by the British people and again fully accountable to them.'

His words on economics are brief, and those on defence are thin: 'Dire warnings on security are bizarre. Does anyone seriously think the UK won't share intelligence and cooperate with our near neighbours on security outside the EU?'

I seriously think the EU might lose its trust in a UK that constantly boasts it punches above its weight yet ignores the bruises it leaves across the continent.

Burns finally hits the hot button: 'For too many years now, immigration has been the number one issue that concerns the British public, but our membership of the EU leaves us powerless to stop people coming here from the continent.'

Winningly, he bends the issue to highlight its impact on the local economy: 'To reduce immigration, the government has been making it harder for people from outside the EU to come here. Anyone who works in a local English language school will tell you the visa process has become harder, so language students are increasingly going to countries like Australia, New Zealand, Canada, and the United States. Our local economy is suffering because we're not free in this country to decide who we invite into this country and who we exclude.'

I frown. It's us versus them again.

Burns rounds off with a flash of outright bombast: 'I have a great belief in the British people. It is their energy, talent, and enterprise that make us the fifth largest economy in the world. I believe they have the common sense and judgement to elect a government to make the laws under which they live. Like them, I have one vote on 23 June. I will be casting it with confidence for Britain to leave the EU and forge a new path as a sovereign nation that trades with the world.'

He sits down with a flourish, and the audience erupts into enthusiastic applause. I knew this was coming and sit impassively. I even clap politely to show I bear no ill will.

Next is John, the wise councillor. With his thinning hair, modest stature, and quiet demeanour, he makes no attempt to dazzle us with rhetorical fireworks, and some at the back find his voice hard to hear. But the case he makes is strong and sound.

After John, the former marine stands up to do his patriotic duty in support of Conor Burns. He delivers a stirring clarion call to rally behind the union jack.

The main event of the evening now follows – the questions and answers. The questions are varied and interesting.

To round things off before a final vote, the two main speakers each give a one-minute review. I'm first. I pick up a few loose ends from the questions and give them each a few words of gloss, but it's not stirring stuff.

Burns takes a quite different approach. Disdaining the details, he makes a grandiloquent declaration of praise for the British heritage, with proud nods to Shakespeare and the English language; the traditions of monarchy and the peerage; the parliamentary achievements of the great Victorians; the British Empire in all its mighty pomp and circumstance; and the proud military traditions of the victors at Trafalgar and Waterloo, the famous few in the Battle of Britain, and doubtless more to come. Here is a nation bathed in glory, crowned with greatness, too blessed by far to let the bureaucrats in Brussels bind it to march in lockstep with the lesser nations of Europe.

The result of the vote is preordained. Leave wins by a big margin. When people stand up to go home, Burns is soon surrounded by a tumult of fans eager to touch his hem.

A video crew interviews me. They're making a news segment for a Japanese TV company. The Japanese interviewer holds out a mike while his assistant begs me not to look at the camera.

He asks: 'Do you think Britain will vote to leave the EU?'

'It's hard to predict, too close to call,' I reply. 'But I think the majority will probably vote to remain. The practical arguments for staying are too strong to ignore.'

'Why do you think so many people want to leave the EU?'

'Well, you heard Conor Burns say why. The idea that Britain is a special country, with a proud tradition and a history of empire, that we can make new trade deals worldwide, is somehow exciting. And most people in Britain think immigration is a problem we need to solve.'

'Why has the debate gotten so angry, so political?'

'Because the issue runs deep. As I see it, this whole debate is a classic case of head versus heart. The head says remain in the EU to enjoy the economic benefits. But the heart, for many people, says leave and let the UK resume its traditional course as a proudly independent nation. Naturally, for most people in Britain the heart wins every time.'

———

I speak in another local debate, this one in a village a few miles away, where the population is heavily stacked with pensioners on the verge of supporting UKIP. The event is in early June, and the national dialogue has taken a turn for the worse, thanks to a hard focus on immigration.

The latest UK immigration figures are the trigger for the new mood. Nigel Farage isn't the culprit this time. Boris Johnson bears most of the blame.

Boris the clown, the former mayor of London who likes to play the fool but is now an MP with a voice in the Commons, bigged up the issue by boosting the wild idea that millions of Turks might suddenly come to Britain. He chose not to say he's one of the few people who favours Turkish membership of the EU, and then only because it would sink it.

Johnson is on the hard right of the party. Conor Burns has taken his entire case on immigration from him. Boris was with David Cameron and George Osborne at Oxford, where the three of them wined and dined together in the Bullingdon Club. I detest the club not only for its elitism but also because it resembles the drinking clubs in Heidelberg, where students duelled with swords to put noble scars on their cheeks.

Johnson the clown went viral in February with a speech that began, characteristically for him, thus: 'Let me tell you where I've got to, which is, um, I am, um … I've made up my mind.'

He made up his mind to promote the Leave cause. Just a few minutes beforehand, he texted his chum Dave with the news, thus undermining Dave's entire government strategy.

The impact of this defiance of Dave was not long in coming. Other MPs around the country began to declare for the Leave cause too. Even Robert Syms tweeted that he'd decided to support the Leavers. I was dismayed and vowed to fight on for Remain.

In the village leaning to UKIP, I'm billed as a supporting act. The main speaker for Remain is Roy Perry, a former British MEP and now the chairman of Hampshire County Council. But I find the case he makes unconvincing. He seems to feel no British voter who thrills to the resonant tradition of the Westminster parliament would willingly tie its destiny to the lame efforts of the European talking shop to control the Brussels juggernaut. I'm saddened.

The main speaker for Leave is a member of UKIP and a candidate for parliamentary office. We're meeting at his business premises. The UKIP case he makes is true to type.

Then it's my turn again.

I begin by channelling Hamlet: 'In or Out? That is the question. In means sharing our future with friends and neighbours. Out means pulling up the drawbridge of Fortress UK.'

It's an edited version of my tennis club talk. My big picture is down to a single line: 'We live in a global village where news travels instantly and divisions of language and race are history.'

I find a new point to make: 'The EU bureaucrats draft technical legislation that could overload national parliaments, so our parliamentarians can focus on serving British voters.'

Another new theme is the integrity of the United Kingdom itself: 'Voting Leave means Britain closing its borders and risking the loss of Northern Ireland and Scotland. Little England would look like a rump state.'

I end as before and sit down to polite applause. The UKIP military man who follows earns a more spirited response.

The audience is agitated in question time. After a few tame questions go by, one old fool, quivering with either senile dementia or barely controlled anger, stands up:

'What about the Turks? We don't want 77 million Turks coming over here, taking our jobs and living on welfare handouts. We need to close our borders now. We're full up!'

A murmur of mutinous solidarity spreads like a wave around him. The mutineers look ready to take up arms against the Turks.

I reply: 'Turkey is not a member of the EU and there's no chance it will be as long as Angela Merkel in Germany has any say in the matter. But let's not start bashing the Turks.'

I explain how Germany has integrated its Turkish minority, but this does nothing to quell the mutiny.

The event runs its course, and a final vote by show of hands gives an overwhelming victory to the Leave side. A few younger people come up to me to share their sympathy, and I settle for that.

Driving back home in my BMW, I muse. My car is my lifeboat in case the national mood keels over. Mob rule might yet force me to pack my bags in a hurry and seek refuge in Germany.

———

The referendum campaign takes a sombre turn on 17 June, when the Labour MP Jo Cox is shot and stabbed to death on the pavement outside her constituency surgery. She was the mother of two young children and a campaigner for Remain.

I read that the killer was a man called Tommy. '*Britain first,*' he shouted as he attacked her.

The brutal murder is a sobering moment in British political life. The European question is raising political passions above the usual British tepid level. Such passions were strong in Germany decades earlier, not because Germans were more hot-blooded than native Brits but because the issues were real and vital.

In an interview published two days later, David Cameron recalls the issues: 'At the moment the case for Brexit, as they are pushing it through your letterbox, is based on three things that are completely untrue.'

He slaps his thigh three times: 'One, that Turkey is about to join the EU; two, that 350 million pounds a week goes to the EU; and three, that there's going to be a European army and Britain's going to be forced into it.'

Relenting on his thigh, he continues: 'If people, after serious thought and consideration, want to leave this organisation, of course we must leave. But to leave it based on three things that are not true would be a pretty desperate outcome.'

In summary, he says: 'I really do believe that there is a very, very clear case for Remain … The right answer is to remain.'

———

I attend a final debate that Tuesday, two days before the referendum, at Bournemouth University. The two Bournemouth MPs are speaking for Leave and Remain respectively and answering questions. The moderator for the event is my young friend Rachel.

The venue is a small semicircular lecture hall in a new block built in a bold and elegant style.

It's a hot, sunny afternoon, and I don't expect a big audience. By this stage in the campaign, most people are fed up with the whole business, and local students have better things to do than listen to two MPs argue with each other.

I turn up in my cream linen suit over an open blue shirt, with perforated white rubber water shoes. I meet Rachel at the entrance. She looks lovely in a little white skater skirt that leaves her long, smooth, graceful legs bare as they descend to tennis shoes.

'Hi, good to see you again,' I blurt. 'How have you been?'

'Good to see you too, Andy!' She makes pleasing eye contact. 'I'm good, thanks. Glad you could make it today.'

'Too nice a day to be arguing over politics, but how could I resist? Anyway, how was the online response for tickets?'

'Pretty good. We'll fill the hall if they all show up.'

She looks behind us and sees the MPs approaching. 'Excuse me, Andy, I have to attend to our guest speakers. Catch you later.'

'Sure.' I go in and find a seat.

Conor Burns MP looks the same as ever with his ruddy complexion, stooped stance, and crumpled dull suit, the parliamentary uniform. Rachel greets him warmly.

Tobias Ellwood is the MP for Bournemouth East. He's also a Conservative, but as a junior minister in the Foreign Office he's well known as an internationalist. He has a military background and a solid and capable bearing, and he supports Remain.

By the time everyone is assembled, the lecture hall is more than half-full. I recognise a few people from my efforts to liven up the local Young Conservatives.

Rachel sits beside a low table, with the two MPs on the other side of it, as in a TV interview. She begins:

'We're here today to discuss the referendum question – should we stay in the European Union or leave it? To help us make up our minds, we have here as guests our two Bournemouth members of parliament, Conor Burns and Tobias Ellwood. Conor will present the case for voting Leave, and Tobias will do the same for Remain.'

Conor makes the case I've heard too often already. Tobias then offers his five minutes of wisdom.

Rachel holds up well in face of their star power. She utters smooth words of thanks and claims her prerogative to ask the first question, a softball starter to Conor.

'Conor,' she begins, with oily charm. 'You mentioned introducing an Australian-style points-based system to control immigration. I can see how that might work for doctors or engineers, but how would you use it on students, who don't have the qualifications and work experience that you'd need to give them points?'

The bullish Conor makes short work of this, but does so in a genial and friendly manner, exempting Rachel from his usual cutthroat style. She turns to face him and smiles indulgently.

I raise my hand and ask a question to even the score: 'Tobias, you said our membership of the EU makes military cooperation on logistical questions easier. Can you tell us more about how our membership can facilitate procurement cooperation too, so that we get the full benefit of kit standardisation in NATO?'

Tobias does so happily. I smile – a razor cut on Conor.

Further questions ensue. Rachel umpires the exchanges with consummate poise, until one precocious student member of the Young Conservatives whom I know well speaks up.

'Conor,' he says, 'You said that once we were free from Brussels rules, we could do trade deals with other countries all around the world, but doesn't the EU already have trade deals with most of those countries, and wouldn't it take far too long to make replacements for all those deals?'

I agree. He's right to see this as a critical question, one the Leavers are far too cavalier about.

But Conor is unimpressed: 'I see you've suddenly become an expert on trade questions. I can assure you that we can make new bilateral deals fast enough to make up the loss of trade with the EU and indeed make us better off in very short order. Perhaps you should study the facts before you take sides on this issue.'

I imagine hearers gasping at Conor's snide tone. Before my friend has time to flounder, I spring to his defence.

'Conor,' I say, 'At present, the UK does nearly half of its international trade with EU member states, less than a seventh with the United States, only about six percent with China, and even less with Commonwealth countries.' I improvise from my daily skim of the *Financial Times*. 'Most economists agree that Britain runs the risk of suffering reduced trade and reduced GNP for many years. Our student colleague is right to flag up this issue.'

Conor fulminates with scorn in reply, but his bluster leaves me unruffled.

Soon enough, Rachel winds the proceedings elegantly to a close.

As we all rise to go, Conor walks up to her and kisses her on both cheeks. I frown to witness such a liberty.

I walk out with Tobias and engage him in closer debate on defence and security policy. We part outside, in the bright sunlight, and I stand waiting for Rachel.

She comes out with a pair of female colleagues. I approach the trio: 'Hi, Rachel, that was an excellent event, well done. Your moderation was flawless, of course.'

She flashes me a wide smile. 'Thank you, Andy! It was lovely to see you again – and thanks for your questions. I thought the debate went very well.'

'Well, I'd better be going. Do keep in touch.' I step forward, reach out to hold her upper arms, and kiss her on both cheeks.

She pulls back gently: 'Yes, keep in touch. See you!'

She extends her right hand firmly and we shake hands. We're partners in politics.

10. 'We're out'

On the day before the referendum vote, David Cameron airs his final thoughts on Brexit: 'As far as I am concerned this referendum should settle the matter. I believe it will one way or another be decisive. Britain will not want to go through this again. On the other hand, if we vote to leave, this really is irreversible.'

I fear the worst. The day marks an anniversary that symbolises the worst all too vividly. It's the 75th anniversary of the start of Operation Barbarossa, Nazi Germany's invasion of the Soviet Union, which came at the darkest hour of the Second World War from Britain's perspective, when Winston Churchill stared defeat in the face and saw only the faintest glimmerings of hope.

The Barbarossa Blitzkrieg led to the most titanic struggle in human history, with millions of troops on either side, millions of deaths, hundreds of thousands of war machines consumed, and an outcome that changed everything. By the time Stalin and the Soviets could rally and fight back, the Nazi onslaught had very nearly taken Moscow. But then America joined the fight, and years of struggle and more megadeaths later, the world was rearranged, with two superpowers as winners and the British Empire among the losers.

For me, Barbarossa shows why Britain must remain fully engaged in Europe. The spillover from such volcanic eruptions will burn or bury the people on the British Isles anyway, so it's far better to hang on in there and help shape the course of events. A British disengagement would be a colossal unforced error.

———

I spend the anniversary walking on the beach. I head south along the playground peninsula of Sandbanks, where tourists flock in summer and the villas of the rich stand empty for most of the year, to a chain ferry that runs across the harbour mouth between the tips of Sandbanks and Studland.

The Studland peninsula is a wilderness paradise. It stretches south to the larger, hilly peninsula of Purbeck, whose southern cliffs form the eastern end of the famed Jurassic Coast of Dorset and Devon. There the rocks are filled with fossils from the ages before the dinosaurs, when the coastal waters were filled with ammonites and trilobites.

Several miles of unspoiled beach border the eastern side of Studland. At its southern end, a shop in a weathered wooden shack beside the sea serves drinks and snacks to hardy beachgoers.

The day starts overcast, and I stupidly set off without a hat and without sunblock on my face. When the sky clears and the sunlight beats down fiercely, I keep on walking. By the time I've enjoyed my snack at the shack – a full English breakfast with coffee – and hiked back north again to home base, I've copped a serious dose of solar radiation. Boy, is my face red that night!

———

I rise early on referendum day to blue sky and a sunny outlook. After a brief coffee over the news, I run to the local polling station in the village library, set in a stone cottage shaded by trees beside a clifftop park. There I vote Remain before running back for breakfast.

That evening, in my dark suit with collar and tie, I attend an overnight party at the Poole Civic Centre. This palatial building dates from 1932 and is a splendid example of art deco style. Now in dire need of expensive renovation after years of austerity, it's still the daily workplace for hundreds of municipal civil servants. Here the local politicos watch the results roll in on television.

For the big night, the reception hall, set at ground level below an ornately appointed council chamber, is equipped with three giant TV screens. Banks of plastic chairs face the biggest screen, and refreshments are laid out on tables around the perimeter. As usual at such events during austerity, the refreshments are less than gourmet fare, just finger food for paper plates, and the main drinks on offer are tea and coffee from big stainless-steel urns.

A few members of the Westminster and European parliaments, kitted in campaigning suits and party outfits for the cameras, mix freely with local officials clad in their usual working grunge. Two TV crews work on their cameras and lights on the raised areas at both ends of the hall.

At one end, Robert Syms is happily engaged in an interview with a national news correspondent.

He holds forth with his habitual confidence: 'My vote in the referendum counts the same as anyone else's, no more and no less. We're all free to vote as we choose, but I've already said I'm voting to leave the EU. I've done so because I want to see Britain regain its sovereignty and bring it back to parliament in Westminster where it belongs. We need to take back control – control of our borders, control of our taxes, control of our spending, and control of our laws and regulations.'

The interviewer asks: 'If we end up with a fifty-fifty result, with no clear majority for Leave or Remain, do you think we should stay?'

'I'm sure the result will be clear enough to set the future course of the government. Ask me again tomorrow!'

At the other end of the hall, my former debate partner and current member of the European parliament for the local region, Julie Girling, is being grilled by a regional news presenter.

The presenter asks a pertinent question: 'As an active MEP, you must be worried about your own future career tonight. What will you do if Leave wins?'

'Well, I hope they won't, of course, but if they were to win and the government decided to leave, I would continue to serve as a sitting MEP until the process completed, which would take a minimum of two years. That means I retain my seat until the next European elections in 2019, which is about the same level of job security I have in any case.'

We all watch the results roll slowly in for the various regions of the UK on television. First the outlook is disturbing, then it's alarming, and finally it's desolate.

At 4:40 in the morning on Friday 24 June 2016, on our big TV screens, veteran BBC news anchor David Dimbleby announces: 'The British people have spoken, and the answer is: We're out.'

I'm sitting beside Julie as he speaks. After a moment of stunned silence, I say: 'Out, with a four percent lead – that's really shocking.'

Julie looks horror-movie shocked. Her face has turned ashen. 'This is a huge mistake. A historic blunder. We shall have to live with the shame of this for years.'

We talk on, but I can see she just wants to go home and nurse her grief in private. I watch her go but decide to stay a while longer to sense the mood in the hall. I wander across the room to overhear another TV interview with Syms.

The interviewer asks him: 'It looks as if you'll get your parliamentary sovereignty back. Is this a happy moment for you?'

Robert nods slowly: 'Happy, yes. This is certainly a historic result. We can all be glad the democratic process has delivered a clear result, as indeed it usually does. I'm sure most of my party colleagues will also be satisfied with the public's decision and ready and waiting to get on with the job of getting us out of the EU as soon as possible. But there's a lot of hard work ahead of us to follow through on this result. It will be a bumpy road ahead for a while. We live in interesting times!'

I exchange quiet words with a few local councillors. But my mood is sinking fast, so I soon call it a night and drive back home, to bed, to sleep, perchance to dream.

———

Later that Friday morning, I take my time over brunch to digest the news online and on television.

The market reaction is fast and cataclysmic. Sterling falls ten percent to its lowest value since 1985. Global markets lose two trillion dollars in their biggest one-day drop since 2007. A few canny hedge fund managers make millions from the carnage.

Cameron announces his resignation as prime minister. He says he'll stay until October to give the party time to elect a replacement.

A clear majority of UK voters opted to leave the EU. The Leave vote was 52 percent of the votes cast, the Remain vote 48 percent, to give a majority of well over a million for Brexit.

I have a date that afternoon at a garden party hosted by a local widow named Elsa. As a loyal Poole Conservative, Elsa makes her family home – her empty nest – available for the event to help raise funds for the party coffers. I park in her street behind the big, new, white BMW driven by the PCA treasurer. He's an old stalwart called Nick who made his fortune working for a global oil giant in the Gulf. I help him to unload a couple of canvas canopies and carry them into the back garden.

Elsa is old and frail, and she delegates the deployment of the garden furniture to the young bloods in the group. This means me and Mohan, the big councillor, who still looks presidential in a polo shirt and chinos despite the summer heat. I feel boyish in my shorts and sandals but help manfully to erect the canopies.

The event is a bleak affair for me. The referendum vote is the topic of the day, and try as I might, I can't see a positive side to it. Mohan tells me a European freedom of movement that doesn't extend to Indians looks unfair. I try to explain the economics, but it sounds thin. I drive back home later with a sense of foreboding. My former life is sinking fast.

The result has hit the EU like a bomb. The German ambassador to the United States, Peter Wittig, says: 'This is a really serious setback. We have to prove to the citizens that the European Union is there for them, that it is a union for the citizens and not a union for the bureaucrats.'

By contrast, Russian politicians, journalists, and nationalists are revelling in the result. Russian TV anchors speak gleefully of victory for Little England and call it a nightmare for Brussels. In the Kremlin, Vladimir Putin is no doubt feeling cheered.

The outcome exposes a generational divide. Surveys before the vote showed that most young Brits favoured remaining in the EU, while most older Brits chose to leave. A graph showing the ratio of Remainers to Leavers falls from three-quarters at the young end to one quarter at the old end. Seniors voted against their kids.

The reinstalled UKIP leader Nigel Farage is jubilant at his win: 'We have the potential to keep a lot of the voters that we've got … the response to us on the referendum was huge.'

Over the weekend, an online petition demanding a second referendum passes three million signatures. The signatories call upon the government to implement a rule that sets minimum thresholds for the majority and the turnout next time.

Brexit turmoil continues into the next week. Global markets react without mercy. The Footsie indexes fall by several percent and the pound falls by a total of fourteen percent.

For a few days, Boris Johnson is the frontrunner to become the next Conservative party leader and prime minister. Theresa May is emerging from a crowded field of likely also-rans as the leading 'stop Boris' candidate.

Despite the carnage, Boris is upbeat: 'This EU referendum has been the most extraordinary political event of our lifetime. … This will bring golden opportunities for this country.'

But Johnson has already caused grave offence in Europe by likening the European project to the dreams of conquest that Hitler foisted upon the continent. Johnson's claim that Brexit will trigger events that unravel the entire project is like a declaration of war against the united leaders of a continent at peace.

On Tuesday, Cameron gets a frosty reception at his farewell EU summit. The other EU leaders refuse to talk about a new deal until the UK formally invokes the provisions for leaving the union.

German chancellor Angela Merkel sums up the mood among the continental leaders: 'We will ensure that the negotiations will not be run on the principle of cherry-picking. ... Whoever wants to get out of this family cannot expect that all the obligations fall away but the privileges continue to remain in place.'

Dutch premier Mark Rutte is more emphatic: 'England has collapsed politically, monetarily, constitutionally, and economically.'

The Brexit leaders have no plan. British politics is in disarray. Within hours of the referendum result, Sinn Fein calls for a vote on reunifying Ireland, Spain calls for joint control of Gibraltar, and nationalists in France and the Netherlands call for their own EU referendums. The Scottish Nationalist Party wants Scotland to remain in the EU, and confusion reigns in Westminster.

In the Conservative party, support for Theresa May begins to surge, putting her ahead of Boris Johnson in the race for the top job. She soon becomes the betting favourite to win.

In Germany, Angela Merkel is ready to give Britain more time to decide on Brexit. She knows the economic impact of Brexit will be damaging and fears it will reduce European influence in the world. She probably wants to see Brits bury the whole idea.

As for how to do Brexit, there are at least four models or options for the UK, codenamed Norway, Switzerland, Canada, and Albania. Norway is in the European Economic Area, Switzerland is outside the single market, Canada has a free trade deal with the EU, and the Albania model has a lonely fan in Michael Gove.

On Thursday, a confused and ruffled Johnson withdraws his bid to be prime minister after Gove 'reluctantly but firmly' concludes that Boris isn't up to the job and proposes a Gove candidacy instead. Inevitably, Boris supporters accuse Gove of treachery, and the proposal dies a well-deserved death. Theresa May now launches her campaign.

With the British economy in peril, George Osborne sounds a retreat: 'We will continue to be tough on the deficit, but we must be realistic about achieving a surplus by the end of this decade.'

By Friday, my red face is shedding flakes of skin quite alarmingly. In the office, an unusually brisk and cheerful Robert, who seems quite buoyed by the referendum result, comments on the cancer risk. I'm dismayed enough by my loss of face to take the rest of the day off and lurk in the shade at home.

On Saturday, I venture out for two pub gatherings with party hacks and councillors. Buoyed by their fatalism, I drink four pints of beer – a lot more than usual for my weekends.

On Sunday, I read a German novel by Walter Kempowski set in Prussia in early 1945, when the Red Army was advancing fast, with a title that translates as *All in Vain*. With Europe weakened, Russia resurgent, and Britain an island fortress again, the progress of seventy years could vanish.

Brits are now casting about for someone to blame. In a Sunday newspaper, former Oxford historian Niall Ferguson offers his view: 'The Tory leadership contest is like Oxford student politics. Oxford graduates David Cameron and George Osborne were defeated, then one former president of the Oxford Union debating society (Gove) knifed another (Boris Johnson), while a former Oxford Union treasurer (Nicky Morgan) decided to back Gove against a former Oxford Union returning officer (Theresa May), who is married to a former Oxford Union president.'

I'm saddened to see just what a bodge those alumni of my *alma mater* have made of their efforts to run Britain. In an act of penance, I sit in front of my television and watch *The Riot Club*. This movie skewers the Bullingdon Club, the mob that put Cameron, Osborne, and Johnson on the road to ruin.

On Monday, Bully boy George gives billionaires a break. He says he plans to cut corporation tax to less than fifteen percent to tempt business into investing in Britain. The OECD warns that the UK could turn into a tax haven economy.

The Brexit drama is playing out as if scripted and staged by the Bullingdon bovver boys for the benefit of the disaster capitalists who want to make fat profits at the expense of the EU. To them, the EU is a defenceless cash cow or an economic dinosaur like the USSR in its twilight years, whereas the UK government is poised to turn Britain into a deregulated haven for buccaneers. The masters of disaster are no doubt already planning acts of piracy against the continent from their sally port in the British Isles.

One result of this revaluation of all values is a sudden surge in the number of alarmed Brits seeking to become nationals of other EU states. Descendants of Jewish refugees who fled to Britain from persecution in Nazi Germany are even seeking German nationality, where their right to claim it is anchored in the postwar German constitution.

Oxford biologist Richard Dawkins is furious at the damage the referendum drama has done to the international world of science. He fires an angry blast on behalf of scientists everywhere: 'The prime minister recklessly gambled away the future of Britain and Europe. Lacking the courage to tell the yobs in his own party to take a running jump, he played Russian roulette with the future of Europe and the world. His decision to hold the referendum was a monstrously irresponsible gamble.'

I've had enough. On Saturday, I pack my bags for Germany, ready to set off bright and early on Sunday morning.

PART 2
PROCRASTINATION

July 2016 – May 2019

'I want a red, white, and blue Brexit.'
Theresa May

11. Driving into Germany

A week after reading Kempowski, I'm on my way to Germany to see old friends and explain the shock vote to abandon Europe.

I'm glad at least that peace still prevails. I can still hop over to France and drive on through, which I used to manage in a single day when I went through the Eurotunnel. Apart from checking my passport, the only complication is to remember in time to buy the fiddly stickers I need for my headlights.

On this occasion, I take the scenic route. I book a voyage on the ferry that runs daily between Poole and its twinned town Cherbourg in Normandy. The ship takes several hours to make the crossing, but today the sea is calm, so I linger over lunch and try to read a French magazine.

As dusk descends, I pause my drive through France for an overnight stay in Amiens. This city was on the front line in August 1918, when the Brits won a decisive battle there on what chief of the German general staff Paul von Hindenburg called the 'black day' of the German army. The city was then bombed by the RAF in 1944 during the campaign to liberate France from the Nazis.

I find nothing much to do there after I've got lost in the dark and asked for directions in a MacDonald's. But I'm glad of the chance to test a hotel and enjoy a good French dinner and an hour of French television. My onward drive the next day is a joy.

Back on the German autobahn, the joy is even better. Here the traffic rolls faster, with more jockeying for position. After years of mournful penance on British roads, I'm in driving heaven. I can press the pedal to the metal again and feel the speed. Motoring past Mannheim revives all the old memories. I'm back home.

I drive into the little town of Schwetzingen, my home base until three years ago, and settle in a small hotel. It's a family business, sited next to the palace and its formal gardens where the Palatinate princes lived and where Mozart staged some of his musical works. The town has good memories for me.

On my first day back in town, I meet up again with Matthias, a young Lutheran pastor who runs a local congregation. Matthias is an energetic and practical man who takes the pragmatic stance of a social worker toward his Christian vocation. He's also a redhead, with a redhead wife and a redhead schoolboy son. His idea of a good time is playing folk guitar with his flock around the campfire or hiking in the woods and visiting rustic hostels with them.

Matthias and I sit over coffee at a sunlit outdoor table in the central square in Schwetzingen. I'm in my cream linen suit again, with my white rubber water shoes. Matthias wears jeans and a green polo shirt, ready for robust action in the service of the Lord, and his baseball cap covers a buzzcut fuzz that he offsets with a trimmed beard and round-framed glasses. I usually speak with him in German, but since he speaks fluent English, we revert to the tongue of angels when we discuss the latest news from England.

'It's a complete disaster,' I say, spreading my hands in despair. 'David Cameron had to resign, and I have no idea what Theresa May can do to rescue us. The government will probably feel bound to honour the vote, or at least try to, and this means political chaos for at least a year or two while they sort it out.'

Matthias looks concerned and sits forward: 'This is terrible for Europe. Germany relied on Britain to balance the European Union. Without Britain as a member, it looks like a German economic empire, like a Fourth Reich. If France were to vote for Marine Le Pen, the whole union could fall apart.'

'Yes, this could unravel everything. We could go back to the law of the jungle in Europe. Back to nation states strutting like fighting cocks and Russia looming in the east. But what can we do? Nation states can't be wished away. All politicians try to make people feel patriotic, like all those Leave voters in Britain who voted for Queen and country.'

'In Germany we try to feel less for nationalism and to feel pride for Europe. It's the big lesson we learned from the disaster of the Second World War.' Matthias says this like an incantation, but he means it.

I try a dose of philosophy: 'Global politics must integrate above the nation state. National communities are language communities, and with machine translation via Google and so on those divisions are history.'

'But national community feeling is a fact, like regional feeling here in Germany,' he says. 'We used to think it was an achievement to think like Germans. Now we must work harder to think like Europeans. It needs an effort to rise above our roots.'

'That should be easy for a Christian,' I say with a smile. 'We're all humans in the sight of God, and our nationality is no more important than our street address or our fashion sense. Or am I being too free in my take on the faith?'

'No, of course, that's right. God loves us in our individuality, our particularity, our soul, and not for the colour of our flag or our skin.'

I smile: 'Take away God, and I think that basically chimes with the philosophy of Immanuel Kant, too.'

'If you say so. I never read Kant in detail.'

'Well, the European Union is basically Kantian philosophy made flesh.'

We talk on in the market square. But the afternoon is too good for politics, so we turn to lighter matters.

———

On the next day, I meet up with a former office colleague called Otto, who tells me our erstwhile employer is holding its big annual summer party in a few days' time. We worked in the same team at

SAP, which has an enormous, new, and state-of-the-art campus beside the otherwise sleepy village of Walldorf.

The SAP summer party is a major event on its social calendar, where the entire campus is briefly turned into a big outdoor party zone, with beer tents, hot-dog and burger stalls, and fun and games for all the family. Employees are encouraged to bring their spouses and kids along to join the party and let the good times roll.

Otto reminds me that ex-employees are welcome too – our payroll numbers are allocated for life and for retrieval at any SAP terminal – so I'll have no trouble getting an entry pass. Two days later, I show up on the campus and check in at the pass desk.

It feels good to be back among the SAP family. The company vibe is young, fresh, and global. New digital technology is transforming the human world, and the internet makes all the old divisions that carved the people of the world into tribes obsolete. With modern science and new technology, everything that divided people – their skills, their knowledge, their language, even their genetic identity – is fungible, up for grabs, in a common currency of data that the engines of the revolution can process and analyse and reconfigure faster than the speed of thought.

SAP is a pioneer of that revolution. It's corporate Europe's answer to Microsoft, a global behemoth creating new streams of value in the lives of everyone in the global economy. SAP makes the business software that runs the operations of most of the biggest corporations in the world. Its customers rely on the legendary strength of German engineering to build the solid software architectures that keep their business afloat.

The SAP campus is physical proof of the extraordinary success of SAP software in the global marketplace. It hosts offices and machines worth billions and employs many thousands of mostly young men and women. Everything is clean, modern, functional, and efficient, inspiring and intoxicating at once, all smoothing the way for the smartest brains on the planet to produce working code to run the world.

Walking in the afternoon sun between the tents and the kiosks serving beer and fast food, selling fresh works of art, and promoting the best of SAP business, I revel in my immersion among the employees and their young families. Here it's very heaven to be alive.

As I'm walking, there's my former colleague Klaus, who worked in a team on Java scripting for business process transactions. My team worked on developing a superfast new database engine. Klaus and I joined SAP at the same time, and we attended the same introductory classes at SAP University. He's also fluent in English, since he studied maths as an Erasmus student in Cambridge, before earning his physics doctorate with hard mathematical labour among the field equations of quantum chromodynamics.

I see Klaus first. His unusually tall body, with head held high, prominent nose to the wind, face shaded under a baseball cap, is unmistakable. I greet him in German. He responds with a start, then dawning joy, before switching to English out of politeness.

'Well, this is a pleasant surprise. What brings you here?'

I smile. 'I couldn't keep away. This is so much better than being among the nationalists in Britain. The referendum result has emboldened the racists and xenophobes.'

'Yes, what happened? Are you here to stay?'

'No, not now anyway. I'm here for a week or so, just to say hi to everyone. I'm working part-time for our local member of parliament, and this is our summer recess.'

Klaus turns in surprise: 'Ah so, you're working in politics now? I had expected the Remain side to win. This must be hard for David Cameron and his team.'

'They're all toast now, collateral damage. This is a boost for Boris Johnson and the Brexiteers, the hard-line extremists in the Conservative party.'

'Boris Johnson? I thought he was the party clown. What was he – mayor of London?'

'Yes, former mayor and famous for his drinking exploits in an Oxford student club.'

'Weren't he and David Cameron at school together?' Klaus has obviously done some reading here.

'Yes, both went to Eton before Oxford. The British establishment is a very small world.'

'The Queen and her government,' he intones grandly. 'Now we see that Great Britain is not so great after all.'

'It never was. It's only the empire that made it seem great for a century or so – and made it rich, of course.'

'Ah, the empire,' he reflects in an amused tone. 'Living like God in India – it's a German phrase, you know.'

'Yes, I remember. Now the Indians with brains work for SAP here in Walldorf.'

'I was in Bangalore last month, upgrading the process for working via satellite.'

I glance at him. 'I remember our team's Indian colleagues well. They were smart.'

'Of course – our technical director, Vishal, is Indian. He works mostly at our institute in Berlin.'

'Yes, he was a fan of my team's new database engine. He got a bunch of researchers in Berlin – and in California and in Shanghai – to help us.'

'I worked with him in California a couple of years ago. His PhD is from Stanford, so he knows everyone there.'

'All this is so much more fun than British politics!'

He pauses and looks concerned: 'Sorry, Andy, I really have to go now and find my wife and kids. I left them in the canteen, and I need to rescue them before they think I've forgotten them.'

'Sure – great to see you again. Give them my fond regards.'

Klaus and his wife are committed Christians. I once travelled with Klaus to a weekend workshop in Marburg, where he'd hoped to convert me, but I stuck doggedly to my secular humanism.

I wander on through the crowd, reliving the sense of being at home I'd felt at SAP. Soon I reach the main open-air arena, where a big stage at one end will be the platform for SAP's customary very loud rock concert later in the day. Now, in bright sunlight, the company board members are taking turns on stage to deliver their annual review of the year's successes.

SAP co-founder and chairman of the board Hasso Plattner is holding forth with his characteristic eloquence, on this occasion in German, on the need for continuing prudence following the global financial crisis and the European sovereign debt crisis. Hasso is a billionaire and could retire to a life of leisure racing his ocean yachts, but he loves the business and is still active as a professor in the computer science institute he's founded with his own money in Potsdam. He's a colourful character, beloved by us all.

Next on stage is the SAP chief executive, an American everyone calls Bill. I listen as Bill explains in his Californian-accented English the company's devotion to its employees' welfare. Hasso insisted years earlier, when I was still on campus, that Bill could only take over if he promised to adopt German standards of generosity to the workforce. Bill now seems much mellower and more benevolent than in those early years, when my colleagues mistrusted Dollar Bill as a typical brash American interested only in earning a fast buck.

I learn later that Bill had suffered an accident that changed his whole life. Now he wears dark glasses to disguise a lost eye. They say he'd been drinking at a formal company reception when he walked down a flight of steps with a glass of wine in his hand. He tripped and fell, and as he hit the floor, he inadvertently rammed the broken glass into his eye. I reflect on the way adversity can some-times impart a wisdom unattainable by gentler means.

—

A couple of days later, I meet up with Angie and Rolf again in the central square in Schwetzingen. We meet in the early evening, with the square flooded from the palace end by yellowing sunlight, and as usual we sit outside. We drink locally brewed beer from tall half-litre glasses as we wait for our savoury pancakes – a local ersatz for pizza – to arrive.

Clad in sloppy sweatshirt and jeans as usual, Angie tells me about a few of the recent physics books she and her team have published. She adds proudly that both their kids have now started university, while I dutifully offer my congratulations.

Stroking his short silver beard and smiling, Rolf explains how his publishing enterprise is making enough money to let him take flying lessons. He's even thinking of buying his own aircraft, and he explains various options to help pay for it.

I fight down a sick feeling of despair that Brexit Britain offers me no such options: 'It was so good to see the SAP campus again – and to see all those old faces from my time there.'

'I'm sure it was,' says Angie, who always seemed happy in Germany. 'At least they're international there. You must be frustrated with British politics.'

'Frustrated is an understatement. The average British mindset seems to have retreated back to the Forties, with Britain alone against the world, and Johnny Foreigner as the enemy.'

She shakes her head: 'They all seem to have gone mad over there. I'm very glad I'm settled here with my book series and my physics friends. All that politics is something I can do without. Angela Merkel is a reasonable person, and I'm happy to leave it all in her safe hands.'

'You would say that – she has a doctorate in physics too.'

'Yes, she's sensible. She did the right thing welcoming in the Syrian refugees, but she's getting a lot of criticism for it.'

'Voters in England didn't understand it at all. They thought the Germans had lost it. They thought she'd betrayed Europe, or maybe that she only did it to get her face on the cover of *Time* magazine. They thought it was just inexcusable.'

Rolf joins in: 'Many Germans thought she was losing it too. But the birth rate in Germany is low, so I think she was importing more guest workers to take new jobs and pay our pensions.'

I nod thoughtfully: 'That would be wise thinking. State pensions in England are much lower than here.'

He locks eyes on me: 'Will you come back to live in Germany?'

'Maybe, once I see how the Brexit story plays out.'

Dining in Schwetzingen with Angie and Rolf in the gathering twilight is my last pleasure for this trip. Driving back the next day, toward a quarantine island where an epidemic of xenophobia has broken out, is the first duty on my new mission to fight the plague.

Flying lessons – if only!

The ferry heads northward out of Cherbourg. The passenger deck is full of monoglot Brits. Back in Poole, I peel off my headlight stickers and sigh.

12. From Dunkirk to Joan of Arc

Within days, I'm down in Swanage, a quaint little town a few miles south of Poole on the Purbeck coast. I'm acting as an extra in the shooting of a major motion picture for a Hollywood studio.

The movie is a drama set in the Second World War, where I play a Home Guard volunteer – Dad's Army – greeting troops back from France. I guess the movie is about the 1940 evacuation of British troops from the beaches of Dunkirk. Englanders imagine this disaster, where the Germans forced the British army to fall back to England without its kit, was a blessing in disguise. The Germans chose not to kill or capture the Brits, allowing Winston Churchill to fulminate about fighting on the beaches and so on until the Battle of Britain annulled the risk of a German invasion.

Swanage is a town straight out of the Forties or Fifties. To serve tourists who value its walking proximity to the Jurassic Coast, it boasts a lot of hotels and guest houses that thrive in summer. In winter, it's all but dead.

The day is clear and sunny, and the shoot will be after nightfall. I show up at a school hall beside a big car park, where the movie's travelling circus is camped out, and get fitted for my Home Guard outfit. The hall is full of young men kitting up in army battledress in all stages of disrepair, as if they've just escaped death by dive-bombing or by drowning in diesel oil.

The wardrobe mistress takes great care to outfit me correctly. She finds civvy shirt and tie and shoes to go with a heavy wool serge jacket and trousers in the regulation army tone of dark khaki. Now I'm properly kitted and accoutred, I find to a mirror to admire the effect. Smart old soldier!

I join the other extras for an informal meal in the canteen tent. The kitted-out battle vets wear the heavy regulation black hobnail boots that were notorious in wartime for chafing. I feel like I'm in an army canteen.

Soon it's time to march off for a briefing before we join the shooting war. The company heads out onto the streets in clattering hobnails, totally out of step with each other, toward the briefing room. Older locals stand and gape, reminded of those desperate days in 1940.

The briefing room is in the local Conservative Club. To get to the upstairs meeting hall, we go through the downstairs bar, where the local old boys gulp over their beer as we thunder past them and up the stairs. The hall soon fills, and another wait begins.

Once we're all seated, I look around. It's a typical Conservative Club meeting room, lined with dark wood panelling, furnished with hard wooden chairs, and sporting, in pride of place above an ornamental mantelpiece, a classic and iconic painting of Churchill in one of his famous wartime poses. To complete the illusion, I imagine the dulcet sounds of Vera Lynn singing *We'll meet again* – the hit of the season for the troops back then.

The briefing officer arrives. He's a Hollywood guy, in sneakers and jeans and a Hawaiian shirt under a sleeveless tan vest with bulging pockets. His build is slim, his head is bald, and he has a loud and camp manner. He explains in his California drawl the evening scene we're about to shoot at the railway station.

Once we're briefed, we take to the streets again for the march to the station. By now the day is fading, but not before I can see what the movie crew has done to the site. This little branch line terminus looks good on a normal day. Now it looked spiffing.

The MP for South Dorset, the wealthy landowner and former army officer Richard Grosvenor Plunkett-Ernle-Erle-Drax, said in the local paper: 'The Swanage railway plays a vital and integral part in promoting tourism ... Those romantic days of steam are played out every day on this scenic stretch of line.'

My platoon of Home Guards peels off from the squaddies and marches down to the railway lines beside a signal box. There, under a darkening sky but lit by bright lights, we confront rows of trestle tables bearing refreshments for the returning troops. Again, I'm amazed by the attention to detail. Cigarette packs and chocolate bars, the wrappers empty but printed correctly for the period, are stacked next to arrays of tin mugs and groups of big teapots, ready to give each lad a nice hot cuppa and a packet of fags.

The movie crew hands explain the staging of the scene. They have plastic flagons of mud-coloured liquid to fill up the teapots.

The guy who fills my teapot tells me what to do: 'Just pour out mugs of tea and hand them to the troops when they march along here to the trains. And give them cigarettes and chocolate bars. Make it look natural. You're just trying to cheer them up. They're exhausted and they think they've just lost the war.'

'Yeah, I get it. Make them feel happy to be home again.'

He nods firmly: 'You got it.'

Further along the track, a camera crew is setting up its heavy gear on a rolling dolly, looking to me like a wartime crew manning an ack-ack gun. A group of serious chaps walk along inspecting things and fussing over details. Among them is presumably the director. I'm wide-eyed with wonder at this whole bizarre memorial to Britain at bay, steeling itself to fight the Nazi foe and save the island race.

The director and his entourage walk straight by. Soon after them comes a bunch of lads I guess are star talent. They're kitted out like the returning soldiers, but their sculpted punk hair spiking modishly above the regulation short back and sides and the cheeky smirks on their faces give them away. They stop beside me and my Dad's Army mate at the teapots for a friendly word.

'Good show you have here,' says one with a somehow familiar face. 'Hope you're ready for the action. We might need a few takes.'

'We're ready,' I reply stoutly. 'How long will it take?'

'Could be hours. But thanks for taking part. We appreciate it.'

They walk on to the next bunch of extras. I'm told the face was Harry Styles, the teen idol, the hottest star in the universe.

On the first take, I watch a column of weary-looking troops trudge along the railway lines, over the wooden sleepers and the granite stones beneath them, hobnails crunching, toward us.

I step forward with mugs of tea and packets of fags: 'Welcome home, lads, here's a hot cup of tea for you.'

The troops say nothing – we aren't paid to speak lines – but they take the mugs and fags and crunch onward.

Take one looks fine to me, but the director is evidently looking for more. Take two follows, and three, and four, and more, as the darkness around the set deepens. I lose count, but at each take the weariness in the troops is a little more authentic, the seductive fantasy of the whole scene a little more compelling. I'm in the zone, no longer acting but living the Dad's Army dream.

Finally, the take is wrapped and canned, everyone relaxes, and we march back to the wardrobe hall. I put on my civvies and drive home in a German car with an Iron Cross on the back.

———

August is another off-duty month for me. The weather is hot and sunny, but rather than waste my days on the beach, I close the curtains and sit in front of my Mac screens instead, emerging only in the early morning for a quick swim down at the beach before breakfast and then again in the cooler evening to go shopping and the like. This is the crepuscular lifestyle I adopted in Germany, where high summer can be fiercely hot and sunny compared with the usual wet and windy English summer.

I spend my days solving tricky and challenging problem sets in maths and physics on a website that lets people test their skills in competition with other users. The problems are grouped and graded, and users are ranked. With a few weeks of work, I raise my game far enough to put me up in the top rank.

The key to my new obsession with solving maths problems is my new weekend job. A few months after the 2015 election, the Poole Conservatives ran too short of funds to keep paying me. I'm still working for Robert Syms MP for a notional two days a week, but the rest of my time is my own.

Rather than rot in idleness, I've found a deserving A-level student of mathematics and physics in the area who is both in want of some expert tuition and in possession of a rich father who's happy to sponsor his son's higher education.

It's a marriage made in heaven. I enjoy hours of bliss buffing up with maths and physics texts for the tutorials. The student, a sober young man who shows flashes of real talent, is well behaved and eager to earn, so the sessions are fun.

The job keeps me on the straight and narrow path of virtue. It also prompts me to explore more advanced texts again, on the fringe, where the details are hairy and weird. Soon I'm back in a dreamer's heaven, puzzling over how I might bend my wacky ideas in logic to sort the paradoxes of quantum theory.

The new work on my first love puts my mind back in balance. The long perspective I cultivated in Germany is still there. But a continuing mental itch leads me onward.

The problem of Islam has bothered me ever since the 9/11 attacks and the New Atheist response led by folks like Sam Harris. I'm tempted to rant like Sam about religion. But my new student is Iranian, and his exemplary demeanour prompts me to consider what I can salvage from his Islamic heritage.

So, in September, I write a review essay titled *The Messenger of Monotheism*. In it, I tackle Islam head on, focusing on a pair of books I've just read by the exiled Iranian writer Kader Abdolah.

To reassure readers, I begin gently: 'The Prophet Muhammad

brought the message of monotheism to the tribes of Arabia … In doing so, he raised the Arabs … to become the leading agents of a force for progress that dominated the region stretching from the Indian subcontinent to the Atlantic Ocean for a thousand years.'

Soon my inner Kant pops up: 'Even in a secular worldview informed by modern science, there is a clear meaning to the central concept of monotheism that Muhammad espoused … The core insight … is that the self … is the logical instrument for reflecting and understanding God.'

I'm in my heaven of psychology and philosophy: 'The biblical God … becomes a superself of mythic proportions, magnified in every subsequent theology to big up the divine ego to yet more cosmic dimensions, until in the view of later philosophers such as Friedrich Nietzsche the entire enterprise collapsed under the weight of its own absurdity.'

But I see a message here: 'Updated to build on more modern logic and science, … first, the self is a logical construct more general than we humans often imagine, and second, neuroscience can show us how sacred dramas can … achieve psychic transformations in the believer.'

Inevitably, I spin back to the problems of formal logic: 'The logical vortex of self-reference had drilled through all of reality as we know it in mathematics and science.'

Then I pounce: 'It may seem intuitively obvious that what Muhammad aimed to do in his channelling of the divine message was impossible … But it takes logic to nail the refutation of his audacious claim.'

We're back to the ice-cream cone universe. But now I call it the mushroom cloud. The atomic paradox of the empty set explodes to become a billowing cumulative hierarchy: 'The idea that makes this formalism more than what Hermann Hesse would have called a glass bead game is that we are … inside this mushroom cloud.'

Here I enjoy revelation: 'If our fate as temporal beings is to be trapped within the mushroom cloud, the image of God looming above us is mapped to a V-set within the cloud. Its limitations and its imperfections become flaws in our conception of God.'

I bow politely to the Prophet: 'Muhammad was right to intuit that a divine perspective was available in principle … [But] a … rigorous methodology … can suffice for us as scientists to make assertions … with at least the same claim to transcendent authority that Muhammad claimed for his revelations.'

I sing in praise of scientists: 'Muhammad was the last prophet because scientists are the new prophets, and they scorn the label. For them, the title of being a scientist is more noble.'

At last, I return to the start: 'Kader Abdolah has performed a great service in making Muhammad and his work more under-standable and accessible … His biography of the Messenger and his annotated edition of the Qur'an … put the violence and disorder within Islamic societies … into some sort of perspective.'

My target publication in New York doesn't take my review, so I post it on my website. At least my mind is clear again. A summer love has borne fruit, even if my quantum ideas haven't.

My bonus, the cherry on top, is my other love. To my delight, I find myself quite lovestruck by Rachel following the gala dinner at the Italian villa. I haven't seen her since then and don't dare reveal more than polite interest in what she's doing, but I do imagine seeing her on my walks along the sunlit prom beside the beach.

It could happen any day. I know Rachel likes beach life and swims and surfs with confidence, so whenever I see a pack of kids playing beach volleyball, I dream I might spot her there too. This is enough for me. I'm too old and ugly to wish to be seen – nor do I yearn to meet any other ladies from my English past.

It feels like salvation.

———

Also in September, Nigel Farage speaks at a rally held by the far-right party Alternative for Deutschland in Spandau Citadel, Berlin, where the Allies imprisoned Hitler's deputy Rudolf Hess.

Farage was invited by the party's deputy leader Beatrix von Storch. She's a member of his parliamentary group of MEPs. She was expelled from the mainstream group of conservative MEPs after she called on European border guards to open fire on illegal immigrants. She later called her comments a tactical mistake.

In Spandau, Farage says: 'I regard Beatrix as a friend. I believe we have strong, shared, similar values.'

Duchess Beatrix of Oldenburg studied law in Heidelberg while I lived there. Her grandfather was Hitler's finance minister. I'd advise her to choose her British friends more carefully.

But I'm glad she let Farage speak in Spandau. She's effectively outed him as untouchable for all but the most outrageous Brits.

Later in September, Theresa May, the new prime minister, sets up a special new department of government, the Department for Exiting the European Union, DExEU, to be headed by the relaxed and unflappable party veteran David Davis.

In a dire official statement, Davis sets out his principles for the coming negotiations with his EU counterparts in Brussels: to build a national consensus around his negotiating position, to put the national interest first, to make his position loud and clear, and to reaffirm the sovereignty and supremacy of his parliament.

May's new cabinet features a fat surprise. Her new foreign secretary is Boris Johnson, who remains undead after Michael Gove stabbed him in the back.

Boris is more impressed by his new appointment than I am by the wisdom of putting him anywhere near real power. He loves the grand office he now occupies in the Foreign Office in Whitehall: 'This was once the nerve centre of an empire that was seven times the size of the Roman empire at its greatest extent.'

I find the whole thing – the new Brexit department, the new Brexit minister, the undiplomatic principles, the new chancer in the Foreign Office, the harping on about past glories – deeply ominous.

———

At the Conservative party conference in Birmingham in October, Theresa May outlines her plan: 'We will introduce, in the next Queen's Speech, a Great Repeal Bill that will remove the European Communities Act from the statute book.'

I watch her on television and see a British Joan of Arc, leading her country into a new hundred years' war.

May explains: 'That was the act that took us into the European Union. This marks the first stage in the UK becoming a sovereign and independent country once again.'

She's seeking to enact what she imagines to be the will of the people: 'The referendum result was clear. It was legitimate. It was the biggest vote for change this country has ever known.'

She's swallowed the Kool-Aid.

Suddenly, she's determined to get Brexit done: 'We will invoke Article 50 no later than the end of March next year.'

Article 50 of the EU Treaty starts the clock on a two-year notice period before the departure takes effect.

I'm horrified. There are so many reasons to hold back.

The referendum was bungled. Dave should have insisted on a super-majority for something as consequential as leaving the EU. He should have said a referendum outcome can only be advisory. He should have stayed in office to clean up the mess he made.

May and her party colleagues seem to be interpreting the referendum outcome as a thoughtful appeal by an informed electorate to reconsider the technical arrangements by which British governance is implemented.

Wrong – it's a cry of outrage from voters crushed by austerity, a loud *Fuck you!* to the whole rotten establishment.

I recall seeing May in Shaftesbury when she spoke for Remain. Now she's the prisoner of an evil inner party cabal.

Theresa May is not known as a deep thinker. She's a provincial English vicar's daughter who read geography at Oxford. As home secretary, she tried and failed to implement effective immigration controls. Her whole outlook is classic English Tory.

Now she's reborn as Saint Theresa: 'Our laws will be made not in Brussels but in Westminster. The authority of EU law in Britain will end. We are going to be a fully independent, sovereign country.'

She underscores her provincial Tory outlook with a phrase that will echo in infamy: 'If you believe you're a citizen of the world, you're a citizen of nowhere.'

———

I sit in the office with Pam. I'm scrolling through a surfeit of emails from constituents. Pam, cheery as ever, takes the day's snail mail from the postman.

Amid the usual heap of litter is a long carboard tube. As the postman departs, I look up: 'Take care, it could be a bomb.'

We've been warned about security. Ever since Jo Cox was murdered, constituency offices up and down the country have been doubling down on the personal security of MPs and their staff.

Pam scrutinises the cardboard tube: 'It's from central office. I think it's safe.' She opens it and pulls out a poster. 'Oh, it's Theresa – an official portrait of our new prime minister – just right for the office wall!'

I stand up for a better look: 'Let me see. Quite a good one – I like the Frida Kahlo bracelet. But it's too big for our frame.'

The official portrait of Dave the ex-PM hanging on the wall is more modestly dimensioned. Now it's obsolete.

Pam admires the May portrait: 'I like it. Nice one, Theresa. I'll go and buy a bigger frame in the lunch hour.'

Hours later, Pam puts up the framed portrait and I check it

hangs straight. The frame is enormous, so now the thing dominates the office quite absurdly.

'Very imposing,' I say. 'Now we can get back to work.'

'Yes, it looks good,' says Pam. 'Can you take Dave into the back room and replace the old one of him in there?'

I take Dave away. As ever, Winston glowers out over anything and everything we do. Portraits of The Greatest Englishman seem as common in modern Britain, in Tory circles, as airbrushed images of Josef Stalin were in Soviet Russia.

To be fair, portraits of the Queen are probably even commoner, but we're in a sad state when the only way to leave the war behind is to double down on the medieval ancestor cult of the monarchy.

I admire another artwork in the back room, the placard of images of the flying boats that formerly flew out of Poole. The flying boats are a local link with the empire of old.

When I was a kid, I loved to see the big aircraft land and take off in the harbour. My boyhood imagination was enraptured by them. I would have bought an Airfix model of one if it hadn't cost the princely sum of ten shillings and sixpence. Ever since then, that model has symbolised for me the value of ten bob.

Soon after that, decimalisation turned a ten-bob note into a fifty-pence piece, which will buy a single apple in my local supermarket. The pound has sunk faster than the euro. Blame Brexit.

———

Buoyed by joy from the Messenger review, I write a similar long review of *Sapiens* and *Homo Deus*, the two big books by Professor Harari on the past and future of our species.

American politics is getting interesting.

13. The Trump apocalypse

In America, the business mogul and media celebrity Donald Trump is getting lots of airtime in the presidential election campaign. To my dismay, many local Conservatives admire him.

In October, an old video clip emerges of Trump reflecting on his power over women. He boasted he could 'grab them by the pussy' and get away with it.

I expect Hillary Clinton to win. I think Americans are on her side. Even Robert Syms says he wants and expects her to win.

Yet the Brexit surprise makes me uneasy. British voters were told they could have their cake and eat it. The truth, as Eurocrat Donald Tusk says, is that they'll go hungry: 'There will be no cakes on the table, for anyone. There will be only salt and vinegar.'

The Brexit confrontation on the menu is only a starter. In 1914, Brits declared war on an upstart Germany for invading Belgium. They thought they'd teach the Krauts a stiff lesson in neighbourly behaviour and said it would all be over by Christmas. But it dragged on for four years and dragged in the whole world.

Four months after the referendum, I meet Steve and Graham and Steve's wife Anne again in Poole for lunch at a local restaurant.

I treat them to my revelations from the world of Tory politics: 'Theresa May is trying to play clever with Boris Johnson. She knows most of the party faithful would rather see him at the helm, sticking it to the Europeans with his boisterously puckish British wit, so she's made him foreign secretary. Either he shows he can handle it and gives her a reason to let him loose or he fouls up so badly that everyone can see his career is over.'

Steve demurs: 'I don't think she had much choice in the matter. She's running scared of her own party, trying to outrun the Leavers.

Boris on the back benches would be too much to handle, so she brings him into the cabinet to keep him in line. Now she can sack him if he attacks her.'

Graham sees the problem: 'But Boris acts like a complete buffoon. How can Theresa May put him in charge of British relations with the world? How can the Europeans take him seriously?'

I smile ironically: 'Well, sure, but that's not the point. At least he's a true-blue patriot who's not ashamed to wave the flag – that's how the party faithful see him.'

Anne, who's Scottish, intervenes: 'That's how the English party faithful see him. In Scotland they see him as just another Westminster Tory, determined to ignore the Scots and forget the inconvenient fact that they voted to remain in Europe.'

Steve gives his verdict: 'All this is a power grab by Westminster. "Take back control" is cover for concentrating more power in central government, where once Theresa May is gone, someone like Boris can rule the roost and start governing like a dictator.'

I frown. 'Like the early days of the Third Reich.'

'History is full of such power grabs,' he says.

'This is terrible,' says Graham. 'Can't the Europeans stop it?'

'How?' I ask. 'The EU is a voluntary club, like a family we've married into. Our MP, Robert Syms, says the marriage has broken down and we're just looking for a decent divorce settlement. As a divorced husband himself, he knows how hard that can be, but he says it's better than staying in a loveless marriage.'

Robert was married to a lady of Russian extraction called Fiona until they divorced in 2016. They have two children, and he now wants to put them through college on his MP's salary. Fiona was his second wife, after an English lady called Nicky, who drops into the Poole office occasionally to chat with Pam. Robert employs both of his ex-wives as parliamentary assistants, putting me in a humbling third place on the payroll.

Graham moans: 'But being in Europe was a good marriage. How can the Tories justify tearing apart forty years of progress for the sake of their own party extremists?'

'The Tories feel vulnerable on their right flank,' I tell him. 'The coalition with the Liberals lost them votes to UKIP and Nigel Farage. Now they want their voters back, and to get them they need to man up.'

Steve adds: 'It's like Republicans going for Trump in America.'

———

A few days later, I meet Rachel again for an evening date at a restaurant in Poole. We've kept in touch on social media. I presume she plans to leverage my lust to calibrate her adjustment to a life in politics. She now works in London and is down for a family visit.

I'm too old and modest in my habits to wish to consummate the affair in carnal concupiscence. Instead, I let my brain soak in a warm bubble bath of happy hormones. The dosage is strong enough to beguile my mind when nothing urgent intervenes, but not bad enough for more. That said, a physical meeting is welcome.

To keep it cool, I opt for a casual look: open shirt under a blue pullover, with smart dark jeans and clean sneakers. Over this outfit, I add a black nylon update of the tough old waxed-cotton biker jackets that scrambler riders used to wear in my teens.

I arrive first and loiter with a beer in the bar, sitting on a sofa with the pub's newspapers. Rachel arrives looking as lovely as ever, with her long wavy hair shining and bouncy. She holds out her hand for mine.

'Hi, Andy, I hope you haven't been waiting too long.'

'No, I came early to relax with the papers. It's good to see the print editions from time to time. Can I get you a drink?'

'Thanks. A soda and lime would be fine.'

We settle knee to knee on the sofa. She removes jacket and scarf, to reveal again the airy blouse, black trousers, and flat shoes with bare feet in them I recall from the gala dinner. She looks wonderful.

'It's good to see you again,' I begin, 'I trust you're keeping well in London.'

'Yes, fine. I didn't tell you, but I'm working as a parliamentary intern for Conor Burns now. He remembered me from the debate I moderated and hired me.'

'Oh, no – really? Burns the Brexiteer of all people! Has he converted you to the Leaver cause?'

'No, nothing like that. I do policy research, back-office things.' She pauses for a moment. 'The referendum result was a shocker, wasn't it? I'm still getting used to it.'

'Yes, me too. I was totally gobsmacked. I watched the count with Julie Girling, and she was gobsmacked too. A couple of weeks later I went back to Germany, and my old friends there just couldn't understand what had happened. It was like a betrayal, like an act of treachery.'

'I can imagine. It must look bad from their point of view.'

A waitress invites us to take our places in the restaurant.

Over dinner, Rachel asks me about the books I've written, and I explain my entire philosophy, at length.

This is an ideal date for me. Socratic exchange of ideas means more to me than exchange of body fluids, welcome as that was in my younger years. If Rachel reflects on me as fondly as I do on her, she needs brain food to make the seed bear fruit. As a philosopher, I have this duty to my new disciple.

After the feast, knee to knee on the sofa again with drinks, we converse more intimately. I recall our words on Germany.

'As I said, my friends in Germany really don't know what to make of this whole Brexit thing. They can't help thinking back to the Nazi period and making comparisons.'

She looks reflective. 'Me too. My grandparents escaped from

Germany in 1939. Now I can imagine the sort of feelings they must have had.' She pauses. 'Actually, I'd like to go and visit Germany and get to know it better.'

I smile suddenly. 'I'd like to go with you. I could show you around, help you with the language and so on. How about it, next summer?'

'It's a nice idea. I'd love to just go there and get to know the culture.'

'Well, I'd go too and help you. Do you still have relatives there?'

'Yes, but none I know well. My grandparents were Jewish, and most of their family died.'

I pause and look down: 'Tragic … but the Jews haven't all gone. There's a big new synagogue in Heidelberg. I can show you that too if it makes you feel better.'

'It's a lovely thought …'

Her mobile emits a musical trill. She takes the call quietly.

'That's my boyfriend. He's come to take me home.'

'Oh, okay,' I sigh. 'I was just getting warmed up.'

She stands and picks up her jacket. 'Would you like to meet him? He's just outside with the car.'

'Sure.' I stand up and follow her out. I shake hands with boyfriend Crispin, a tall, thin chap who looks very young and gentle. Then I shake hands with Rachel, and then I watch them go.

———

May fought the law, and the law won. The British High Court ruled that MPs must vote on whether the UK can start the process of leaving the EU. May can't invoke Article 50 without them.

A tabloid the next day leads with mugshots of three High Court judges above the headline ENEMIES OF THE PEOPLE.

Days later, Julia Neuberger, the senior rabbi of the West London Synagogue and a baroness in the House of Lords, writes her response: 'I'm a rabbi, and I'm applying for a German passport.'

The dame is doing the right thing. I wish I'd done the same while I was still living in Germany.

———

Donald Trump wins the election to become the next president of the United States. With Trump in America and Brexit in Europe, the liberal world order of yore is sinking fast.

I recall the transatlantic Nylon axis running between New York and London that dominates global finances. With Trump ranting about immigration like a Brexiteer, the borders of the Nylon world are about to slam shut, to leave naked self-interest raging rampant as a wrecking ball. If this is disaster capitalism in action, it's taken on a whole new dimension.

On Thanksgiving, a bunch of prosperous Brexiteers, including the Barclay brothers, who own the Ritz hotel and the *Telegraph* newspaper, and Arron Banks, who spent millions of pounds on the Vote Leave campaign, throw a reception at the Ritz to thank the UKIP founder and new interim leader Nigel Farage for his leadership on Brexit and his support for Trump's presidential campaign.

It's all about the money.

President-elect Trump picks Steve Bannon as chief strategist. Bannon has a murky history as a libertarian extremist.

Trump picks Rex Tillerson, chairman and chief executive of ExxonMobil, as secretary of state for foreign affairs. Tillerson has a long history of business ties with Russia. In 2013, Russian president Vladimir Putin even awarded him the Order of Friendship.

Trump's pick for vice-president is Mike Pence, a fundamentalist who opposes abortion and denies the theory of evolution. His pick to head the US Treasury is an investment banker who made billions from the housing crisis. His pick for labour is a fast-food boss who disdains the minimum wage. His pick for the Environmental Protection Agency is a man who agitated against the agency.

His pick for defence is retired Marine Corps General James

'Mad Dog' Mattis, the warrior monk, who once summed up his martial philosophy thus: 'If you fuck with me, I'll kill you all.'

Trump is rattling the cage. I fear he might try to play softball with his friend Putin in the Kremlin.

The Baltic States of Estonia, Latvia, and Lithuania were all parts of the Soviet Union for decades but are now member states of the EU and NATO. In response, Putin is boosting his military presence in the neighbouring Russian exclave of Kaliningrad, which was an eastern province of Germany until 1945. In British war games, a Russian push into Latvia led to nuclear war within days.

Global thermonuclear war is back on the menu.

Trump is encouraging Theresa May to get tough too. In January 2017, she stands on the deck of a Royal Navy ship in the Persian Gulf and says: 'We seek a new and equal partnership between an independent, self-governing, global Britain and our friends and allies in the EU.'

I wince as she declares: 'I want a red, white, and blue Brexit.'

———

I watch President Donald Trump deliver his inaugural address. He walks unsmiling onto the Washington stage with his fist aloft under a grey sky. He speaks in a declamatory monotone:

'We, the citizens of America, are now joined in a great national effort to rebuild our country and to restore its promise for all of our people.'

He airs his philosophy: 'A nation exists to serve its citizens. Americans want great schools for their children, safe neighbourhoods for their families, and good jobs for themselves. These are the just and reasonable demands of a righteous public.'

I hear a Bible-belt dog whistle.

He intones a litany of American problems and declares: 'This American carnage stops right here and stops right now. From this moment on, it's going to be America First. … America will start winning again, winning like never before. We will bring back our jobs. We will bring back our borders. We will bring back our wealth. And we will bring back our dreams.'

He delivers a one-two knockout to the naïve hopes of the free-market Brexiteers: 'We will follow two simple rules: Buy American and Hire American.'

I smile: Come on, Brexiteers, wake up and smell the coffee.

Trump states his pledge of allegiance: 'At the bedrock of our politics will be a total allegiance to the United States of America.'

He's riding on a rhetorical high now: 'When America is united, America is totally unstoppable. There should be no fear. We are protected, and we will always be protected … by God.'

He gets real: 'Now arrives the hour of action. … Whether we are black or brown or white, we all bleed the same red blood of patriots, we all enjoy the same glorious freedoms, and we all salute the same great American flag.'

Blood and the flag!

His grand finale: 'Together, we will make America strong again. We will make America wealthy again. We will make America proud again. We will make America safe again. And, yes, together, we will make America great again.'

I'm stunned. Americans have dived into deep doo-doo.

———

A week later, I rise early from my bed. I put on a white shirt, blue necktie, dark suit, black shoes, and my biker jacket. I run down to my sporty BMW and drive off to the Royal Motor Yacht Club on the millionaire peninsula of Sandbanks. I park near the slot reserved for the club commodore and walk in.

A waiter ushers me up to the dining room. It has a panoramic view of the harbour and the island where Lord Baden-Powell once lived in his castle. The marina below me has a fine array of motor yachts wintering in the placid waters.

The twelve of us assembled here for breakfast gather around a long table. We're awaiting the arrival of the guest of honour, Robert Syms, our member of parliament.

This is a party event we call a cabinet breakfast. The diners are local businessmen who pay the price to breakfast with their MP and hear his views on the state of the nation. I'm here to support him and to keep my finger on the pulse of the local power elite.

As we stand waiting, I talk with Ken, the founder and chief executive of a company that uses expensive American machines to do something technical. Ken is younger than me, dynamic in manner, and intelligent in his outlook on the world.

'Trump really doesn't know what he's doing,' I say. 'He's new on the job, he didn't expect to win, and his whole take on the world is framed by his background in real estate, gambling, mobsters, and sleazy sex. This is not a nice man.'

Ken differs: 'I'd rather give him the benefit of the doubt. He's smart, he's fought his way up the hard way, and his conservative instincts are sound. This is a man we can do business with. Imagine if Hillary had won. She's a Washington insider, a liberal disaster zone. We'd get no mileage there at all on trade deals.'

'But she knows what she's doing. She understands the machinery of government.'

'Crooked Hillary,' he retorts. 'It would be a stale rehash of the Bill Clinton years, with a whole lot of politically correct baloney about equal rights and no thought at all for the business community that generates the wealth that pays for the whole shitshow.'

'I guess we'll have to agree to differ. Here's Robert.'

We all sit down for a full English breakfast. When it comes, on heated plates bearing the RMYC crest, I face a fried egg, two rashers of crispy bacon, a blackened slice of blood sausage, a brown square of fried bread, a dollop of baked beans, and a fried half of a tomato. Not quite my usual fruit and granola.

Robert speaks: 'The government is working hard to get ready for the Brexit negotiations, and David Davis is preparing to represent our interests strongly in Brussels. Contrary to all you might have read about him, I think he's the right man for the job.'

Robert presses on: 'Theresa May is determined to keep up the momentum and deliver the Article 50 notice soon.'

And Robert is going to back her all the way.

He continues with an anecdote I've heard a few times before: 'As usual, the Labour opposition in Westminster is in complete disarray. I was talking in a lift with a Labour MP the other day, and he was almost suicidal.'

He moves on to Trump, NATO, China, and Europe.

He sums up: 'Altogether, then, things are looking quite good. The Brexit preparations are proceeding at pace, the government is looking forward to working with the new US administration, and we Conservatives can look forward to winning the next election. These are interesting times, but I think we can look ahead with optimism.'

Later that day, I see Theresa May has her first date with Trump at the White House. Wearing her best bright red dress and eager to secure the special relationship, she holds his hand as they walk along the veranda beside the Rose Garden. It's shameful.

———

Trump pulls the United States out of the Trans-Pacific Partnership. He then appoints Steve Bannon to the National Security Council. Bannon once said: 'I want to bring everything crashing down and destroy all of today's establishment.'

Bannon spoke at the Vatican in 2014 and praised Julius Evola: 'We, the Judaeo-Christian West, really have to look at what he's talking about as far as traditionalism goes.'

Evola called himself a traditionalist 'superfascist' and became a darling of Benito Mussolini's Italian Fascist movement. He also inspired the Russian traditionalist Aleksandr Dugin, who in 1997 proclaimed a new 'fascist fascism' for Russia and then founded the Eurasia party. His big ambition was to establish a Eurasian Union stretching from the Atlantic to the Pacific.

Dugin drew inspiration from the earlier philosopher Ivan Ilyin, who had imagined a Russian Christian fascism. Ilyin praised Hitler as a crusader against Bolshevism and dreamed about fascism from exile in Switzerland. He said the Leader would rule every aspect of political life, and elections would be ritual of submission.

In the new millennium, Russian president Putin not only works with Dugin in the Kremlin but has also rehabilitated Ilyin as a court philosopher. Putin is building a new brand of populist fascism.

Trump wants to build a Washington–Moscow axis that would destroy NATO and the EU and pave the way for a fascist Eurasian Union.

I drive up to Oxford for a graduate seminar on transatlantic security in the Trump era. The speaker is Dr Anthony Wells, an Anglo-American intelligence analyst.

The transatlantic intelligence collaboration began in 1941 to fight Nazi U-boats. It continued during the Cold War to coordinate deployment and targeting of Polaris nuclear missiles fired from nuclear submarines and continues in the Trident era.

The wider collaboration is now established in the 'Five Eyes' intelligence community that underpins the security of the West.

———

A German word I like from my time there is *Fazit* – pronounced 'fart-zit' – which means conclusion, result, or upshot.

Fazit: Trump and Putin are no friends of Europe.

14. She pulled the trigger

I lie sleepless in my narrow British bed. My thoughts are churning. Brexit means trouble.

Modern London is a global metropolis. London is banker to the planet. Leavers say they're reclaiming London for the nation, but financial companies plan to move elsewhere. Trouble.

The UK delegation in Brussels proposes a British candidate to chair the EU working group on tax competition between member states. But the UK opposes EU plans to outlaw tax havens such as Bermuda, the British Virgin Islands, the Cayman Islands, and Gibraltar (former Crown colonies) and the Channel Islands Jersey and Guernsey and the Isle of Man (Crown dependencies). Trouble.

The Brexiteers plan to separate the UK from the EU. The UK unites four states with antique institutions and ancient traditions. The EU is a union of 28 states with modern institutions and new programs. The EU looks better than the UK. Trouble.

Brexit poses a giant economic problem for all Europeans. The British economy is as big as those of the twenty smallest EU member states combined. Trouble.

Brexit also destroys the political equilibrium of the EU. In the European Council, a blocking minority needs just over a third of the EU population. The northern member states favour free trade and have a combined population of a third of the total. Against them, the southern 'Club Med' states favour protectionism and have a similar share. After Brexit, Club Med will dominate. Trouble.

Brexit is no joke.

I lie sleepless no longer. I spring out of bed and look out on a new morning. I plan to spend the day exploring the mathematics of quantum computing. It makes more sense than Brexit.

———

On 22 March, a terrorist attack near the Houses of Parliament kills six people and injures at least fifty. A car mounts the pavement and crashes, then the Islamist driver jumps out and runs toward the Palace of Westminster, armed with a knife. Confronted by the cops, he kills one before others shoot him dead. Foreign minister Tobias Ellwood tries and fails to revive the cop. More trouble.

That Saturday, a 'Unite for Europe' rally blocks the streets of central London to protest Brexit and to celebrate sixty years since the signing of the Treaty of Rome that founded the EU. A hundred thousand people are there. I wish I were there too.

Four days later, Theresa May signs her Article 50 letter giving notice that the UK intends to leave the EU. Her man in Brussels delivers the letter. The die is cast. Yet more trouble to celebrate the birthday of the union I cherish.

—

On April Fool's Day, I meet my old friend Graham, who's visiting Poole. We walk down the high street into the heart of the old town, to a restaurant run by immigrants from eastern Europe.

We stride briskly through the gathering twilight past a street scene of closed shops, many of them charity outlets and some of them boarded up. For anyone who knew the town decades ago, the new look is depressing and the gathering gloom a mercy.

With his leather jacket and silver stubble, Graham is hardly a posh gent, but his academic life in London separates him from all this. As we pass rough sleepers in doorways and drunks stooping unsteadily in the deepening shadows, he tries to stare ahead.

'This looks really awful,' he says at last. 'When did it get this bad?'

'Since austerity. The financial crisis hit harder here than in London. With no money for local authorities, the council has had to cut back a lot further than anyone wanted. Add to that the shift of retail trade online, and in no time at all you get, well, this.'

'But the Conservatives are to blame for austerity. How can you defend working for them?'

'Well, Maggie Thatcher is to blame. It was under her watch that Britain went for broke in the global finance sector and let industry go to ruin. We bet big on Brits being traders and bankers to the world. Then the crash in 2008 put the kybosh on that.'

'Yes, I was there in London,' he says. 'The City was booming for years. But obviously what we need now is more public spending. The last Labour chancellor, Gordon Brown, was right to pump billions into the economy. Austerity is madness.'

'Yes, but then a basic conservative instinct kicks in. Don't run up debt unless or until you know how you can pay it back. I sympathise with that. In Germany the government still runs a surplus. Industry is strong there, and it's a massive export earner. Britain made a strategic mistake.'

'But how can you defend working for the Conservatives?'

'Because that's where the problem lies. When you have a problem, you go to the point where it began to fix it. Conservatives need to learn that the path to prosperity is to renew British industry.'

Graham looks incredulous. 'Renew industry? The markets are gone already. Look at the car industry – dead, dead, dead.'

I recall he drives a BMW too: 'Not quite. We have a thriving trade in components and final assembly for cars sourced internationally. That's the future. All the best industries have gone global. We should start by hosting as many big German and American companies as we can here.'

'But then the profits go overseas. We lose control over them.'

'Not at all. The companies operate in a legal frame. We just make sure the laws give us a share of the profits, a fair tax return, decent working conditions, and so on. All this should be obvious – and the Conservatives should learn that lesson.'

'Or to get it wrong again by going for Brexit.'

I see the restaurant: 'Here we are. Time to think about eating.'

It's in a stately building that during the war was a naval command headquarters for amphibious operations in support of the
D-Day invasion. Now it's aiming for a Mediterranean vibe, with
Chianti bottles hanging in fishing nets and so on. The diners look
prosperous and civilised.

We're soon eating and drinking well. The waitress who serves
us has only basic English, but she looks friendly and conforms well
to the imperial ideal of submissive servitude. We continue our
debate on the state of the nation and the world.

'What worries me is travel,' says Graham. 'We have a holiday
cottage in France, and we like to drive down there at short notice,
just for a few days. If we have to fuss about visas and insurance and
so on, it'll be no fun at all.'

I smile: 'Tell me about it. I have just the same issue with
Germany. We both agree that the whole thing is a nonsense, and we
both hope the government will come to its senses. But now I'm
trying to think about physics, to grapple with the new ideas.'

'Yes, you told me. What are you hoping to achieve?'

'Not a lot. I'm too old to follow most of the maths now. But I
kept plugging away at it in Germany, more just to try to keep up
than to do any new work. I like to understand the ideas.'

He shrugs. 'I haven't really kept up with it. The maths was too
much. Even computer science is more than I can keep up with now.
My work was mostly administration by the time I retired. Now I'd
rather think about boating and the family and so on.'

'Fair enough, but as a single man I need something to keep my
mind busy. And physics is linked to my old logical ideas.'

'Why didn't you get married in Germany? You were there long
enough.'

'Yes, I was, and I developed crushes on a series of German girls
over the years, but they all had boyfriends already. The girls who

didn't were less appealing. Sad story, but not worth fussing about. I'm living the life of a philosopher now.'

The deeper story comes to mind, but I'm not about to dig it up here and now. I kept plugging for a partner, but I couldn't forget my murky past. The years with Judy and their aftermath left me unable to conceive a higher high and terrified of plunging to a lower low. Better to play safe until the shadows of the past recede.

'I still see Judy in London occasionally,' he says. 'I suppose you know she's no longer an MP.'

'Yes, I checked the results. But all that's a lifetime ago. I have a completely different lifestyle now, with Germany and so on.'

A more boring lifestyle too. Judy and I managed to have a lot of fun together. After that, life as a single seems rather dull.

'Did you imagine your life would turn out this way when you and Judy were together?'

'No, I was still lost in a world of dreams. But I do remember that when we spent the summer of 1974 in Berlin, I realised that the German experience was far too interesting to let a life with Judy in England get in the way of it.'

'Ah, yes, the summer of 1974 – that was the end of our year in the student commune in Ealing.'

'Right. When that split up, Judy and I went straight to Berlin. The commune in Berlin was far more radical than Ealing.'

Graham smiles: 'Ealing was radical enough for me. Jeff and I were glad to go back to a quiet life in our flat in Hampstead.'

'Oh, right, Jeff. What happened to him?'

'He made a fortune in banking. He got married soon after I married Jules, but not to anyone you've met.'

My deeper story is shifting in its grave, undead, a zombie.

———

European officials in Brussels publish a draft document on Brexit that says any agreement between the EU and the UK relating to

Gibraltar must be acceptable to the Kingdom of Spain.

For most Europeans, the status of Gibraltar is an outrage. Brits have let this rocky outcrop on the southern tip of Spain become a tax haven, a gambling paradise, and a source of Spanish fury.

The European claim is a source of fury for Brexiteers. Foreign minister Boris Johnson issues a patriotic blast pledging to defend the Rock by military force if push comes to shove.

Many Germans see Brexit as betrayal. Klaus Weber, who leads the centrist EPP group in the European parliament, says: 'Some of the politicians in London have not understood what leaving the European Union means. It means being alone.'

But Theresa May is not to be diverted. In mid-April, fresh back from a walking holiday in Wales, she calls a snap general election, to be held on 8 June. Her party colleagues see the strong possibility of a substantially increased parliamentary majority. Thus emboldened, she takes the bait and names the date.

Two days later, she confirms that the UK will leave the EU at the stroke of midnight (European time) on 29 March 2019: 'This is an historic moment from which there can be no turning back.'

———

Days later, I meet with Steve in Poole. He's driven down (in his BMW – he has one too) for a day trip, not only to see me but also to enjoy a bracing springtime hike along the Dorset coast.

Oh, to be in England now that April's here. Today, there's a light breeze and a veil of high cloud but no rain and no chill. Steve is kitted for the hike with a waterproof jacket, country trousers, rucksack, hiking boots, and a floppy hat. I too have hat, jacket, and rucksack, but I dare cargo shorts and walking sandals.

We set off southward at a brisk pace to Sandbanks, and from there we take the chain ferry over to the natural paradise of Studland. Here the heath is bordered for miles by a wide sandy beach. As we walk along the shoreline, we fall into conversation.

'Trump is a menace to the civilised world,' says Steve. 'With him and Brexit together, we're entering uncharted territory.'

'Well, indeed,' I reply, 'I think we all need to take a deep breath and try to understand what's happening. This is a new turn in the politics of the Western world, and it brings a whole new landscape into view.'

'Trump is Putin's man in Washington. He's undermined the integrity of Western democracy.'

'There too we need to take a step back. Better relations with Russia are just what we need so soon after the Cold War. But we also need to reconsider what democracy means in our world.'

'True. The old model of voters as reasonable people voting in the national interest is obviously wrong – proven wrong in Britain and in America.'

'Exactly. We need to get to the bottom of that – and European philosophy offers us a way to do so.'

'Okay, you're the philosopher. Tell me how.'

'Well, I locate the start of it all in German philosophy. Ever since the time of Kant and Hegel two hundred years or so ago, German thinkers have pushed ahead and created a new foundation in thought for the humanistic world we live in.'

'Is this just your opinion?'

'It's not just me. We've moved on from the ancient Greeks. That world is still where Anglo-American thinkers tend to start from in the West, but the fact that we don't understand Trump and Brexit shows the need to rethink.'

'That sounds logical enough. Can you give me any examples?'

'Look at the voter model we use to defend our brand of demo-cracy. We're not rational egoists who optimise our choice between alternatives subject to moral constraints about treating everyone equally. Modern neuroscience says the rational model is wrong, and common sense says we don't treat everyone equally, whatever we say about equal rights.'

'Did the German philosophers foresee this, or is this modern neuroscience?'

'Good point. The philosophers saw a gap. The neuroscientists filled it. Look at Marxism, which is a sort of plain man's parody of Hegelianism. Marx said people follow their class interests, not the dictates of pure reason. That's just one way to fill the gap, and since then we've learned to do better. The Marxists were the first crude revolutionaries who stormed the liberal ramparts.'

Steve frowns: 'But the Anglo-American world never fell for all that Marxist dogma. We kept the faith with liberal humanism and defeated the Marxists in the Cold War.'

'Not so fast, young man. Our first assault against the Marxists came from Nazi Germany, and that was no liberal paradise. You may recall that German nationalism grew historically from Prussian nationalism.'

'Okay, I can agree with you on that.'

'Well, the other dialectical strand in Hegel's philosophy was a robust defence of Prussian nationalism, as embodied in monarchy, Christianity, and military discipline. Martin Heidegger took up that strand in his philosophy.'

'Heidegger? But he was a Nazi.'

'Well, Heidegger was briefly a Nazi before the war, but yes, it was damaging for him. Anyway, he emphasised the importance of a sense of one's own identity, rooted in a kind of religious mysticism. Anyone who feels love for a Christian nation will understand.'

'And hence Trump and the evangelical right – is that it?'

'Yes, exactly. The Brexit story fits too, as a last echo of the Church of England. But the same model also fits Putin's Russia, Catholic Poland, nationalism in Hungary and Greece, and so on.'

Steve is dubious. 'I'm not sure about the Church of England – we're all atheists now – but I see the rest.'

'The historical analogy for Brexit is the founding of the Church of England in opposition to the Church of Rome. The European Union is obviously the secular analogue of Catholic Church, and the Brexiteers are doing the same sort of thing that Henry the Eighth did when he broke off from Rome.'

He nods: 'Yes, that makes historical sense.'

We push on, through the ancient village of Studland with its huddle of stone cottages around a Saxon church, over the grassy Purbeck hill offering a grand view from its windswept top, down a winding gravel path southward, and into the town of Swanage.

We're in the fiefdom of Richard Drax MP, who lives in a splendid manor house within a vast walled-off Dorset estate that's listed in the Domesday Book of 1086. We push on.

We continue to Durlston Castle, set on a craggy promontory south of the town. Here we pause for a snack before heading back.

It's been a long day. I climb into my narrow British bed. She's pulled the trigger. The rest is physics. And a bloodbath.

15. The Queen's hat

On the last Saturday of April, I stand on the stage of a village hall in Poole and look out over a sea of faces. I aim my camera and take a series of photographs of the crowd arrayed before me. The people look cheery and hold up identical blue placards, and in front of them a smiling man holds up his right arm in a gesture of triumph.

This is the Poole Conservative Association adoption meeting for its next prospective parliamentary candidate. The hall is in the richest ward in Poole, home of our most powerful party members. The smiling candidate whose adoption I record is Robert Syms. My best pap snap is the keynote image for the campaign.

I won't serve as the election agent this time. I let my wily conspirator Isaac do it. Robert, with his usual easy way on practical details, is fine with the change. He knows his seat is safe from anything but an avalanche and plans to do as little as possible to bang his own drum.

I'm glad Isaac is prepared to take on all the aggro. I'm not on board with the party's campaign message. I'd rather stick to the fun stuff like writing propaganda and monitoring parliamentary mail than try defending the indefensible on doorsteps.

Much like Isaac, the British establishment is Orwellian in its disregard for inconvenient truths. A Downing Street statement says Theresa May held a 'very constructive meeting' with Jean-Claude Juncker over Brexit. In fact, Juncker later told Angela Merkel that May lives in another galaxy, and Merkel told her MPs in Berlin that London is 'under illusions' about the Brexit negotiations.

The EU bureaucracy has calculated a Brexit bill of around sixty billion euros to present to the UK. May says the UK doesn't have to pay a cent. She also demands immediate talks on a future trade deal. The EU team wants to sort out the basics first.

On 7 May, in another sign of the growing gulf between Brexit Britain and continental Europe, Emmanuel Macron wins a clear victory over Marine Le Pen in the presidential elections in France. Macron is the voice of Europe against the threat of 'Frexit' under Le Pen, so it's a win for Europhiles across the continent.

I see France and Britain going opposite ways. Two nations, so similar in population and economic output yet so different in style and culture, have a lot of shared history and a rivalry they rarely overcome. I know who's right and who's wrong in this case.

———

A church in Poole holds a soapbox meeting to parade the field of prospective parliamentary candidates before the voting public. It's a chance for the voters to ask their burning questions.

Robert is only persuaded under pressure to take part in it. He turned down a request from the same vicar in 2015 on the grounds that his sharing a platform with other candidates was only giving them more legitimacy. I tell him it's the duty of privilege to bend to popular will and expose his butt to a kick or two.

The church in which Robert reluctantly agrees to appear is a beautiful building, last restored in the Georgian era, and still in use as a parish church. It sits in a patch of grass surrounded by a warren of ancient streets and old stone cottages, all lovingly restored to preserve an antique community style that looks like a Disneyland theme park. The Poole Xenophobe party that runs the ward is proud of the precinct and votes against anything that might spoil its kitschy charm.

I attend the event as a member of the audience. My date for the evening is Susan Lever, the lady I helped to run for the council against the Poole Xenophobes.

It's shady and cold after a sunny day when I meet her on the grass outside the church. I wear my biker jacket over my dark suit, with a blue scarf to show my party affiliation. Susan's long dark hair tumbles onto a black coat and scarf over a black skirt and boots.

We meet, kiss cheeks, and head for the church door past a gauntlet of hucksters holding out leaflets. Their pet peeve of the season is that the Tory council is saving money by closing public conveniences. Protesters say people who need to pee or poo in a hurry will be tempted to foul the local greenery or risk soiling their pants, hence endangering civilisation as we knew it.

One huckster, a local UKIP man who was once a Conservative, shouts: 'Selling out to Brussels again? When will you lot learn?'

I stride on. A reply is more than he deserves. Robert is doing his opponents a favour by showing up here. With his majority he can afford it, but it's a no-win night for him.

Susan and I sit on a pew near the front and wait for the nave to fill. The vicar looks pleased at the crowd. Beside her, seven stooges sit in a glum row, waiting for the action to start.

The vicar opens the show with a confident voice and outlines the details with an efficiency honed by years of practice. She then invites each candidate in turn to speak for three minutes, so that in half an hour the questions and answers can begin on time.

Robert casts himself as the candidate for competent and steady government, not flashy but attuned to the real issues and determined to do the right thing. He earns polite applause, though Susan and I loyally clap a while longer.

The Labour candidate is a feisty woman with a loud and brassy voice whose message I don't recall. The Liberal Democrat candidate is a chap with a chip on his shoulder whose passionate call for social justice seems too unhinged to be let loose at parliamentary level. The Green is a gentle young man who airs fuzzy vacuities.

The UKIP man is a former Conservative, a canny financial operator who thinks his sharp suit and posh accent will win votes, but whose claim that getting out of Europe will let people like him make more money is a guaranteed loser as an election pitch. The

Poole Xenophobe is another former Conservative who thinks the old town is a historic national treasure.

Finally, the protest vote candidate, the joke candidate, is Percy Payne, the army veteran with a peg-leg who now looks awkward in a smart suit. He's so inarticulate that I have no idea what he's trying to say. He gave his best clue with a selfie on social media sporting a pirate costume, complete with leather hat and a sword.

When the vicar calls a brief pause, Susan and I stay seated.

'I thought Robert came over well,' she says. 'We need him re-elected to get Brexit over the line so that we can get on with our lives again.'

'Get Brexit over the line?' I sneer, 'Get it banished and deep-sixed for all eternity, I'd say.'

'Don't you want to see us freed from Brussels regulations?'

'We need a stable regulatory frame. Or do you want to see a return to robber-baron capitalism, red in tooth and claw?'

'I want a return for hard work, not creeping socialism and state bureaucracy.'

'That's code for grab all you can and refuse to share it out. Selfishness on steroids.'

'Are you really a Conservative, Andy?'

'Let's agree to differ. We're about to start again.'

The vicar fields questions from the floor and answers from the panel. But one exchange causes a glorious stir. It's about how a future government can make better provision for the National Health Service, and several panellists give boring answers.

But the Liberal Democrat gets excited: 'It's a national disgrace, just appalling! What with privatisation, no money for new equipment, the shortage of ambulance drivers and qualified doctors and nurses, absurdly long working hours for staff and waiting times in A&E, it's utterly unacceptable. Jeremy Cunt should be ashamed of himself!'

There's a hushed pause in the audience, then a couple of muted giggles.

The Lib Dem realises what he's said: 'Oh, God, I'm sorry!' He looks heavenward: 'Forgive me, God, here of all places.' He turns desperately to the vicar.

She seems unfazed. After waiting for the giggles to die down, she lets the evening grind on to its normal conclusion.

I see Susan safely to her car and then head off to a more remote car park for my Beemer. Just another night out.

Next morning in the office, I'm doing my thing as usual when Isaac walks in with a spring in his step and a twinkle in his eye.

'Did you hear him?' he asks, addressing Pam and me equally. 'The Lib Dem candidate, did you hear him? Jeremy Cunt! In a church! He'll never live this down! They reported it in the paper. Didn't use the word, of course, but it got around. I posted the story on Facebook, and it's got hundreds of clicks already. He's done for, completely scuppered.'

I smile at him, bemused by his animation: 'You really think it's a big deal?'

Isaac pulls an evil grin: 'Absolutely! He has no chance of recovering from this one. We'll nail him down and dance on his grave.'

'You really want to make an issue out of it?'

'You kidding? He hands us a silver bullet, we use it. That's the power of propaganda. Never miss a chance to dish the dirt on your opponents. That's the way to win.'

———

Theresa May writes the intro for the Conservative party manifesto: 'The next five years are the most challenging that Britain has faced in my lifetime. Brexit will define us. Now more than ever, Britain needs a strong and stable government, Britain needs strong and stable leadership, Britain needs a clear plan.'

The manifesto is a total disaster. A proposal to ask wealthy old people to help fund any extended care they might need in old age, as dementia and the like take their toll, is so badly formulated that the press calls it a dementia tax and a death tax. A pledge to lift the ban on foxhunting is lampooned mercilessly by the same press critics. And so on – the manifesto seems designed to nobble the Tories from the start.

The only thing that saves them is the leader of the opposition, Jeremy Corbyn. His red-rag socialism is so rebarbatively Marxist that he should have no chance at all.

The no less rebarbative Nigel Farage helps her too by reminding voters of why UKIP is unelectable: 'The British government will … never forgive me for being successful … I admire Vladimir Putin. As a political operator [he's] the best in the world.'

Farage – Putin – Trump – Brexit – three men and a dog.

Trump flies over to Italy in the last week of May. Graciously, he describes his meeting with Pope Francis as a great honour. Francis gives Trump a copy of his encyclical on caring for the environment, in which he accuses capitalists of turning the Earth into a big pile of filth. Trump won't read a word of it.

Trump goes on to wreck the Group of Seven global summit in Sicily. He refuses to endorse the Paris climate accord and berates NATO members for not spending enough on defence. He also has a new beef to air: 'I have a problem with German trade. Look at the millions of cars they sell in the US. Terrible. We'll stop it.'

Days later, back in Germany – in a Munich beer tent, to be exact – Angela Merkel responds with cool diplomacy: 'We must fight for our future, as Europeans, for our destiny … of course in friendship with the United States of America, in friendship with Great Britain, and as good neighbours … with other countries.'

With this elegant statement, Merkel makes clear that the Brexit vote has changed her view of the UK on the world stage. She lumps Britain together with America as an unreliable ally.

On the first day of June, Trump pulls America out of the Paris climate accord. He says it's a bad deal for the United States. He thinks climate change is a hoax invented by the Chinese, and he's convinced the way forward is to keep on burning fossil fuels.

—

On Thursday 8 June, British voters go to the polls to elect their next government. I run early again to my local polling station to do my duty. That night, before the polls close at ten, I stride into the Poole Arts Centre with a big blue rosette on my lapel and collect a pass on a lanyard. I'm here to help at the overnight count again.

Compared with 2015, this is an easy night. There are only the votes for the next MP to count, without more fuss for councillors. Two constituencies are being counted in parallel, not only Robert's fiefdom of Poole but also Mid Dorset and North Poole, where the Conservative incumbent is Michael Tomlinson, a fine young man with high parliamentary ambition and high Tory views.

Both Robert and Michael are there at the count, along with Isaac, whose energy amazes me. He speeds relentlessly around the counting tables in search of technical infractions he can use to call forth mighty vengeance from the invigilators. I check a few counts too, but only to pass the time. The chance of a serious counting irregularity is tiny.

Isaac pauses on his tireless rounds to ask me: 'Any indication about the result yet?'

I shake my head: 'Not really. It's clearly a big win for Robert, but I can't say how big.'

'Yeah, that's about my estimate too. As big as last time, do you think?'

'Maybe, but I wouldn't bet on it yet. I'm more fussed about the national picture, to be honest.'

'Hey, remember my post about that Lib Dem twat? I've got over a thousand likes on it now, and it's still increasing. It's my most popular post in the whole campaign.'

'Well, good for you. I guess that's his career down the pan.'

Isaac speeds on his way, looking for new evidence of skul-duggery among the counters. I move on too, until I spot the warty face and bulging gut of Percy Payne, whose pirate campaign is doomed to lose him his deposit again.

'Hi, Percy, how's it looking?'

'No chance, obviously, but I never expected to win.'

'Why do you keeping doing it?'

'It's the chase. It's exciting, nothing like it. Plenty of time to get over it later.'

'Well, good for you. Can't really say good luck, but you get my meaning.'

Percy smirks and stumps off. I turn to a table and pretend to check the count while I admire the fine fingering of the girls at the table. I wonder if they like being watched.

Hours pass as the painstakingly manual ritual inches toward its climax. Sheaves of paper bundles, counted and recounted, sorted into hundreds in coloured wrappers, collect on the long central tables where the overall result will be tallied. Already, the lines of blue bundles are longer than all the other lines together.

At last, the presiding officer makes the call. Robert Syms, Conservative, has gathered almost 29 thousand votes.

A bit of huddled arithmetic with Isaac extracts the meaning of this number. Robert has 58 percent of the vote, about twice as many as the runner-up, the Labour lady. He's done significantly better than in 2015, which was his previous best result. It's a landslide. Poole is his private fiefdom.

Meanwhile, over on the tables counting the votes for Michael Tomlinson, a similar result is emerging. His seat was a marginal in 2015, but now it's his own safe seat, by a handsome margin. His main opponent, the Lib Dem candidate Vikki Slade, whom I know from her council work and almost admire for her feisty spirit, had hoped to win. Her bitter disappointment is plain to see as she concedes defeat.

All the while, I've been regularly ducking out of the counting hall to check the national scene on the big television in the foyer beside the bar. There things look less rosy for the Conservatives. In fact, the outcome looks set to be a squeaker.

I'm glad. This is the best way of getting through to Theresa May and her team that their chosen course of pushing ahead with their Brexit policy even though half of the electorate hates it is, to say the least, unwise.

Later in the day, after I've gone home, slept for a few hours, and caught up with the news again, the situation is clear enough for Tory hearts to sink across the nation. May has lost her majority.

With all the results in, her prospects look dismal. Conservatives have lost thirteen seats and with them their overall majority. Labour has gained thirty seats, mainly at the cost of the Scottish National Party. Liberal Democrats gain four, and the Democratic Unionist Party of Northern Ireland gain two, to give them ten seats. UKIP is crushed, with no seats, and its leader quits.

May refuses to concede defeat, but Tory grandees are furious. They curse her for gambling away their majority. May begins talks with the DUP and bribes them to make a 'confidence and supply' deal to support her. She's fatally weakened.

The show limps on. Tourists in London on 22 June are treated to all the traditional pomp and pageantry of mounted soldiers in fancy uniforms and a horse-drawn gilded carriage straight from Disneyland bearing Her Majesty the Queen on a ride to the Palace of Westminster for the State Opening of Parliament. There, amid further pageantry involving people in wigs and garters, a black rod, an old hat borne aloft on a stick, and a pair of thrones set against a wall so encrusted with gilded decoration as to rival any studio prop in Tinseltown, the Queen enacts the rites to mark the opening of a new session of parliament.

She reads out a speech that heralds Brexit, but her hat says otherwise. Her suit is in a shade of blue resembling the blue of the European Union flag, and her big, bold hat is in the same shade of blue. It's even studded with yellow or golden stars, or at least quasi-stellar objects, resembling the golden stars on the EU flag.

I blink: Is the Queen coming out as a Remainer?

Her speech, written for her by the new prime minister using the signifier 'My government' as an elegantly ambiguous form of words, omits most of the unfortunate manifesto pledges, to leave a thread-bare package dominated by eight items on Brexit.

16. Dunkirk all over again

British troops stand in orderly queues on the beaches of Dunkirk. Stuka dive-bombers fly down toward them, their sirens wailing, and drop bombs that throw sand and smoke in all directions. Machine-gun bullets spatter all around and zing off metal plates.

I'm riveted by *Dunkirk*. Directed by Christopher Nolan, the movie features a night scene at a railway station with me nowhere in sight. I see it in a new Bournemouth cinema with a state-of-the-art sound system and feel every bomb and bullet as if I'm the target. Okay, the Messerschmitt fighter and the Heinkel bomber aren't quite authentic (they're from the postwar Spanish air force and have Merlin engines) and the Royal Navy destroyer is an impostor (a postwar French navy destroyer, to be exact) – and there are far too few Tommies on the beach and the burning Spitfire at the end is absurdly missing an engine – but all this could be fixed with some computer graphics.

Less forgivable is the overall tone. The movie is a sentimental celebration of Brits abandoning hostile Europe and returning to the comforts of home, enjoying a nice cup of tea with the family behind the white cliffs of Fortress UK. I'm glad I'm out of it.

Walking back along the seaside prom to Poole, I reflect on my luck at being born into a generation where the armed confrontation with Europe seems like ancient history. The downside is that some voters think it's safe for Britain to cut its ties with the mainland.

It's a sunny day, and as I walk alongside the holidaymakers on the sand, my head is still ringing with the sounds of the bombs and bullets those troops endured on a beach much like this. These girls in bikinis and boys in shorts would look up with innocent curiosity if a warplane flew by, as they do every year during the air show. They wouldn't dream of ducking for cover.

—

The first Sunday in August is sunny. I go on a hike southward along the familiar trail over miles of golden beach beside wild heathland, through the ancient village, over the grassy hill with a view, down the winding path, into Swanage, and along the seafront to another grassy hill and a rocky promontory.

On the promontory, the grass gives way to cliffs and a rocky peak. There a Coastguards station stands watch over a seascape stretching to the southern horizon and the foreign shores of France beyond. Above the station flutters a union jack, and in the glazed cabin stands an officer scanning the skyline through binoculars.

The scene is idyllic. A few clouds drift across the blue sky, the grass shines bright green in the sunlight, and a few distant figures lend a placid air to the vista. I take photos, and one delights me, with the station on the left, flag flying, and an infinite seascape to the right – a little outpost guarding Fortress UK from dark threats below the horizon.

That photo inspires me for the next four weeks as I write *Britizen Jon*. No novel written in four weeks is a classic, but that's not the point. I'm making a statement, sketching a vision of what Brexit might bring, and setting the nightmare into mad relief.

I write a deliberately ambiguous blurb: 'This is the tragic story of Jon Ball, who became a Conservative prime minister in the UK only to blow it spectacularly, with the result that Britain became a socialist republic within the European Union.'

I'm used to the drill here. Once I have a print-ready text and the cover art as PDF documents, I send the files to an American print-on-demand publisher. In early September, I have the first copy of my new statement in my hands.

A few weeks later, I'm cheered when Rowan Williams, the former Archbishop of Canterbury, responds to a copy I sent him: 'It's important to be reminded how easily democracies lose their grip, morally and politically, and how societies slide towards re-pression and self-destructive policies in pursuit of short-term goals. I read it as a plea for a more grown-up politics.'

———

In Brussels, the government's Brexit talks are deadlocked. The main stumbling block is still the divorce bill.

Brexiteers mime apoplexy as they compete to express their outrage. Some say the UK should send the EU a bill in the billions for reparations to mitigate the historic damage 'we' suffered at the hands of federalists in Europe. I sigh at their antics.

Theresa May has secured a narrow parliamentary majority with a billion-pound bung to the Democratic Unionist Party. The DUP is a bunch of hard-line extremists, and her deal buys them only for as long as she does what they want.

What they want is not only the continuing peace in Ireland brought about by an open border with the republic but also a pledge never to allow Northern Ireland to be treated differently in any way from the rest of the UK. This makes a meaningful Brexit deal all but impossible, as everyone involved soon sees.

If Britain had proportional representation, Theresa May might now be leading a coalition that found a way to bury all this Brexit nonsense.

Later in the month, Germans show that PR can work well. The federal elections in Germany send a warning to Angela Merkel when her Christian Democratic Union and its sister party the Christian Social Union suffer their worst result since 1949. Undaunted, she simply seeks to build a black-gold-green 'Jamaica' coalition to stay in power.

In France, Emmanuel Macron reaffirms his loyalty to Europe: 'Europe alone can give us a capacity for action in the world in the face of major contemporary challenges. The only path that assures our future is the rebuilding of a Europe that is sovereign, united, and democratic.'

I think Germany and France are the right models for Britain in its attempts to update its creaky old political system.

———

The 2017 Conservative party conference in Manchester is a demoralised gathering relieved only by black comedy. The grand finale is for Theresa May to stand at the podium and deliver a speech.

As she does so, a dozen of the loose letters spelling out a slogan on the blue screen behind her quietly fall off, one by one in a spellbinding drama, to turn BUILDING A COUNTRY THAT WORKS FOR EVERYONE into a blankety-blank puzzle. Also, she starts coughing, which strangles her voice so completely she's often almost inaudible. Then a comedian from the audience pops up and hands her a sheet of paper, a P45 form of the sort handed to fired employees, before heavies hustle him away.

It's a fitting burial for a geriatric party. The average age of party members is around sixty. Party workers define young voters as anyone under the age of fifty. Party pollsters say the only voters they can ignore more totally than young ones are dead ones.

Old Conservatives imagine they're on the cruise ship HMS Brexitannia on a voyage across the wide blue oceans, conquering new markets as their imperial ancestors did before them. This is religion, the opiate of the dying, not politics.

———

Later in October, I read with youthful joy that LIGO gravity-wave astronomers have seen and heard a pair of neutron stars colliding. This cosmic crash gives us our first view of how the heavy metals in the universe were created. I've been following the back story for decades, ever since Cambridge man Fred Hoyle first showed how big stars could cook up all the heavier elements in the universe.

About then, I host another visit by Graham and Steve. We walk along the seafront to Bournemouth and sit at an open-air café in the central square. We face a leisure complex including the *Dunkirk* cinema, with a towering new hotel block behind it. To the north, a well-kept parkland flanks a stream flowing southward. Before us, throngs of tourists parade back and forth in summer outfits.

Graham, now a suave professor emeritus, admires the scene: 'This looks a lot better than Poole. They must be doing something right here.'

I nod: 'Yes, tourism is certainly a big earner, and of course the language schools here are still doing well. All those students from Europe make the place come alive.'

Steve takes a more jaded view: 'Brexit will change that. I think we can predict that some of those language schools are not going to survive.'

'Absolutely,' I reply. 'The local MP is worried about it, even though he's posing as an arch-Brexiteer. He hopes students from China and Africa and so on will make up the difference.'

The local MP hired my beloved Rachel. I haven't seen her for months, but she says on social media she's thinking of standing for election as a local councillor in London.

Graham responds: 'The student problem affects science too. We'll get fewer European students, and then fewer collaborations in European research projects – bad news all round.'

'Tell me about it,' I say. 'My former colleague Angie in Heidelberg is worried about that too. She publishes collaborative research in physics, and she's sure she'll have fewer British authors.'

Steve leans forward. 'I really don't follow Conservative thinking here – or perhaps Conservative thinking is an oxymoron anyway. Does Theresa May really think going through with Brexit to appease the right wing of the party is worth the pain for science, industry, tourists, and all the rest of us – not just here but right across Europe?'

'In short, yes,' I say. 'Like most of the party faithful, she feels the need to deliver on what Conservatives promised less than two years ago. They think the damage to democracy caused by not going through with it outweighs all the problems.'

'But that's crazy,' cries Graham. 'The political embarrassment to the Conservative party outweighs the massive economic damage – running to billions and billions – for the rest of us. It's tail wags dog!'

'Go tell that to Theresa May!' I lament. 'And Boris Johnson, and Conor Burns, and Jacob Rees-Mogg, and so on and so on. This is representative democracy in action. They represent us, so they call the shots on policy.'

Steve shakes his head: 'Madness.'

———

The Honourable Robert Syms MP becomes Sir Robert. No one says why Theresa May selected him for this honour, but presumably his tireless work for many years as a party whip and as chair of various parliamentary committees played a role. I suspect his winning a record majority in her disastrous election might have helped.

The Poole association holds a party for him at a local church hall. Pam organises it. She's happy to prepare the sausage rolls and the sandwiches, and the orange juice and the bubbly, and to stand by serving us as we chat in the draughty hall.

Sir Robert looks sleek and happy, and when he gives his little speech of thanks to the company, he expresses serene confidence that Brexit will probably turn out fine, after the first few turbulent months. I have my camera with me and move around taking snaps. Most of the guests are oldsters, but the young and beautiful wife of a hunky young businessman is bold enough to show up fresh from sports in a tank top and a little white tennis skirt.

One local party activist – and a Trump admirer – is Bryan, a former colonel in the US Army who served in Afghanistan and is now married to a local councillor whom I helped to get elected in

2015. He cuts a lean and wiry figure, no doubt thanks to army fitness training, and has hawkish features that belie a friendly and likeable temperament.

'Hey Andy,' he says, 'I really liked your novel.'

A few weeks ago, I distributed hard copies to some of my party colleagues, and I'm beginning to think it's time for a few to come back with reader reactions.

I perk up: 'Really? Thanks for the feedback. You're the first reviewer beyond a few friends and family. Tell me what you liked about it.'

'I thought it was well written. I didn't see any typos or grammar mistakes, and I liked the three-part story. I thought the military action was good, too.'

I depicted the decline of Brexit Britain into a xenophobic hell where Muslims are interned in camps, prompting an international effort to liberate them in the sort of invasion Tom Clancy fans might like. My years of obsessive interest in modern weapon systems paid off in fine detail that only a war nut would relish.

I smile with relief: 'The scenario might be a bit over the top, but – you know – these things can happen.'

'Sure, and they do. Anyway, you wouldn't have much of a story left without them.'

Fair point. I'm cheered anyway.

———

In November, the party holds a fund-raising dinner at a posh hotel in Sandbanks. The guest speaker is Jacob Rees-Mogg MP. He's the chairman of a bunch of Brexiteers called the European Research Group and the honorary president of the Port and Policy group run by the Oxford University Conservative Association. The group was recently in the news when members drunk on port were heard to bellow 'my castle is bigger than yours' and 'I'll buy their families' when refused more booze.

A staunch Brexiteer and Trump defender, Rees-Mogg is a hard-right Tory, from climate-change denial to praise for disability cuts, from attacks on the BBC to abhorrence of regulation. As a hedge-fund multimillionaire, he wants to cut taxes and says this will bring in more revenue.

I take the time to run around with my camera. The young lady from Sir Robert's party is there, showing off her boobs in a low-cut green silk dress, and she lavishes attention on the Mogg. Susan Lever is there too, dressed in black lace, with her husband, looking happy.

I talk briefly with the star guest, who tours the tables to woo us into feeling we've got our money's worth.

I offer a token of good will: 'I used to like reading your father's editorials in *The Times*. I thought they were rather good.'

He looks pleased to hear it: 'Thank you.'

That's about all I can say. When in doubt, shut up.

Days after the dinner, the media have a feeding frenzy over the leak of the 'Paradise Papers' – millions of files revealing how the world's biggest businesses, heads of state, and celebrities shelter their loot in the tropical island tax havens under the British Crown. Rees-Mogg is said to be a principal beneficiary.

The back story here is a tale of depressing venality. In 2015, Britain rejected EU plans to combat tax avoidance that would undo the UK network of tax havens, and British MEPs voted against EU plans to punish countries or territories worldwide that fail to curb tax evasion. Wealthy Brits saw that the EU rules were due to take effect in 2019 and scheduled Brexit accordingly.

Protected wealth is a sore point in the UK. In response to the financial crisis of 2008, the Bank of England decided on a policy of quantitative easing, also known as printing money. They pumped hundreds of billions into the economy, but it went straight into property. The wealthiest ten percent of households got richer, but the inflation left the poor poorer.

Following the 2010 general election, the new coalition government began the task of restoring order to its finances by imposing austerity. The bankers were bailed out, but again the poor were made poorer. The UK suffered the longest period of declining real incomes in recorded history, and life expectancy fell.

Yet the government fails to tackle tax avoidance. The global balance sheet consistently shows more liabilities than assets, with a discrepancy of some nine trillion dollars representing wealth hidden by rich people in tax havens. The UK is widely seen as the worst offender because its leaders won't crack down on dodgy dealings in its global archipelago of islets left over from the days of empire. The moral failing is inexcusable.

The UK has an old-fashioned rentier economy. Those with property assets, final salary pension schemes, and inherited wealth benefit at the expense of a growing underclass. Brexit Britain is set to continue this feudal brand of capitalism and further degrade the drudges at the bottom of the social pyramid.

—

In December, the village of Wimborne in the constituency of Mid Dorset and North Poole hosts a 'punch after lunch' event starring Michael Tomlinson MP. This is another toff show.

The event is staged in the stately home of Sir William Hanham, thirteenth Baronet of Wimborne. Set in extensive grounds, which offer plenty of muddy parking space for guests, the house is very old and must need a retinue of servants to run it. The baronet lives there, like his ancestors before him, in a manner that would have seemed familiar in the Georgian era.

The action unfolds in the ground-floor rooms and involves standing around chatting politely over canapes and drinks. Several local councillors are there, and I catch up on local gossip.

When it's time for Tomlinson to give his little speech, he does so in the baronial living room. This is quite a hall, with a grand fireplace for a massive pile of logs, burning brightly. Fierce heat is radiating out over the brassware and onto a pair of sleeping dogs on the hearthrug. Around the room are bookcases filled with leather-bound volumes, as well as old portraits of the baronet's ancestors, and behind the row of comfortably sagging sofas is a grand piano, where a winsome young lady in a modest frock is playing light classical melodies.

The lord of the manor relaxes in his well-worn armchair beside the fire, with his walking stick propped beside him, as the capacity crowd of party guests assemble to hear the young toff speak.

The young Tomlinson is a tall, slender man with neatly trimmed fair hair and soft, rounded features behind wire-framed spectacles. He's a lawyer by profession and a member of Rees-Mogg's European Research Group by persuasion.

Tomlinson begins his oration thus: 'I have been representing you in parliament for two and a half years now, and I must say I feel extremely privileged to be doing so, especially since you re-elected me with an increased majority after my first two years in the House. I am very conscious of my obligations to you all, as indeed I am grateful to our gracious host this afternoon ...'

I listen with the best humour I can muster, but soon the words flow without meaning as I bask in the warm glow of the fire.

After the speech, back in the room with the canapes, I exchange a few personal words with the young reactionary.

'I don't know if Sir Robert told you,' I begin, 'but I wrote a little novel this summer about British politics, and I'd like to give you a copy.' I pull out a copy of *Britizen Jon* from my pocket and hold it up for him.

He looks disconcerted for a moment, then gathers his wits and takes it with delicately extended fingers to scrutinise the cover. He scans the blurb for a while and replies: 'Why, thank you, thank you very much, That's most kind of you. I'm so grateful that you thought of me in this way. I shall look at it with interest.'

I don't expect him to read the thing.

———

The Christmas party for the Conservative councillors of Poole is held at the hotel that once served as terminal for the flying boats.

Janet Walton, the leader of the council, is there. I still recall with pleasure our joint outings to the museum of erotic art and to the Royal Navy frigate, plus one or two other such occasions.

When councillors start dancing to canned music pumping out at high volume from an adjacent bar, I start dancing with her. Soon we're swaying scandalously, cheek to cheek, before retreating to a quiet corner to chat. We discuss Brexit.

No doubt the other councillors will fear the worst and start to gossip. No need. I'm still nursing my little flame for Rachel.

But Brexit still bugs me. It's a disorderly retreat, Dunkirk all over again.

17. Typhoons over London

I attend a meeting of the Conservative Policy Forum in January. These gatherings let local party members discuss national issues in a structured setting. Central office sends out briefing points and collects replies to help set party policy.

We meet in the back room of a local pub. The topic is housing policy. The government has issued a paper on German experience, and I've briefed Sir Robert on its contents.

Over a pint of beer, Sir Robert airs his views, conveys his confidence that the housing crisis will soon be resolved, and cautions about releasing more land for building.

I make a statement: 'Only about two percent of the land in Britain is free for building on. This raises land prices for housing and means most people can't afford to buy their own house. I think the simplest way to resolve the crisis is to release more land.'

Susan Lever replies: 'But most homeowners have a large part of their wealth invested in their property. Releasing more land for building will lower house prices and make them poorer.'

I shoot back: 'But homeowners have profited disproportionately in recent years from rising property prices, so letting prices sink to make housing affordable to more people who now have to rent seems only fair. Someone has to suffer, so let it be those who can best afford to do so.'

'That sounds like socialism,' she says.

———

The European Union publishes a draft withdrawal agreement. It proposes a transition period from March 2019 to December 2020 in which the UK abides by all existing EU rules but has no say in changing them or making new ones. A backstop will keep the peace in Northern Ireland.

On Friday 13 April, I'm in the office with Pam and Sir Robert. He has no visits planned, where I serve as bodyguard, chauffeur, photographer, and expert counsel.

As usual, Pam prints out all the emails deserving Sir Robert's personal attention, and he dictates his replies to them. Email pages fly from printer to waste bin at high speed as the letters on parliamentary notepaper pile up. Once that's done, Robert relaxes.

Between surgery appointments on such quiet days, Robert and I often shoot the breeze on pet themes.

I kick off: 'Robert, what do you think the top policy priority of the government should be?'

Looking casual with his collar askew, jacket rumpled, and bright socks flashing between old trousers and scuffed shoes, he leans back on his office chair and muses: 'Terrorism, I'd say. National security is our first responsibility. Then Brexit and so on.'

I shake my head. 'I don't think so. It's climate change. That's far more important than terrorism, which I'd rank below Brexit as a priority.'

He shoots back: 'That's your opinion. I'm not sure I trust the scientists on climate change. They can't be certain about it.'

'They can be certain enough. I've read their work, and I'm convinced. The consequences if we let temperatures and sea levels rise are catastrophic, so we need to err on the side of caution.'

'But not if we can only do so by sacrificing the economy.'

I try again: 'What do you think of the new draft withdrawal agreement? Do you think your colleagues will go for it?'

He shakes his head: 'No chance. During the transition period we'd be a vassal state, taking rules but not making them. And the Irish backstop is impossible. It treats Northern Ireland differently from the rest of the UK and puts a border down the Irish Sea. It won't survive a vote in the Commons.'

'Okay, but you know the EU team is not likely to compromise

on those things.'

He looks morose. 'If not, then it's no deal. That would be better than becoming a vassal state or breaking up the UK. A clean break is better than a messy divorce that drags on forever.'

'I don't see why there should be a divorce at all. We were all getting along fine until the referendum spoiled things.'

'The relationship was rocky before that. Once a marriage hits the rocks, it's better to get it over and done with and make a clean break. That's how I did it when I divorced Fiona. It was still messy, but it could have been a lot worse.'

'Divorcing Britain from Europe seems unnecessary to me. We still have to get on with our neighbours, and that's easier inside the club.'

'I think it's too late for that. We kept the peace in Europe before we joined the EU. We can so after we leave.'

'But we kept it by fighting two world wars! What kind of peace in Europe is that?'

He starts shuffling a sheaf of papers: 'We have the bomb now. If the Germans start acting up again, we can nuke them.'

'And kill a few million people? Is that the British way to keep the peace?'

He reaches for the stapler, puts a wad of papers between its jaws, and thumps his fist down hard on it. He stares at the result — the staple is askew and broken: 'The stapler doesn't work.'

Pam, who's sitting quietly getting things done as usual, joins in: 'It does if you press it more gently. It always works for me.'

———

Graham visits Bournemouth over the weekend. We meet there on Sunday evening at his seafront hotel. As teens, we and other likely lads from school used to visit the Bournemouth clubs and discos, including one in the basement of this hotel. It brings back pleasant memories of dates with girls from language schools.

I'm early and loiter in the lobby, checking out the changes over forty years. I'm in my black velvet tux over a black tee and jeans and my black water shoes.

Graham shows up, walking fast and apparently preoccupied with an invisible presence a few feet in front of his face. He wears his brown leather jacket over a pullover and jeans.

He has a plan: 'I know a good tapas restaurant on the other side of the square, if that suits you.'

'Sounds good.'

We set off at a brisk pace, past the tall new hotel and the big new cinema. I recall his Irish Catholic heritage and ask:

'What do you think of the Irish backstop in the Brexit deal?'

'It makes sense from an Irish perspective,' he says. 'But I don't think the Unionists are going to like it. I'd vote for it if it leads to a reunification of Ireland. What's the government line?'

'As you'd expect, the backstop is intolerable to the Brexiteers. But they can't admit they don't care about a hard border, so they're stuck, defeated by simple logic.'

'If they go through with a hard Brexit, I predict the IRA will be back and we'll see blood on the streets again. I'm glad I've got an Irish passport now, just in case.'

I blink. 'You have? When did you get that?'

'Just recently, as a precaution. Jules and I can escape to Ireland if it gets too bad here. Would you go back to Germany?'

'Sadly, it didn't occur to me to apply for a German passport while I was there. Soon I'll have been away for too long to get one. I'll have to start all over again with the residency requirement.'

'Let's hope you won't need it.'

———

In America, President Donald Trump pulls the United States out of the nuclear nonproliferation deal with Iran and presents China with a trade ultimatum.

America is on the warpath. China looks like the main target. Its economy is booming, and the Chinese slogan 'Made in China 2025' reflects its bullish mood.

A hundred years ago, the First World War was born when the German economy was booming, and 'Made in Germany' was the sign of the times. Britain chose to punish the upstart, and now America looks like doing likewise.

But Trump is lashing out all around. He announces steep tariffs on steel and aluminium from Canada, Mexico, and the European Union. He can't fight the whole world at once.

Trump has turned the Republican party base into a fan club. His testy tweets have made him the pivotal figure in American politics. Another pivotal figure rose eighty years ago in Germany.

I'm alarmed. The Trump phenomenon in America is too much like the Brexit phenomenon in Britain. The Anglo-American world has lost its foothold in the landscape of truth and reason – in the moral high ground.

—

In June, I go to another Conservative Policy Forum evening, this one at the Parkstone Yacht Club. Its topic is Brexit, and again Sir Robert is the keynote speaker.

The clubhouse is shiny and new. It flanks a marina crowded with boats and serves as a social hub for most of the local yachting crowd. The membership is less socially elevated than in the RMYC, but it's still conservative to the core.

Sir Robert begins his talk with a full account of Theresa May's plan to steer her deal through the Commons in time to allow the UK to set sail on the high seas on 29 March 2019.

He ends thus: 'I'm optimistic that we can not only get the deal through on time but also negotiate reasonable trade deals with the EU and with other trading partners worldwide, including the United States, where I'm sure President Trump will be happy to strike a deal that's good for both of us. This may take time, and there may be a few bumps along the way before we can finalise the deals, but I'm confident it will all turn out fine in the end.'

Questions and answers follow, but I hold back. The tone of the meeting is aggressively pro-Brexit, and I don't want to take a hammering. I stay silent and play photographer.

One face grips me. Susan Lever and her husband have fixed their attention on Sir Robert. She's in black, as usual, as gothic as a Tory wife can look, and her face is set in an icy rictus that sends chills down my spine. I'm reminded of the Third Reich.

———

Whitehall civil servants draw up three scenarios for a no-deal Brexit: mild, severe, and Armageddon. In the severe scenario, the port of Dover collapses on day one, shops in Cornwall and Scotland run out of food in days, hospitals run out of medicines in weeks, and officials need to charter aircraft or use military airlifters to supply remote parts of the UK. Armageddon is a lot worse.

Boris Johnson is unmoved: 'Imagine Trump doing Brexit. He'd go in bloody hard … But actually you might get somewhere.'

In June, Professor AC Grayling holds a guest lecture at Bournemouth University with a fighting title: *Brexit must be stopped*. Grayling is an Oxford philosopher of about my age who taught for years in London. He's very liberal, but he's also a thoroughly decent fellow with a good reputation among professional philosophers.

I like what he has to say, but I'm unmoved. His words are clear and logical enough to convince any rational listener, but Brexiteers and their voters are beyond reason, beyond experts, beyond liberal preaching. Their brains have been hijacked by raw anger,.

Boris is back in the news a week later. During a Foreign Office reception for the Queen's birthday, career diplomats say he was asked about fears in the business community over Brexit, to which he replied: 'Fuck business.'

Meanwhile, Theresa May claims to have united her cabinet
behind a soft Brexit that would keep Britain in parts of the single
market. She calms their fears during a special cabinet meeting at
Chequers, her official country residence, in early July.

That Sunday, Brexit secretary David Davis resigns.

On Monday, Boris resigns too.

On Tuesday, I take time out to drive to London for the Royal
Air Force Centenary celebrations, where I have a ticket for the VIP
reception in Horse Guards Parade, behind Downing Street. I go
alone, with my camera, hoping to blend in as a photographer.

I walk around the static display of aircraft parked on the fine
gravel of the parade ground. It features mock-ups of the Tornado
and the Typhoon, plus real examples of a Harrier jump-jet and of a
Chinook heavy-lift helicopter.

I spot an older aircraft. A Dakota transport plane with invasion
stripes recalls the parachute drops on D-Day, but I see it's painted
to resemble a plane that served during the postwar Berlin airlift,
when Stalin besieged the city until Allied air power prevailed. In a
tent to the side, two Spitfires, one from 1940 and one from 1945,
attract the war nuts.

The VIPs include senior RAF officers in their dress uniforms,
sporting oodles of scrambled egg on the front to show their status,
as well as wives and other ladies in fancy hats and pastel dresses. I
mingle discreetly with my camera lowered.

The action begins. Huge screens above the aircraft show monstrously magnified images of the central balcony of Buckingham
Palace, where the royal family has assembled, the males in their best
comic-opera military uniforms. A military band on the forecourt at
the palace strikes up the strains of the national anthem. Suddenly
the VIP types around me stand still, to attention, facing the monarch
as she poses scowling on her balcony. A besuited chap next to me
sees me moving and hisses: 'Stand still!'

I have the strange feeling I'm in a tinpot military dictatorship in a banana republic. The ruling junta is lined up on the palace balcony for the adoration of their humble subjects. The show goes on, with more martial music and marching troops on the big screens, while the VIPs chat quietly below. Then the national anthem sounds out again. This time, I stop in mid-step and stand in silence.

Finally, as the climactic *coup de theatre*, the air display features an extended fly-by of a hundred RAF aircraft (or so they say), all carefully choreographed for maximum dramatic effect. Among them is the Battle of Britain Memorial Flight, this time consisting of the Lancaster flanked by three Spitfires and two Hurricanes. The cherry topping on this aerial circus is a gloriously deafening formation of Eurofighter Typhoon jets positioned to spell out the digits '100' in the grey cloudscape.

Donald Trump would have loved it.

Later that day, I'm back in my media cockpit. On the eve of his visit to the UK to visit the Queen, Trump weighs in on the British cabinet crisis: 'Boris Johnson is a friend of mine. He's been very, very nice to me. Very supportive. And maybe we'll speak to him when I get over there. I like Boris Johnson. I've always liked him.'

On Wednesday, once Air Force One has landed in Europe, Trump holds a meeting with NATO officials and airs an unscripted opinion: 'Germany is a captive of Russia.'

I sigh with exasperation. What a patzer!

On Thursday, Theresa May and her husband greet Donald and Melania for a formal dinner at Blenheim Palace, the ancestral home of the Spencer-Churchill family and the birthplace of Sir Winston Churchill.

On Friday the thirteenth, following a nice cup of tea with the Queen, Trump outlines his hopes for trade with the UK following Brexit: 'We want the UK to trade with us. We have a tremendous opportunity to double, triple, or quadruple trade.'

I'm exasperated again. Fantasy numbers!

Trump has his expected showdown with Angela Merkel and vents his anger that Germany is spending too little on arms.

On the next day, Monday, he holds a summit meeting with Russian president Vladimir Putin in Helsinki, where he sides with Putin against US intelligence and law enforcement agencies.

Republican senator John McCain responds: 'Today's press conference in Helsinki was one of the most disgraceful performances by an American president in memory.'

Meanwhile, back in the UK, Theresa May's 'softer Brexit' white paper is said to be 'dead in the water' after four wrecking amendments enrage Remainers. For them, it's soiled toilet paper, good only for flushing away.

———

A week later, I drive to Farnborough to enjoy the air show. I used to love this show as a teenager. I recall the Hunter and Lightning fighters, the Vulcan and Victor bombers, and British airliners like the Vickers Viscount and the Bristol Britannia. On a later visit, I saw the beautiful Concorde, with a low pass so deafening it tamed all later rock concerts for me.

Now times are harder, and the show must pay for itself.

I walk around with my camera. Here's a US Air Force Eagle fighter, there a US Army Chinook transport helicopter, there a US Army Apache helicopter gunship.

There's more for history buffs. Over here is a smartly restored US Army Air Force Mustang, and a little further along a line-up of other US war veterans.

I return to home base in sombre mood. Britain is a vassal state of America. President Trump is top gun on Planet Earth.

18. Genocide and tank warfare

August ends with a miracle. I meet Rachel again. She's down in Bournemouth for the weekend and has an afternoon date with some other people, so we agree to enjoy lunchtime refreshments at the restaurant on Bournemouth Pier. It's a pleasant day of alternating cloudy and sunny spells.

We meet on the crowded forecourt to the pier. I show up in a khaki bush jacket over a loose blue shirt and cut-off cargo pants with sandals.

Rachel looks lovely, as ever, with her long hair hanging free and her manner as loose and untroubled as I recall. She's in a white hoodie, unzipped, over a plain white T-shirt and blue jeans, with flip-flops flapping on her feet. She smiles widely, showing off fine teeth fringed by pink gums.

'Hi, Andy,' she says as we shake hands.

'Hi, Rachel, great to see you again. How are you?'

'Fine, feeling good. It's great to be back here again.'

'Surely. How's life in Westminster?'

'Hectic. Conor keeps me busy, and there's a lot to learn.'

We walk the length of the pier to the restaurant at the end. The boardwalk leads to a theatre and gaming hall, with the restaurant beyond it, surrounded on the seaward sides by wide planked areas. We order cold drinks at the bar and settle at an outdoor table.

I ask about her opposing Brexit yet working for Conor Burns, who was parliamentary private secretary to Boris Johnson when he was foreign secretary. She tells me she sees politics as just a job, less about getting your way than ensuring due process, engaging with people, keeping them on board. I'm cool with that.

She asks me what I've been doing, and I say I've written a few essays over the summer. The one I've just finished looks at Islam, reviewing a controversial book by Douglas Murray.

'What did it say?'

'Murray argued that Muslim immigration into Europe risks a social disaster that threatens the entire civic order on the continent. But I say we're strong enough to take the risk.'

She smiles. 'That reminds me of what Angel Merkel said about the million refugees into Germany in 2015 – "We can manage it," or something like that.'

I nod appreciatively. 'I think she's right, but I know people in UKIP and on the Tory right disagree. It's the fear Boris Johnson played on in the referendum campaign.'

She says she has good Muslim friends but fears normalisation of traditional Muslim attitudes toward women. I tell her what little I know about the bloody history of Islam.

She says right-wing attitudes to Muslims remind her of Nazi attitudes to Jews. I point out that today it's Muslims who demonise Jews as they agitate against the state of Israel.

I handle all this in my easy academic manner, trying not to be distracted by her naïve and passionate beauty. It's like a philosophy tutorial with a uniquely charming student.

As we part with airy promises to keep in touch, we shake hands again. Our hands fit perfectly together. Walking back to base along the seafront, I relive the encounter and think of the paedophilic Humbert in *Lolita*. I'd rather die than cause her any embarrassment or offence – but that's what they all say.

———

Reading my review's words on fears of an Islamised Europe again after all Rachel said, I find a paragraph that stands out:

'For centuries, the tragedy behind Christian ascendancy was the marginalization of the Jewish people in Europe. ... The demise of the ruling narrative, and with it the eclipse of the Jewish God, led to a backlash of unprecedented ferocity. When Hitler and the Nazis accused Jews of seeking to replace the Christian bedtime stories with a Marxist litany of class war and expropriation, the dam burst, and genocide followed.'

This was the primal sacrifice that lay behind the foundation of the European Union. A Muslim genocide would destroy it.

———

Another essay I wrote this summer is a review of Boris Johnson's 2014 book *The Churchill Factor*. It's more a review of Boris himself.

I begin with a fact: 'Boris Johnson … has obvious ambitions to become British prime minister.'

I end with a wish: 'Perhaps Boris will … undergo a Damascene conversion to the Remainer cause. That might save us all.'

I post a printout to Boris and get an anonymous parliamentary postcard in reply. Nothing personal.

On the anniversary of the last British declaration of war on Germany, Johnson's *Telegraph* column starts thus: 'And we begin the final round of that international slugfest, the Brexit negotiations … In adopting the Chequers proposals, we have gone into battle with the white flag fluttering over our leading tank.'

But the public is getting fed up with it all. An opinion poll shows sixty percent of UK voters say: 'I no longer care how or when we leave the EU, I just want it over and done with.'

I recall Dr Goebbels' famous 'total war' speech in Berlin in February 1943, where the crowd no longer cared how bloody or horrific the war would be, they just wanted it over and done with.

At the Conservative party conference in early October, Johnson airs his contrarian view of May's chosen course: 'For me, Brexit should be part of a really self-confident and glorious campaign to revitalise the UK economy.'

The former foreign secretary goes on: 'If we bottle Brexit now, believe me, the people of this country will find it hard to forgive. … This is not what we voted for. This is an outrage.'

For me, like anyone else not bedazzled by the Tory pixie dust, Britain after Brexit looks set to fall into a downward spiral of failure and upheaval that could turn truly toxic.

I watch the conference TV coverage with horrified disbelief as Theresa sways onto the stage to the tune of Abba's *Dancing Queen* to deliver her closing speech: 'Leadership is doing what you believe to be right and having the courage and determination to see it through, and that's what I've been doing on Brexit.'

The rest of her cabinet choose not to dance along with her. Days later, the new foreign secretary, Jeremy Hunt, compares the European Union to the Soviet Union and attacks the EU for saying the Chequers plan won't work. I can see it won't work just by using logic to combine its proposals.

In their insular mix of pride and prejudice, the Brexiteers are still out of tune. Former Brexit secretary David Davis writes a piece showing he's lost it: 'Brexit panic has started on the continent. ... Now is the time when we can start to exact concessions from the EU. ... Now we must drive a hard bargain.'

Not to be outdone, Boris mobilises his bottom (parliamentary slang for gravitas) to emit a blast of Churchillian defiance in the direction of Brussels: 'The EU are treating us with naked contempt – we must abandon this surrender of our country.'

———

Steve and I make a day trip to the Bovington Tank Museum.

The tank museum was one of my childhood haunts. My mate Harry and I often cycled there on a Saturday to make notes for our models. In those days, the museum was barely more than a giant shed that reeked of scrap metal, paint, and diesel oil, and the tanks were jumbled together in lamentable disrepair. We loved all that.

I still have an interest in tanks that leaves me with an excess of erudition about armoured warfare. But the museum is transformed. The giant shed has been rebuilt as a world-class museum with slick exhibition halls and the exhibits polished, arranged, and labelled to present a coherent historical narrative.

The story I read from it is one of global power politics in the twentieth century. It begins with the rise and fall of nationalist Germany as a continental challenger to British imperial dominance in the first half of the century and continues seamlessly into the rise and fall of Soviet communism as a global challenger to the liberal-capitalist Anglo-American world hegemony in the second half. The two rises and falls were the waves on which America surfed into the new millennium.

For me, tanks offer a window onto this global story. Steve is a history buff, but he has no faith in my neo-Hegelian take on history as a long arch bridging the evolution of science and technology from humble beginnings to a planetary force. I hope to convert him to the faith.

We climb out of Steve's big BMW with its heavy-duty wheels and springs (good for British roads and potholes) and make for the modernistic front entrance to the museum. I'm in my tan cargo pants and bush jacket over a sky-blue shirt – I've liked the colour combo ever since Tony Blair and George W Bush aired it on their visits to the troops in Iraq.

We start at the beginning with the World War One tanks. Then we follow a sign for *The Tiger Collection* pointing us to a hall with five colossal German tanks from the last years of the Second World War. These are buffed to a showroom shine that looks good as new.

Steve is impressed: 'Wow, that was quite a jump. This is, what, twenty-five years later?'

'Yup. The technology moved on. For me, this is evolution in action. Just like today, when the changes with drones and electronics and so on seem faster than ever before.'

'If the Germans had tanks like these, how come they lost?'

'Simple. Mass production. The output of all these Tiger models together came to less than five thousand by the end of the war, whereas the Americans produced over fifty thousand Sherman tanks and the Soviets made even more T-34s. No contest.'

Steve studies the beasts: 'A Sherman wouldn't stand a chance against these things. How did they fight back?'

'Right, the kill ratio was maybe ten to one for a Tiger. But air power was the killer. With squadrons of Typhoons and Thunderbolts flying over the battlefield, picking off Tigers in France was like a turkey shoot.'

'Scary way to go into battle, in a box like this.'

We tarry a while longer, then go to the evolution hall, where the tanks are set in their operational context.

'Okay, here we are back in the First World War.'

Steve looks onward: 'And there are some armoured cars, for policing the empire. That looks like what Lawrence of Arabia used, and what the army used in the mass murder at Amritsar.'

We move on to the Panzers that led the Blitzkrieg in France.

We study the posters explaining Blitzkrieg tactics. Then Steve looks on and sees a Soviet tank, a T-34. We study its rough metal casting and lumpy welds.

'Looks quite primitive,' Steve ventures.

'Right, quantity, not quality. Compare it with the Panther.'

The German Panther beside the T-34 is a big, beautiful beast, with a long gun barrel, smooth castings, and neat weld lines.

Steve nods: 'That looks like quality engineering.'

We move on to the section with British D-Day tanks in it. We look at a few, and I tell him what was wrong with them.

'The first good British tank was the Centurion,' I say, as we study a Centurion. Parked near it are other Cold War tanks.

I point at one of them: 'The Leopard there was a big break for German designers. It was fast and mobile.'

Steve looks around: 'What about this Soviet one?'

'Ah, yes, the T-55. They were basically designed during the war but not built until the war was won. The Soviets produced it in bigger numbers than any other tank, ever. You see still see them in Middle East wars.'

'These tanks look quite modern. What's happened since then?'

'Basically, electronics. Now they're full of computers.'

'But still easy pickings for helicopter gunships.'

'Sure. They're sitting ducks on a modern battlefield. The next step in the evolution will be robot tanks. Then you can deploy them by the thousand and not mind losing a few.'

He smiles. 'Terminator here we come. Shall we take a break?'

We walk up a curving ramp to the restaurant and settle at a table with a panoramic view over the tanks below.

'As I was saying, with a big robot tank army you could occupy any country within days, and you'd need nukes to stop them.'

'With nukes you can stop anything, so what's the point?'

'You can't finish a war without boots on the ground. If you nuke everything, everyone loses, so that doesn't help.'

He sits back. 'So, what's your big lesson from all this?'

'The evolution of mechanised warfare, right up to drones and nuclear missiles, has transformed human civilisation. The Germans and the Soviets both gave it a big push. Next, I guess it's the turn of the Americans to push the boat out further.'

'I can see that with someone like Trump in charge, they might be mad enough to try, but why?'

'To take down China. But China and Russia have close military ties. And after Brexit, the European countries might well do deals with Russia to appease Putin.'

Steve smiles: 'I thought we'd get back to Brexit somehow.'

———

On Saturday 20 October, several hundred thousand people rally in central London to demand a 'people's vote' on Brexit. I watch them on television and wish I'd gone along too. The rally is proof that many younger Brits see Brexit as a wanton and wilful divorce that brutally wrecks our European home.

Brexiteers fail to understand the European project or what it means to be European. They see the UK as an imperial power and imagine Britain was a beacon for the world. After Brexit, they dream it will shine again.

By November, Theresa May has a plan to secure a Brexit deal and win the backing of parliament. The EU will write a customs deal into the withdrawal agreement to avoid a backstop, an exit clause will reassure Brexiteers that the UK won't be in the EU for ever, and a promised future economic partnership will sort out the rest.

But it's all in vain. On 9 November, the government minister Jo Johnson issues a public statement: 'My brother Boris is as un-happy with the government's proposals as I am. … I have today written to the prime minister asking her to accept my resignation from the government.'

Jo Johnson is a passionate Remainer, but brother Boris is the leading Leaver, while their sister Rachel supports holding a people's vote. Both brothers are old boys of Eton and Oxford who dined in the Bullingdon Club and have worked as journalists. If they can't agree, who can?

Jo adds: 'I now appeal to every Conservative to ask themselves if the choice being offered to us between vassalage and chaos can truly represent the national interest.'

Days later, the new Brexit secretary Dominic Raab resigns too. Tories prepare for a vote of no confidence in their leader.

Out in the wider world of voters, a petition demanding a fresh Brexit referendum is signed by more than a million people.

May calls off a planned Commons vote on her deal. Hardline Brexiteers help her survive a vote of no confidence, leaving her a puppet in their hands. Under her command, HMS Brexitannia is committed to leaving its dock in the EU on 29 March 2019, with or without a deal, to follow the siren call to sail the high seas on Her Majesty's service. Brexiteers see no need to rock the boat.

I recall the Imperial Japanese Navy battleship Yamato sailing out on her last voyage in April 1945, only to meet a massive air attack launched from US Navy carriers that sank her under a mushroom cloud four miles high. Yamato is an old name for Japan, so the portent was clear.

Brexit Britain is doomed if it sails a sovereign course against mainland Europe. Germans did the right thing by forming a union with their formerly hostile neighbours.

But Germans are too slow to map out a new future for Europe. Their booming economy may be a fool's paradise. In 2018, German exports of goods and services exceeded imports by about a quarter of a trillion euros, by far the widest trade surplus in the world. To EU neighbours, this imbalance looks unfair.

Nationalists across Europe cry foul at German dominance. Yet they also see the risk of disaster if they rebel against it in the way Greece did. Britain is the only European country with a world-class financial industry, so its citizens don't see a problem.

I'm concerned about the mischievous role of Putin in all this. Brexit is to Putin what Dunkirk was to Hitler – it removes a big player from the continental chessboard. That helps him checkmate the Brussels politburo and push for a new union with Russia.

Putin is a former intelligence officer in the Soviet Union. He's worked hard to undermine faith in democracy. But he's won an impressive victory over the American superpower that broke the former Soviet Union. Donald Trump probably owes his presidency to him. Across Europe, similar Putin puppets are gaining in political power, so he's obviously doing something right.

A much bigger physical disaster looms in the wings. A new report by the Intergovernmental Panel on Climate Change sets a target of 1.5 degrees (Celsius, on a scale where each unit step is a kelvin) for global warming.

In December, at the 2018 UN Climate Change Conference in Poland, negotiators agree to try to limit global warming to less than two degrees. The delegate from China says: 'Climate change is the greatest challenge of mankind. In front of it, no country is spared, and destinies are shared.'

———

On 15 January 2019, Theresa May holds the meaningful vote she promised on her Brexit deal. The Commons defeats her motion by the biggest majority against anything in its modern history.

Irish pundit Fintan O'Toole sums up the British predicament: 'Brexit is a choice between two evils: the heroic but catastrophic failure of crashing out or the unheroic but less damaging failure of swapping first-class for second-class EU membership.'

British novelist Hari Kunzru senses a lurking Freudian fear: 'The English cult of heroic failure, exemplified by the charge of the Light Brigade and the evacuation from Dunkirk, suggests that the secret libidinal need of [Brexiteers] is actually for their noble project to fail in the most painful way possible, as an immolation on the altar of past glories.'

I agree with O'Toole and Kunzru. But whatever the flaws of the EU, learning to live with its ambitions is a great leap forward compared with struggling to continue the UK narrative.

Just in time to commemorate the British bombing of Dresden in 1945, which killed some 25 thousand German civilians in a firestorm with no military value, historian Helene von Bismarck points out that Europe faces big challenges. She says the German government, if asked to choose between punishing either the UK or the EU for Brexit, won't hesitate. British hopes that Germany might broker a face-saving Brexit deal are doomed.

———

On Valentine's Day, I discuss Brexit with a chap called Ben Aston at Bournemouth University. As a BU alumnus and a young tech entrepreneur in the Dorset area, Ben cuts a dynamic figure, radiant with street cred, and has a smart camera rig he's eager to use.

As the organiser of the *Dorset 4 Leave* group, Ben is ambitious to debate Brexit with an articulate Remainer, and to do so on video. His idea is to bring his fresh presence into the public eye in an encounter that can set the issue alight for students who may have missed the great SUBU debate Rachel organised in April.

It was Rachel who put me in touch with Ben. She told me her friend was eager to record the big issues of the Brexit story for the wider world and needed a sparring partner who could offer an even match. I vow to do my best.

The debate takes place in a quiet corner with no spectators and lasts for about a hundred minutes. Ben posts the entire video on YouTube, where it slowly gathers a few views.

That's my last blast of warning before the looming cliff edge. Britain is on a suicide course to plunge over the edge in two weeks. There's nothing more I can do to stop it.

I pack my bags for Germany.

19. Flying over Germany

Soon after dawn on Saturday 23 February, I drive to the Port of Poole for the next crossing to Cherbourg. I wait in line and drive onto the good ship *Barfleur*.

Once I'm in France, basking in bright morning sunlight and revelling in driving on the right again, I motor steadily on through to Amiens, where I stay in a good hotel and dine well. Bright and early the next morning, again under a clear blue sky and on autoroutes bearing only light traffic, I drive onward into Germany, back onto the autobahn that runs straight through to Mannheim. I take the Heidelberg exit.

Back in Heidelberg, I'm on home turf, surrounded by a street scene I know and love from decades in the city. I press on into the hills, to the sunlit upland village of Gaiberg, to visit Rolf and Angie. They've invited me to stay with them for a couple of weeks at their family home.

Their house sits squarely on a hilltop over a sloping garden fringed by trees. It's a modernist fortress, built in the Sixties to a generous design as a base for a previous dental practice.

Angie is eager to learn more about the unfolding Brexit drama on the islands she once called home. I try to explain – and to stay calm as I recall my anger and despair. Rolf is cool about it all, quite unfazed by the idiocy of politicians and eager to get back to a feature article he's writing on quantum computing.

A night of talking and a new morning of sunlit peace lift my mood. Gazing at the garden over a bowl of muesli with fruit and yoghurt restores my Zen mind.

On Monday, Rolf invites me to join him on a joyride in his gyrocopter, which is based at Mannheim City Airport, to fly through the cloudless blue sky over the Rhine–Neckar region. Rolf is now a keen pilot who celebrated his certification by writing and publishing a textbook on the process.

Mannheim City Airport is a small and sleepy place, but modern, and we explore the offices on the way to the hangar. Rolf bought his little aircraft new and looks after it carefully, and I admire his professionalism as we check the mechanical systems before setting off. Rolf rolls it by hand, like a motorbike, out from the hangar and onto the apron.

The motor is a small gasoline engine with a boxer layout, and it's very noisy. Inside an alarmingly fragile fibreglass cabin, we wear soundproofed headsets and talk with each other by radio. But there isn't much to say, and I have my hands full with my camera – I'm determined to get a good haul of images from the trip.

Along the runway we go, gathering speed. We lift off, then climb to the prescribed height and tour the airspace over Mannheim, Heidelberg, the Rhine and Neckar rivers, and the green hills around us as far as Gaiberg and beyond. I see from above all the places I haunted during my years in this patch of paradise.

The ride is a joy, in utter contrast to the experiences in precisely this airspace just 75 years earlier, in 1944, when American and British bombers pounded Mannheim, Ludwigshafen, and the rest repeatedly, heavily, and mercilessly.

The first RAF bombing of Mannheim was in December 1940. British bombers continued their raids over the years, until a big one in March 1945 caused a devastating firestorm in the city. In all, the RAF dropped 25 thousand tons of bombs onto it.

Naturally, the German defences over the city grew stronger. Flak batteries multiplied, and young pilots defending their homes and families became aces in their night fighters by shooting down lumbering Lancaster heavies from England.

Toward the end, rookie pilots even went up against American day bombers in jet and rocket planes. The new aircraft were so hastily designed and built that the pilots were more likely to be killed in an accident than shot down by the long-range Mustangs that by then were swarming over Germany. I imagine Rolf would have been up there too, flying a fragile fighter into the bomber streams to do what he could.

Half an hour later, we land smoothly, and Rolf wheels the copter back into its hangar. A little later, over lunch at the house in the hills, Rolf and I debate our views on the future of computing. It's a field I think I know well, and our exchange probes the limits of what I've learned over decades of tilling it.

When Angie returns from her office in Heidelberg, she brings with her an advance copy of the latest book in her frontier series for me. It's an introductory textbook on modern cosmology by Delia Perlov and Alex Vilenkin that goes all the way to quantum foam and multiverse scenarios, and I immediately dig into it whenever I get a few minutes to launch my mind into space.

On Tuesday, Rolf has another excursion lined up. The giant chemical company BASF is headquartered nearby in Ludwigshafen, and Rolf has a couple of passes to attend its press conference where the latest annual results will be announced. Rolf is an accredited journalist and tells them I'm one too.

The BASF headquarters is modern and magnificent. Its style reminds me of the SAP headquarters in Walldorf – there's a German corporate style cloned all over the map – and I feel transported back to some of the happiest days of my life. The conference hall is big and bright, with a stage for the board members and plenty of space for journalists and cameras.

I listen and follow from the media pack as chief executive Dr Martin reveals good results and a sound plan for going forward. He speaks mostly in English, as usual for big German companies. The big-banner slogan for the event is 'With optimism into the future' printed over a rainbow.

At the break for refreshments following the conference, Rolf and I talk with Martin. He outlines an impressively sophisticated overview of global developments when I quiz him on the perils and promise of increasing trade with China. I recall similar sophistication at SAP and decide modern corporate bosses are far more likely, for various reasons, to know what they're doing around the world than most politicians, or at least than most English ones.

On Wednesday, I visit my friend Matthias in Schwetzingen, where he's busy running a Christian soup kitchen to welcome and support the Muslim refugees who showed up in the town following Angela Merkel's national welcome to immigrants in 2015. Matthias seems to be more disturbed by my tale of the Brexit tragedy than by his new neighbours. Soup and salvation are business as usual for him, but betrayal and hatred are not.

On Thursday, I go for a walk in the woods. I park on a quiet street west of Speyer, next to an army training ground, where the forest stretches far and wide into the Rhine Palatinate. I've walked and jogged from this spot countless times. It's always calming and refreshing to wander for hours among the trees.

On Friday and Saturday, I make efforts to find an apartment, in the fond hope that I can fix all the formalities for a permanent move to Germany by the end of the month. As I get started, I realise it's not going to happen. There's far too much to do, with too many unknowns, and the best I can do is to rest my fate in England with the gods until the Brexit storm blows over.

On Sunday, I go along to meet up again with my old friends in the Schwetzingen congregation. Matthias performs the customary Christian rites, and I enjoy them as theatre.

On Monday, I visit Frau Wolf at the Heidelberg civic office for foreign registrations, where that redoubtable lady gives me a verbal clip about the ear for imagining I can still acquire German citizenship after so many years back in England. That evening, with Angie and Rolf at a local pub restaurant, I air my frustration at the small-minded officials and politicians who seem determined to make life difficult for the soaring philosophical eagles of this world.

On the Tuesday known as pancake day in England, I station myself in central Heidelberg with my camera to witness the annual Fasching parade, or Heidelberg carnival. As the carnival floats and the costumed figures from the local community parade by, I reflect on how *ethnic* it all seems. It's a living example of the *Volk* community that Heidegger praised as the killing field of the pious ideals of liberal ideology. Blood and soil mean more in such communities than the refined abstractions of political philosophy.

On Wednesday, my stay in the Rhineland paradise comes to an end. I pack my case, say farewell to Rolf and Angie, and strap myself into my little white BMW. In bright sunlight under a clear blue sky, I drive out of the hills, onward past Mannheim, and onto the fast route to Amiens, where again I enjoy a night of French hospitality before cruising on westward to Cherbourg.

The Thursday evening sea voyage from Cherbourg to Poole is stormy. Winds whip up big waves to rock the boat, and torrents of rain lash the windows. Driving off the ramp and back onto British soil is like entering a quarantine island during a plague epidemic – the first sign to greet me at the customs checkpoint is a warning that if I'm an illegal immigrant then I'm not welcome and if I'm any kind of foreigner then I may need a visa.

Whatever, I feel like the outsider now. In my German car with an iron-cross sticker and my headful of German language, I'm now less truly native than most bloody Tories on English soil.

———

On Friday, I go back into the office to check my mailbox. Once I've made a pass over the backlog and listened to Pam's update on local news, I talk about Germany with Isaac the local chairman and Sir Robert the Lord Commissioner of the Treasury (or so the copy of the parchment document from the Queen that Robert has stuck on the office wall tells us). We discuss *The Rise and Fall of the Third Reich*, a classic history first published by the journalist William Shirer in 1960. That book impressed Isaac and Robert so much that it still colours their feelings about Germany. I read it as a teenager and was impressed too, but since then I've moved on. They haven't.

Over the next few weekends, I binge-watch a box set I bought in Heidelberg, *Babylon Berlin*, a TV drama set in the Weimar republic. It's won wide critical acclaim for the authenticity of its gritty and alarming portrait of Weimar life.

The Berlin drama reminds me of my stay in Berlin in the summer of 1974, which is already equidistant between the 1929 of the Weimar drama and the 2019 of Brexit Britain. I now feel I understand the predicament that led to the calamity of the Third Reich. Happily, my predicament in Brexit Britain is less dire – so far.

—

There's still no Brexit deal. Unless something dramatic happens first, the UK will cease to be a member of the EU an hour before midnight on Friday 29 March 2019.

Theresa May's government is still trying to polish a turd. The 2016 referendum result detonated a bomb under politics as usual in the UK. Russell Brand came up with the best line on that result: 'People saw a bright red button that said *Fuck Off Establishment*, and they pressed it.'

Brexiteer rebels led by Jacob Rees-Mogg and Boris Johnson are reading the result as permission to crash out of the EU without any trade deal, to break the Good Friday agreement and erect a hard border in Northern Ireland, to refuse to pay any bills presented by the officials in Brussels, and to do all this with no transition arrangement. As an upstanding Catholic, Rees-Mogg will doubtless say 'Hail Mary' as he jumps over the cliff.

People in Ireland are aghast at the aggressive ignorance of

English Brexiteers. Business leaders everywhere are outraged by their cavalier disregard for the economic consequences of Brexit. Brexit threatens bloodshed in Ireland, secession in Scotland, and chaos in Dover.

But the English have form in Ireland. Rees-Mogg awakens a lot of old ghosts in his opinion of Irish resistance to Brexit. In words that remain unattributed: 'We simply cannot allow the Irish to treat us like this. The Irish really should know their place.'

The untold story behind this farce is about money. The UK is possibly the largest financial centre in the world. More than a third of global foreign exchange trading takes place in London, plus a similar proportion of derivatives trading. The British banking sector is sized at more than ten trillion euros and manages more than a third of all European financial assets. A no-deal Brexit could easily trigger a global economic crisis.

Brexit is the latest wheeze of the world's disaster capitalists, or rather the vulture capitalists who stand ready to feed on the corpses of the victims of their manufactured disasters. Those who are properly positioned in the money market, as Rees-Mogg no doubt is, can profit handsomely from the turbulence of a no-deal Brexit. All they need are strong nerves and suitably prepared footprints in the UK's archipelago of tax havens.

I ponder how their get-rich-quick schemes factor in the rise of China. The Chinese economy now boasts an annual output of some 25 trillion dollars and is set to become the most powerful economy in world history. But the People's Republic deplores the cynical exploitation of individual rights that regularly leads the Western democracies to the brink of disaster. Chinese communists will treat tax havens with the contempt such sinkholes deserve.

The European Union is ambivalent about China. It's China's largest trading partner, and China is the EU's second largest, behind America. In 2018, China accounted for about a fifth of EU goods imports and more than a tenth of its exports. Chinese investment in Europe is increasing, and Europeans are feeling uneasy.

Germany and China have a lot in common. Germany needs access to Chinese technology, yet also worries about Chinese companies acquiring German technology. I recall these worries at SAP, where I wrote a handbook on my team's new database engine. My managers hesitated to endorse it because I teasingly touched on a few technical tricks of the trade. A pair of our team's developers from Shanghai said it was a good book – good for them!

Both the German and Chinese economies are driven by exports and run large external savings surpluses. But German economic strategists alone can't compete with China's integrated approach to policy. To fight back, Westerners need to coordinate their activities on a continental scale.

In this context, Brexit Britain is a wilful loser, a fallen domino. It's committing an act of self-harm with no upside. The days when Leavers talked about the sunlit uplands are over. They now have only one reason for Brexit: the 2016 referendum. People voted for it, so it must be done. Warnings from big business are an excuse to talk tosh about the Fourth Reich. The case for Leaving has sunk to xenophobic nationalism.

Two months after the Commons first rejected Theresa May's proposed deal, the Commons reject it again, again by a huge margin. They pass a motion to reject a no-deal Brexit in March as well, also by a big margin. Newspapers run bold headlines with such words as MELTDOWN and CHAOS.

With only a fortnight to go before the UK is due to leave the EU, May's strategy for delivering an orderly departure is in tatters. She's fatally misread her opponents.

Moved to creative fertility by the political drama, I write another essay: 'A democratic political system is a formalised way of enacting the will of the people. Since no individual politician can credibly claim to know the will of the people directly, the system forms a snapshot of that will by collecting the votes of the people and subjecting them to some simple procedure, such as counting, to assemble a pixelated image.'

Amid chaos and crisis, I've written a brief treatise on the theory and practice of representative democracy in the age of social media. My final message for its patient readers:

'UK parliamentarians have acted in genuflection to the 2016 icon without due appreciation of the need for a better portrait of the people. The 2017 general election offered no royal road for voters disaffected by the icon and thus deepened their disaffection. The obvious solution is to commission a new portrait.'

This is as close as I dare go in advocating a second referendum. I know politicians are now scared of the prospect and will never freely consent to it. I think simply revoking Article 50 is the better solution, but I fear that might put blood on the streets.

On Tuesday, with just ten days to go, Theresa May writes to Donald Tusk asking him to postpone Brexit until the end of June, with the option of a longer delay.

On Friday, EU leaders give Theresa May three weeks to come up with an alternative Brexit plan if MPs reject her deal again. If she passes her deal, they allow another forty days to pass the technical legislation.

The reprieve comes just in time to prevent the activation of Operation Yellowhammer, which was due to start on Monday. The operation would have put thousands of troops on standby and called up reservists to support them around the country. Hard Brexit would have triggered Operation Redfold, run from a crisis room in the nuclear bunker deep beneath Whitehall.

20. Bollocks to Brexit!

On the last Saturday before the Brexit deadline, I rise early and board a coach bound for London. The coach has been chartered by the *Dorset 4 Europe* mob of anti-Brexit activists and is full of Europhiles clad in EU blue and yellow. We're off to the next 'People's Vote' mass rally.

I'm filled with hope in my blue hoodie with EU stars on the front and my blue cap with more EU stars on the brow. With jeans and sneakers, I'm ready for any street fighting we might face.

I sit gazing into space, surfing a tide of heroic thoughts in my head. With this fresh demo fodder around me, plus a million more if we're lucky, there's no way the Brexit Old Guard bog of Empire loyalists, English nationalists, vulture capitalists, UKIP Faragists, and diehard nativists can stop us. We're fighting for a future of friendship and cooperation with our European neighbours.

When the coach arrives around noon, we jump out and make our cheery way to Hyde Park. It's a fine day, cool but not cold and overcast but not rainy, a fine day to be marching for the cause.

The crowds in the park are already enormous. The dew is still fresh on the grass as I cut between the trees. Around me, many thousands of demonstrators, decked out with marching outfits and flags and banners, form into fluid groups.

The flags and banners around me sport a wild profusion of symbols and words. The most popular symbol by far is the EU flag, followed meekly by the union jack. Other banners flutter too, but there's no sign of Conservatives or UKIP here.

Suddenly I see my brother-in-law David, standing tall and gaunt with his beaked nose and goatee beard. Beside him is Helen. Both wear EU blue and hold placards bearing witty slogans. I go up and say hi, smiling through their surprise.

At last, the big drums pound and the shrill whistles blow and off we all go, shuffling down Park Lane as we chant slogans and sing out our love for 'EU'.

'What do we want?' – 'People's vote!'

'When do we want it?' – 'Now!'

The crowd slows us down, but I rejoice to see the gems of wit and wisdom on the placards. Being here, feeling righteous solidarity with my fellow citizens on a matter of vital importance, feels like the best exercise of true democracy my indignant soul could want.

Real democracy has very little to do with the vote I cast once every few years either for or against an MP with a cast-iron majority. That pathetic exercise, casting one quintennial bit of information, represents an average transmission rate of just a few nanobits per second, which in the age of gigabit broadband is laughable. Real democracy is about making a fuss, causing a media storm, getting the message out, marching on the streets.

As we shuffle down Park Lane, we start a new chant:

'Bollocks to Brexit!'

This one's a winner. One voice shouts the slogan in a shrill voice and the crowd repeats it in a lusty roar.

Video crews are recording the show. A girl with a microphone beside a chap with a camera stops me and shouts:

'Why are you marching today?'

I shout back: 'Because I want to stop Brexit!'

'What do you want the government to do?'

'Revoke Article 50 before it's too late!'

'Why do you want them to do that?'

'Because all the studies show that Brexit is bad for Britain and bad for Europe!'

I smile and bow, and the crowd moves us on.

Between the chants, we sing lines from favourite songs:

A Beatles riff: 'We love EU, yeah, yeah, yeah!'

A Whitney Houston riff: 'I will always love EU!'

A Liverpool Express riff: 'EU are my love!'

And a Rick Astley classic: 'Never gonna give EU up.'

The crowd shuffles along in a crush as it turns from Park Lane into Piccadilly. Above us, a television helicopter bathes us all in its choppy downwash as its crew records the event for the national news. And another helicopter, and another.

There's still a long way to go before we reach Parliament Square. Helen. David, and I decide to turn off from Piccadilly into Green Park. We walk across the park to the Victoria Memorial in front of Buckingham Palace and head east along Birdcage Walk.

As we approach Parliament Square, the crowd gets denser. We'll never get near the stage where the speakers are holding forth. So, as soon as we see a speaker on a big TV screen over the heads of the crowd, we declare victory and retreat.

For me, the rally was like being in a medieval army, marching off to depose an evil monarch and launch a revolution. It reminds me of my days as a student activist at Oxford, when my rebel ways were recorded as blots on my copy book. But you can't make an omelette without breaking eggs, as someone once said.

———

Media reporters say the rally brought together a million marchers. It's the clearest sign yet that Remainers are a force to be reckoned with. There's still time for reasonable people to win.

For several days, an online petition has been running that calls on the government to revoke Article 50 before it's too late. On the Sunday after the march, the petition passes five million signatures. A lot of people are sick of the Brexit circus.

Theresa May meets Star Chamber lawyers at Chequers for crisis talks on Brexit. The Brexiteers in Rees-Mogg's European Research Group now call their 'elite' team of lawyers the Star Chamber. The original Star Chamber, a criminal court in Stuart England, was so harsh it was abolished in 1641. The hardcore Brexiteers have even taken to calling themselves the Grand Wizards, like the leaders of the Ku Klux Klan.

On the next day, Monday, MPs pass a motion as amended by the former Cambridge philosopher Sir Oliver Letwin, the MP for West Dorset, allowing the Commons to take control of the agenda to hold indicative votes on Brexit options.

On Wednesday, Theresa tells Conservative MPs she'll resign as prime minister if only they oblige her by backing her Brexit deal. Now it's dead, Boris Johnson says he'll back it.

On Friday, hours before the original Brexit deadline, MPs reject May's withdrawal agreement for a third time, again by a massive margin. The deadline slides past.

The weekend is eerily calm.

On Monday, April Fools' Day, the House of Commons defeats four proposals to limit the damage Brexit might do. The public petition to revoke Article 50 now has over six million signatures.

On the second day of April, the prime minister – no one's fool – accepts the need for a further extension of Article 50.

On the third day of April, she turns for help to Jeremy Corbyn in the hope they can agree on a way forward.

On the fourth day of April, a rainy day, business in the Commons is interrupted by a noisy gush of water from a leak in the roof of the chamber. The House is adjourned.

On the fifth day of April, Theresa May writes to Donald Tusk asking for an Article 50 extension up to the end of June, or earlier if a deal is reached, and promising continued preparations to hold European parliamentary elections.

On the sixth day of April, the bill forcing the government to extend Article 50 receives royal assent.

On the ninth day of April, May visits Angela Merkel in Berlin and Emmanuel Macron in Paris to brief them on the crisis.

On the tenth day of April, Tusk grants the UK a 'flextension' until the end of October. He adds that until then the UK still has the option of revoking Article 50 and cancelling Brexit altogether. The UK has won a stay of execution until Halloween.

I rejoice that day. Scientists have processed astronomical data to create the first-ever visual image of a black hole.

———

Back in Poole, I attend a meet-and-greet event deep in the old town. The campaign has begun for the next local elections. I volunteer to help Isaac, who's now both PCA chairman and election agent.

The meet-and-greet is for the Conservative candidates in the Old Town ward. First among them is Buzz, the incumbent Tory councillor for the ward, standing again. Second is Xena Dion, who has a long council record including stints as mayor and sheriff, and who has let go of her previous safe seat to help win back the problem ward from the Poole Xenophobes.

The third candidate is a mildly pleasant young chap with flawless party credentials called Tom, who read history at Oxford and now runs his own antiquarian book business. With his drab clothes and polite manners, Tom is blue to the bone.

We stand in a draughty church hall, chatting with a few elderly ward residents as we snack on orange juice, crisps, and biscuits.

Among us at this pitiful event is Bryan, Xena's husband, the former US Army colonel. I talk with him:

'How do you rate our chances in this ward?'

He looks combat-ready in his field jacket, jeans, and hiking boots. 'Pretty good, I'd say. Xena knows what she's doing, and people remember her from when she was mayor. We're getting good reactions on the doorstep.'

'I thought the reactions were good here back in 2015. It didn't help me get elected, though. The Poole Xenophobes are dug in deeper than bugs in a rug.'

He grins and pats my arm: 'Don't take it personally! The
Xenophobes are a problem, sure, but we can handle it. And if Xena
doesn't make it, hey, no problem. Remember I'm standing in her
old ward, so we have two chances here.'

'Well, sure, but look at the national scene. We had everything
going for us in 2015, but now the government could fall any day.
Westminster could lose Scotland and Ireland. The whole UK could
go down the tubes. We're heading for trouble.'

He rocks his head. 'Yeah, maybe. I see that, but we can buck
the trend. Gotta give it our best shot, anyway!'

I sip orange juice. 'What do you think about Trump's chances
of getting a free pass in the Mueller report?'

'Trump? Oh, he'll brush it off. The main facts have been out
there for two years, and they haven't hurt him yet. He's got a rock-
solid base among the rednecks. They'll need a smoking gun to shift
him.'

'I think Trump is Putin's man. The connection is too big to
ignore. It undermines our eastern front in Europe.'

'Well, maybe, but Trump is tough on defence. He's not about
to let Germany fall to the Russians.'

'It's not what he wants or intends, obviously, but he's a patzer
when it comes to grand strategy, whereas Putin is a heavyweight
grandmaster. Putin is running rings around him.'

Bryan shrugs and pulls a grin: 'Hey, cheer up! America is still
Number One. Putin doesn't have a hope of invading Europe.'

'I'm more worried about Trump invading Britain. After Brexit,
Britain will have to make a trade deal with Trump America. Do you
really think he's going to play nice? We'll be screwed, a vassal state
of America.'

He laughs: 'Come on, Andy, Trump's not gonna be there forever. We'll make good deals, and everyone will be happy.'

'We already have good deals with Europe. Our whole added

value is bridging Europe and America, not taking sides.'

He looks over at Xena: 'Hey, I gotta go. Nice talking with you.'

———

While Britain is consumed by Brexit, schoolgirl Greta Thunberg is making waves on the global stage: 'Our house is falling apart. Our leaders need to start acting accordingly, because at the moment they are not. If our house was falling apart, … you wouldn't hold three emergency Brexit summits and no emergency summit regarding the breakdown of the climate and the environment. It's still not too late to act.'

A few days later, she explains further: 'This is not just young people being sick of politicians. It's an existential crisis. It's something that will affect the future of our civilisation.'

———

Later in the month, I visit Buckingham Palace together with my scientific friend Violetta, who's a professor at the University of Lodz in Poland. We collaborated in Germany to edit a volume of conference proceedings. She's in London to visit Polish friends.

Personally, Violetta reminds me of my old flame Judy, updated to account for the passage of the years since then. Like Judy, she's a natural redhead of average height and build who was beautiful in her younger years. I like Violetta's sharp intelligence.

Judy was animated by Marxist ideas I didn't like. Violetta is immune to all that after growing up in Poland. Now that a Polish pope and the Polish Solidarity movement have put an end to Soviet rule, and Poland has joined NATO and the EU, she feels just as European as I do.

I meet her at an elegant Polish guest house in central London. Her landlady there is a friend and a wealthy investor.

We sit over coffee in her guest room while we decide what to do. The Queen's Gallery in Buckingham Palace is hosting an exhibition titled *Russia: Royalty and the Romanovs*. It looks good.

We set off to the palace. I keep up a cracking pace, as usual, while she struggles to keep up and catch her breath. Once there, we relax and take time to enjoy the show.

I wave at a wall chart showing a long Russian royal family tree: 'Look how far it goes. There are people all over Europe here. Queen Victoria too, the whole lot.'

Violetta peers at the chart: 'Yes, monarchy is an international institution. In past times, diplomacy was royal family politics. Only today we have career professionals and political parties.'

'Except here in the United Kingdom, where the Queen still works hard on the diplomatic front. You know she holds a weekly audience with the prime minister, where she can steer government decisions.'

'Yes, I saw the movie *The Queen* about the death of Princess Diana.'

'Well, you can see the problem. The prime minister is her loyal servant, a servant of the Crown, a flunkey, a nobody. This is a monarchy, not a democracy.'

'The last Polish king was Stanislaw the Second in the eighteenth century. But Polish history is quite a mess. Polish borders are not fixed on the map like British borders.'

I recall a fact of history: 'Didn't a Polish king defend Vienna against the Turks in the seventeenth century?'

'Yes, King Jan the Third led the army that ended the Ottoman siege of the city in 1683. He saved Europe from the Muslims. But Poland already lost Ukraine to Turkey.'

I shake my head. 'The year 1683 was big for that Norwegian gunman a few years ago. Remember him?'

She nods: 'I remember – horrible. He was mad about Muslims.'

'Right, he thought Muslims were taking over Europe and that people like him should rise up and kill them all.'

She frowns: 'We in Poland don't want Muslim immigrants. We

like to preserve Polish Catholic culture.'

I look at her more carefully: 'Are you religious?'

'No, not at all. Catholic identity is cultural tradition. And it was partly responsible for allowing the Nazi death camps in Poland. So, I can never accept that chapter in the history of Catholic Church.'

'Fair enough. The Catholic Church is based in Rome. Here in England, the Queen is the supreme head of the Church of England. She's a religious leader as well as a national head of state.'

'I never understood that. Why do you have a national church?'

'It was Henry the Eighth back in the fifteenth century. He broke off from the Church of Rome because he wanted to divorce his wife so that he could marry someone new and have a son and heir.'

She looks puzzled: 'This is very strange for a Christian. I know religion is strange always, but today we accept that church and state must be separate. Why not in England?'

'Just another historical nonsense. In Britain the monarch is crowned by the Archbishop of Canterbury in Westminster Abbey. And Church of England bishops have reserved seats in the House of Lords. The only other country in the world that has reserved places for religious people in the legislature is Iran. The Islamic Republic of Iran and the Christian Kingdom of Great Britain have that in common. A fossil of history, but true.'

'This is your British problem – your nationality is your religion. For you Brits, European citizenship is like … blasphemy!'

'Absolutely. Not for me, of course, but I'm an exception.'

She waves at the gallery around us. 'This palace is so historical, so old-fashioned. Why don't people like you rise up and make a revolution?'

'If we could, we would. But we saw how things turned out in French and Russian revolutions. Once you start trying to modernise the establishment, you can't stop, and that can get bloody.'

'I'm bored with all these portraits of old kings and queens,' she says. 'Shall we go?'

We go down to the gift shop, where tourists face mountains of tasteless royalist kitsch at shamelessly inflated prices. Gilded and crested dinner services, monogrammed bed linen, toy soldiers with red coats and bearskin helmets, toy marching bands in kilts and fancy garters, model red buses and black taxis, novelty teapots, calendars and postcards, tins of biscuits and boxes of chocolates – all such tat. Shame on the royal estate!

We tear ourselves away and make off for Exhibition Road, the site of the Science Museum and the Victoria and Albert Museum, to visit a rather posh Polish club offering a good afternoon tea.

———

Local campaigning for the council elections continues. One Saturday, I go down into central Poole with Isaac, Tom, and Buzz to distribute leaflets to shoppers in the high street.

Isaac and I stand on either side of a mall entrance and give out leaflets. But some shoppers seem to dislike seeing us handing out our worthless propaganda.

One chap, a scrawny man of middle years in untidy clothing, responds indignantly: 'Are you a Tory? You've got a cheek, asking for our votes. There's no way you're getting my vote!'

I respond with serene cheer: 'We're the ones who can offer good governance and responsible administration of public affairs.'

'Good governance? You should be ashamed of yourselves, cutting public services and imposing austerity on us, ashamed!'

I smile sunnily back. 'We couldn't spend money that wasn't there. Would you rather we got into debt and had the World Bank dictate how we should cut services?'

'The cuts are shameful! People who need services, the poorest, the vulnerable are suffering. And all you lot can do is protect the wealthy and go on about lower taxes. It's disgusting! You should all be thrown out!'

I'm still smiling. 'Better to let people who know what they're doing make cuts than let politicians splash money around like water and put us all into debt.'

He's now bobbing around and shouting: 'You're all a bunch of scoundrels and I wouldn't vote for you if you were the only ones standing. You're all despicable!'

Isaac comes over and tries to calm him down: 'It's okay, you're entitled to your opinion. Sorry if we bothered you.'

The man stares at me blankly, then turns and walks away.

'Best not to wind them up,' Isaac says to me. 'They only cause more trouble. He won't vote for us anyway, so let him go.'

A big chap in a dark suit comes out of the mall to confront us. He tells Isaac: 'I must ask you to move back, away from the doors. You have no right to block the entrance.'

Isaac replies: 'We have a permit from the council to be here. We're just handing out leaflets.'

I come over: 'We're Conservatives.' I put my hand on Isaac's shoulder: 'This man is an eminent senior councillor and a former mayor of this borough. He's our local chairman.'

Bouncer repeats his line: 'I must ask you to keep away from the doorway. We don't want you upsetting our customers.'

Isaac shrugs at me: 'Fair enough, let's go for a coffee.'

———

The British establishment is thin on supporters of the European project. The inner circle thinks Britain should aim to divide and conquer in Europe. Even the Europhiles tend to see the EU as a commercial project and obsess about profits and losses.

British businessmen are so used to treating their fellow Brits as cash cows to be milked for money they think it's okay to prey on fellow Europeans that way too. They're eager to deny the founding values of the EU and restore a more primal disorder across Europe in which dog eats dog in a Darwinian mud fight.

Across the pond in the Americas, President Trump is even more shamelessly determined to do the same. And yet, after two years of digging in the dirt, Robert Mueller and his team have found 'insufficient evidence' of a criminal conspiracy.

I think Putin actively helped both Trump and the Brexiteers. Nigel Farage, Arron Banks, and Andy Wigmore call themselves the Bad Boys of Brexit. Banks had several meetings with the Russian ambassador and Russian officials in early 2016. On the same day Leave.EU held its press launch, Banks and Wigmore visited the Russian embassy and were invited to buy a group of gold mines plus stakes in a diamond company.

—

On the second day of May, I vote for the two Conservative council candidates standing in my ward.

By Saturday, the fog of war has lifted to reveal carnage. The Tories have lost way over a thousand councillors nationwide and lost control of over forty councils. Altogether, the UKIP vote has almost halved, the Conservative vote is way down, and even the Labour vote is down. On the upside, the Lib Dem vote has more than doubled and the Green vote has almost trebled.

The new Bournemouth, Poole, and Christchurch unitary council has lost its Conservative majority. Janet Walton is out.

My beloved accomplice Rachel has also lost her council bid in London. The Conservatives have suffered their worst drubbing in local elections for decades.

Amid all this carnage, a Downing Street spokesman confirms that the UK will hold European elections later in the month.

I'm cheered. Maybe Brexit can still be revoked.

PART 3
INDIGNATION

May 2019 – December 2019

'I'd rather be dead in a ditch.'
Boris Johnson

21. Shilling for Europe

I try to stay calm: 'Most of the votes cast in England in the 2016 referendum on whether the United Kingdom should leave the European Union were in favour of leaving. The result was marginal and unexpected, and it was widely seen as having been driven by a mixture of anger and pride. Cooler heads continue to say it provides no good basis for redirecting national policy.'

I go on like this until my essay concludes: 'There is still time for UK politicians to resile from that decision. For the sake of all we hold dear, defying the populists who would drag us all into anarchy and chaos, they should show some resilience.'

Between those two endstops, *Resilience* surveys a vast landscape of big ideas from high Earth orbit. The history of the UK, the ideals of the EU, the philosophy behind Western civilisation, challenges of global governance, big issues that defy us, and a closing riff on democracy and the internet to zoom back in on how the EU offers a forum for the UK to play its part – it's all there.

Neither Sir Robert nor Boris Johnson responds to it.

———

The ninth day of May is celebrated across Europe as Europe Day. I spend the evening at a restaurant in Bournemouth debating the Brexit question. I'm here as the front man for the *Dorset 4 Europe* group, and my sparring partner is the movie man Ben who fronts the *Dorset 4 Leave* group and debated with me in our Valentine video. Ben is eager for a Europe Day rematch – this time in a live event with tickets available online.

Expecting a crowd, we sit in the restaurant at the appointed time and chat amicably. I dream Rachel may show up by surprise and wait with bated breath to see her radiant face again.

Fifteen minutes later, a couple walks in. They look like yuppies.

I recall their names as Daniel and Sarah as we all shake hands.

Ben smiles: 'I guess you're here for the Brexit debate we advertised on Facebook.'

Daniel replies: 'Yes, we were expecting a crowd here already. Are we too early?'

Ben shrugs: 'No, but you're the first to arrive. We don't expect a big crowd.'

I close the slide show I've prepared on my laptop. 'We don't really need a crowd at all. We're just here to debate the issues. If others want to join in, fine. If not, no problem.'

'Seems okay,' says Sarah to Daniel. 'I'd rather this than a big meeting where we just sit and listen.'

He nods and takes off his jacket: 'No problem for us either. Let's just take it as it comes.'

Ben waves expansively around the room: 'Great ... you can get stuff at the counter. They stayed open for us, so they'll be glad to see you.'

Sarah goes to the counter. We settle around the table.

Ben begins: 'So, ah, Daniel, what's your connection with the Brexit thing?'

'Actually, I lecture in social theory at the university,' he replies. 'For me, this is a central issue in how politics is changing in the age of social media and global mobility. I could make a whole course on how Brexit illustrates the issues. How about you – what do you do?'

Ben keeps his voice level: 'Cool. That's really interesting. I'm a software developer. I'm in a small company that wants to be big in augmented reality apps – you know, projecting data and instructions and ads and so on into a field of view.'

Daniel smiles: 'Wow, awesome. It's great that we're doing stuff like that here in Dorset. And, ah, Andy, how about you?'

'I'm the oldie here. I work part-time with the local Conservatives, but I'm retired from a career in a big software company in

Germany. It was business software, for global and multinational corporations, where Brexit is really just a big headache.'

Sarah returns with a tray. We get started. Time passes.

'Actually,' I say, 'when we go beyond the economic issues about trade and the political issues about sovereignty and the British union, the big thing for me is global clout. The world has organised into three big power centres – America, China, and Europe. After Brexit, we're out of all that, just a tiny island group against the superpowers.'

Ben disagrees: 'Physical size isn't an issue in the digital age. We have unique talents, and we need to be free to express them and take full advantage of them.'

Daniel holds up his hands: 'Wait, guys, the world has changed in the last twenty years. We no longer live in a world where big power centres can rule the planet, like villains in a James Bond movie. People with social media can outsmart all that.'

I pull an ironic smirk: 'Go tell that to Vladimir Putin or Xi Jinping! Putin and his team are using social media more smartly than we in the West are. And Xi is locking down the internet in China, so no one here is about to outsmart anyone in China.'

Ben shakes his head: 'No, that's all wrong. We need to reinvent social media. What we have now is just one form, with very simple user dynamics. People post text and videos and buy stuff, but behind the scenes the big corporations are hoovering up all the data and building predictive user models. It's the corporations we need to be worried about, not the governments.'

'Quite right,' I add. 'The corporations have the real power. But politicians stake out the playing field. Once you get that right, corporate power is benign. What the corporations want are happy customers and happy employees – and profits, of course. Governments can either help them or get in the way and get shoved aside. The global corporations can play them off against each other.'

Daniel intervenes: 'Slow down, guys, this is all too easy. People don't want corporate control any more than they want government control. Governments and corporations do things for them, and they want those things done well, but they won't fall into the mould of – what did you call them? – predictive user models.'

I shrug: 'Maybe they will, and maybe they won't. With neuroscience telling us free will is an illusion, the prospects for predictive user models look quite good. We need to step back further. Science and big tech are pushing on fast. Soon people will be paying big money to turn themselves into cyborgs. That's a powerful incentive to accept the rule of big corporations because they're the money machines. But that only works in an organised global environment, with coordinated laws and taxes and so on. We need global government just to keep the money machines running efficiently.'

Ben shakes his head: 'No, we need global freedom, so that new ideas can be developed. Britain can be a centre of innovation once we get the bureaucratic monster from Brussels off our backs.'

Sarah has been quietly observing this male-on-male fight. She joins in: 'I can't help feeling you're all missing something big here, which is nature, not just human nature but the environment, the climate and so on. Mother nature will find ways to stop all this stuff. Trees are being burned down, insects are dying, new diseases are evolving, species are disappearing, the polar ice caps are melting, the weather is getting more extreme. We can't just ignore all that.'

I nod: 'Quite right. That's another argument for global governance, to let wiser policies prevail. The first step is working in the EU, which has relatively enlightened environmental policies.'

'We humans are an animal species,' Sarah adds. 'We can't go against nature.'

I feel smug. I ploughed through all this in *Resilience*. But Rachel didn't show. Bummer.

———

A week later, I go along to a meeting at a local church in preparation for the European elections. The church is in a block between Poole and Bournemouth. The evening air is still pleasantly warm, and I rock up in my linen suit over a blue shirt, with sandals, and a round blue EU badge pinned to my lapel.

I walk past a clutter of tables around the periphery, where little interest groups bask in their moment of fame and volunteers tout their wares and distribute leaflets. I hang around awhile, sensing their vibe of earnest commitment.

There are plenty of people I recognise, and I exchange a few hellos and brief words, but I don't feel like sitting with them. Then I get lucky. I see my old teenage date Deb with her husband Colin standing near the front. I walk up to them.

'Deb,' I say. 'Great to see you again!'

She smiles with genuine delight. 'Andy, great to see to you too.' We shake hands warmly.

'Colin. Good to see you,' I add. We shake hands too.

The main event is about to start. I sit next to Deb. She's wrapped in a warm jacket, but the feeling of her next to me is unexpected balm to my solitary soul.

At the communion rail in front of us, the vicar introduces the proceedings. The candidates standing for election as members of the European parliament for southwest England and Gibraltar are an uninspiring bunch, but that goes with the new terms of the job they're seeking. Given Theresa May's chosen course, the winner is doomed to serve mere weeks or months in post before the Brexit tsunami sweeps them away.

We listen politely as the candidates step up to speak. Like me, Deb and Colin both clap whenever someone says anything in favour of remaining in the EU.

I'm unimpressed by most of the speeches. The Conservative candidate, a young lady I've never seen before and who lacks any visible charisma, is particularly dismal. Her pitch is simply that she wants as our elected member to make herself redundant again just as quickly as possible. Only the diehard Tories applaud her.

The Lib Dem candidate is a more capable lady who presents a coherent vision of what she might do as an elected member and how Britain might play a constructive role in the European parliament, and I clap warmly. The Green candidate is good too – she's an economics professor who knows what she's talking about.

The Brexit Party candidate is a horror beyond belief. Nigel Farage worked fast to set up his new 'party' – more of a business start-up with no more than money, a message, a logo, and a leader – and his recruitment of candidates for these elections was hurried and slapdash. His lead candidate for this region is the venomous former Tory Ann Widdecombe. She states her case for Queen and country and against Europe with the clear elocution of a seasoned public speaker, but her rant is so unhinged and jingoistic that I hear it as a Monty Python lampoon. The hardcore Brexiteers applaud it with whoops of joy.

The Labour candidate hasn't even shown up. Instead, the Labour peer Lord Adonis is here to stand in for her. This turns out to be the salvation of the event for me, as he's a good speaker and gives far and away the best of the speeches.

In words he recorded later, this is his pitch: 'The European Union withdrawal bill is the worst legislation of my lifetime. I feel duty bound to oppose it relentlessly in the House of Lords. Brexit is a dangerous populist and nationalist spasm worthy of Donald Trump.'

So far, so good. Then he puts the boot in: 'Theresa May seeks to override parliament on Brexit. Her assertion of government sovereignty must be rejected by both the Lords and Commons. The fiction that Brexit is about parliament taking back control is in truth a power grab by the right wing of the Conservative party.'

That's my take too. He continues: 'Brexit is not a done deal. Opinion polls show a majority against Brexit and a surge of support for continued EU membership among younger voters.'

We applaud warmly. He continues: 'The Brexit obsession is a distraction from real UK challenges. Britain is facing a crisis in housing, education, healthcare, employment, and the incessant rise of social and regional inequalities. All this is feeding populism and undermining the national fabric.'

More warm applause. Adonis ends with party politics centre stage again, so I tune out.

During the interval, while Deb and Colin go in search of coffee, I tour the tables again. Behind one piled with Lib Dem leaflets, I spot a face I know. Vikki Slade is my old friend Isaac's pet hate on the council, the one against whom he pitches his most pointed propaganda. I like her sharp and spirited attacks on my councillor friends, who need to be challenged firmly and often to stop them getting lazy, as well as her commitment to decency and common sense in civic affairs.

Vikki isn't so tall, but she's trim and fit, and her face and tone are remarkably fresh and animated. I used to admire her in action in the Poole council chambers, where I observed the proceedings from the public gallery on my team's side, looking over to the opposition front bench where Vikki performed. She recognises me too.

'You work with Robert Syms, don't you?' she says. 'What's your position on the European elections?'

'Yes, but I'm opposed to Brexit and can't possibly support the Conservative candidate here. Given the choice, I'd vote Lib Dem. You have the best policy on Europe.'

She smiles widely, revealing good teeth. 'I'm glad to hear it. I know your sister. She does good work in the housing association.'

'Yes, she tells me about it.'

Soon I return to my seat beside Deb for question time.

As we part with airy promises to keep in touch, Colin tells me he's a Lib Dem activist. Good for him – Deb chose well.

—

I go along to the first meeting of the new BCP council. The Bournemouth council chambers will be the seat of the new assembly, but they're not ready yet, so we meet at a lecture hall in the university instead.

I sit stoically as the ritual election of council officers unfolds on the stage before me. I watch my party colleagues struggling to put on a brave face against the assorted liberals and anarchists who are about to rule the roost and impose a new brand of chaos on the conurbation.

When the vote is held for the role of council leader, the winner is Vikki. She leads a Unity Alliance combining Liberal Democrats, Poole Xenophobes, Labour, Greens, and various independents.

I'm rooting for her.

—

German chancellor Angela Merkel says the European political order needs burnishing: 'Our political power is not yet commensurate with our economic strength. … This is a time when we need to fight for our principles and fundamental values.'

I see a Europe of nations emerging. The big decisions are being made by national leaders acting in concert. This is better than a union run by technocrats. Citizens are free to vote out their leaders. It's a good order.

Back in unruly Britannia, Theresa May and Jeremy Corbyn end their talks with no agreement on a way forward.

May says she'll step down as party leader in June. Boris Johnson instantly says he'll run for the leadership. The race has begun.

22. Tears in Downing Street

Thursday 23 May is election day in the UK for the European parliament. I stroll to my local polling station and vote Lib Dem.

On Friday, Theresa May, clad in a bright red suit, steps out from the familiar black door of 10 Downing Street, strides forward, and addresses the nation from a sunlit podium. In her flawless Oxford-trained elocution, she delivers a momentous speech.

'Ever since I first stepped through the door behind me as prime minister, I have striven to make the United Kingdom a country that works not just for a privileged few, but for everyone. And to honour the result of the EU referendum. …'

On she goes, summarising her three years in high office with clarity and incisiveness, until she comes – with a voice that begins to falter – to the emotional climax.

'I will shortly leave the job that it has been the honour of my life to hold – the second female prime minister but certainly not the last. I do so with no ill-will, but with enormous and enduring gratitude to have had the opportunity to serve the country I love.'

It's too much for her. In that last sentence, and the word 'love' especially, her composure breaks, her face folds into a mask of bitter regret, and the tears began to flow. Hastily, before the pain becomes unbearable, she turns away and hurries back to her sanctuary behind the black door.

Strife over Europe has claimed another British prime minister. A new one will take over in July.

Boris Johnson will likely be next. He's already vowed to renegotiate the withdrawal agreement with Brussels. He plans to force Brussels to back down – yet Brussels shows no sign of budging.

If Boris is elected, he'll face the same parliamentary arithmetic as before. One option would be to disregard parliament altogether.

The existing law will then take the UK out of the EU on Halloween unless he intervenes to stop it.

Boris could even prorogue parliament until D-Day has passed. Or he could behave so badly in Brussels that his partners there decide to kick Britain out of their club regardless. In any case, he faces an exciting set of options – and it's his game to lose.

But can the old Etonian who cuts such an abominable diplomatic dash steer his way out of the corner he's painted himself into? Siding with the Leave campaign because his rival backed Remain, and then failing for three years to come up with a plan for what to do after leaving the EU, was a monstrous dereliction of his duty as a public servant. Is he smart enough to reinvent himself?

Johnson would be the least qualified prime minister of modern times. His only ministerial experience was that dire two-year stint as foreign secretary. But first, to be propelled into office, he must survive a series of run-off polls among Tory MPs and then win a poll of party members nationwide – a tiny and absurdly skewed sample of the population, two per thousand of it to be exact, with an average age of about sixty.

Despite all his gaffes and buffooneries and character flaws, the rank-and-file members of the Conservative party still adore their Boris, so his chances are good, in betting terms. Yet selecting him would be a huge gamble.

Johnson is abhorred and abominated by European politicians. Good Europeans will never forgive him for having once compared the EU to the Third Reich.

—

The results of the European elections take time. Most EU member states vote on Sunday, so the UK results are left sealed until Sunday and only then counted at regional centres around the British Isles. The results for southwest England and Gibraltar are counted in the afternoon and evening at the Poole Arts Centre.

I'm there again, serving as an invigilator. I show up on time at the Arts Centre in my dark suit and a white shirt, but this time without a rosette. My blue tie is EU blue, not Tory blue, to match an enamel EU flag badge on my lapel.

The drama is less than in a general election, and I don't see many stalwarts from previous counts. But my canny old mate Isaac is here, his beady eyes on the lookout for any trickery among the counters. And the counters are just as nimble-fingered and industrious as ever.

For this count, candidates and agents from all over the south-west region are present. I don't know most of them, but I stride around the tables with lordly assurance anyway, just for fun.

Then, beside me again at a counting table, is Percy Payne, his warty face and pot belly wrecking the dignity of his sober suit. I pull a wry smile and await a rude greeting.

Percy smirks: 'Brexit Party winning by a mile, no question. I'm looking forward to Ann Widdecombe taking them by storm in Brussels.'

'She'll embarrass us there, that's for sure,' I say, recalling her Monty Python performance at the church hustings. 'No way back for Britain in Europe once they hear her.'

European elections use a proportional representation voting system, and there are six seats available for this region. Each party submits a list, and their overall vote share determines how many people on the list are returned, so the top candidates for the top parties are all but guaranteed seats. Since the Brexit Party is tipped to win in this region, and Ann Widdecombe tops its list, she's in.

'Conservatives have no chance,' boasts Percy. 'They're on a ticket to nowhere.'

'No doubt,' I concede. 'My money is on the Lib Dems to win at least two seats.'

'At most two. Brexit Party will get at least three, maybe four.'

'At most three. Greens will get one.'

I move on. A few minutes later, I come across Tom, the book man, looking good in his dark suit and Tory tie.

I try to be cheery: 'Hi, Tom, how's it going?'

He pulls a glum face: 'Looks bad for us, but I wasn't expecting a miracle.'

'Take it with a smile. It's all part of the Tory plan to get us out of Europe as soon as possible.'

He smiles wanly. 'But not if it means giving good publicity to the Brexit Party.'

'If you start a revolution, you have to roll with the punches. I think you'll find that Boris can take out Farage without any great difficulty.'

'I hope you're right. Are you backing Boris?'

I pull a clownish face: 'Are you kidding? I'd rather go back to Germany and become a political zero again. No, Jeremy Hunt is the man for me – moderate, sensible, a safe pair of hands in turbulent times.'

Tom demurs: 'I don't think he has a chance against Boris.'

'Probably not, but Boris is an opportunist. He has no political principles. He just wants to be Number One. As foreign secretary he was dire. If that's any indication, he's a no-no for me.'

'I think he could flourish once he was in office. Remember in the Foreign Office he had to work under Theresa May. With all due respect to her, that spoiled it for him.'

'That's a bad sign. It means he's not a team player – I think we have the results.'

Up at the front of the hall, the civic officer presiding over the count gathers his team and reads out the vote totals for the party lists. As expected, Nigel Farage's execrable new Brexit Party comes first, followed by the 'Bollocks to Brexit' Lib Dems, and then the Greens. All the rest are out of the running.

Isaac bounds up obliquely: 'It looks like what I was predicting, but I need some help with the maths here.'

I explain the mathematical formula for the voting system to Isaac and Tom. Together, we predict the six seats for southwest England as follows: Three seats go to the Brexit Party, two to the Lib Dems, and one to the Greens – to the smart professor of economics.

As everyone expected for a Crown territory that depends on good relations with Spain, Gibraltar voted overwhelmingly for the Lib Dems. The thirty-odd thousand British citizens of the Rock find the Brexit nonsense in the mother country deeply unsettling. But their votes go into the regional totals, so, like it or not, they now have three Brexit MEPs failing to represent them in Brussels too.

Tom looks crestfallen: 'Pity – I'd been hoping one seat would go Conservative. Ashley Fox will be disappointed.'

Ashley Fox is the leading name on the Tory list for the region. He's been a staunch MEP since 2014 and was the leader of the British Conservatives in the European parliament. I watched him speak in Poole and thought him a fine fellow – until his efforts to follow the May line put him out of sorts with the EU.

The three of us go out of the hall and check the national results on the big television beside the bar. The poll predictions are still uncertain, so we agree to hang around over a drink before we head off home. Drinks in hand, we settle around a table.

Isaac is combative, as usual: 'We have to fight back against the Brexit Party. We can't let them steal all our supporters in Poole.'

Tom nods: 'We need to back Boris. He's our best hope now.'

'Too desperate,' I say. 'When disaster looms and hope is almost lost, vote for the last scoundrel standing and pray for salvation.'

Isaac pulls an evil smile: 'Sounds like good sense to me. We can't afford to go soft on Brexit now. What better than the hardest Brexit hitter we have in Downing Street?'

I get serious: 'What's better is a government that pulls us back from the cliff edge and restores sanity before politics in this country goes completely bonkers.'

Tom protests: 'Boris isn't bonkers. He's got good party credentials and he knows what he's talking about on Europe after his years in Brussels.'

Isaac agrees: 'He's got a lot of support in Poole. He's our best bet.'

I sit back with an air of finality. 'Well, count me out. Unless he surprises all of us very soon, he's not a man I can support.'

'If Boris can't save us, we're dead,' says Isaac. 'Brexit will have killed the Conservative party. It'll be a choice between Nigel Farage and the Lib Dems.'

Tom looks gloomy: 'These are desperate times.'

Isaac finishes his red wine. 'I'm off to bed. The results can wait until tomorrow.'

I check the results in the morning.

The seats for the UK are allocated as follows: 29 to the Brexit Party, sixteen to the Lib Dems, ten to Labour, seven to the Greens, four to the Conservatives, and four to various nationalists. Tories are humiliated.

As the fog of battle lifts across Europe, the new European parliament elected by the citizens of all the member states looks quite decent. The centre-right and centre-left groupings remain the biggest, but liberals and greens make gains. A far-right group was set to make big gains, but the rest hold them in check. Proportional representation has rescued Europe for the moderates.

———

Days later, I ponder on Nigel Farage. He speaks up for people who feel excluded from the old-boy club that defines national politics. He listens to the regular chaps in the pub and refuses to dismiss their griping about immigrants as racism or bigotry.

On the other hand, the liberal establishment, which includes most of the Remainers, listens to people in business and the professions, to young people who want a better future, and to anyone else who's woke enough to know right from wrong. British political life has polarised into two sides, and neither of them understands how the other side sees things.

In both Britain and America, a deep crisis of conservatism has been building ever since the end of the Thatcher government and the Reagan administration. Transatlantic conservatism as they knew it died with the 'greed is good' mantra of the Masters of the Universe, which met its end in late 2008.

In Britain, Conservative party membership has been dwindling for decades. Gone are the halcyon days of millions of energetic and idealistic members. Now it's down to a hundred thousand-odd ageing diehards. A decade of austerity has taken the shine off their finance-led revolution to build a new global empire.

Under Margaret Thatcher, the Tories promoted a generation of brutally Darwinian dogs of war and yet retained enough civic good sense to leave intact the main threads of the social fabric. But as the cannibal dogs turbocharged the global economy, and as the rest of the world began to catch on, things began to go wrong, first slowly and then faster, until the rising costs of preserving the threadbare fabric exceeded any remaining gains from the turbo boost.

I don't regard the rise of populists like Trump and Farage as a new incarnation of conservatism. Their rise reveals its inner decay rather than its renewal. Traditional conservatives were often smug and complacent, but they weren't usually angry. Trump and Farage depend on white male rage to mobilise their base.

British conservatives direct their rage at the European Union. Its efforts to promote business and the single market are too mild and cautious for the zealots. They resent the growth of the EU into a power centre overshadowing the Westminster establishment. The

EU sees politics as about compromise rather than conviction and holds liberal values. All this antagonises the cultists. Euroscepticism gives them new energy.

The logical culmination of the disease of conservatism to which Tories fell victim was the Brexit referendum. When Trump then won his presidency with a campaign based on lies and delusions, conservative populism looked like a fad with a future.

But populist conservatives have no tools in their toolbox to get a handle on the climate issue, the crisis of confidence in capitalism, or the explosive rise of inequality. Trump and Farage are symptoms of the disease, not the cure.

Farage is the most egregiously extreme exemplar of the pre-crisis 'greed is good' thread in British politics. He opposes anything that hinders his *nouveau riche* accomplices. If he had his way, most of the poor dupes who voted for him would be working harder and longer, for less money and with less protection, to feed his greed. He hates the EU because it defies his social Darwinism.

Farage spotted a political opportunity and went for broke to exploit it. His previous vehicle was UKIP, but that outfit is now worn out. To replace it, he launched a vulture capitalist start-up, with crowd-funders for members. His Brexit Party is an outfit for one event only: no-deal Brexit. It's his Halloween costume.

The Brexit Party made a killing in the European election. The corpse is moderate Conservatism. Farage is putting huge pressure on the government to deliver Brexit on Halloween, deal or no deal. For him and his rich pals, it's either the trick of nuking the Tories or the treat of making millions from betting on a no-deal Brexit.

The United Kingdom is in trouble.

23. Enter the joker

I'm still animated by the spirit of physics. I love the science behind the visual image of a black hole released in April. When an online vendor offers a black T-shirt bearing the image, I buy one.

On the first Sunday in June, Wendy and Dick Bragg hold an afternoon party at their new house in Poole. The build is new and sports an open, modern design, with the lounge running from front to back and an open flight of stairs in the middle, plus a kitchen range and bar on one side.

Wendy and Dick are retired investment bankers. They're both smaller, slimmer, and younger than me, and both are nerdy and clever. Wendy is a councillor I supported for election. Dick began life as a student of physics, but now he's a Bitcoin trader.

The other guests are mostly party and council contacts I know by sight at least. I'm in my linen suit over my new black-hole tee, with black water shoes and an EU badge on my lapel.

Dick, holding a glass of wine, presses a finger at my chest: 'That's the black hole image – you bought a T-shirt for that.'

I open my jacket to show it off: 'Sure I did. I think it's well worth celebrating. As a former physicist too, you should appreciate the achievement behind the image.'

'I do. But not my field anymore. My doctorate was in electrical engineering.'

'So how come you ended up in banking?'

'More money. What better reason could you want?'

'How's the Bitcoin trading going?'

He shrugs: 'Can't complain. Paid for this house, anyway.'

'Nice place. Obviously pays better than philosophy.'

Dick moves on. I latch onto a staunch party member I recall from cabinet breakfasts, a prosperous local businessman.

I frown: 'Hi, ah, Cliff, isn't it? Sorry, I'm not so good at names.'

'Yes, Cliff. You're Andy, right?'

'That's me. Are you still going to the cabinet breakfasts?'

'Yes. I don't see you there anymore. Any particular reason?'

'Not enough payoff for me. I can talk to Sir Robert whenever I like – well, any Friday at least.'

'I see,' he says, pulling a frown. Then he spots my lapel badge: 'That's the EU flag – you're not a Remainer, are you?'

'I certainly am. I think Brexit is the biggest political mistake in Britain in my lifetime.'

'Are you serious? Joining the EU in the first place was the biggest mistake since Chamberlain appeased Hitler in Munich.'

'The European project is precisely what we need to avoid that sort of problem again.'

'It's a betrayal of British sovereignty!' He's almost shouting.

I reply firmly: 'It's a betrayal of all the people who died in World War Two not to support the European project.'

His anger is rising. 'The betrayal is having anything to do with Germany. The European Union is the Fourth Reich!'

'That's an absurd accusation. The EU is a peaceful project to pursue prosperity as an orderly community.'

'Taking marching orders from Berlin! If you support that, you don't belong in the Conservative party!'

I reply flatly: 'No, if you can't stand modern Berlin, you don't belong. You should join UKIP or the Brexit Party.'

His wife intervenes: 'Cliff, please. The Germans are not all Nazis.'

—

On Monday, President Donald Trump and First Lady Melania land in London for a three-day state visit before a memorial service in Normandy for the D-Day landings in 1944.

That evening, the Queen hosts a state banquet at Buckingham

Palace for the First Couple. Her words as she welcomes them to the banquet are exquisitely diplomatic.

Watching her performance on television, I'm impressed by her professionalism. This is a consummate actress at work, playing the part with total conviction.

The Queen speaks with her tight, plummy diction: 'Visits by American presidents always remind us of the close and longstanding friendship between the United Kingdom and the United States.'

I guess she means this. Her view of transatlantic relations was forged by her political mentor Winston Churchill, whose special relationship with Franklin Roosevelt was historic.

She continues: 'Tonight, we celebrate an alliance that has helped to ensure the safety and prosperity of both our peoples for decades, and which I believe will endure for many years to come.'

I see now that she really does mean it. For her and her dynasty, an Anglo-American bond based on shared delight in the tongue of angels and James Bond movies means far more than a marriage of commercial convenience with the continental powers.

The state visit was originally supposed to include a ride in a horse-drawn gilded carriage along the Mall leading up to Buckingham Palace, which Donald had been childishly eager to enjoy, but security concerns led to its cancellation. Instead, protesters fly a big blimp shaped and painted to resemble baby Trump in a diaper over London.

When the travelling circus moves to Normandy for the D-Day event, Trump recalls his time with the Queen with his own special brand of hyperbole: 'There are those that say they have never seen the Queen have a better time, a more animated time.'

I smile to read it. The wicked old witch of Buckingham Palace has put her spell on the Donald. I see it in the photos: Queenie has an evil leer on her face in one image, and the Don looks like a clumsy, gauche schoolboy in another. Her regal scam, honed over generations of dazzling the masses with ancient bling, has trumped his mafia-don brand of devilry.

Trump also airs his opinions on Brexit: 'Get it done. Get the deal closed. I would walk away. If you don't get the deal you want, if you don't get a fair deal, then you walk away. I wouldn't pay fifty billion dollars.'

He calls Boris Johnson 'very talented' and adds a personal reference for his job application: 'I think Boris would do a very good job. I think he would be excellent. I have always liked him.'

Why am I not surprised? The Tweedledum-and-Tweedledee coincidence of the two blond bombshells in American and British politics is a meme. Their matching hair crimes cry out for a double act that sets their rhetorical tics to music.

I've been brooding about bigger things. I type out my thoughts as an essay directed to an unknown audience. I'm thinking out loud, groping in search of readers who might redeem my efforts to attain a higher clarity.

The Great Reboot is its name. It's an extended review of a list of books on Buddhism, the Enlightenment, doughnut economics, the climate crisis, and quantum computing. I tie their themes together in a winding argument for a 'great reboot' of Western civilisation.

A keynote paragraph says: 'Any sustainable future for Western civilisation must involve a radical rethink of classical economics and democratic politics. Continuing the path that we as a species on Earth have been following for decades will spell our certain doom before the century is out. ... We shall only master the crises we have precipitated if we learn to identify with all life on Earth.'

After some food for science fans, I conclude: 'All humans alive – in the past, present, and future – are members of a family with a common purpose. With this truth, suitably fleshed out, as our master narrative, our challenges look more tractable.'

Once that essay is done, I brood anew on Tweedledum and

Tweedledee. Like Trump America, Brexit Britain is wallowing in a psychodrama of national humiliation. But this self-pity is ludicrous. The empire is long gone. Absurdly, Brexit depends on the idea that Britain is too generously endowed with lingering imperial glory to rest content with being an ordinary European country and that burial in the EU is impossibly humiliating.

I say admitting some glory on the European continent can be liberating. If Brits are proud of being among the victors in two world wars against Germany, then Germans should feel no less proud for painfully regaining worldwide respect and admiration.

Conservatism in the wider sense is as much a German as a British phenomenon. But recent British Conservatives have forgotten its roots in a historic tradition that distinguished it with a set of values higher than the market. Brexit Conservatives have lost the stoic faith of German conservatism and preserved only the British imperial myth that trading commodities for profit is the jewel in the crown of their faith.

Worse, Brexiteers are trapped by a more recent myth spun around the Second World War. The result is a cartoonish morality that elevates resolve over reflection, in which every leader is either a Chamberlain or a Churchill and foreign policy is a question of appeasement or defiance.

The Conservative party has become an apocalyptic cult, ready to torch the UK itself in a bid to 'take back control' of its destiny. A party that once prized pragmatic common sense now judges its leaders by the fervour of their belief in Brexit.

The Brexiteers are like the legendary British citizen abroad who thinks that if he shouts enough, Johnny Foreigner will scurry to do his bidding. Through the sheer power of their indomitable will, the Brexiteers will force the continental Johnnies to renegotiate the withdrawal deal. If the Johnnies refuse, the hardliners will walk Britain off the plank on Halloween.

Johnson reminds us of his Brexit views in his *Telegraph* column in mid-June: 'After three years and two missed deadlines, we must leave the EU on October 31. Delay means defeat. Delay means Corbyn. Kick the can and we kick the bucket.'

The words also remind me of the crass stylistic tics Boris has picked up in his years as a hack journalist meeting too many tight deadlines by dictating superficial garbage to beat the clock.

BoJo goes over the top: 'In everything we do we will seek to strengthen the union of our four nations, that invincible quartet, the awesome foursome that makes up the UK, the world's soft power superpower.'

I grimace. The mettlesome mophead from Eton is seeking to invoke the spirits of the awesome foursome of mopheads from Liverpool in support of his defence of an ancient and dilapidated union against the merits of the modern and more efficient union across the Channel. It's worse than Cool Britannia.

After that, I'm relieved to read the words of Max Hastings, a historian I respect. I once persuaded Max to inscribe a little signed message in my first edition copy of *Finest Years*, Max's 2009 book on Winston Churchill as warlord from 1940 to 1945.

Hastings explained his interest in 2012: 'Boris Johnson worked for me as EU correspondent of the *Daily Telegraph* and then as a columnist when I was the paper's editor, and I have seen plenty of him since. He is a magnificent journalist and showman.'

More Max: 'Boris is a gold medal egomaniac. His chaotic public persona is not an act. He is also a far more ruthless, and frankly nastier, figure than the public appreciates. He is not a man to believe in, to trust or respect, save as a superlative exhibitionist.'

Max updates his words in 2019: 'Boris Johnson has remodelled himself as a serious political figure. As to his period as foreign secretary, many mandarins speak of him with contempt.'

He adds a final encomium to sugar the pill: 'Behind the easy charm and effortless humour there lurks a giant brain. He is without a doubt one of the most intelligent politicians I have met.'

I smile. Trump the 'very stable genius' is teaming up with 'giant brain' Johnson to mastermind a new Anglo-American apotheosis. Trump will defy China, Johnson will defy Europe, and the pair will rule the Earth. Or not.

The *Evening Standard* is a London newspaper edited by former chancellor George Osborne. It backs Boris to be the next prime minister for the infantile reason that if anyone can give Britain back its mojo, it's BoJo.

In a Tory party poll, two-thirds of members say they want Brexit even if it damages the economy and leads to Scotland and Northern Ireland leaving the UK. They say Brexit means more than the survival of the party. Half of them would even be happy to let Nigel Farage be their new leader.

In the fifth round of polling among MPs for the party leadership, Boris Johnson comes first, Jeremy Hunt second, and Michael Gove third. Boris has more votes than the other two combined.

That's it. Gove is eliminated, and Johnson and Hunt will vie for the votes of the party's national membership. But no one is in any doubt about the outcome. It's practically a coronation.

I find more from Max Hastings: 'The sight of Boris Johnson in full flow convinced me years ago … that he was temperamentally unsuitable to be entrusted with any position of power.'

Endorsing that verdict, Sonia Purnell says of him: 'When I worked as his deputy in Brussels in an office of two, it took a long time to get used to what became known as his "four o'clock rants" in which he hurled four-letter words at an innocent yucca plant for several minutes at deadline time every day to work himself into a frenzy to write his creative tracts against the EU.'

She continues: 'His attitude to women – endless affairs leaving a string of women behind him – has long been one of entitlement and lack of respect. He has boasted to other men that he needs plenty of women on the go as he is "bursting with spunk" – descriptions of women as "fillies" in earlier years sullied his reputation with many women as an unreconstructed sexist.'

Party members nationwide have a month or so to decide between Johnson and Hunt. The result is as preordained as gravity.

Halloween looms liked an event horizon. Beyond it, I sense the spacetime warp of a supermassive black hole.

—

One Saturday in late June, I find Johnson is struggling to keep his campaign on course after police were called to his home. Neighbours were disturbed by the noise of a late-night row, presumably between Boris and his partner Carrie Symonds. He's living in sin with this lady, who's evidently a temperamental filly.

Bozza will obviously survive the embarrassment. For his fans, it's merely a sign that he's bedded a spirited wench. It's proof, if proof were needed, of his virile potency in spaffing the surfeit of spunk that gathers in his testicles.

Talking of balls, Sir Vince Cable is retiring as Lib Dem leader after his success with the 'Bollocks to Brexit' slogan. Leadership hopeful Jo Swinson follows suit: 'Three years since the European referendum, we have a Conservative leadership contest in which both candidates are seeking a mandate for a disastrous Brexit. ... Bollocks to Brexit, and Bollocks to Boris.'

To sway the popular vote his way, Johnson tours England in a coach dubbed the Boris Bus to make his case to party members in the provinces. One stop on his tour is at Bournemouth Pavilion, where he plans to fire up the oldsters I've been wooing for years.

With miraculous serendipity, I secure a ticket just in time and check with Rachel on social media that she'll be there too, tagging along as parliamentary assistant to Conor Burns. We agree to meet after the main event.

The pavilion is a massive brick building backing onto a plaza that overlooks the pier and the beach. First opened in 1929, its main hall resembles a big traditional cinema, with serried ranks of folding seats covered in red velvet and swish curtains revealing a wide stage. It's a favourite location for popular theatre and bedroom farces in the seaside tradition – just right for the Boris pantomime.

I sit up on the steeply banked balcony, safely remote from the action. I'm in my linen suit again, with sandals for the season, plus a little blue enamel Poole dolphin in my lapel – I don't dare wear an EU flag in this blatantly Brexiteer company.

Conor appears on the stage with minimal ceremony, his beetling posture of aggressive humility instantly familiar. This is his turf, so he does the warm-up act for the main man. In his most pompous parliamentary manner, he gives a wordy introduction to say in effect that Boris needs no introduction, then steps back. I guess Rachel is down in the front row, admiring her man in action.

Boris comes on to a burst of enthusiastic applause and lusty shouts of 'Boris'. Straight away, he goes for a pantomime vibe, telling his audience there are 'three things' the next leader has to get done: 'And the first is what? What?'

The pensioners in the ranks turn down their hearing aids and shout back in a ragged chorus: 'Brexit!'

Johnson roars back: 'Yes! Get Brexit done!'

I notice the answering chorus is feebler for his other points: uniting the country and defeating Labour. The speech soon goes downhill, but Boris gets through it with brio and ends to an avalanche of acclaim.

As the crowd spills out from the event, I go and loiter outside on a forecourt big enough for a fountain feature and turning space for carriages. It's a sunny evening.

Rachel comes out in the company of a tall young man. She looks happy, with her long hair free over a light blouse and a dark miniskirt, carrying a bulky bag. Her escort looks like a typical young Conservative, with short hair and a dark lounge suit over a white shirt with a blue tie. She sees me and waves.

'Hi, Andy,' she calls, 'Hope you haven't been waiting too long.'

She approaches and thrusts out her right hand.

'No problem.' I shake it gently.

She glances at her escort: 'Edward works with Tobias. We work together in London.'

I smile for the young man and extend a hand. 'Hi, I'm Andy.'

'Hi, Andy, Ed.' He has a fresh open face and good teeth. My teeth no longer look so good, but as a philosophical senior citizen I don't need such props. His handshake is too firm, as if a man-to-man greeting must be a trial of strength, but I grip hard.

I smile at Rachel and reply to Edward: 'I work with Sir Robert down here in Poole.'

'I already explained,' she says, and turns to him: 'Well, Ed, it was good to touch base.'

He nods. 'Yeah, sure, have a great evening. See you in the office some time.' He steps away: 'Good to meet you, Andy.'

Rachel and I stand uncertainly. 'I need a drink,' she says.

'Are you hungry? We can dine down on the seafront.'

'Not really. Maybe a quick beer. How about the Moon?'

'Okay, off we go … can I help you with your bag?'

She looks down at it in surprise. 'No, it's not heavy. Just a few overnight things.'

We set off. The pub is only a few hundred yards away through the lower gardens. We talk about work. She's busy with Conor. He's still on close terms with Boris after serving as his parliamentary private secretary. This is the Commons equivalent of what in Eton they call a fag, or in more normal terms a dogsbody. All this means Rachel interacts with Johnson's team quite a lot. My role with Sir Robert now seems lazy.

I'm curious about how she handles her boss. 'How do you get on with Conor? Are your relations honest and professional? Does he treat you in a sexist way? Does he hit on you at all?'

She laughs. 'He's gay, didn't you know? He behaves entirely correctly, like a gentleman, and he treats me well. I have no complaints there at all. The work is interesting and challenging, and he supports me and takes an interest in my welfare.'

I sigh with relief. My Lolita is still intact. My philosophical disciple is still open for my wisdom. But I need to probe a little further: 'How about your boyfriend? Is he cool with the setup?'

It's her turn to sigh. 'Crispin had no problem with Conor, but he did have a problem with London. We've been living apart since the local elections. It's difficult, but I hope we'll work it out in time.'

I smile. My disciple is doing fine. My challenge is to stay cool.

We reach the pub, which is busy, and I order a couple of pints of lager. We find a small table in a quiet corner.

Rachel takes a deep swig of lager. 'Ahh, that's better! I was getting hot and thirsty in that theatre. I'm still feeling sweaty and sticky from the train journey.'

'I sympathise. But I had a swim earlier and a cold shower before I came out again, so I feel fine.'

She smiles, as if ruefully. 'Glad to hear it … would you excuse me while I go to the ladies?'

'Be my guest.' I attend to my pint while she's away. Many people here are tanking up quickly before going on to fancier dates. It's a pub with cheap beer.

Rachel comes back with bare legs and her black tights balled up in one hand. 'Excuse me, but I had to take them off. They were getting scratchy and uncomfortable.' She stuffs them in her bag and guzzles down her lager. 'Ahh, I think I could enjoy another one.'

I let my mirror neurons share her relief in airing her legs as I drink down my lager. 'I'll go and get a second round.'

'Okay, thanks. Then I must be going. My parents will be waiting for me. They expect me for dinner.'

Over the second round, we discuss political philosophy, with special reference to the question of whether Boris stands any chance of doing a Brexit that might benefit Brits. I'm sceptical, of course, but she expresses a guarded optimism that I read as her attempt to rationalise working for Conor and Boris.

We leave the pub and go our separate ways. We part by kissing cheeks, but I stay cool. I'm not her teacher, but at least I can aspire to a Conor level of decorum.

——

A crisis is looming. Boris Johnson is saying he intends to take the UK out of the EU by Halloween, do or die. But most MPs are opposed to this, and the EU refuses to renegotiate the deal they hammered out with Theresa May. Boris is threatening to leave without a deal and refuses to request a new extension.

Boris believes in the power of positive thinking. When he was foreign secretary, he told a junior colleague: 'I used to captain rugby teams … You say to them: "It's great, we can do this" … You've got to build their morale and make them feel pumped up and feeling it's going to be great. The more they say it's going to be great, the greater it's going to be.'

In heroic accordance with his belief, Johnson says the EU will cave at the last minute to avoid a no-deal Brexit and offer him better terms. He knows his voters: 'I think people are yearning for this great incubus to be pitchforked off the back of British politics.'

During his visit to Britain, Trump called the special relationship 'the greatest alliance the world has ever known' and dangled the prospect of a 'phenomenal' new trade deal with America.

Boris is betting on it. But in the trade talks, Trump's demands will certainly include throwing open the UK food and healthcare markets. This will be enough to end free trade with Europe.

Brexiteers prattle about resuming the glory of times gone by, but I fear a ship of English fools is about to set sail.

On the final rally of thousands of party members in London for his leadership bid, Boris waves a plastic pack containing a smoked fish – a kipper – above his head:

'If you want to understand why it is that we must leave the EU and the advantages of coming out, I want you to consider this kipper … [A kipper seller] is utterly furious because after decades of sending kippers like this through the post, he has had his costs massively increased by Brussels bureaucrats who insist that each kipper must be accompanied by this, a plastic ice pillow.'

He waves it: 'Pointless, expensive, environmentally damaging health and safety, ladies and gentlemen. When we come out therefore, we will not only be able to end this damaging regulatory overkill, but we will also be able to do things to boost Britain's economy and we will be able to establish an identity as a truly global Britain and get our mojo back.'

After the event, fact checkers soon point out that EU regulations are not at fault here, but British ones, quite independently of Brussels. But it's too late. The media damage is done.

The results of the nationwide Tory ballot are announced on 23 July. Johnson bags about two thirds of the votes.

The victor stands before a crowd of jubilant party supporters and spells out his mantra: 'Deliver Brexit, Unite the country, and Defeat Jeremy Corbyn … unfortunately it spells DUD.'

Boris burbles on: 'We are going to energise the country. We are going to get Brexit done on 31 October and take advantage of all the opportunities it will bring with a new spirit of can do.'

He adds E for Energy to his mantra to make 'dude'.

Enter the dude, the joker in the pack.

24. Burning the bridge

The UK is about to install its eleventh Oxonian prime minister since the war. Boris Johnson graduated from Oxford in 1987. David Cameron, Michael Gove, and Jeremy Hunt all did so in 1988. Margaret Thatcher had done so in 1947 and was prime minister in September 1988, when her speech in Bruges gave Brexiteers their battle cry: 'We have not successfully rolled back the frontiers of the state in Britain only to see them reimposed at European level, with a European superstate exercising a new dominance from Brussels.'

Kid Boris went up aiming to become president of the Oxford Union. This debating society is like a teenage House of Commons and aspires to achieve the same level of witty English banter.

He did become president, but he failed to get a First in Finals. His sister Rachel said it later fell to her to 'break the terrible news' to him that their more swotty brother Jo had got a First.

Oxford's training degree for government is PPE, short for politics, philosophy, and economics. In 2016, the PPE graduates in Cameron's cabinet, including Dave himself, were Remainers. The Leavers were Boris (Classics), and Gove (English).

I too read PPE at Oxford. I paused physics and maths for later. My first step back to them was to work for a master's degree in logic and science in London. In my second year there, I shared a commune with several other Oxford PPE graduates.

One of them was Judy, another was Graham, and yet another was a young lady called Maggie. The commune also embraced Jeff (Classics) and Mark (English). Other friends made up the numbers to about eight. Our home base was a Victorian semi on a quiet street in Ealing in west London.

We ran a civilised commune, but it was radical. All the rooms were shared, in principle, and we each slept in any of them. Clothing was optional, the bathroom was unlocked, and meals, friends, and joints were all shared.

Our experiment in communism enabled us to rediscover how conservative we were in our personal lives. Basic levels of propriety, privacy, territoriality, and sexual fidelity stayed largely intact. But honesty and openness improved.

I rediscover Maggie via Facebook. She and her new husband Roger have retired to a country cottage in Dorset. I make a date to meet them for Sunday lunch at a trendy new restaurant in Sandbanks, near my usual jogging trail and swimming beach.

When Maggie shows up with Roger, I recognise her right away. She vaguely resembles the model in Leonardo's *Mona Lisa*, but her hair is a lighter shade of brown and her appeal is more English. Also, she's a bit older now. Roger is a big man with a thick moustache, a stooping gait, and the grizzled air of an outdoor type.

Once we've found our table, we catch up on our back stories.

I start the interrogation: 'So, Maggie, what have you been doing for the past few decades?'

'Well, after a few years in industry, I settled at the Department of Trade and Industry and shuttled back and forth between London and Brussels. What else was I going to do with a degree in PPE and A-levels in French and German?'

'Oh, right, I can see why this whole Brexit drama has left you fed up with British politics.'

Her voice rises in pitch: 'It's an absolute disgrace! Completely disastrous. It makes me ashamed to be British. But what about you? How did you get involved with the Conservatives?'

'Good question. When I came back from Germany ...' I tell my story. 'The whole Brexit nonsense just blew up out of nowhere and blindsided me.'

'It blindsided a lot of us. But you were never Conservative as a student. Do you still see Judy? How does she react to it?'

'I don't know. I haven't seen her since she became an MP. But I was never on board with her student Marxism.'

Maggie turns: 'Roger is a Marxist, aren't you, Roger?'

He leans forward: 'Yes, actually. I'm a Labour man. I support Jeremy Corbyn.'

I raise my eyebrows theatrically: 'Oh my gosh, a Corbynite! I'll try not to hold it against you. Seriously, why? Do you believe in class war and nationalising the commanding heights of the economy?'

He smiles: 'Not just like that.' He launches into a defence of his views that I'd have recognised as a student.

I reply with a measured defence of the regulated capitalism I've seen in action for decades in Germany. He says British capitalism is different, after the Thatcher years, and we hit the dialectical ball back and forth a few times.

Maggie joins in: 'Andy, you can't just assume our government will make changes just because they see them working in Germany.'

'No,' I concede, 'but we must admit reforms are needed.'

She smiles: 'Quite so, we agree on that. But they don't. Boris Johnson is not about to reform government and business.'

I sigh: 'The Boris premiership is a symptom of the problem, not the cure, sure. If that's the best the Conservatives can do, then it's not the party for me. But again – Corbyn is not the answer.'

Roger disagrees again. I reply, and off we go again. Corbyn's ideas are too parochial, I say, too British.

Maggie replies: 'We all accept that some problems need solving internationally. I'm as European as anyone, and so is Roger.' She prods him: 'Aren't you, dear?'

Roger nods: 'I support the European Union too. It guarantees workers' rights and environmental standards. The Tories can't be trusted to maintain them.'

I sit back: 'Right …' I couldn't disagree with that.

We talk on. My old memories flood back. Then we step out into the solar radiation field and depart.

It's a hot summer. Temperatures exceed forty degrees Celsius across Europe. Talk of climate change dominates the media.

—

July brings the fiftieth anniversary of the glorious culmination of the Apollo mission to put men on the Moon. I was a teenager back then, and the Apollo climax was a defining experience in my life. My basic faith in the power of physics and mathematics to solve human problems was implanted then. I'm an Apollo man.

My long march through the institutions – through Oxford, the Ministry of Defence, the German business world, and the Conservative party – never quite erased my ambition to achieve clarity on the deeper questions of physics and maths.

But my thoughts lead me to views I find hard to explain. Still, I keep trying, and my swansong attempt emerges in the high summer of 2019 as a long essay titled *Omniscience*.

As with my earlier essay *The Answer*, this is key.

I recall my big idea: 'A mindworld is a virtual reality, and we, the gamers, are avatars inside that reality. … Modelling a mindworld as a ranked universal set is a natural first step toward formalising the science of consciousness.'

I recall psychology: 'An embodied mind is an agent, or an implementation or realization of a rational ego, and the ongoing drama of how such an agent grapples with the sensorium is the drama of cognition.'

And physics: 'The Standard Model … fails to accommodate general relativity, which remains our best theory of gravity, and so the problem of building a theory of quantum gravity is our next frontier challenge.'

And my Hamlet question: 'In my set theory model, a ranked mindworld is defined by a set of bits, whereas the next mindworld that is in the process of becoming appears as a vista of qubits. The process of stepping forward from mindworld to mindworld is a matter of popping the qubits to define the next rank of bits in our newly ranked mindworld. We might even define an existential question: "Does this mindworld exist?" A qubit poised between 0 and 1 codes the answer.'

Then comes breaking news: 'A more recent proposal that now excites me is that entanglement relations define the Planck network underlying spacetime. … My gloss on entanglement is that it shows spacetime growing, budding forth at the leading edge.'

My brainstorm: 'By reducing the arrow of time to the logic of disentanglement, to the process of popping qubits down to bits, as if the course of history were a long march over a cosmic sheet of bubble-wrap, a theory embracing entanglement would represent a complete revolution in our understanding of spacetime.'

A last hurrah: 'Our minds expand to universal dimensions and maintain a grip on the truth as they do so. This is reassuring, even to humble human beings whose minds are mostly preoccupied with relatively trivial things.'

—

Back on Planet Earth, President Trump pits America against Iran and China, without allies, a goal, or a plan.

His unholy godfather Putin says liberalism is obsolete. Putin's claim chimes with those of Trump and the Brexiteers.

Meanwhile, Boris has boxed himself in. He's set a hard deadline of Halloween to do or die. A no-deal exit will force him to return to the table with the EU after wrecking his negotiating position.

Trump tries again to boost his UK sidekick: 'We have a really good man who's going to be the prime minister of the UK now, Boris Johnson. Good man, he's tough and he's smart. They're saying Britain Trump [*sic*] … He's going to do a good job.'

Fintan O'Toole says Johnson has learnt too much from his boyhood hero Winston Churchill, whom O'Toole dismisses as an unprincipled opportunist, a serial bungler, and an untrustworthy egotist. Boris is the natural new Churchill for old England.

For O'Toole, Johnson's true genius is to create popular complicity with his clownish persona. His brandishing of a kipper to defame Europe yet again was camp self-parody. The performance was everything, not a lie but a pantomime joke.

To back up his cabinet, Johnson appoints Dominic Cummings as his chief special advisor (or 'spad' in the lingo). Cummings is an Oxford history grad who spent years doing odd jobs in Russia before getting hired by Faragists and Brexiteers to mastermind the Vote Leave campaign in 2015.

Cummings is fizzing with wild ideas and seething with unresolved hostilities: 'Before the 2016 referendum, I and a few others knew that the systemic dysfunction of UK institutions and the influence of grotesque incompetents provided an opportunity for extreme leverage. … Vote Leave hacked the referendum. Such opportunities are rare.'

Chief spad Cummings tells the new cohort of spads their first loyalty is to Johnson and their primary objective is to achieve Brexit.

Toward the end of July, Johnson visits the Faslane Trident submarine base in Scotland and boards HMS Victorious, one of the Royal Navy's four V-class nuclear submarines carrying the British nuclear deterrent. There he poses with his finger on the button, ready to unleash thermonuclear fire and fury on his foes.

His Brexit strategy is mutually assured destruction, MAD. His 'Brexit war cabinet' assembles on Monday. Every minister is 'turbocharged' to prepare for the great no-deal offensive on Halloween.

Johnson visits the four nations that make up the UK. He wants the world to know he loves the awesome foursome, even though for English nationalists, Brexit really means England First.

Johnson and his team are threatening the EU with MAD. A cabinet minister says: 'The EU will give us a better deal because if they don't, Ireland is fucked. No-deal will destroy it. No-deal hurts us, the EU, and Ireland, but it hurts Ireland the most.'

Brexit is now a hostage drama. Johnson is the shooter, Ireland is the captive, and the backstop is the ransom. He says: 'Drop the backstop or we'll kill the hostage in a no-deal shootout.'

In August, a newspaper publishes leaked details of Operation Yellowhammer. This is the plan to run a no-deal Brexit from the Brexit war room. It empowers ministers to impose curfews, redirect food supplies, and change laws on the fly.

The war plan assumes that France will impose controls on UK goods, French customs will hold up lorries going to Calais, UK citizens will face new border checks, supplies of medicines and fresh food will be disrupted, data sharing will end, financial services will be cut, a hard border may be reimposed in Ireland, Spain will harden the border with Gibraltar, UK nationals will lose their EU citizenship and rights to services, the UK may block EU and EEA fishing vessels from its waters, and many prices and costs will rise. *Ouch!*

The Queen approves Johnson's request to 'prorogue' parliament until 14 October. MPs cry foul. A petition calling on Johnson not to do so is soon signed by well over a million people.

To escape the madness, I watch the annual Bournemouth air show over the seafront. Again, it features a patriotic memorial to the British air war in World War Two.

A Spitfire flies alongside a Spanish Buchon fighter, which is a licence-built Messerschmitt 109 powered by a Rolls-Royce Merlin instead of a Daimler-Benz engine. It's the one that flew in the movie *Dunkirk*.

Together with this pair, an American pair comprising a Mustang and a Thunderbolt complete the awesome foursome of warbirds performing their aerial ballet over the seascape.

I watch their mock combat end with smoke trailing from the

Messerschmitt as it flies off low. The idea is that the good guys have seen off a bad guy.

I'm offended by its vulgarity. I recall Joseph Goebbels' advice to Germans suffering total war that they should ask how they'd be portrayed in the postwar movies and go down like heroes.

In this hot summer, Greta Thunberg reminds me of such aerial theatre when she says: 'They keep saying that climate change is an existential threat and the most important issue of all. And yet they just carry on like before.'

—

On the last Saturday of August, I walk briskly along the seafront from Poole to Bournemouth. It's a sunny morning.

I'm on my way to the 'Stop the Coup' rally that *Dorset 4 Europe* are holding in Bournemouth Square. The coup is Johnson's attempt to prorogue parliament and do or die on Halloween.

A big group of protesters has assembled. I hang around on the fringe as it moves into the gardens. A parliamentary employee like me shouldn't take sides in public.

In the gardens, the group gathers around a wooden box stage flanked by loudspeakers. I walk around taking photos as various punters take the stage. Half an hour of thrilling live action later, I've had enough and sneak off for the beach.

On the morning after this rally, Boris Johnson says to a BBC TV camera: 'We need to get a deal done. Parliament has had three whole years for delectable disputations on this matter without successfully resolving it. ... We're trying to put a bit of a tiger in the tank, put our pedal to the metal, foot to the floor.'

On Monday, he threatens to 'remove the whip' from Tory MPs who voted in the Commons to block a no-deal Brexit. The whip here is the privilege of being a member of the parliamentary Conservative and Unionist Party, and it's administered by an MP called a whip who makes sure members vote along party lines. Sir Robert was a whip for years, and it gives him clout within the party.

The UK is an elective dictatorship. Because it's based on an unwritten constitution, it's wide open to rogues. Johnson is now using prorogation to foreclose parliamentary opposition to his hard line on Halloween.

The UK constitution boils down to a statement in the 1689 Bill of Rights: Whatever receives royal assent in parliament is law. The idea is that the Crown delegates its sovereignty to anyone commanding a majority in parliament. This gives a prime minister what used to be known as the divine right of kings.

On Tuesday, the Commons passes a motion to make it illegal for the UK to leave the EU on Halloween without a deal. Johnson says this only makes it harder for him in Brussels. He says EU leaders will relent only when they see the UK is about to jump.

A snap election would be the quickest way out of the mess. Voters would face a choice between Johnson and a probable no-deal Brexit, and Corbyn and an extreme left-wing government. Tory wits say the choice is between the strong possibility of chaos on the one hand and the absolute certainty of it on the other.

But Johnson is losing control. He can't even call a snap election. After this defeat in his first Commons vote, he takes his revenge. He strips the whip from the Tory rebels.

On Wednesday, Johnson prepares to face his first prime minister's questions. As I watch it on the parliamentary TV channel, it sinks into slapstick farce. Corbyn is Caracas! It wasn't funny when he first used the gag years ago. The opposition is shit! Corbyn is a big girl's blouse!

Johnson waffles when Corbyn asks about the Brexit negotiations. The Joker is refusing to take parliament or the negotiations seriously.

The Commons has voted to defer an election until the Brexit delay bill is law. Johnson wants to fight that election. He wants to frame it as a contest between parliament and the people and to tar his opponents as collaborators with the European enemy. He calls the bill to block a Halloween Brexit 'Corbyn's surrender bill'.

On Thursday afternoon, Johnson delivers a shambolic speech to police cadets in Yorkshire. He takes the stage late and speaks gibberish. At home, I watch his meltdown and groan.

Someone asks him a question: 'Can you comment on your promise to never seek a Brexit delay from the EU?'

His reply reveals his despair: 'Yes, I can. I'd rather be dead in a ditch. What on Earth is the point of further delay? I think it's totally, totally pointless. I hate banging on about Brexit.'

———

On Friday, I'm in the office as usual when Sir Robert comes in. He mumbles curt greetings, sits at his table, and attends to his papers.

After a while, he stands up with a paper and strides toward the photocopier. He looks down at me with blank eyes like a deer caught in headlights and asks: 'Everything okay?'

'Well, as okay as you might expect when parliament is on the point of meltdown. What's happening there?'

He pauses to answer: 'We always knew it was going to be turbulent. We just need to box through in parliament until it sorts itself out. Without a majority, it's hard to do anything, so the best we can do is push for an election as soon as possible.'

I don't buy it: 'But prorogation? Suspending the whip from party moderates? This is a dishonourable way to behave. I suppose you all think it's business as usual.'

'No, it's not business as usual. This is not normal, this a knife fight.'

'Well, I'd call it outrageous. The government can't just ram Brexit through like this, without proper procedure or time for debate on the backstop problem and the rest. That's not the way we do things in Britain, or it never used to be, anyway.'

He sighs: 'I know, it looks bad. But parliament has had three years to debate Brexit, and all we're doing is going around in circles. We need to get on with it, get it done by the end of October. Then things will look better again.'

'Get Brexit done with no deal? Have you read the Operation Yellowhammer report? It would be a disaster. No one is prepared.'

He flutters his forgotten paper: 'The civil servants who wrote the report were over-egging it. Life will go on. It will all look better by Christmas.'

I sigh: 'I very much doubt it.'

He sits down again and attends to his work. Then he looks up, turns on his chair, and says: 'Boris Johnson is still feeling his way. He needs a few more weeks to get settled in the saddle. Once Brexit is done, he'll relax, and things will get back to normal again.'

I'm still way out of line: 'Boris is thrashing around as if he's drowning. He's making a horrible mess. After his … disappointing stint as foreign secretary, I find it hard to see how anyone in the party can repose any confidence in him.'

'It wasn't that bad,' he says quietly.

'It was bad enough. It wasn't the performance you'd expect of a future prime minister. Do you really trust him to deliver?'

'Yes, I think he can still rescue the situation. He's very popular in the party, and if anyone can deliver Brexit on time, he can.'

'For me, that's precisely the problem. Half the population isn't ready for this.'

'Well, I'm prepared to trust him.'

'And I'm not. I find him insufferable.'

Robert goes back to his papers. Minutes later, he packs his bag and walks out, with barely a word to Pam and me.

The bill to prevent a no-deal Brexit on Halloween clears the House of Lords. It will become law on Monday when it receives royal assent.

On Saturday morning, I walk along the sunlit seafront to Bourne-mouth again. I'm off to another 'Stop the Coup' rally in the gardens. I've agreed to speak.

The rally is much like last week. My EU hoodie is too hot. I go to the sales table and see a fine blue *Dorset 4 Europe* tee on display. I buy it and put it on.

The organiser turns to me at last: 'Our next speaker, Andy, is a local political activist, is that right?'

'Yes, that's right.' I take the mike and step onto the stage.

I begin: 'I'm a local activist and I've worked quite closely for years with the Poole councillors. For me, the national situation is clear. A no-deal Brexit will be disastrous for us all. Anyone who reads the Operation Yellowhammer report can see we're not prepared for a no-deal Brexit. Half of the population is not prepared for any Brexit. This is no basis for the government to push us off the cliff on Halloween.'

I'm getting good applause. I continue: 'All the evidence shows that there is no strong popular mandate for Brexit. Vote Leave and the Brexiteers won their majority in the 2016 referendum with lies and trickery. Rich backers with Russian money and Dominic Cummings together plotted to poison the referendum with propaganda and false promises. The result offers no good basis for Brexit. The government needs a new mandate before doing something so big and so irreversible.'

More applause. 'Boris Johnson is a Brexit extremist. He and the other members of the ERG are presenting a completely distorted picture of the EU. The EU is not the enemy. The old guard who still think in the stereotypes from the war are the enemy. They are spreading the nonsense that EU members are out to trick us or cheat us or exploit us. That whole picture is nonsense.'

I add some oomph: 'The EU is an organisation dedicated to

peace in Europe and to the continuing prosperity of its members. In the EU view, the Brexiteers are behaving like the nationalists in Hungary or Poland, or like Putin or Trump. This is dangerous. We want to remain friends and partners with people in Europe.'

I get personal: 'I worked for a couple of decades in Germany. No one I worked with had a problem with the EU. We all saw it as a good thing, good for peace and good for prosperity. We all agreed that working with each other is better than working against each other. There is no danger for Britain there. Again, the EU is not the enemy.'

I begin to wrap up: 'We need to stop Boris Johnson from going ahead with his hard Brexit. Most people agree we'll have a general election soon. That will be our chance to get rid of Boris and his band of Brexiteers.'

My conclusion: 'But the opposition is divided. The only way to be sure of getting Boris out of power is to think and vote tactically. Look at the candidates on offer and vote for the one who not only opposes Brexit but also has the best chance of being elected. We need a second referendum at least. If possible, we want to revoke Article 50 before it's too late. We have to get the Brexiteers out of power, and the only way to do so is to vote tactically.'

The applause is spirited.

I've broken free.

25. Apollo, Enigma, and goodbye

Amber Rudd says on Sunday morning television she's resigning as secretary of state for work and pensions and surrendering the Conservative whip.

My phone beeps with a text message from Sir Robert: 'Why do I have voice mails from other association officers and a couple of journalists all wanting me to ring them about you?'

I tell him: 'I spoke at a "Stop Brexit" rally in Bournemouth on Saturday. … I guess I will have to resign.'

He replies quickly: 'Wish you had talked to me first … I know you feel strongly about Brexit.'

I text back: 'Okay, thanks for five fascinating years. You know my problem with Boris.'

Job done.

———

I rise early on Monday and jump into my BMW. I drive to London, park in Richmond, and take the tube into central London.

I stride briskly from South Kensington tube station through a tunnel to the Science Museum. This is my favourite museum, where I've spent countless hours over the years.

I make straight for the Energy Café, where Steve and Graham are patiently waiting for me over coffee. In a museum where many of the visitors are kids, I'm startled to see a pair of white-haired old men looking my way. I buy a coffee and join them.

'I did it,' I tell them. 'I burned my bridge to the Conservative party. Resigned yesterday after giving a speech at an anti-Brexit rally in Bournemouth on Saturday.'

Graham smiles: 'Good for you! Does that mean you're out of a job now?'

'Yes, that's the downside. It was a nice top-up for the pension.

But when your boss is a Brexiteer you can't really go speaking in rallies against Brexit.'

Steve looks thoughtful: 'How long had you been there?'

'Five years. Long enough to know what the party line is and that I had no chance of changing it. For them it was Brexit or bust.'

'I don't see how anyone could support Boris,' says Graham. 'What's happening now in parliament is a horror show.'

'How do you think it will turn out?' Steve asks.

I frown: 'There's sure to be an election soon, and Boris will be the front runner. The opposition is divided and unlikely to come together quickly or solidly enough. But the Brexiteers are united. Nigel Farage is not going to rock the boat for Boris when they're so near their dream goal. So, altogether, I'd say we have a problem.'

Silence falls.

We start our tour in the space hall, where missiles of all shapes and sizes are on show around a real Apollo capsule and a full-size mock-up of the Eagle lunar lander. We pause in front of a display of missile models, all to the same scale, from the wartime German V2 rocket up to the Apollo Saturn Five booster.

I point at them: 'Amazing to think that one man, Wernher von Braun, took us from the V2, there, all the way to the Saturn Five, there.'

Graham looks interested: 'Was he where it all started?'

'Pretty much, yes. His V2 was the first serious rocket, first used in 1944. He led the project – it was even bigger than the Manhattan project. After the war, the Americans snapped him up and got him building rockets for the US Army. Then he joined NASA, the rockets got bigger, and he ended up building the Saturn Five for the moonshots. Incredible career progression.'

'He was very lucky,' says Steve. 'He was a Nazi, and his first rockets were built with slave labour.'

'Yes, but you can forgive him a lot when he gives you a delivery system for your nukes and years of supremacy over the Soviets.'

'What about the Soviets?' Graham asks. 'Weren't their rockets even bigger?'

'No, there's a Vostok launcher for comparison. The Russians have been using derivatives of it ever since. Again, they started with a bunch of Nazi rocket scientists. But the American Nazi rocket scientists were smarter than the Russian Nazi rocket scientists.'

'They had more money, at least,' adds Steve.

'I'd say von Braun was a genius, a true visionary. He imagined fleets of spaceships colonising the solar system.'

Steve shakes his head: 'That's just Nazi megalomania.'

'Why were the Soviet rockets smaller?' Graham asks.

'They never sent men to the Moon. But the Soviet intercontinental ballistic missiles for delivering nuclear warheads – there – tended to be bigger than American ones.'

Graham nods: 'Aha, that's what I thought.'

'The Americans didn't need such big ones because they'd mastered the art of miniaturising their nuclear warheads. And they were more accurate, so they could use warheads with lower yields. The Soviets used big multimegaton warheads so that even if they missed, they'd destroy the targets.'

'What about the Brits?' asks Steve. 'What did we use?'

'Well, at first we used bombers like the Vulcan to deliver nukes. Then we bought American missiles – Polaris Poseidon, Trident.'

'Maybe Brexit is all about the missiles,' he muses. 'If you have to choose between Europe and America, choose the people who make the missiles for your nukes.'

We examine more rockets, then decide to go up to the top of the museum and work down. We start with the flight hall on the third floor, where aircraft hang from the ceiling over our heads.

I wave upward: 'Ah, look at that Supermarine floatplane – what a beauty!'

266 ANDY ROSS

'What's special about it?' Graham asks.

'It won the Schneider Trophy in 1931 – and it won the world airspeed record. It was clocked at over four hundred miles an hour. Its designer went on to design the Spitfire. And its engine was made by Rolls-Rolls – it was a predecessor to the Merlin.'

Graham smiles: 'Oh, okay, I suppose that's historic, then.'

'What's that one up there?' Steve asks.

'That's a Messerschmitt 163 – the world's first rocket plane. It flew in combat in 1944 against American bombers. It could fly at over a thousand kilometres an hour, but it only had enough fuel for a few minutes of flight.'

Steve looks puzzled: 'Was it any good?'

'In principle, yes. But they were dangerous and difficult to fly. The Germans didn't have time to refine them.'

Graham looks up: 'What about that one, British, isn't it?'

'Yes, the Gloster Whittle jet. That was a test plane that first flew in 1941. It was the first British jet plane.'

'Ah, a British first then.'

'Not quite. The Germans got there first with a Heinkel jet in 1939. And the German engine design was better. The Whittle jet used a centrifugal flow system, whereas the Germans used axial flow from the start. All modern jets use axial flow.'

'You're obviously the expert on all this,' Steve says. 'Tell us which other planes we need to see.'

We move on to the mathematics and information halls on the second floor. We admire the big Victorian-era Babbage engine for calculating trig and log tables. Peaceful stuff.

Graham declares: 'I want to see the "Top Secret" exhibition in the basement before we run out of time.'

Steve agrees: 'Yes, me too. Let's go down there now.'

Down we go. The exhibition room has a low ceiling and a labyrinthine layout, but it suits the spy story.

'I suppose Alan Turing is the star of this section,' says Steve.

'Yes, probably,' I reply. 'Another genius from Cambridge, after Newton and Darwin.'

'Would you put him in that league?'

'I think so, yes. His Turing machines were computers. That's big. People call him the father of computer science. I studied the mathematical background of all this. I read his original paper on what he called the decision problem. It was important.'

Graham asks: 'He broke the Enigma machine, didn't he?'

'Yes, but I think the movie simplified the story a bit. A bunch of Polish logicians before the war had done the basic work. He scaled up their solution and tweaked it to run fast enough on a big machine to crack the code in hours.'

'Why did the Nazis trust the Enigma machine?'

'For the same reason that banks around the world today trust prime factor encryption – because the basic maths of it suggests we're orders of magnitude away from being able to crack it. The Nazis hadn't reckoned with advances in machine decryption.'

'How did the Enigma machine work?'

'It jumbles up the letters of your messages according to a secret recipe. You need to run the machine in reverse to sort them out again. They changed the code every day, so Turing only had a few hours to crack it. They thought it was secure.'

Steve asks: 'How come you know all this?'

'In Germany, in publishing, I worked for years with a professor in Munich who'd written a mathematical textbook on decryption. I helped him translate it into English and prepare a new edition. It was a brilliant book, but quite hard going.'

Graham frowned. 'Turing built the first computer, didn't he?'

'Not quite. His Colossus machine, the one that cracked Enigma, was maybe the first important machine, but it first appeared in 1943. A German chap in Berlin built a computer in 1941.'

Steve smiles: 'Really?'

'Yes, Konrad Zuse. I translated his autobiography into English. He was a student and built it at home, but the RAF bombed them and destroyed it.'

'Okay, but Turing made something useful.'

'So did Zuse. He built machines for calculating aerofoils for aircraft manufacturers and for building flying bombs, the fore-runners to the V1 buzz-bombs, if you remember those.'

'Yes, of course,' he says. 'But Turing actually won the war. That counts for more, I think.'

'Well, at least he did more to win the war than anyone else except Winston Churchill, perhaps, but it was a team effort. And the Colossus machine was optimised for just one task.'

Graham was thinking. 'Don't Americans say they invented the first computer?'

'Yes, it was called ENIAC. After the war, John von Neumann used it to design the H-bomb. That was the first general-purpose, Turing-complete computer, as we say.'

'Fascinating,' muses Steve. 'So, after all that, where is Britain now in all this top-secret stuff?'

I wave at a nearby scale model of the General Communications Headquarters in Cheltenham: 'There it is – GCHQ – where our secret services read our emails and conduct cyberwar and so on.'

Steve studies it: 'Bletchley Park on steroids, I suppose.'

'Yes, exactly, this is the British contribution to the Five Eyes global spy network.'

Graham nods knowingly. 'Big Brother.'

Soon we move on to the posh Polish club across the road from the museum to get a good meal before going our separate ways.

———

I catch up with political news the next morning. MPs have passed a motion to release the Operation Yellowhammer documents. Boris

Johnson has lost his sixth parliamentary vote in six days, and MPs have again rejected his call for an immediate election.

The Westminster parliament is finally prorogued in the early hours after midnight to scenes of chaos and anger in the House of Commons. As the speaker John Bercow begins the formal proceedings for prorogation, a group of opposition MPs carrying signs reading 'silenced' drown out the ceremonial figure of Black Rod as she tries to enact the ancient ritual.

Several MPs get into a scuffle near the speaker's chair. It's like an attempt by members in 1628 to prevent the speaker proroguing parliament at the behest of King Charles the First, who was then beheaded. That little spat led to the English Civil War.

While Bercow completes the formalities in the House of Lords, opposition MPs sing rousing songs, including the socialist classic *Red Flag* (with its great line 'We'll keep the Red Flag flying here'), *Jerusalem* by William Blake ('And was Jerusalem builded here, among these dark satanic mills'), *Scots Wha Hae* by Robbie Burns ('Let us do or die!'), and the hymn *Bread of Heaven* in Welsh, with harmonies.

It isn't quite civil war, but it's close. I then take time composing my resignation letter (inspired by Amber Rudd's letter from the weekend) and mailing it to my parliamentary inbox.

I keep it diplomatic: 'I am grateful to have had the honour of serving you in your parliamentary duties for the last five years or so. My departure is not due to any personal dissatisfaction with our working relationship but is entirely motivated by my inability to reconcile my conscience and sense of the national interest with the recent conduct and policies of HM Government.'

On the next day, 11 September, I go into the office to enact the last rites. I dress down in blue jeans and a blue polo shirt.

Sir Robert and Pam are both there. Robert sits looking anxiously friendly and Pam sits facing her computer screen as usual.

'Hello,' I begin, 'I've come to give you my resignation letter.

First, I have to log on and print it out.'

'Go ahead, no pressure,' says Robert. 'I'll sit and wait.'

I log on and print the letter. *Shit.* 'I'm sorry, I've left a typo in it. I'll have to go back home to fix it, then come back to print it. Sorry – I'll be back in half an hour.'

Robert smiles tightly: 'No problem. I'll still be here.'

I race back home, fix the typo, update the date, mail it again, and race back to the office. Back in my chair, I print it and sign it.

'Here you are, Robert, my resignation letter.'

He reads it quickly and lays it gently on a pile of papers. Then he stands up and extends his hand.

'Well, I'd like to thank you for your work. You've been a great help to me, and I've enjoyed our conversations.'

'Thank you,' I reply, 'It's been a pleasure working for you, and I wish you well in the rest of your parliamentary career.'

'Yes, all the best,' he says. 'Will you manage on your pension?'

'I hope so. If I go back to Germany, there are plenty of ways I can earn money, teaching or editing or translating.'

'Well, take care.' He sits down again.

Now Pam stands up. 'Let me say goodbye properly,' she says.

We embrace for a few seconds, cheek to cheek.

'Goodbye,' she says, 'And thanks for all your help in the office.'

'It was a pleasure. Oh, I was going to cancel my party member-ship.'

Robert speaks up from behind: 'You can do that later. Perhaps you'll change your mind – there's always hope.'

I smile: 'Okay, no hurry.'

Pam adds: 'You can drop in any time for that – or just to say hello.'

'Indeed, no problem. Well, goodbye.'

And off I go. A chapter in my working life is over.

—

Later that day, Scotland's highest civil court rules against Johnson's suspension of parliament. They judge that both his advice to the Queen and the prorogation were unlawful, null, and of no effect.

A government spokesperson immediately says Downing Street will appeal against the ruling to the supreme court in London.

A European parliament resolution says the UK government 'insists that the backstop must be removed from the withdrawal agreement but has not until now put forward legally operable proposals that could replace it' and says MEPs won't ratify a trade agreement unless the UK agrees to maintain high levels of environmental, employment, and consumer protections.

In short, there's still a lot of ammunition for battles over Brexit or over any future trade negotiations.

If Johnson gets his Brexit on Halloween, his backers stand to make hundreds of millions out of the disaster. Most of them backed him in 2016 too, when they funded the Vote Leave campaign and took short positions on the referendum result.

The prime minister has an obvious conflict of interest. The vulture capitalists bankrolling him can expect rich pickings from the sinking of HMS Brexitannia.

26. Leopard joy, hippy chick

This Saturday is Tiger Day at Bovington Tank Museum. I drive there in my BMW. My sister Helen, her husband David, and her son Dane and daughter Andrea go together in David's roomier car. For all five of us, the trip is like a day at the races, an opportunity to see a field of tanks show off in the big stadium.

It's a sunny day with a cloudless blue sky, and I have my camera. I wear bush hat, tan shirt, and old US Army camo pants.

The parked display we admire before the action starts includes a lot of old German army gear from the war, lovingly preserved by unpaid hobbyists, who seem especially fond of Wehrmacht motorcycle combos with machine guns attached.

We enter the stadium for the main event. It's crowded on the grass. I soak up the circus vibe as the punters from suburbia chat and wait patiently for the gladiators to enter the arena.

The combat zone is laid out as a circuit, with a trench and a bridge and a big grass patch in the middle. A wartime German assault gun, looking squat and ugly under its armoured top on a Panzer hull, is parked on the grass to set the tone. Just beyond the circuit, screened by trees, more tanks are waiting to lurch out and face the crowd.

The first tank to roar into view is a modern British Challenger. I guess it's here to outshine the older hardware that follows. The show aims to excite young boys to dream of an army career, where they can continue the proud British tradition of humbling overseas foes in victorious feats of arms.

Next on are the bikers, riding their old German combos around like Hell's Angels, but looking quaint and puny compared to the heavy metal in the stadium. Then comes a wartime US Army half-track mounting a quad pack of heavy machine guns for shooting down aircraft but used most famously in the Korean War as a 'meat chopper' to cut men down by the score.

The next act is an old dame called 'The Princess Royal' – a Matilda tank, as fielded by the British army in France in 1940 and in the Western Desert against General Rommel's Afrika Korps. This princess has heavily armoured skirts, but they slow her down badly, and her main weapon is a puny little two-pounder gun that looks like a peashooter.

Without more ado, the Matilda is followed by the main act – the mighty Tiger, the most dreaded weapon in the wartime German arsenal so far as British troops were concerned. I know this Tiger well and have admired it from both near and far many times. British troops captured it intact in Tunisia in 1943, and Winston Churchill took a good look at it before it was shipped off to England.

For me, this big beast, with its thick armour, its powerful Maybach V12 engine, and its fearsome 88-millimetre gun firing a sixteen-pound armour-piercing shot, is a good reason to respect German engineering. Tanks like the Matilda were no contest for it. Even after D-Day, against up-gunned US Sherman tanks, the kill ratio was at least five to one in favour of the Tiger. The only consolation for the Allies was that there weren't many of them.

In fact, the Tiger was too heavy, too complicated, too expensive, and too much fuss in the field. Its interleaved road wheels spread the load evenly on soft ground, but they were hard work to replace. All modern tanks have separate road wheels.

As the Tiger chugs and clatters around the circuit a few times, lurching every time the driver pulls a brake lever to steer right or left or wrestles with a gearchange, all the while emitting the sweet rumble of a well-tuned motor from its fat exhaust stacks, I sigh.

The next act is a wartime British Churchill tank, fielded at about the same time as the Tiger but no competition for it. It has a six-pounder gun, like the guns that with three hits dinged the captured

Tiger and prompted its crew to bail out. Then come a few more boring old-timers.

The next fun tank for me is the Sherman that starred in the movie *Fury*, with a grizzled Brad Pitt as its commander. This war veteran is glammed up for the show, with bags and boxes and cables and logs all over it, plus mud and a few dents, to give it that battle-hardened patina that makes a hunk of heavy metal look like a war machine.

After the Sherman comes a British Comet tank, designed with the Tiger experience in mind but too late for more than a few weeks of combat in Germany. It was the first British tank to be able to put up a decent fight against a Tiger.

Then comes a real delight for me. It's a German army Leopard from the Cold War era. Designed to avoid the weaknesses of the Tiger and built to take on the best Russian tanks, which were consistently better than Anglo-American tanks in World War Two, the Leopard in action is a joy to behold. Built by Porsche and packing a powerful modern diesel engine, not weighed down with too much armour, and sporting a big NATO-standard gun, the Leopard bounds around the arena, sending up big clouds of dust as it follows through on its handbrake turns.

Then the British Challenger comes back to round off the show.

Fazit: Tanks can be more fun than politics.

———

As I relax from Tiger Day, Liberal Democrat leaders at their party conference in Bournemouth on Sunday pledge to cancel Brexit if they're granted the power at the next general election. Members vote for the policy by an overwhelming majority. Their new leader Jo Swinson affirms: 'We will do all we can to fight for our place in Europe and to stop Brexit altogether.'

Sir Vince Cable explains: 'Liberal Democrats will campaign to cancel Brexit by revoking Article 50. Following a general election, should our party win a majority, that would be a sufficient mandate to revoke. [We] could close down the Brexit issue and overhaul UK constitutional arrangements in a democratic revolution.'

I'm pleased to hear it. That's exactly what I'd like to do.

I'm beginning to take a shine to the Lib Dems. The party is enjoying a resurgence from its coalition debacle by returning to the political centre and standing firm as the party of Remain. No one sees Jo Swinson as a prime minister, but her party could easily hold the balance of power in a hung parliament.

As a philosopher, I like that the Lib Dems occupy the moral high ground. As Chuka Umunna says: 'To be a Remainer is not only to be an advocate of our continued membership of the European Union, it is to hold a set of liberal, internationalist values.'

While the Lib Dems enjoy their moment in the sun, at least one Conservative thinker fears his party has gone over to the dark side. The Tory peer Daniel Finkelstein, also known as the Right Honourable Baron Finkelstein of Pinner, says: 'Boris Johnson's decision to prorogue parliament was wrong and unwise.'

Fazit: British voters now face a clear moral choice.

———

Friday is Climate Action Day. Mass demos are being staged in big cities worldwide to protest government inaction on climate change. July 2019 was the hottest month ever recorded: People in hundreds of cities worldwide endured temperatures above thirty-five degrees Celsius. The years since 2014 have been the warmest since records began. The heat is due to greenhouse gas emissions, say scientists, but getting this through to politicians is hard.

Climate Action Day is warm and sunny down in Dorset, and I decide to join the rally in central Bournemouth. Clad in cargo shorts and my *Dorset 4 Europe* tee, with bush hat, dark glasses, and sandals, I stride briskly past early beachgoers along the sunlit seafront to the square. There I join the crowd of people waving banners and flags and watch as a few noisy chaps shout their stump speeches. One I recognise is the leader of the Poole Xenophobes, the chap who held the council seat I failed to win in 2015.

I take off my glasses and scan the crowd. Yes, another little miracle – I spot the familiar face of my beloved Rachel. She turns and sees me too, and her eyes register a jolt of recognition. I push through the crowd to get beside her.

'Good to see you again,' I say. 'Are you down for the weekend?'

She smiles. 'Yes, visiting the family. How are you?'

'I'm fine. I resigned from my job with Sir Robert and left the party.'

She looks surprised. 'Really? What happened?'

'I spoke out against Brexit here in the gardens just a few weeks ago. Conor Burns naturally complained to Robert, and I resigned on principle. I really can't support the government's Brexit policy, and I can't endorse Boris Johnson as leader, either.'

'Wow,' she gapes. 'Conor complained – did he say more?'

'It was clear enough. I'd advocated tactical voting in the next general election, which would have been against Conor in this seat, obviously.'

'Conor can be hard sometimes. He feels an obligation.'

'Anyway, enough about me. How about you?' I look more closely at her. She's wearing ragged denim cut-off shorts and a loose green T-shirt with an Earth image on the front. Her hair is tied back in a twirl, and her face is as fresh and natural as ever.

She looks good. 'I'm still working for Conor, but I'm getting more involved in other issues, and I may leave him at the end of the year. I'm helping out in a lobby group to legalise cannabis.'

I know about her cannabis work from the group's email actions to lobby MPs. The medical uses of cannabis are becoming ever more attractive, but the government refuses to legalise it. I'm for legalisation, obviously, but Sir Robert isn't.

'I'm glad to hear you're thinking of leaving Conor. His fagging for Boris makes him an enemy for me.'

She looks startled: 'Fagging? What do you mean?'

I grin at her. 'It's what they call being the dogsbody for someone at Eton. Junior boy Conor is the pooper scooper for shaggy dog Boris. Haven't you heard the word?'

She grins back and shakes her head: 'In the abstract, yes, but not for parliamentary work. It's official business.'

'Official or not, Conor fags for Boris. So, if you fag for Conor, then you fag for Boris too. If you're happy with prorogation, sacking moderate MPs, and so on, fine. But count me out. My honour as a philosopher demands no less.'

The crowd is making too much noise. I pause, shake my head, and look out over the audience at the current stump speaker, whose words are almost drowned out.

'I'm getting too hot here,' says Rachel. 'I'm going to stand in the shade – perhaps under those trees.'

'Me too – shall we go and get a lemonade at the café there?' I wave at the nearby café in the centre of the square.

'Ah, yes, under the canopy, by the door, for shade.'

We go and sit under the canopy, where a small table for two stands vacant. She shucks off a small rucksack and sits down with a sigh. I take off my hat and glasses and go inside to buy two glasses of lemonade, then sit down beside her.

'I don't think the rally is going to do much,' she says.

'I agree. I'd rather be on the beach.'

She reaches down and loosens her sneakers, then slips them off and flexes her feet in white sockettes. 'The beach would be worse, for being too hot, I mean.'

'I like to go early in the morning before the crowds arrive.'

'Tell me about the political philosophy of Vladimir Putin.'

'Okay …'

Many minutes later, lemonade glasses empty, we sit back and muse quietly on the pearls of seminal wisdom I've produced for my intellectual mistress. I've said what little I know about Marxism, Leninism, and the fascism of the Russian philosophers that Putin admires, and I've related them to German philosophy and hinted at the limits of Anglo-American orthodoxy in face of such ideas.

'I want to walk down to the seafront,' she says suddenly, climate protest now forgotten.

'Great idea, me too.'

'But the shoes are too much.' She stares down at them.

'Put them in your rucksack.'

'Yes.' She reaches down to peel off the sockettes.

I look at the sack doubtfully. 'Is there room in it?'

'Yes, all I have in it are cards and keys.' She opens it and thrusts a hand in. 'Oh, and my bikini top.'

I smile. 'Just the top?'

'I'm wearing the bottom.' She pushes the shoes in – they just fit – and zips up the flap. 'Ready to go.'

I pay the bill, we walk out across the smoothly paved square to the lower gardens, and the disappointingly small rally continues tamely behind us.

I glance at the slender hippy chick walking beside me and recall a new movie: 'Have you seen *Once Upon a Time in Hollywood* yet?'

The film is Quentin Tarantino's take on the Sharon Tate story. I love its nostalgic evocation of the summer of '69, the climactic summer of the Apollo project.

'Yes,' she smiles and glances at me. 'I know, in these shorts I look like that hippy girl, what was her name?'

'Pussy, that's what they called her.'

'In the story, yes, but it was Margaret someone, the daughter of Andie McDowell.'

'Oh, right.'

'I thought she was good. And I thought Brad Pitt was sexy.'

I recall Brad's role in the tank movie *Fury* but decide not to mention it. 'Yeah, maybe,' I muse, 'More than me, anyway.'

She turns to look at me: 'Do you want to look sexy?'

'Not really. Not my scene at all. I'm a conscientious celibate.'

'Suits you – for a philosopher, I mean.'

We walk down to the beach, wander around for a while talking philosophy, decide not to go swimming, and walk back to the bus stops near the square, where she has a bus to catch.

As we say our goodbyes, she looks into my eyes, or rather my sunglasses. 'Thank you for spending time with me today. It was really nice meeting you again and hearing your news.'

'My pleasure entirely, thank you,' I reply as I move in for a kiss. She turns her head deftly and catches a modest smacker on either cheek. But her hands on my naked arms and my hands on her naked arms convey a tantalising hint of carnal concupiscence. Our hands slide past each other in a moment of haptic intercourse.

I walk back to home base cheered. I held onto my code of conduct, but I felt a bit of a buzz anyway.

Fazit: Even a day at the seaside is a chance for philosophy.

———

I'm still puzzling over why the Anglo-American world has fallen victim to its new maladies. With the help of thinkers like Martin Wolf on the *Financial Times*, I begin to see the flaws in AA capitalism that led to the sudden descent into reckless populism.

I'm tempted to agree with Wolf that the problem is the rise of rentier capitalism. Rent is the economists' jargon word for reward over and above ideal market levels – think of a landlord being paid more rent by his captive tenants than he ploughs back into the properties they occupy. Rentier capitalism is what you get when market and political power enables privileged groups to extract such rent from everyone else.

I say AA capitalism has gone bad. In America, Trump has cut taxes for big corporations. In Britain, Brexit is a scheme to let rich investors run free. After Brexit, deregulated London will be a casino for fund managers to place their bets on disasters and crises galore. The UK will be the go-to haven for Big Money while populist politicians dazzle the masses with pixie dust.

My old flame Judy would offer a simple diagnosis: When economics goes wild, politics is sure to follow – that's Marxism.

———

A fresh rupture in the negotiations in Brussels is looming over Downing Street's underwhelming Brexit proposals. Johnson's government demands that the EU treat its documents as 'Her Majesty's Government property' and not distribute them to member states. EU officials say all the proposals need to be available for analysis. Officials in Brussels are in despair.

The Queen is in no position to insist that her prime minister play by the rules, because in her realm there are no rules. The UK's unwritten constitution has only a few old conventions that amount to a gentleman's agreement on good manners and fair play. The Queen claims to be above politics, leaving her prime minister free to act like the uncrowned king.

The British supreme court in London agrees with the Scottish court that Johnson's prorogation was unlawful. This throws his cunning plan to ram through Brexit on Halloween into disarray.

Johnson is at the United Nations in New York at the time, doing some alpha bonding with President Trump. He simply says: 'I strongly disagree with this decision of the supreme court.'

The president of the supreme court is Brenda Hale, Baroness Hale of Richmond, who gains fame by sporting a spider brooch when she explains the court's unanimous ruling. She says the prime minister's advice to the Queen was unlawful, the prorogation is void and of no effect, and parliament has not been prorogued.

House speaker John Bercow instructs the House authorities to prepare for the resumption of business. MPs return to the House and take up where they left off.

But the government isn't out of tricks yet. Party hacks now propose a motion for a three-day parliamentary recess to give time for the Conservative party conference in Manchester.

MPs defeat the motion – the seventh defeat for Johnson in the seven parliamentary divisions since he became prime minister.

A stormy sitting in the Commons follows. Johnson harangues MPs and says they must deliver Brexit. His language is Trumpian – he rants about surrender and betrayal and brands all those who voted in the Commons to oppose Brexit as traitors.

Johnson is mobilising his base of angry Leavers. He wants to be seen doing battle in the name of the people. This gives him his armour-piercing ammo for the next general election.

All this cutthroat drama leads to a breakdown of trust between the Queen and her prime minister. An unnamed Whitehall source says on behalf of the royals: 'They are not impressed by what is going on, at the very highest levels of the family.'

A palace courtier explains: 'Boris joins Cameron and Blair. Not in the Queen's lifetime will any of them ever receive the garter.'

The garter is the highest honour the Queen can bestow. To be more exact, the Order of the Garter, founded by King Robert the Third in 1348, is the most senior order of knighthood in the system. Legend has it that the Countess of Salisbury was dancing merrily at a court ball in Calais when her garter slipped from her leg. As courtiers sniggered, the king picked it up and returned it to her, saying, in French, 'Shame on any who thinks ill of it!' – which became the order's motto.

The last prime minister to 'receive the garter' was Sir John Major, who's a man of impeccable decency and honour. He's also an active and very vocal Remainer.

———

American Democrats have a plan to impeach President Trump. It seems Trump tried to strong-arm the president of Ukraine to dig for dirt on Joe Biden's son in a bid to swing the 2020 presidential election.

Press pundits say it's an impeachable offense.

Trump hits back: 'These animals in the press … They're scum … I don't know if I'm the most innocent person in the world. I just said I'm the most presidential except for possibly Abe Lincoln when he wore the hat – that was tough to beat. Honest Abe, when he wore that hat, that was tough to beat. But I can't do that, that hat wouldn't work for me. Yeah, I have better hair than him.'

Boris Johnson is an animal from the press too, but his impeachable offence isn't his hair crime. It's Brexit.

I watch the TV coverage of the Conservative party conference in Manchester.

Government ministers file into the conference hall and take their seats to a standing ovation. Stanley Johnson, the new king's father, and Carrie Symonds, the new king's consort, receive a yet warmer ovation. Jubilant exultations fill the hall as the king himself makes his grand entrance.

Boris says Brexit is a breeze and parliament is wasting time. Arguments over Ireland are boring technicalities. If the Irish thing doesn't work out, he can always blame the EU or parliament. He says it's his plan or no deal.

But not long into this free-form oration, the Incredible Hulk has said all he wanted to say and begins to ad-lib. He throws in a few gags that weren't funny when he told them years ago, until it all begins to sound desperate. Party members in search of a vision are fobbed off with a vacuous after-dinner speech.

The European parliament Brexit steering group issues a statement: 'The UK proposals do not match even remotely what was agreed as a sufficient compromise in the backstop.'

Her Majesty's government promises under duress that in the absence of a deal, Johnson will write to Brussels seeking an extension to Article 50, as required by Hilary Benn's surrender act.

Brexit is down to a final extra-time shootout. The shootout is a winner-take-all drama with everything still to play for. After three years of play, the future of Britain is still in the air.

The UK is in crisis.

Brexiteers assume Britain will bask beside the United States in the special relationship. But Trump wants to Make America Great Again. He doesn't give a damn about preserving Great Britain.

27. Marching for the people

On 11 October, EU officials give the green light for the Brexit negotiations to enter 'the tunnel' – the phase where a final deal is hammered out behind closed doors.

I have a date with fellow Remainers at a hotel in Bournemouth, where Lord Adonis will speak on the folly of Brexit. I recall him from the European elections in May, when his eloquence rescued the evening I sat beside Deb and Colin.

It's a rainy evening, and I show up in my nylon biker jacket over a blue fleecy and the *Dorset 4 Europe* tee. I see a few familiar faces among the Remainers in attendance. But I spy no one like Rachel, so I sit alone, swaddled in my stormproof jacket.

I let my thoughts drift back to the Ealing commune in early 1974, when Judy and I sat in meetings very much like this. At her bidding, we campaigned for the local Labour candidate in the February general election that pitted Harold Wilson against Edward Heath and resulted in a hung parliament. The local Tory candidate was the son of a wealthy gin baron and had no clue about how to integrate the Indian community in Ealing, who faced racist discrimination, whereas the Labour man would treat them decently.

The meeting I recall most vividly was one where the Labour hopeful, from the National Union of Railwaymen, introduced himself. Unaccustomed to public speaking, he mumbled these first words: 'Well, I'm a dialectical materialist myself.'

However bad this Remainer meeting turns out to be, it won't be that bad. The dashing Adonis will save it. I wait.

The Labour lord shows up late, flustered, held up by a delayed train. But his minders calm him down, and he's settled when he takes the stage. It's an informal delivery, a chat with people on his side, and there's no need for big oratory.

Andrew Adonis, ennobled as Baron Adonis of Camden Town, served as a minister under Tony Blair and as transport secretary under Gordon Brown. A former Oxford academic and a journalist, his fluency with words is impressive. He's tall, thin, bald, and much younger than me, and he projects an air of nervous dynamism. I listen carefully.

He says about the same as he did for the European election, with differences only in the delivery. But I'm struck by one point especially. In words he used later: 'The fatal flaw of Brexit is the act of putting the UK outside the EU and its future. If we end up in a blind Brexit without a credible plan for our national future, we and our children will pay a steadily greater price until the day we rejoin the EU.'

A brief break precedes the question-and-answer session. People mill around and buy drinks at a bar beside the stage.

I say hello to Vikki Slade, now the leader of the Unity Alliance on the BCP council.

'Hi, Andy, glad to see you here.' She glances at the *Dorset 4 Europe* logo on my T-shirt. 'You ought to come and join us in the Lib Dems. We'd love your support to help us mobilise locally and to get the Brexit message across to our voters.'

'Yes, I'm considering it. I need to do something, and you have the right message. I want to do what I can to spread the word.'

Vikki smiles: 'Great. We look forward to seeing you at one of our meetings.'

The audience settles again for the Q&A session. Once that's done, I go up to Adonis to exchange a few words before he dashes off to catch his train. He's signing copies of his new book, a compilation of words by British prime ministers about Europe.

'Thank you for the speech,' I say. 'I agreed with it all, of course.'

Adonis looks down at my tee without quite reading it: 'I like your logo. *Bournemouth 4 Europe* seems to be well organised.'

'Yes, *Dorset 4 Europe* is a good group. But I'm worried that Boris Johnson has a strong and simple message with "Get Brexit done" while Remainers are still all over the map.'

Adonis looks unworried: 'The polls are in our favour. If young people come out to vote – and vote tactically – we can win.'

'Not in Bournemouth. The older vote dominates here, and they're almost all Leavers. Look, you said you admire Winston Churchill, and you know Boris well. Can't you persuade him that Winston would have backed Remain?'

Aides are pressing Adonis to go before he misses his train. He looks anxious as he grabs his bag and coat: 'I don't think I can change his mind – sorry, I have to go now.'

I watch him go and then go too. Adonis can't turn things around. Boris is unopposed.

On Monday, as the culmination of the orgy of pageantry for the state opening of parliament, the Queen sits on a throne in the Palace of Westminster and delivers a party-political broadcast on behalf of the Conservative party.

———

The Brexit train emerges from the tunnel. On the first day of the big EU summit, European Commission president Jean-Claude Juncker tweets: 'Where there is a will, there is a deal – we have one! It's a fair and balanced agreement for the EU and the UK and it is testament to our commitment to find solutions.'

In parallel, Boris Johnson tweets: 'We've got a great new deal that takes back control – now parliament should get Brexit done on Saturday so we can move on to other priorities.'

It doesn't get done on Saturday. Northern Ireland's Democratic Unionist Party decide not to support the deal. The EU and the UK propose to avoid a hard border on the island of Ireland by asking Northern Ireland to apply EU customs and tariffs rules overseen by the European Court of Justice – a red line for the DUP.

The proposed deal would give Northern Ireland a special status within the UK. Also, it would leave most British citizens poorer. Average personal incomes under the deal would be more than two percent lower than under continued EU membership.

Johnson's deal is mostly identical to Theresa May's deal, but where it differs it's worse. A breakup of the UK is suddenly a real possibility. Yet Brexiteers are undaunted, even jubilant.

As the Right Honourable Jacob Rees-Mogg puts it: 'Let us stagnate no more; let us spring forth and seize the victory people voted for.'

—

On Saturday 19 October, activists assemble for another People's Vote rally in central London. The format is the same as in March, when a million people gathered to glorious effect.

The looming Brexit deadline is less than two weeks away. The hardliners are determined to press on with their bid for sovereignty. The only way to stop them is to vent public outrage.

I must do my bit. The disaster is not yet irrevocable. All it takes is protest on a scale that even Boris and the blowhards can't dismiss as empty virtue signalling. Unfortunately, that looks unlikely. Our action looks set to be a replay of the March rally.

Still, I'm not ready to admit defeat. This time, I drive up to Richmond, where I park and take the tube into the city centre. Otherwise, it's the same procedure – and the same outfit, with EU hoodie and cap. My phone, cards, and keys fit in my pockets.

As before, the crowds in Hyde Park are already huge when I arrive. The dew is still fresh on the grass, and the demonstrators hold up flags and banners, many now with jokes about Boris and Halloween.

As in March, the big drums pound and the shrill whistles blow and off we all go, shuffling down Park Lane, chanting our slogans.

Again, we chant: 'What do we want?' – 'People's vote!'

Again, the second line: 'When do we want it?' – 'Now!'

Again, before long, the favourite: 'Bollocks to Brexit!'

The crowd shuffles along its course, hemmed in by a friendly and polite police presence, and turns from Park Lane into Piccadilly. As before, a few television helicopters hover noisily overhead, recording the event for the evening news. We've surely attracted at least as many people – a million or so – as in March.

We begin our shuffling progress along Piccadilly, but I see it'll take ages to reach Parliament Square. I decide to peel off for lunch beside the way. I step into a side street and find a little supermarket selling the sort of delicatessen fare that appeals to customers in one of the richest parts of London, where Park Lane meets Mayfair.

The little cul-de-sac is crowded in front of the supermarket. The shop has deep-set windows with low sills wide enough to sit on, and diners sit in a row, as well as on the kerbs, knees raised, feet in the gutter, munching food and swigging pop.

I buy a pair of little strawberry-and-cream tarts and a bottle of fresh orange juice, find a space on a windowsill, and get started. Across the street from me, squatting on the edge of the pavement, a pair of girls in short skirts and black tights are noshing like me. With bovine calm, I gaze impassively at their legs as I guzzle down my tarts and juice.

I rejoin the marchers with renewed energy. Further along, the column passes a building where two teenage girls are standing on a balcony overlooking us. One of them, with a loud and penetrating voice, is acting as cheerleader for the mob: 'Bollocks to Brexit!'

The crowd answers back with a volume and a vehemence no one can ignore. She repeats her call, and the crowd responds, again and again and again, until we've moved on. Soon we turn right into St James Street, then left along Pall Mall to Trafalgar Square. From there it looks likely to be a snail's-pace shuffle down Whitehall to Parliament Square.

But when I'm just a block short of Trafalgar Square, a brilliant glimpse of heaven is revealed. A huge television screen mounted above us shows the live proceedings from the House of Commons. The crowd is hard of hearing, thanks to the clamour it's making, but a banner on the screen relays the glad tidings.

On this historic day, 'Super Saturday' as Johnson is calling it, in recognition not only of the amazing fact that MPs are sitting on a Saturday but also because he hopes the day will go down in history as the turning of the tide for Brexit, MPs stop his deal dead. Just moments before I see the news, they inflict another defeat on Boris by passing an amendment withholding their support until the deal becomes law. The margin of victory is five percent.

A whoop of joy erupts from the crowd. Boris is unable to make his Brexit deal law without a majority in parliament – unless his opponents cave in – so he's forced to back down. Under the terms of the Benn act, he's now obliged to write to the EU to request a Brexit delay, and moreover to do so this evening at the latest.

I breath a deep sigh of relief. It's a stay of execution. Halloween is saved.

There seems no further point in subjecting myself to the torture of the mob, civilised though it is, so I dip out and walk speedily up Haymarket to Piccadilly Circus, where I take the tube back to Richmond. Once back in my car, I take off my shoes and socks, breath more sighs of relief, and drive back home barefoot.

———

I catch up with the unfolding story the next morning. Bowing to pressure not graciously but like a vile sneak, Johnson sent three letters to Brussels last night in a bid to make sure the EU doesn't offer him an extension. One letter asks for a delay in accordance with the Benn act, but he refuses to sign it, and a second explains that he didn't write it. In the third, signed letter to Donald Tusk, Johnson says he doesn't want an extension.

Remainers respond with fury and threaten legal action. Tusk says he'll consult with other EU leaders about what to do next. Another Commons vote is expected on Monday.

The cabinet minister in charge of Brexit preparations is Michael Gove, a fussy, precise little man who cuts a boyish figure in the media that belies the icy edge of his clipped manner of speaking for the cause. On the latest moves in the Brexit game, he says: 'If we vote to leave, we get the legislation through. Then there is no extension – October the 31st is within sight.'

After his Super Saturday flop, Johnson yanks his bill, with the intent of reintroducing it later. Too much is at stake to rush it.

Those who expected the Commons sitting on Super Saturday to pass Brexit weren't paying attention. MPs were in no mood to let Johnson bounce them into a do-or-die choice, so they took out an insurance policy against a disorderly Brexit. Johnson's attempts to bully his bill past them have failed.

But far from relenting, Johnson now announces Titanic Tuesday. He asks MPs to vote on the second reading of the bill intended to give legal effect to the deal he's negotiated in Brussels.

Astonishingly, for me at least – I imagined another cliff-hanger here too – they pass it by a comfortable margin.

For Boris, Titanic Tuesday is indeed titanic. The vote on the second reading is the 'meaningful vote' that Theresa May failed to win. It's usually the main obstacle to pushing a bill through the Commons. By contrast, the next step, to read the bill carefully and table amendments, is for most bills a relative formality.

Then the government asks the House to vote for a fast track to pass the bill into law by Halloween. MPs say no, again by a good margin. Johnson responds by accelerating preparations for a no-deal Brexit.

At home, I follow all this on parliamentary TV like a sporting event. If war is politics by other means, politics is war by other means. I'm watching MPs fight the Second English Civil War.

I see the Brexit division as the deepest in British politics since the First English Civil War, which disfigured the middle years of the seventeenth century so badly that it led to the deaths of some four percent of the population in England, six percent in Scotland, and by one reckoning a shocking forty percent in Ireland. That war pitted the Roundheads led by Oliver Cromwell against the Cavaliers led by King Charles the First, who was beheaded for his trouble, and it led to the settlement of 1689 that delegated the monarch's sovereignty to parliament.

The new division between Leavers and Remainers puts a knife between UK sovereignty and an island sovereignty shared with the EU in Brussels. Like the fight between Cavaliers and Roundheads, at stake is the head of the monarch, in this case Boris Johnson.

In 2019, in the new war, diehard Tories are going ape with fury as they watch the party tricks play out in the Commons. A new poll finds that three-quarters of English Conservatives who voted Leave in 2016 would go for Brexit even if it led to Scotland and Northern Ireland leaving the UK. They're backing Boris.

A quick deal still looks possible. The Tory faithful would accept a delay of a few weeks if the alternative were more months of delay for an election. Sir Robert has told me precisely that.

But Johnson's version of Brexit is far too controversial. His shamelessly brutal attempt to bludgeon his bill through the Commons in three days, exploiting a growing national weariness with Brexit, is like a rapist accelerating his assault while his victim is too tired to resist. The notion that an issue with the gravity and magnitude of Brexit – like unwanted sex – should be pushed through without proper consent is an affront to decent people.

Johnson won his 'meaningful vote' in parliament by the same margin that Leavers won their referendum vote in the electorate at large in 2016. But parliament doesn't approve his deal. Many MPs voted for a second reading not to endorse the bill but to amend it – drastically – by insisting on UK membership of a customs union or by conditioning it on another referendum. Johnson is too eager to interpret a vote for a second reading as consent. It isn't, any more than agreeing to 'come up and see my etchings' is consent to sex.

Following Titanic Tuesday, the former UK ambassador to the EU, Sir Ivan Rogers, remarks gloomily: 'I suspect that we will have to live with Boris Johnson for the next ten years.'

The defeats Johnson has suffered since July have only made him stronger. Every path leads to new elections, and he can triumph as the man leading his country to freedom and taking back control. In a December election he could win big.

Sir Ivan is pessimistic: 'We are in deep shit.'

On the evening of the Monday before Halloween, a government motion to hold a general election on Thursday 12 December wins a large majority among the MPs present. But it fails because they're too few to be quorate.

Donald Tusk understands the struggle going on in the UK. He interprets Johnson's three letters as a request for an extension, in accordance with the Benn act. He says the EU will grant a Brexit 'flextension' until the end of January 2020.

On behalf of the Lib Dems, party leader Jo Swinson suddenly reneges on the Remain Alliance agreement to deny Johnson his general election for as long as possible. It's a blunder.

On Tuesday evening, the House of Commons approves the plan to hold a general election on 12 December. If all goes to plan, the next prime minister will be announced the next day.

By the grace of providence, Halloween passes without incident. The devil simply waits to get his revenge on Friday the thirteenth.

Nigel Farage interviews Donald Trump, who says: 'We want to do trade with the UK.'

Other people in the United States are less bullish. A liberal columnist in *The New York Times* says Britain has gone nuts. He imagines historians saying: 'This was their saddest hour.'

Johnson hopes voters will be put off Jeremy Corbyn by the stink of antisemitism and the musty scent of Marxism in Labour. But his Tories are giving out a stink too – a sour tang of toxic masculinity and sweaty armpits – as they wrestle with Farage and the Brexit Old Guard.

On the evening known as Guy Fawkes night, recalling a failed 'gunpowder plot' to blow up the Houses of Parliament in 1605, the prime minister travels in his motorcade to Buckingham Palace and informs the Queen of his intention to dissolve parliament. In the early hours of the morning, it's dissolved.

I binge-watch the TV mini-series *Chernobyl* again. The horrific 1986 reactor accident was a Soviet version of the Brexit referendum – sudden pandemonium, bitter regrets, and the lingering end of a union.

28. Fighting the good fight

This year marks the thirtieth anniversary of the fall of the Berlin Wall in Germany. I still remember my excitement in Heidelberg as I watched the Red sunset on German television. It was a time for joy. The end of the Cold War psychodrama! The end of the four-minute threat of nuclear apocalypse! Communism collapsed, the Soviet empire in eastern Europe dissolved, and within a few years the former satellite states of the region were welcomed into NATO and the EU.

When the Wall came down, I was working in the palatial offices of the science publisher Springer, where one of my colleagues was Angie, who had not yet met Rolf. We worked on physics manu-scripts from all over Europe, including some from inside the Soviet bloc, and I recall with fond pity the typescripts from those authors, looking so much more primitive than the processed printouts most of our authors delivered. I smartened up their work for the global science community.

At the time, the institution soon called the European Union was universally regarded as the latest and greatest embodiment of open, tolerant, liberal, free-market values. Admired from all sides, it was the very model of supranational political organisation, a paragon for emulation worldwide. No one could have guessed that thirty years later, the UK of all countries would be straining to escape the club and go it alone in a world where Russia was still posing like Conan the Barbarian against Western values.

Yet so it is. I'm caught in the most extraordinary nightmare. The Conservative party has abandoned all its old values. My only hope now is to work with the Liberal Democrats.

In a world of sugar and spice and all things nice, I wouldn't hesitate to join the Lib Dems for real and condemn Tory slugs and snails and puppy dog's tails without more ado. But bitter experience has taught me that ideals die first in the real world, and a deal with a rat is often better than buying a cat in a bag.

Now, in November 2019, the Tory rats are about to take the most catastrophic leap of faith in modern times, over a cliff and into an uncharted abyss. Brexit offers no safe sovereign future in a world where little nations are routinely bullied and raped and butchered by bigger neighbours. Brexit Britain will leave its haven in the EU to dock in New England, which offers only humiliating subservience to President Trump just when it matters most.

For me, the priority is to stop Boris from wrecking relations with Britain's European neighbours for the sake of a fantasy alliance with a madcap US administration concerned only to Make America Great Again. In the next British general election, this means tactical voting against the Conservatives. In Poole, it means voting Lib Dem, and for me it means supporting a Lib Dem candidate.

I face another dilemma. I owe my member of parliament and former boss Sir Robert a debt of gratitude and solidarity, and I can see anyway that his majority is so massive that nothing short of a political Chernobyl can sink it. The better course for me is to shift my attention to the neighbouring constituency of Mid Dorset and North Poole, where I owe the 2015 new boy Michael Tomlinson no debt of any sort.

Performing my act of defection from – or treachery to – the Tories against Tomlinson has another advantage. Apart from the fact that Tomlinson is a Grand Wizard in the Star Chamber and a deputy chair to the ERG chairman Jacob Rees-Mogg, the Lib Dem candidate running against him is Vikki Slade. Supporting her will be as much a personal pleasure as a moral duty.

The kick-off meeting for Vikki's campaign is on the evening of the same Saturday that marks the thirtieth anniversary of the fall of the Wall. Her home ward is the Poole suburb of Broadstone, which sits on a hilltop ridge a few miles north of the town centre. The meeting is held in the upstairs hall of the Broadstone sports and community centre.

Liberals are renowned for their informal dress sense. I won't be welcomed with open arms by the young activists of Broadstone if I rock up in a Tory suit and a blue tie. I go instead for boring grunge: a Cambridge-blue sweater over an Oxford-blue shirt, matched with blue jeans and my black biker jacket.

It turns out to be the ideal camouflage for the occasion. All the rest, except for a few older gents who show up in jackets and ties, with their female escorts in twinsets and pearls, look much the same as I do – just decades younger. Here already is a contrast with the Conservatives, where I was the youngster.

Vikki looks a model candidate for national office. Her hair is honey blonde and shoulder length, her outfit is a smart blue-green twinset over a plain neckline and kitten heels, and her smile is dazzling. She's pleased to see me and turns from her VIP guests to give me a booster shot of personal attention.

'Andy, great to see you here! Glad you could make it – we really appreciate it. Did you tell the Conservatives you were coming?'

I smile and shake my head. 'It's good to be here. No, I didn't tell them. But they've had fair warning of my intentions after the garden rallies in Bournemouth.'

'Yes, surely. Hey, maybe you could give a little speech later, when we're ready, telling us why you joined us and what the party means to you, before I speak?'

'As a kind of warm-up act? Yes, I'd be happy to. I can say why I'm supporting you and what it means to the community.'

Vikki smiles: 'Perfect. Steve – over there – will tell you when we're ready.'

I turn toward Steve, a tall young chap with tangled hair and a hairy chin (no one would call it a beard) sprouting over a dishevelled shirt and jeans.

'Hi, Steve, Vikki says you're lining up the speaker acts for later.'

'That's right,' he says cautiously. 'Do you want to speak before Vikki comes on?'

'Yes, that's what she suggests. What shall I say?'

'Whatever you like. What you said in Bournemouth gardens – something like that would do fine. But build it up to Vikki.'

'Okay, thanks, can do. She's the star. I'll think on it.'

Broadstone is the Liberal stronghold in Poole. Annette Brooke, the wife of Broadstone councillor Mike Brooke, was the Lib Dem MP for Mid Dorset and North Poole for years before Michael Tomlinson snatched the crown in 2015. Annette is here with Mike, and I go over to talk with them.

'Hi, Mike, I guess you remember me from the council meetings in Poole.'

Mike looks at me calmly with creased eyes through his glasses: 'Yes, of course, it's good to see you here. Have you said hello to Vikki yet?'

'Yes, I have. She's lined me up as a warm-up act for her speech.'

'Good, the more the merrier. Have you met my wife, Annette?'

'Not yet. Hello, Annette, pleased to meet you.'

She seems distracted: 'Hello, ah …'

'Andy – I used to work for the Conservatives – for Robert Syms in Poole.'

She looks disconcerted: 'Oh. Have you changed sides now?'

'Yes, for this election, at least. Brexit and Boris are more than I can take, more than I could ever defend in good conscience.'

She relaxes slightly: 'Well, indeed, that goes without saying. But why aren't you campaigning for our candidate in Poole?'

'That would be disloyal to Sir Robert. Whereas here the Tory opponent is Michael Tomlinson, whose views I can't help but find reprehensible.'

She smiles: 'Well, yes, they certainly are! You may not know I was the MP here from 2001 to 2015. I think we have a good chance of winning the seat back for the Lib Dems.'

'Yes, I do know. I agree. This seat was a marginal in 2015, so the Lib Dem base must still be there, ready to vote Vikki in.'

'She has a very loyal following here in Broadstone. Everyone knows her from her council work, and I think she's an excellent candidate.'

'I agree – that's why I'm here!' I smile artlessly.

Mike is busying himself with his camera to take a few snaps. No doubt some of them will reappear as images in the party's leaflets in the coming weeks. I've admired some of the recent leaflets, and I'm impressed by their smart layouts and clean editing.

In contrast, to the well-moneyed Tory machine, the Lib Dem operations run on a shoestring. Signs of economy are everywhere, but now at least their literature is good. In earlier elections, I studied Lib Dem leaflets for weaknesses to exploit, and it was too easy. Amateur editing, cheap production quality, wordy waffle for stories, unhinged criticism of pretty good policies – basic mistakes. Isaac and I won the propaganda war hands down.

Time for the speeches. First on is an organiser who talks about campaign planning, with a pitch for people to sign up as volunteers. Then comes a young activist talking up Vikki and her years of tireless work in the ward and on the council. All this goes down well, to bursts of applause from the crowd.

Then it's my turn. I stand in a clear space in the middle of the hall and speak without a mike. The acoustics are fine, but I speak up loud and clear anyway.

'Hi, my name's Andy and I was a Conservative,' I begin, in the style of an Alcoholics Anonymous confession. 'Until September I worked for Sir Robert Syms in Poole as a parliamentary assistant, and before that I'd also worked as the party agent for the local and general elections. But the Conservative policy on Brexit is all wrong. I say – Bollocks to Brexit!'

This draws a spirited round of applause and a whoop or two. I continue: 'Now I can't campaign against Sir Robert, who is an honourable and decent man, but I can campaign against Michael Tomlinson, who is an extremist Brexiteer and a close colleague of Jacob Rees-Mogg and other pantomime villains.'

Pause for more applause. 'Brexit is a terrible policy, conducted for all the wrong reasons, that will damage our economy and poison our national debate for years, if not decades to come.'

I pause again, now for effect. 'And Boris Johnson is a terrible prime minister. He has a long record in journalism as an unprincipled liar, he undermined his own party's government in 2016, he made a complete hash of his time as foreign secretary, and now he's failing to offer anything better than stand-up comedy routines on the most consequential reversal of national policy for decades. He cannot be allowed to continue!'

This earns more applause and another whoop. 'The Liberal Democrats have an opportunity to stop Boris before it's too late. After the Lib Dem successes in the local elections and the European elections earlier this year, the party is poised to win the balance of power in the next parliament. All it takes is tactical voting around the country.'

Here there's no applause, just expectant attention. 'Here in Mid Dorset and North Poole, Michael Tomlinson is vulnerable. Lib Dems have a strong base of support here and a strong candidate with Vikki Slade. I've watched Vikki in council for years and I can testify that she's got the energy, the talent, the wit, and the bite to succeed not only locally but also nationally. In my humble opinion she has what it takes to make an excellent MP!'

The applause here is stronger and more sustained, but I'm not quite finished. 'In the next few weeks, we have the opportunity to defeat Tomlinson and put Vikki in her rightful place in parliament, where she can do nationally what she has done locally, as leader of the council, and fight for our interests, for policies that are humane and fair.'

Thoughtful applause tells me I need to ramp it up: 'Vikki can win this constituency for the Lib Dems again. Then she can fight in parliament against austerity, against Brexit, against the old-boy club that for too long has strangled British politics. She can fight for decent housing, for good schools, for a functioning National Health Service, and for us – the people of Poole!'

That's better. I let the applause continue and bow out.

Vikki is next, with a low-key start recalling her struggle over the years to balance the duties of motherhood against the demands of a business career and the challenges of council work. Then she recalls the people who have helped her on the way, with practical help, with inspiration, and with encouragement to keep on fighting. By the end, the whole audience is rooting for her, eager to help her win the next battle, and the next, for as long as it takes.

In the closing melee, Mike Brooke raises his camera, snapping right and left, and Vikki waves to me. Mike waves too.

Vikki moves up close to be heard. 'I wanted to thank you for your speech. I thought we could have a picture with you in it.'

'Good idea. You can use it with a short story about how a former Tory is backing you.'

Vikki smiles, flashing her teeth: 'That's what I thought. It's a good endorsement.'

Mike waits while Vikki and I pose. I put my arm around her shoulder, she puts her arm around my waist, and we smile on cue.

Mike takes a few snaps of us and asks: 'Can you write a sentence or two for the story, Andy?'

'Sure, no problem. I'll mail it to you tomorrow.'

———

Official Secrets is a movie starring Kiera Knightley about a GCHQ employee who leaks a secret memo exposing an illegal US spy operation related to the 2003 invasion of Iraq. I see it soon after Halloween and let its portrait of the Anglo-American spy world simmer in my brain. I recall that someone in it tried to pronounce the awkward acronym 'UK-USA' with a sound I heard as 'Yakuza' – the Japanese name for underworld mobsters.

I recall the Yakuza from my year In Japan. At the time they liked to tool around the streets in fast BMW cars, sometimes with fancy paint jobs. In person, they often had arty tattoos and amputated pinkie fingers. They were rolling in dirty money from the 'floating world' of sex workers and sleazy clubs, and widely feared.

British and American collaboration on intelligence, as in the Five Eyes network, is the basis for Anglophone control in cyber-space. It's an essential enabling capability for continuing Anglophone hegemony on Planet Earth. I call it *Yukuza*.

The Yukuza underworld is a global reality. Veiled from direct view, it's locked in a secret war with Russian and Chinese antagonists. The elites of the British Empire, the American world order, and the Five Eyes network are defending their top-dog status.

The top dogs build on Anglo-American dominance to continue the civilising mission of the ancient Roman Empire. So long as the UK remains in the EU, Yukuza retains a link with the classical world. Outside the EU, the UK will begin to lose it and become the site of a fissure in the old empire, as when Constantinople broke free of Rome and formed the new Byzantine empire. Washington will be the capital of the breakaway empire. The new Rome will be Brussels or Berlin, depending on how the EU fares.

The American Byzantium, Yukuza, will face new empires in Persia, Russia, and China. The chasm between Yukuza and mainland Europe will grow, perhaps until it resembles the bloodlands between Eastern and Western Christendom a thousand years ago.

ANDY ROSS

The British Isles will be on the front line, perhaps heavily militarised like eastern Prussia years ago. This will be bad for Brits.

I know the importance of military might and warfare in human history. A global struggle between Yukuza and all the rest is looking ever more likely, as Trump America ramps up military spending, as the UK takes sides with it, as Russia attacks Ukraine and threatens the Baltic States, and as China fortifies islands in the South China Sea and threatens Taiwan. It's hard to see anything good for anyone alive coming out of this.

The liberal world order is dying. The tolerant and democratic order behind globalisation is under increasing threat from more authoritarian orders in lands with weak governments. What once seemed enlightened now seems decadent.

A political structure that bows too far toward liberalism to embrace diversity is powerless to prevent the divisive forces of angry intolerance from tearing it apart. The next step in the process, warned Plato, is tyranny.

As I see it, if Yukuza decouples from mainland Europe, Putin's new populist fascism will take over the continent.

Fazit: Yukuza should say Bollocks to Brexit!

29. Farewell, sunlit uplands

On the morning of Remembrance Sunday, I drive to Poole Park. I emerge from my car in dark suit, blue shirt, and black tie, with my black biker jacket on top. I'm here for the memorial service at the cenotaph beside the lake.

It's a cool, clear day, and a small crowd of people has already assembled. I'm here on behalf of the Rotary Club of Poole. I'll meet other Rotarians, and together we'll lay a wreath. A host of local dignitaries will be here too, as well as a priest, a military band, and a crowd of military personnel and cadets.

I spot Sir Robert, standing alone in his crumpled suit, without a topcoat, holding a wreath and looking morose. I walk over to him.

'Hello, Robert. How's it going?'

'Ah, hello. Are you representing the Liberals here?'

'No, the Rotarians. A group of us will lay a wreath together. But I don't think they're here yet. At least, I don't see them.'

'I suppose quite a lot of the Rotarians are military veterans.'

'Yes, some of them remember the war. It's still a moral compass for them. I guess that explains a lot of contemporary politics.'

Robert muses. 'It was a defining event for that generation. We owe them a huge debt for their sacrifice. If not for them, we could all be speaking German now, with secret police rounding up Jews and so on.'

'Some of us still do speak German. But I don't think the secret police would have survived long in Britain.'

'The secret police survived for decades in East Germany. We should be grateful that Churchill saw the danger for what it was.'

'Yes, sure. But we'll never know how things would have turned out if Lord Halifax had become prime minister in 1940 and made a peace deal with Hitler. King George could have gone either way.'

He seems to shudder. 'Well, I for one am very grateful we were spared German brutality and managed to preserve our parliamentary institutions intact.'

'In the early war years, Churchill said something good about that. He said he knew we'd win because we had parliament and the Germans didn't. There was no mechanism to hold Hitler back from his latest idiocies, whereas Churchill was always held back by his parliamentary colleagues, who used to pour cold water on the worst of his mad ideas.'

'Quite right too,' he says firmly. 'The Germans were always too authoritarian. Is there any sign of a replacement for Angela Merkel yet?'

'Merkel? Yes, she nominated a successor recently, a female colleague, but the choice hasn't gone down well, and I don't think it'll stand. I'd rather see Friedrich Merz take over. He's a mature conservative who would steer Germany slightly further to the right, which would head off the Alternative for Deutschland before they can gain a bigger presence in the Bundestag.'

Robert nods thoughtfully. 'Germans have moved on since the war, I will give them that.'

'They made a completely fresh start. There's no comparison.'

He looks around at the crowd. 'I expect your stepfather Don Barr would have been here if he were still around.'

'Probably, yes, although in his later years he wasn't very mobile. His war wound never got properly treated. He could hardly walk in the end.'

'He once told me about that. He was flying off a carrier in the South China Sea and being shot at by Japanese anti-aircraft guns. Incredibly brave. He said that if he'd gone down and been captured, he'd probably have died in a Japanese prisoner-of-war camp. They were vicious, the Japs. I'm very glad we won the war.'

'But you have to see it in perspective. I lived in Japan for a year, and all the people I met were extremely kind and friendly. But the traditional military mindset in Japan is very extreme. It's based on *Bushido*, the way of the samurai, where the honourable thing is to fight to the death and accept death before defeat and dishonour. They thought any prisoners had lost their honour already and should be grateful for a quick death. It's just a different way of seeing things.'

'Very different. You can go too far in trying to understand these things.'

'No, I don't think so. As a philosopher, I think it's my duty to try to understand them. Hence my time in Japan and Germany, plus all my reading in military history and so on. It's part of the job.'

'Well, thank God it's behind us now.'

I see a Rotary colleague. Robert and I nod farewell.

The event is an annual rite. The military band, the local cadet corps, and the civic leaders look much the same as every year. I watch the marching column of people in fancy dress approaching and stand in stoic silence as they regroup at the memorial.

At the appointed times, my Rotary colleagues and I sing the songs, lay our wreath, hang around making small talk, and head off to the civic centre in the wake of the dignitaries wandering back to their hot tea and a bun.

Standing with coffee and cake, I start talking with Bryan Dion, who's now a councillor for a prosperous ward in Poole.

'So, Bryan, did that ceremony at the cenotaph do anything to lift your spirits regarding the great themes of war and peace in the age of Trump and Brexit?'

He pauses to think: 'Yeah, kinda. Made me feel our efforts in the services are appreciated. That's better than what a lot of Vietnam vets had to experience.'

'Good point. Was it any better after the invasion of Iraq?'

He smiles: 'I don't know – I was in Afghanistan at the time.'

'Oh, right. Did you see combat there or were you in a staff headquarters in Kabul?'

'Oh, I was at the front line alright. Flown in on a chopper, making sure to avoid Stinger attacks on the way in. That was hairy enough.'

'Were you in a Black Hawk or a Chinook?'

'Black Hawk – more mobile, smaller target – also a bumpier ride.'

'I can imagine. I flew in a tiny helicopter over Germany earlier this year. Great way to see the view, but it was a very fragile thing to be flying around in.'

He grins. 'It's worse when you're being shot at, I can tell you.'

'The Afghanistan mission – do you think the American strategy there makes any sense? Do you think the right way to reduce the risk of Islamist terrorism is to go in with helicopter gunships and armoured vehicles and drone attacks and so on?'

'I think so, yeah. Gotta show 'em who's boss. If we don't teach them to keep their heads down, they'll never learn any sense.'

'Fair enough, I guess the Brits thought so too a hundred-odd years ago. The nutjobs there still haven't learned any sense.'

He grins again. 'Yeah, it's kind of uphill work. A hundred years is slow learning, though, that's for sure.'

'It's Islam. That's what I think. It seems to breed a uniquely stubborn kind of opposition to all that we hold dear in the West.'

'Maybe. You're the philosopher. I guess we just have to keep hacking away at them.'

'The problem is that all this is a domestic political issue in Europe. We have so many Muslim immigrants that we can't just turn away and let them get radicalised. We need to integrate them.'

'Well, good luck with that. I wouldn't have let 'em come here in the first place.'

'There you've hit on a major factor behind Trump and Brexit.

People here are mad as hell about it. They want to seal the borders, pull up the drawbridge, and let the rest of the world go to hell.'

'Okay, what do you suggest instead?' He spread his hands. 'Open all the doors and watch everything go to hell here too? Good luck selling that policy to the voters!'

'No, but they're here, millions of them, and we can't just expel them all. We don't want to anyway – we need them. We need more young people to keep our economies running.'

'I thought y'all were too overcrowded on these islands. Now you invite all these guys in too – what sense does that make?'

'It's the economy. An economy as we know it is like a Ponzi scheme. If it stops growing, it stalls and crashes. And if productivity is stagnant, the only way to keep it growing it is to import more consumers. That's the nature of capitalism as we know it.'

Bryan shakes his head. 'I never did figure out economics. How is importing terrorists worth the risk?'

'It's the lesser of two evils. A few terrorists we can live with, no money we can't. Also, Christianity is fading here, so we import a slice of Islam to give religious people something more to chew on.'

He pulls a face: 'Christianity fading?'

'Yes. Christians were getting too liberal, so now they're trying to stop the rot by importing hardline Muslims.'

'Well, you got me there.' He widens his eyes. 'I don't see it. American Christians aren't too liberal, I'm darn sure of that. Maybe it's just the Church of England.'

I nod warmly: 'Exactly that. The Church of England cut itself off from the Church of Rome during the reign of Henry the Eighth, and ever since then it's been downhill in England. Now they say the Church of England is the Tory party at prayer. No god, just politics, which in turn has sunk to flag-waving nationalism.'

'I thought y'all worshipped the Queen here in England.'

'Many do. It's pitiful, beneath contempt, just pitiful.'

He shrugs cheerily: 'Don't worry, it's their problem, not yours!'
He's right. I turn to the bites and top up my breakfast.

———

England has not been conquered for almost a thousand years. For most Englanders, the national past is full of nostalgia.

Continental Europe is different. In the five hundred years since the Reformation, war has dominated the European continent for a total of three hundred of them. Now, thanks to the EU and NATO, Europe has lived in relative peace for generations. You can forgive them for wanting to hang onto both.

The two world wars devastated Europe, and Europeans vowed never to repeat such folly. Yet Brexiteers cheer when their prime minister rants about surrender and condemns EU collaboration as treasonous. Nigel Farage even begins his rallies with the sound of air-raid sirens.

Boris Johnson is fixated on Winston Churchill. He puts the power of the British Empire down to pluck, courage, and determination. He dotes on war stories and traces Allied victory to the bulldog defiance of a great leader. He sees Winston Churchill as a 'resounding human rebuttal' to a Tolstoian emphasis on impersonal factors in history.

As for Russia, I sigh when Her Majesty's government decides it's less embarrassing to suppress a new official report into Russian interference in the UK than to publish it. Johnson seems to think the election will distract people from the scandal of its suppression. I'm not distracted.

The USSR banked its dollars in London during the Cold War. This gave the Soviets easy access to global financial markets and generated revenue for the City of London. After the Soviet collapse, London became the sewer for criminal oligarchs to drain cash out of Russia and the laundromat to help them recycle it to fund their lives of luxury abroad.

Vladimir Putin saw his chance and took it. His dream of a Eurasian Union depends on liberating EU member states from the grip of Yukuza. Anything that carves the UK away from the EU is a useful lever for him, and the Brexit fantasies of people like Nigel Farage are ideal. So, he bankrolled bad boys like Arron Banks and supported cyberwarriors like Dominic Cummings for their Vote Leave campaign in 2016.

In the 2019 election campaign, no one wants to talk about Brexit. Johnson is eager to draw attention away from the terrible deal he's signed to get Brexit done. Lib Dems think opposing Brexit is too obviously right to argue about, and Labour have no coherent Brexit policy at all.

I foresee the breakup of the UK. A united Europe offers a better home for English, Scottish, Welsh, and Irish identities. This makes the UK redundant and the EU indispensable.

Boris Johnson is still standing guard over his turd of a deal. He says an election victory will let him get Brexit done and agree a trade deal in 2020. It's scented toilet water to cover a nasty smell.

———

I follow through on my promise to support the Lib Dems. Their campaign office is in Broadstone. I park in front and walk right in.

The chap in charge is Steve with the hairy chin. He sits at a computer screen, surrounded by boxes and stacks of leaflets being sorted and bundled for delivery. He looks busy but projects an air of enjoying the drama.

Three other people sit at side tables. A young lady who looks like a student is working on another computer screen, and a pair of likely pensioners are counting and bundling leaflets.

Steve looks up: 'Hi, Andy, welcome to our chaos. Are you here to help out today?'

'Sure am. Give me a bundle and a delivery round and I'll get to work right away.'

'Great. Helen can give you a round and a map.' With that, he turns back to his screen, then swivels briefly back to me: 'Excuse the lack of small talk, I'm busy on a new leaflet.'

'No problem. Go right ahead. I know the routine.'

'By the way, we're using your picture and your story here. You might as well see it now, then we can okay it straight away.'

'Ah, good, let me see.' I see a tiny mugshot and a quote: 'Vikki has shown star quality for years in Poole and now on the BCP council. As a former Conservative, I think she will be a great MP.'

He looks up. 'What do you think?'

'It's fine. Go with it. You have my approval.'

Helen looks up from her computer screen, where she's working on address lists and delivery maps, and smiles.

Soon I'm on my way. My European parliament satchel is laden with counted and banded bundles of Lib Dem leaflets, map print-outs of the route, and a Royal Mail dibber to prise open letterboxes. The satchel is a relic of my Tory days and sports the name 'Julie Girling' to show European taxpayers funded it.

I park at the end of my target road and set to work. It's a fine afternoon, and this is a good way to get some exercise. Soon enough, I'm done for the day.

Days later, I do another delivery round. That's it. I don't want to overdo it.

—

One night in late November, I attend another hustings event at the church where in May I met the angelic Rachel. I'm braced for a dull evening listening to the prospective parliamentary candidates for Poole explaining why I should vote for them.

I show up early in blue jeans and my EU-blue hoodie with a ring of gold stars on the front, topped by my black biker jacket. The church is half-empty and cold. I walk up to a glum bunch of old Conservative friends standing around their stall.

Canny old Isaac looks as impishly Machiavellian as ever. His sharp eyes glint as I approach.

'What's this costume all about?' He glances down at the gold stars on my chest. 'You got something against being British?'

'Just making a statement. I'm not going down quietly on this one. If we don't make a fuss, Boris is going to roll all over us.'

'I think he's going to win, and then he'll do what he wants. Pissing him off is not going to help anyone. Sometimes you have to know when to admit defeat and move on.'

'Remaining in the EU is not yet a lost cause. By Christmas it might be, I grant you, but I plan to keep fighting until then. The surest way to lose is to give up before it's over.'

He shrugs. 'I can see where you're coming from, but I think you're wrong. The Lib Dems are on a hiding to nowhere. Do you really think Jo Swinson could be prime minister?'

'Not a hope, but that's not the point. Lib Dems could be the kingmakers in a hung parliament. That's a prize worth fighting for. That would be real leverage against Boris and the Brexiteers.'

He pulls a face and nods slowly. 'Yes, that's still possible. But unlikely. Corbyn would have to do quite well, and I don't think he will.'

'Right, that's out of our control. Boris has momentum, I grant you. But I can't stand by and watch his Brexit thugs wreck our relations with Europe for the sake of a *Rule Britannia* fantasy.'

'What about Vikki Slade?' Isaac asks with an aggrieved edge. 'Do you really want her to win? I saw your name on that Lib Dem leaflet. That was a low blow. I know Vikki, and she's not as nice as you think.'

'Well, Michael Tomlinson is not as nice as I thought. Hanging out with Jacob Rees-Mogg and rooting for a hard Brexit is way out of bounds for me. If Vikki can stop him, good for her.'

Tony Reeves moves in. He's the cheerily robust former tank

man who hired me back in 2014.

'Hi, Andy, I hear you've left us for the Lib Dems. What's all that about?' His accent is as local yokel as ever.

'I'm making a stand on Europe. If the Conservatives are going to push for a hard Brexit, I'm going to jump ship before it's too late. That way lies a titanic disaster.'

He smirks: 'Titanic disaster, eh? You think it'll come to that?'

'Think about it. Britain can only survive without Europe if it attaches itself to America. But Trump is Putin's man. Putin wants him to abandon NATO so that Russia has a free hand in Europe.'

He looks askance. 'Yeah, I kind of see that. But do you really think we'll give up on NATO? We've been in it for decades.'

'We've been members of the EU for decades too. Look how fast that went south.'

'You've got a point there. But what does Putin gain by interfering in NATO? We're not in the Cold War anymore.'

'Well, we are stopping him having his way in Ukraine and in the Baltic States. And we have humiliated the Kremlin by stealing away all its former satellite states in Europe. And we have imposed economic sanctions that are crippling the Russian economy.'

He frowns. 'But Brexiteers want to get out of the EU, not out of NATO. They're different things.'

'Sure, the EU is economic and NATO is military, but we're not afraid of Russian aggression because we're economically stronger than they are. They have plenty of weapons, but they don't have the economic strength to follow through with them.'

He frowns. 'Do you think Brexit will weaken us economically?'

'Yes, both Britain and Europe. Germans will start to see themselves as halfway between Washington and Moscow. They'll do deals with Russia and cut their exposure to the ups and downs of living with Brexit Brits and Trump Americans. We'll see a huge strategic shift.'

He frowns again: 'You think Putin is planning all this?'

'He's already said so. He wants a Eurasian Union, which is basically the EU plus Russia, which is only likely once the EU has got rid of Britain. It makes perfect sense from his standpoint.'

'But in a fight between America and Britain versus Russia and the rest of the EU, I'd put my money on America.'

'Don't forget China. Russia and China are already all but allies, whereas Trump is working hard to pick a fight with China.'

He nods thoughtfully. 'Yes, I see, that does look scary.'

'The whole Eurasian land mass would be on one side, leaving Trump America with its British sidekick on the other. America versus the world. Not hard to predict the outcome of that one.'

'Whew! I'll have to go away and think about that.'

I see Keith standing behind Tony, listening in. Keith is a former Royal Marine and an intelligent man, who trades in Gulf securities and lives in a posh part of Poole. He even cultivates an interest in cosmology.

'I couldn't help overhearing,' he says. 'Do you really think Europe, Russia, and China could get together? It seems rather implausible to me, given their historical differences.'

'History is there to be overcome. Look at how Germany and France overcame their historical differences, or America and Japan, and so on. China sees the need in our age to reach out globally. And it sees huge potential in business ties with Europe, through Russia. I'd say it was a very plausible picture.'

He pulls himself up straight – he's taller than me – and purses his lips. 'I see that, but something still troubles me. I can't see all the European countries eager to make deals with China and watch their own economies crumble under the competition.'

'In Germany you'll find plenty of interest – cautious interest, I grant you – in working closely with China. And where Germany goes, the rest of mainland Europe is likely to follow.'

He nods slowly: 'Yes, a Greater Asian Co-prosperity Sphere, expanded to include Europe. How do you think Britain fits in?'

'With difficulty, I'd say. We've tied ourselves to America. If America goes down, we go down with them.'

Keith raises his eyebrows: 'Yes, good luck with that one!'

The proceedings are about to continue. I find a seat.

The candidates each speak for a few minutes. Sir Robert's pitch is the only one I can relate to. He doesn't once mention Brexit, he refers to Boris Johnson only in neutral terms, and he stresses the benefits of pragmatic government in the service of restoring Britain's economic fundamentals. The outsider candidates have nothing new to say.

I wait for the interval and quietly walk out the door, back to my car. There was no further profit in staying.

———

While I'm saying farewell to my former Tory colleagues, the climate crisis is becoming alarming. Huge swathes of Siberia, Amazonia, Indonesia, Australia, and California are aflame. The science journal *Nature* says humanity faces a climate emergency and calls for action.

The main enemy of effective action is the fossil fuel industry. Big Oil has a lock on politics in Trump America.

Impeachment proceedings against Donald Trump are about to begin in Washington. But Republicans in the Senate will stonewall the process.

The UK election campaign saddens me with its wild promises and shameless lies. At this rate, Johnson could get his hard Brexit. If so, Brits are due for a hard enlightenment in 2020, and again in 2021, after the transition period.

30. The Star of David

On Thursday 12 December, I rise early and walk briskly to my local polling station to vote. It's raining when I drive to Bournemouth and hurry into a store to buy a fresh white shirt and a shiny golden necktie. The tie will announce my new political identity at the count this evening.

The counts for the constituencies of Mid Dorset and North Poole, Poole, Bournemouth West, Bournemouth East, and Christchurch will all take place in the Bournemouth International Centre. This is a big venue well suited to such events.

Early in the evening, I stride into the centre, decked out in my gilded stage costume, with dark suit, white shirt, golden tie, and a golden rosette on my lapel sporting the words 'Liberal Democrats' on it. I settle down in a quiet restaurant and read an interesting little paperback I started earlier titled *Why do we get the wrong politicians?* I finish it shortly before the count begins in earnest.

The paperback's author is Isabel Hardman, who explores the process of selecting and electing the members of the Westminster parliament in some detail. Her conclusions are very much like mine. She reviews the local party machines and members; the British unwritten constitution, or rather the jumble of archaic conventions and gentlemen's agreements that pass for a constitution; the old-boys' club that goes by the name of a parliament in the gothic Palace of Westminster; and the bizarre job description, which involves being a social worker, a public relations whiz, a committee expert, and a dullard prepared to listen to boring speeches for hours on end while sitting on green benches resembling the bus seats of fifty years ago. You must admit that anyone prepared to accept all that will be a bit of an odd duck in the first place. Any political acumen is a bonus.

I trek to the counting halls and find they're sited next to a bar with a big television, where the candidates, counting agents, and others can settle down to a long night of thrilling inaction. I enjoy parading through the counting halls, but my mood sinks when I reach the bar and find many of my former Tory friends already there. As soon as they see my golden rosette they turn away. This suits me – an excuse to avoid their witless small talk is just what I want. With the count and the television near at hand, I have plenty of food for good thoughts already.

The first person I click with is Vikki Slade, who shows up well after ten and is quick to admire my rosette. She's in her candidate suit, knowing that whether she wins or loses, she'll have to stand up and speak to thank her supporters and accept the outcome.

I ask her: 'How are you feeling about the result?'

She frowns: 'I don't really think I'll win, but nothing's certain, so let's wait and see.'

'The television reported the national exit poll just after ten – it looks like Boris will win with a comfortable majority.'

She shrugs: 'I guessed he might. The polls have been consistent for days. We just have to keep fighting on. The local results might be a surprise – you never know.'

'It's going to be a few hours yet. I really don't see why they can't do a quick machine count of the ballots just to give us a warning of the result. The manual count could still be the definitive one, but an idea of what to expect would be useful.'

'It's all tradition. We're not going to change it, so let's just enjoy it.'

I stroll around the counting tables, again admiring the dexterity of the young fingers doing their work with the crumpled papers bearing scrawled crosses on them. All this is a century behind the times. But as Vikki said, best just to chill and enjoy it.

Steve, the Lib Dem agent, is there too. He's in a smart suit for the occasion, over an old-fashioned shirt featuring a stand-up collar with the corners folded down and a tie held in place by a golden stickpin. He's also shaved his chin and combed his hair.

I'm curious about his background: 'Have you been to many of these counts?'

He looks ahead imperiously. 'A few. I was a Conservative agent once, back in the days before Cameron stabbed Clegg in the back.'

'Really? I wouldn't have guessed.'

'Have you talked to your former party colleagues here yet?'

'Just a few icy hellos. Most of them are studiously ignoring me. They're offended at my changing sides, just when they've got their dream candidate for prime minister.'

'Anyone who dreams of Boris for prime minister is not worth having as a friend.'

'Quite so. This is a great way to see who your real friends are.'

But I do talk with Isaac, whose sneaking admiration for the Goebbels line on propaganda makes a mere switch to the Lib Dems an easy betrayal to overcome.

Isaac jokes: 'Your rosette has turned an evil, horrible, sickly shade of puke.'

'How dare you impugn my golden badge of distinction,' I reply. 'I see this as my Star of David, the mark of the chosen few among the Tory hacks and functionaries who surround me.'

'Chosen few, eh? Well, there are very few liberals around here, thank God.'

'Seriously, there's no shame in being a liberal. We occupy the moral high ground. No grubby compromises or political fudges for us, no dodgy backroom dealing. We follow the shining light of reason and virtue, even if it means sacrificing political power.'

He leers: 'Sacrificing what matters, you mean. Without power, all the virtues in the world ain't gonna help you change the world.'

'All I can say to that is – God works in mysterious ways.'

'So long as we win the election, I'm happy.'

Sir Robert shows up around then, but he manages to show me no sign of recognition. The golden-yellow rosette acts as a cloak of invisibility. As we both watch the TV announcer declare yet another Conservative win in a marginal seat, I sense Robert cheering with fractionally more zest than comes naturally to him. He's hamming it up for my benefit, to underscore just how far I'm falling as I watch Lib Dem candidates ground into the dust around the country.

But I knew this was coming and I'm prepared for it. A philosopher is no stranger to bitter defeat and soon learns to relish it. The trick is to rise above it. Soon enough, the exhilaration of flying high over vast distant landscapes overcomes the sour taste of failure and seems to herald a nobler victory. Well, sometimes it works.

Hours pass, until way past my usual bedtime, well into Friday morning. I flop down in front of the television to watch things come slowly into focus. That's more fun than standing around watching busy fingers count crumpled bits of paper.

Then it's time to witness the live announcement of the first local results. The crowd from the bar troops to a smaller room with a stage where the candidates will make their little speeches. First, the presiding official reads out the results for the constituency of Mid Dorset and North Poole, where Vikki is standing against Michael Tomlinson.

The result – *Con hold*.

Tomlinson speaks: 'I'm delighted and humbled to be standing here before you today as the victor. I can never forget what a privilege it is to serve as the elected parliamentary representative for the constituents in Mid Dorset and North Poole. I would like to thank …'

I can't be bothered to hear out the rest. I glance at Vikki, waiting at the edge of the stage for her moment in the spotlight. She's visibly downcast.

She speaks up bravely: 'First, let me congratulate Michael Tomlinson on his achievement tonight and wish him well for his next term of office. Naturally, I'm disappointed by the result, but I have no regrets and would do the same again to fight for what I believe to be right. I would like to thank …'

More turmoil ensues for a while, and I push through to Vikki. I embrace her briefly in commiseration and feel she's even more devastated than she appears.

Next comes the announcement of the results for the constituency of Bournemouth West, where Conor Burns is standing for re-election. He's about to step onto the stage when he glances at me, so I stand up tall and sovereign, wearing my golden-yellow rosette with pride.

The result – *Con hold*.

Conor speaks: 'I would like to thank all my voters for placing their trust in me again. I feel pride and humility at the responsibility you have vouchsafed in me, yet again, and vow to do all that is in my power to redeem your faith in my ability …'

I wince at it all and turn away to scan the small crowd. There, not far behind me, I see Rachel, her miracle of long dark hair as shampoo perfect as ever, her fresh face turned toward Conor, her formal blouse mostly hidden under a black jacket. She turns her head and catches my eyes with that jolt of recognition again. I move through the crowd toward her.

'Rachel, how lovely to see you again, a very welcome surprise.'

She smiles and looks closely at me. 'Good to see you too. How are things?' She sees my golden rosette: 'Oh, Lib Dem now!'

'Yes, I had to do it. Boris and Brexit – I told you.'

'You did, Conor and all that. Hey, we should talk some time.'

'Well, of course. How about right now?'

She smiles suddenly: 'I promised Conor I'd join him for a victory drink afterwards, but – yes, why not – a few moments I can spare while they're all speaking.'

I pause to look around. I see Tobias Ellwood, who's running again for Bournemouth East, just a short distance away, looking at me with a bemused air.

'Okay,' I say, 'let's go to the lounge and find a quiet seat.'

We find seats in a corner away from the television.

'So, are you still fagging for Conor?'

She frowns. 'We agreed I'd leave at the end of the year. I've seen him through this election, and that's a good time to go. I have a job in central office for next year.'

'Good for you. A successful career in politics awaits you, at least for as long as you can stand working for Boris.'

She catches my eyes and smiles. 'He's not that bad. I think you're just bothered by Brexit.'

'Well, yes, that does colour my judgement.'

'As I see it, we have to do it, just to get it done. If and when everyone sees it won't work, that'll be the time to pick up the pieces and make friends with Europe again.'

'I fear it may do a lot more damage than that.'

'That's an opinion. My new colleagues think differently.'

I sigh and take a deep breath. 'I'm sure they do. This could be the parting of the ways for us.'

She looks at me soulfully. I sit forward, with my elbows on my knees, and she reaches out a hand to touch my arm. 'Don't take it personally. You must have known it would turn out like this.'

I return the gaze. 'At least I hope I've introduced you to enough philosophy to think your way through all this.'

'Yes, you have,' she says softly, 'And I'm grateful.'

'I am too, for your indulgence of my folly. Maybe you should be heading off to your reception.'

She nods and stands up. I stand too, ready for the farewell. Our four hands meet briefly in a gentle handshake. She speaks softly:

'Take care, Andy.'

'You too. Keep in touch!'

'Definitely!' She smiles, pulls her hands away, and steps back. Soon she's out of sight in the crowd.

I see no further reason to stay. I've made my stand and met my dream lover – that's enough for one night. I head off to my car. Sleep and dreams of lost worlds beckon.

—

On the painfully bright morning of Friday the thirteenth, I sit at my big Mac and check the results online and then again on television over breakfast. It's a clean sweep for all the sitting Conservatives in the constituencies counted in Bournemouth. No squeakers either: All five of them win handsome – if not record – majorities. It's a wipe-out for all the other parties, Lib Dems included.

When all the results are in, Johnson has a Commons majority of eighty seats.

The landslide seems to have vindicated his strategy of going all out for a new Brexit deal and then building his campaign around delivering it. He now has a decisive mandate to go ahead.

Almost unexpectedly, he also has an opportunity to buck his backers and pursue a closer future relationship with the EU. But I know he's mad enough not to take it.

Labour has failed disastrously, catastrophically. Jeremy Corbyn should have been fired at dawn. He's done the UK profound and irreparable harm. If only he'd led his party and the unions against Brexit, Remainers could have won the 2016 referendum already.

Leavers have clueless Lib Dem leader Jo Swinson to thank for their easy victory. Her decision to abandon the Remain alliance, which held Johnson trapped and impotent in a hung parliament, first made his election possible.

The Scottish Nationalists let go too. For them, an election was a chance to sweep Scotland and agitate for independence. They can watch England go to ruin from a safe distance.

Against all the odds, Boris Johnson has triumphed in a way no British prime minister has done since Margaret Thatcher in 1987. That was when I departed for Germany.

Boris has won what he calls a 'stonking' parliamentary victory. Yet relative to 2017, the Lib Dem vote rose by well over a million, the Labour vote fell by twice as much, and the Conservative vote rose by only a few hundred thousand. The British electoral system has notched up another crazy outcome.

Leaving the EU will cause the UK to be weaker and poorer, as well as wrecking it as a unified state. Northern Ireland will be in a different economic and legal space from England, Scotland, and Wales, and will inevitably move closer to the Republic of Ireland. Scotland voted emphatically for the SNP and wants independence. Even the Welsh separatists will be emboldened.

Soon it'll be time for former Remainers to start fighting the battle of England. An independent England could be a strong European nation. Recalling both Churchill and the *Lord of the Rings*, I see that the battle to keep the UK in the EU is lost, but the battle for a European England has only just begun.

The *Lord of the Rings* saga is Wagner's Ring saga made British. I read Tolkien's tale as a fat paperback in 1969, the year of Apollo, and later watched Peter Jackson's movie version many times. Brexit is the new reality of the ring legend. Boris has grabbed the ring of power. The end is nigh.

———

A week after the election, the Queen delivers a speech to parliament for the second time in ten weeks about what her government will do in the new session. On the very next day, wasting no time, the new Tory MPs pass Johnson's Brexit bill to leave the EU at the end of January 2020. Britain is moving with gathering speed toward an apocalyptic twilight of the national gods.

For the European Union, Brexit has been a big headache ever since the UK voted to leave in 2016. For over three years, the EU was forced to divert attention from all its other problems. Some of its member states, such as Poland and Hungary, are already ignoring the rule of EU law, deviating from its standards on human rights, and denying press freedom.

To many Europeans, the new British government looks very like the governments in Poland and Hungary. But those governments are scared that Brussels might cut their national funding and are too aware of the huge popularity of EU membership among their voters to risk a clash. The UK is now free of all that, free to sink or swim, or perhaps to go down in a final bunker scene of redemptive glory.

Meanwhile, in America, on 18 December, the US House of Representatives impeaches Donald Trump. He's his own worst enemy. He looks like an asset of the Russian government. Trump America is going down in flames, about to burn in a bonfire of presidential vanity.

Vladimir Putin is the most successfully subversive politician of modern times. Britain and America have both succumbed to his Machiavellian tricks. The Kremlin grandmaster has brought fascism to the masses and sold it worldwide. I'm filled with admiration. Putin has turned the death spiral of Western democracy into the birth pangs of a new order.

The order now dawning over Eurasia and the Americas is a cult of leadership. Voters who are tired of exercising their rational faculties to make difficult choices in the voting booth are now free to relax and bathe in the manufactured glory of their new leaders. They're liberated from what Germans call the *Qual der Wahl* – that quailing before the choice on the ballot paper. The leader with the most ruthless propaganda machine – the boldest public image – is the One. All the rest is detail. That's the Putin legacy.

On Christmas Day 2019, Pope Francis says: 'God continues to love us all, even the worst of us. You may have mistaken ideas, you may have made a complete mess of things, but the Lord continues to love you.'

After the almighty mess of Trump and Brexit, the English-speaking world is in dire need of God's love.

I hope 2020 will turn out better.

PART 4
CONSTERNATION

January 2020 – February 2022

'This whole system is chaos.'
Dominic Cummings

31. Bongs for Britain

Boris Johnson's chief special adviser Dominic Cummings posts a job ad on his blog. He wants physicists, mathematicians, programmers, and other 'weirdos' to apply for work with him in Downing Street on his Leninist mission to reform UK government.

As soon as I see the ad, I laugh.

Days later, Philip Ball, an editor for the science journal *Nature*, airs his opinion: 'For anyone familiar with this field, it reads more like the efforts of a rookie postgrad spouting a breathless stream of buzzwords and random citations … anyone tempted by this weird job advert is precisely the kind of person you wouldn't want within a million miles of the levers of power and influence.'

I agree. I liked Ball's 2018 book on quantum mechanics, and I know this take on the ad is spot on.

—

Boris Johnson spends his New Year break enjoying a week in the Caribbean with his girlfriend Carrie Symonds. A wealthy patron has let the lovers have fun in his luxury pad on the island of Mustique. Boris thinks he's earned a break after his parliamentary hazing in 2019 and his final victory in the election.

The planetary ecosystem is looking ominous. Australia is still burning, any hope of rain is weeks away, blazes are tearing through ancient forests, and the sky is dimmed by suffocating smoke.

Worse, human use of pesticides is killing off insects. Any driver who knows the windscreen test – as I do from years of speeding across Europe – can confirm that bug splat on windscreens has diminished greatly in recent years. Experts say insect extinction is causing a catastrophic collapse of natural ecosystems. Chinese fruit growers are even hiring help to pollinate their orchards by hand to make up for a collapse in the bee population.

ANDY ROSS

If human carelessness can kill off the insects, could it kill off humans too? In December 2019, first reports emerged from China of a new viral infection originating in the city of Wuhan. The Wuhan health commission is investigating dozens of new cases of viral pneumonia. They fear a food market in the city has let pathogens jump from wildlife such as bats and pangolins to humans.

By 11 January, scientists in Shanghai have posted a complete viral genome from an infected patient to the genome database of the US National Institutes of Health. It's a new coronavirus, related to those responsible for the SARS and MERS outbreaks of recent years. China has warned the world.

The US health and human services secretary Alex Azar tells President Trump days later. The authorities in China, South Korea, Taiwan, and Singapore react promptly and impose drastic measures to contain the outbreak. But Trump dismisses concerns.

Ever since he took office, Trump has diminished the role of science in federal policymaking and challenged scientific findings. Each year, Trump makes budget cuts at such federal agencies as the National Institutes of Health, the Department of Energy, and the National Science Foundation. The cuts are about to hit the fan.

Law professor Wendy Wagner at the University of Texas at Austin explains: 'When we decapitate the government's ability to use science in a professional way, that increases the risk that we start making bad decisions, that we start missing new public health risks.'

Britain is also at risk. Devi Sridhar, the University of Edinburgh professor of global public health, calls for swift action to prepare for the virus. She warned years ago that a virus might jump species from an animal in China to cause a human pandemic.

A scientific team at Imperial College London led by Professor Neil Ferguson says there might already be thousands of cases worldwide and recommends vigilance.

—

Brits are still focused on Brexit.

One Sunday in mid-January, I meet Helen and David for lunch at a waiter-service seaside restaurant between Poole and Bournemouth. It's a sunny day, pleasantly warm, and we enjoy a direct view of the beach. It's the first time we've met since Christmas Day, and the final act of Brexit is still pending.

I join them at the table. We order drinks.

'So, what's your take on Brexit?' Helen asks. 'Is there any way to stop it now?'

I shake my head. 'Nope. It's a done deal. The EU just wants to get it over and done with as smoothly as possible, so that it can move on to all its other problems.'

'This is such an outrage,' she says. 'They're just ploughing ahead regardless of what half of us think. I know our rules say the winner takes all, but they're taking us out of Europe. That's going to spoil it for a whole generation.'

'Go tell Boris Johnson,' I reply with a shrug. 'I did what I could already, and it wasn't enough. Be it all on his head now. I'm out of it.'

'Well, okay then, that's that,' she says with a note of despair. 'What about Trump? Is there any way to stop him being re-elected in November?'

'After the Republicans acquit him of the impeachment charges, you mean?' I pull a fake smile. 'It would take something really big, and I don't see the Democrats managing that. If the economy were to collapse, they'd have a chance, but business is riding high right now. So, barring an act of God, so to speak, we're stuck.'

'Sad.' She shakes her head wearily and turns to studying the menu. We try not to let the dire outlook spoil our lunch.

—

The British government is rearranging the Brexit deckchairs.

The British public is still ambivalent about Brexit – a poll held in early January found that UK voters are split in favour of Remain by a margin of 52 to 48 percent – the opposite split to that in 2016. Most people expect Brexit to be bad for the economy, bad for the National Health Service, and bad for the unity and standing of the UK. Only one voter in nine backs a no-deal Brexit at the end of 2020, yet that's still where the government is heading.

The 2019 version of the Brexit bill ensured that MPs would be involved in the trade negotiations, but the 2020 version shuts them out. They'll have no oversight over the process, no right to be kept updated, and no vote on any final deal with Brussels. The new bill is an open invitation to a hard Brexit at the end of 2020. On 23 January, the Queen gives it her royal assent.

Chinese scientists warn that the new coronavirus has an infectivity rate of up to three. Any rate greater than one implies that the number of cases will increase exponentially, but a rate of three means medical services will quickly be overwhelmed unless governments worldwide impose strict social lockdowns.

HM government convenes a meeting of its scientific advisory group for emergencies to discuss the virus. SAGE is chaired by the chief scientific adviser Sir Patrick Vallance and the chief medical adviser Professor Chris Whitty. They raise the alarm.

On 24 January, the government holds a lunchtime meeting in the Cabinet Office Briefing Room A in Whitehall. COBRA is the government's national crisis committee. It's nominally chaired by the prime minister, but Boris Johnson is absent. Standing in for him, health secretary Matt Hancock says the risk posed by the new coronavirus is still rated as low.

On that day, Johnson is a short stroll away, in Downing Street, where he's signing the EU Withdrawal Agreement into law. He also takes the time to participate in celebrating the Chinese New Year. He poses in front of Number 10 to paint in the eye of a dragon as a good-luck gesture, to greet the Year of the Rat.

From the British side, Brexit is now done and dusted. The next step is for the EU to finish the job.

The new president of the European Commission is the former German defence minister Ursula von der Leyen. She's the daughter of Ernst Albrecht, a senior German politician who worked in the European Commission from 1958. She grew up attending international schools, developed a love of horse riding, and qualified as a medical doctor.

When she was still an undergraduate in Germany, the police advised her father to move her away. She spent the academic year 1978/79 at the London School of Economics, where she avoided publicity by calling herself Rose Ladson, the name of her American great-grandmother. Ursula recalls her stay thus: 'London was the epitome of modernity: freedom, the joy of life, trying everything. This gave me an inner freedom that I have kept until today.'

On the last Wednesday of January 2020, the members of the European parliament overwhelmingly ratify the Brexit withdrawal agreement. After their vote, they sing *Auld Lang Syne*.

President Dr von der Leyen gives a speech to the assembly and closes it by addressing the UK with these (English) words: 'I want to use the words of the poet, George Eliot. She said: "Only in the agony of parting do we look into the depths of love." We will always love you, and we will never be far. Long live Europe!'

I'm moved to tears. *Ach du liebe!*

Later that day, because Croatia holds the rotating six-month presidency of the EU, the Croatian ambassador Irena Andrassy is chairing the UK's final EU meeting as a member state, and she ends with these words: 'Thank you, goodbye, and good riddance.'

These are the last words of any EU official to the UK before its membership expires. Andrassy says she made an error of translation and that what she meant to say was something like 'good luck' – but I know a Freudian slip when I hear one.

Naturally, the Brexiteers propose a festival of almighty celebrations to mark their 'Liberation from Europe' day. If they had their way, there'd be not only colossal firework displays over the white cliffs of Dover but also parades of troops in redcoat uniforms and bearskin helmets accompanied by mounted lifeguards with silver breastplates and sabres, as well as marching brass bands with kilts swinging and bagpipes playing, along the Mall up to Buckingham Palace, plus an aerial flyby of the Battle of Britain Memorial Flight and an aerobatics display by the RAF Red Arrows, plus a mass hoist of union jacks around the United Kingdom while all true patriots sing *God Save the Queen* and salute the flag.

One idea that's swiftly nixed is to have Big Ben bong on the stroke of eleven, Greenwich Mean Time, to mark the moment of liberation. The clock is being expensively renovated and won't be available at that hour unless a truly excessive sum is allocated to pay for the interruption of the renovation. A public finance committee says no, and the idea rightly withers.

Unfortunately, an echo of the idea lives on in the minds of the Downing Street villains responsible for the whole Brexit shitshow. They arrange a dazzling festival of lights in Downing Street, with lasers projecting red, white, and blue imagery over the brick facades of the buildings and generating spectacular scenes for the television news – accompanied by hugely amplified audio recordings of Big Ben bongs to mark the moment.

I'm at home watching the BBC reportage on the final hour of Britain's EU membership in the comfort of my living room. When the view cuts to Downing Street and its spectacularly meaningless light show, resembling the sort of flashing chaos the BBC normally warns viewers prone to epileptic seizures to turn away from, my eardrums are suddenly banged by bongs of preternatural volume, resounding around my living space with a portentous gravity more suited to a funeral ceremony than to a festival of liberation.

As I hear the bongs, I recall the poet John Donne's words: 'No man is an island … If a clod be washed away by the sea, Europe is the less … I am involved in mankind, and therefore never send to know for whom the bell tolls; it tolls for thee.'

I fall to contemplating the Brexit battlefield I'm now leaving in ignominious defeat. With a wistful smile, I recall Joseph Goebbels' advice: *Go down like a hero.*

I decide not to follow it. Patience and logic tell me the wiser course is to play a longer game. Look to science and count your blessings.

Despite all the doom and gloom on the human front, I know it's been a golden decade for physics. Astronomers have created an image of a black hole and have learned how to study the sky using neutrinos and gravitational waves, both offering deep new insights. They've discovered thousands of planets orbiting other stars. And we've discovered the Higgs boson, exactly as predicted. Whatever the political mess, physics gives me reason for hope.

More practically, the UK government is acting to mitigate the climate crisis. It plans to cut greenhouse gas emissions to 'net zero' by 2050. It's putting up new wind farms around the UK.

To back up the wind farms, the government hopes to revitalise its nuclear power capacity. The UK Atomic Energy Authority is still participating in an international project to build a giant experimental fusion reactor set to fire up in 2025.

The UK government has done less well on the medical front, where all the science in the world can't make up for years of under-funding of the National Health Service.

The NHS was a political football from the start. Founded in 1948 by the Labour government in the years following Churchill's abrupt dismissal from office in 1945, it survived years of Tory neglect and deprivation. So far, none of their tricks have budged this bastion of socialism in the heart of post-Thatcher Britain.

But I know change must come to the NHS. Change must come to the medical sector worldwide. The problem is that progress in science and technology makes ever more medical treatments and services available, at ever rising prices. The medical sector can make good use of all the money we can throw at it, given the chance.

That chance will come. The big winner among the sciences in the twentieth century was physics. Physicists delivered the nuclear bombs and electronics that allowed new levers of political power. But molecular biology will be the big winner in the new century.

A global revolution in medical science and health services will transform politics worldwide. I predict an integrated global eco-system that uses medical service delivery to control human life from cradle to grave, or rather from test tube to recycling centre.

In Britain, the NHS is likely to be the delivery structure for this revolution. The main obstacles are rich Brits who rely on expensive private medical services and dislike funding a socialised system for the masses. But rising costs will hurt them too.

Brexit is a problem for the NHS. Thanks to a chronic shortfall in the number of medical training places in UK higher education, the NHS relies heavily on physicians from overseas. One in every nine of its physicians come from an EU member state, and most of these are considering leaving the UK because of Brexit. Record numbers of EU nationals already left the NHS in 2016.

Among nurses and ancillary workers, the crisis caused by Brexit is devastating. Without EU immigrants to staff these positions, the NHS might quickly collapse. The only way to tempt enough native Brits to consider taking such jobs is to improve the pay and working conditions beyond recognition.

The NHS funding crisis is just the clearest sign that the UK is not prepared for a pandemic. Stockpiles of personal protective equipment (PPE) have dwindled and aged. Also, the government has put training to prepare NHS workers for a pandemic on hold for years. An exercise in 2016 showed the NHS would collapse in a crisis, but its recommendations were ignored.

———

To mark the fiftieth anniversary of the World Economic Forum, Professor Schwab announces a new Davos Manifesto stating that companies should pay their fair share of taxes, show zero tolerance for corruption, uphold global human rights, and compete on a level playing field. Because this sounds like mood music from Brussels, the Brexiteers scoff.

They scoffed too when Swedish climate activist Greta Thunberg spoke at Davos in 2019. She speaks there again in 2020: 'Our house is still on fire. Your inaction is fuelling the flames by the hour. We are telling you to act as if you loved your children.'

Davos 2020 is enlivened by the attendance of the heir apparent to the British Crown, Prince Charles, who says: 'We can't go on like this, with every month another record in temperatures being broken. … What good is all the extra wealth in the world, gained from business as usual, if you can do nothing with it except watch it burn in catastrophic conditions?'

Perhaps the Brexiteers will be brought to heel by such words from the presumptive future king of their United Kingdom. But probably not – they think he's a tree-hugger.

President Trump is at Davos too. Someone asks him: 'Are there worries about a pandemic at this point?'

Trump replies: 'No. Not at all … we have it totally under control … It's going to be just fine.'

Days later, the World Health Organisation declares the Covid-19 epidemic a global emergency.

32. Viral apocalypse

Brexiteers are still locked in their tragicomic war of words with Brussels. European negotiators say there can be no new trade deal if Brits insist on diverging from EU standards.

Boris Johnson has a different opinion: 'There is no need for a free trade agreement to involve accepting EU rules on competition policy, subsidies, social protection, the environment, or anything similar.'

In America, President Trump is focused on other things. In his State of the Union address, he says: 'In just three short years, we have shattered the mentality of American decline and we have rejected the downsizing of America's destiny. … We will never let socialism destroy American health care!'

On the next day, Republican senators vote to acquit Trump of the impeachment charges filed against him.

In Britain, a Foreign Office memo says officials may no longer use the words 'deep and special partnership' in connection with the EU or refer to the 'implementation period' in 2020 and must describe their options as 'Canada' for a hard Brexit or 'Australia' for a no-deal Brexit. The Newspeak memo says the UK will 'restore our economic and political independence' on 1 January 2021.

Johnson starts work in February by speaking at the Greenwich Royal Navy College. He says: 'This country is leaving its chrysalis … as a campaigner for global free trade.'

He goes on to venture a farcically inept metaphor: 'And … when there is a risk that new diseases such as coronavirus will trigger a panic and a desire for market segregation that go beyond what is medically rational … then at that moment humanity needs some government somewhere that is … ready to take off its Clark Kent spectacles and leap into the phone booth and emerge with its cloak flowing as the supercharged champion of the right of the populations of the Earth to buy and sell freely among each other.'

He hammers the point home: 'We are embarked now on a great voyage … championing global free trade.'

The prime minister reshuffles his cabinet. He lets go Sajid Javid as Chancellor of the Exchequer and replaces him with Rishi Sunak, a young Hindu millionaire who's reliably on message on Brexit. First elected to the Commons in 2015, the Oxford PPE graduate and former Goldman Sachs financier argued during the 2016 referendum campaign in favour of leaving the EU and has backed Brexit ever since.

But all that's work. This Friday is Valentine's Day, and Boris plans to spend the next twelve days at his government's 'grace and favour' mansion at Chevening with his girlfriend Carrie. True, he hasn't yet divorced his wife, and the four children from the marriage are said to be unhappy at being left behind, but Boris says he's settled with his ex, so all will be well. I'm not amused.

Two weeks later, the global spread of Covid-19 is looking alarming. As containment begins to fail, afflicted countries worldwide introduce social lockdowns to slow the spread and spare their medical facilities. This is critical in the UK, where the NHS is already overstretched.

The mortality rate of the new coronavirus seems to be around one percent. Its victims often feel fine at first – and even later in some cases – so it could easily infect millions.

On Tuesday 25 February, Johnson returns to London from Chevening for a Conservative fundraising ball, where a rich former citizen of the Soviet Union pledges a ridiculous sum to the party for the privilege of playing a game of tennis with him.

Scientists warn ministers that unless they take drastic action the UK faces a disaster, with perhaps 25 million people infected and a quarter of a million deaths. They urgently recommend a lockdown.

On Friday, stock markets worldwide plummet. Investors have got the message, and they're seriously spooked. At last, Johnson announces: 'The issue of coronavirus is something that is now the government's top priority.'

In America, Trump administration officials are still in denial. But investors are digesting the bad news. Global supply chains are already disrupted, and investors put corporate capital expenditure on hold. In the last week of February, equities are decimated: They shed a tenth of their value in a mass selloff.

Boris and Carrie go off for a weekend away in the country. On Saturday, Leap Day, the happy couple tell the world that Carrie is with child and she and Boris are engaged to be married. A besotted follower tweets: 'I like to think Carrie made the most of the leap day and proposed to Boris Johnson.'

The news is big enough for the Brexiteer rag I dub the *Sunday Excrement* to lead with an upbeat headline: BABY JOY FOR BORIS AND CARRIE. More jaded press hacks make sarcastic jokes about bastards in Downing Street and complain that the prime minister is absent without leave yet again at a critical time for the nation.

That weekend, I indulge in a Sunday lunchtime date at the West Hants Club with my miracle babe Rachel. She's down from London for the weekend, and her parents' house is only a walk away from the club, making it a natural place to meet. She plays tennis at the club when she's down, and this Sunday she plays a match with a partner who has a lunch date elsewhere.

I know the club already from visits with my political contacts. This Sunday is bright and sunny, with a promise of spring in the air, and members are playing tennis outdoors in anticipation of the summer season to come.

I show up at the reception in a blue shirt over baggy white shorts and flip-flops, trying for a sporty vibe, and flash my party card to the girl at the desk, who smiles indulgently and lets me in.

On my way to the bar, I glance into the indoor courts but don't see Rachel there.

I settle at a free table with a glass of alcohol-free beer and wait. She shows up soon after, with her hair still damp from a shower, dressed in a loose blue tee bearing a Conservative tree logo over navy yoga tights and flip-flops. She dumps her sports bag and raises a hand as if to say no.

'I'll get myself a drink, thanks,' she says and heads for the bar. After a brief chat with the barmaid, she returns with a big glass of soda and lime. She plonks herself down and smiles.

'So, how are you?' I ask, 'I see you're looking well.'

'Good, thanks.' She glances down at her hair and strokes it. 'Very busy in London, at party headquarters, so it's nice to get away and relax down here. Do you play tennis?'

'Me? No. Not for, um, going on forty years. My last game was in Japan, against one of my students, a wife and mother, and she beat me. I decided that was humiliation enough and never played again.'

'But you still look quite fit,' she says, apparently seriously.

'Yes, running and swimming are enough for me now. I'm a marathon reader, but that doesn't do much for the muscle tone.'

'No,' she muses. 'Did you really teach philosophy at Oxford? You once told me you did, but I didn't quite get it.'

'Yes, for a year. I was hired to teach a few logic classes and some students in philosophy of mind. That was one of my topics.'

Rachel nods slowly and smiles. 'You told me about neuroscience. Is that the same thing?'

'It is now, yes, but it hardly existed in those days. We've moved on a long way since then. In Germany I got back into it all and started going to conferences on the science of consciousness. I realised that we'd made progress, and soon enough I had enough stuff for my book on it all.'

'I see. And now you're trying to teach me enough philosophy to survive Boris Johnson.'

I smile. 'Yes, funny how life turns out.'

Suddenly she looks directly into my eyes. 'I got the impression you had a more personal interest in me. Do you?'

I look back steadily. 'Yes, in a way. It's hard to teach anyone anything without taking an interest. I see enough promise in you – and that's a personal thing, obviously – to make it seem worth the bother. But don't worry. I have no plans to seduce you. I'm a house-trained philosopher, an intellectual lover, not a Humbert.'

She looks puzzled. 'Humbert?'

'The lecherous old man in *Lolita*. Did you ever read that, or see the movie?'

'Ah, Lolita. I get the idea. I'm not that young, but I see it. So, why aren't you teaching philosophy somewhere now, for a living?'

I take a deep breath. 'I decided it was too quiet and dull. I wanted action. I got myself recruited for the Ministry of Defence, to work at the heart of the action in Whitehall.'

'So why aren't you there now?'

'Well, I was wrong. In the lower ranks it was even duller than philosophy. It was just boring paperwork, trivial stuff, with no scope for creative thinking. My lust for action was science calling, and that took me to Germany. The rest, as they say, is history.'

She's nodding slowly. 'I get it. I got the impression you were trying to hit on me, so I led you on a bit. I hope you don't mind!' She looks up and smiles suddenly.

'No problem. It was a natural thought. I'm glad your radar was good enough to see the risk. I don't want you seducing me either, by the way.'

She blinks. 'Really?'

'Really. It would probably be disappointing, rather like tennis with the Japanese housewife.'

'Aha, good, I see. That's settled, then. I wanted to tell you about our work in central office and hear your thoughts on it.'

'Go ahead. I'm listening.'

'Well, as you probably know, the chief special advisor in Downing Street is Dominic Cummings, and he's quite a revolutionary.'

'Right, I read some of his long blog posts, and I see a disrupter. Certainly not a deep or organised thinker, but still a dangerous chap. He needs watching carefully.'

'Great,' she smiles. 'I think other people agree with you.'

I pause, realising she's taking me into her confidence. 'I don't think he's right for government service at all. He was hired originally as a mercenary for Brexit. He worked for years in Russia and then came back and hacked the referendum for Vote Leave. That's not the kind of chap you want as the spad to the prime minister.'

'But Boris has the right to choose his own staff,' she says, looking down, then looking up at me again. 'So, what do we do?'

'We get rid of Boris. Can't the party throw him out?'

'The party base loves him. Don't you remember the Bournemouth Pavilion crowd last summer? They want Boris in Number 10, at least until the Brexit transition is over at the end of the year.'

'And I want him out before then, so that we can back down and start to undo the damage he's done.'

She looks calm, almost pitying. 'Maybe you need to back down and see both sides.'

'There's only one side to Brexit. It's a get-rich-quick scheme for tax dodgers and speculators. The British public will pay the price.'

She weighs this up for a while, then sighs and swigs a deep draught of soda. 'Is this all because of Germany?'

'What, my detestation of Boris and Brexit?'

'Yes.' She looks into my eyes again.

'Yes. I don't want British nationalists wrecking my years of work in building trust with Germans and other Europeans.'

'I'm sure the Germans can live with Brexit. It's a chance for them to reorganise the EU without British opposition.'

I smile. 'True. But it leaves me marooned on an island run by a bunch of people who only care about money.'

She pauses, then says quietly: 'Join the game. Earn money.'

We both fall silent, then she looks at the clock and jumps. We part hastily, with no-contact handwaves, leaving me to return to reality in my book-lined clifftop hermitage by the sea.

After his baby joy, Boris Johnson is back in zestful action on Monday. He chairs a COBRA meeting in Whitehall and signs off on a 'battle plan' to mitigate the spread of the virus. But there's an awkward delay as he and his advisers debate how to implement the plan. The SAGE scientists urge a full lockdown, but economic advisers are tempted to wait for the public to develop herd immunity. When the scientists explain how many excess deaths this will cause, they grudgingly accept a lockdown.

Johnson missed all five prior COBRA meetings on the epidemic. A Downing Street source explains why it matters: 'There's no way you're at war if your PM isn't there. And what you learn about Boris was he didn't chair any meetings. He liked his country breaks. He didn't work weekends ... he didn't do urgent crisis planning. It was exactly like people feared he would be.'

On 3 March, Johnson holds his first televised press conference with his chief scientific adviser and his chief medical officer, who say an estimated eighty percent of the population could become infected, and one percent of them could die.

Johnson tries breezy good cheer: 'We should all basically just go about our normal daily lives ... The best thing you can do is to wash your hands with soap and hot water while singing *Happy Birthday* twice.'

But he's in sharp focus on Brexit. He still rules out an extension of EU trade deal negotiations beyond the end of 2020. And he's already ratting on the political declaration and on the customs border in the Irish Sea, clashing with EU rules on state aid, and fighting for regulatory freedom. From its side, the EU wants to prevent unfair competition. There's no deal that will let both sides declare victory.

Still dreaming big, the UK government publishes its objectives for an Anglo-American trade deal, which it sees as its jackpot prize. Analysts say any such deal will at best enrich the two countries by a few parts per thousand.

American billionaire Wilbur Ross is Trump's secretary of commerce. He once saved Trump from going bust. His job is to uphold the Trump trade doctrine, which is to reduce the US trade deficit, strengthen US manufacturing, and boost US growth. I can see that Brexiteer hopes of economic rescue from Trump America are hopeless fantasy.

On 6 March, in a White House briefing, epidemiologists warn that Covid-19 could infect four-fifths of the US population and kill over two million Americans.

On Wednesday 11 March, World Health Organization officials say the spread of the coronavirus is now a global pandemic.

On Thursday, the Dow futures market nosedives. The US stock market enters bear territory for the first time since 2008.

Her Majesty's chief scientific adviser makes a dire admission: 'Our aim is to … build up some kind of herd immunity, so more people are immune to this disease.'

Johnson now decides to strike a Churchillian pose. He starts holding daily press conferences flanked by the chief medical officer and chief scientific adviser. He's trying to show the public he's mastering the crisis. This is his update of Churchill's first days as prime minister, when that old bulldog confronted a Blitzkrieg on the other side of the Channel and presided over an evacuation from Dunkirk. Johnson is determined to live up to his moment.

But he's already far too late. Also, thanks to the bee in his bonnet on Brexit, he's insisted that the UK quit the EU pandemic early warning system and leave the European Medicines Agency.

On Sunday, UK health secretary Matt Hancock hints at a new approach: 'We have a plan, based on the expertise of world-leading scientists. Herd immunity is not a part of it. That is a scientific concept, not a goal or a strategy.'

A week passes, with no sign of a plan but with daily press briefings from 10 Downing Street to mark the deepening crisis in the NHS as hospitals fill up and nurses and resources such as PPE begin to run out. It's like following daily government briefings in the summer of 1940 when the RAF struggled to hold back swarms of Luftwaffe bombers and when Spitfires and their pilots began to run out.

On Friday 20 March, Johnson announces the imminent closure of pubs, clubs, and restaurants: 'We're taking away the ancient, inalienable right of free-born people of the United Kingdom to go the pub. … I know how difficult this is, how it seems to go against the freedom-loving instincts of the British people.'

Boris loves his channelling of Churchill as the living symbol of the sovereign birthright of the British people to live free and drink their fill. As he wrote of his hero: 'With his ludicrous hats and rompers and cigars and excess alcohol, he contrived physically to represent the central idea of his own political philosophy: the inalienable right of British people to live their lives in freedom, to do their own thing.'

This innate English nonconformity is a myth. Boris is citing it to sweeten the pill of lockdown. He's grasping at straws.

———

China is claiming victory in its campaign against the coronavirus. Mass quarantines, a travel ban, and a shutdown of most daily life nationwide are said to have stemmed the tide.

By contrast, I can see that the United States is struggling and on course to fail. The European Union looks clueless too. This leaves the role of global crisis leadership wide open for China.

In Brexit Britain, a new setback hits the embattled government. On Friday 27 March, Boris Johnson and his health secretary Matt Hancock say they're infected with the coronavirus. Dominic Cummings is infected too. The UK government is no good at following its own advice on social distancing and hand washing.

I sense the demise of the Anglo-American world hegemony. Trump America and Brexit Britain are down and out. The crisis puts China back on top, to be once more the Celestial Empire it was centuries ago, before the Western barbarians rudely interrupted its tranquil communion with heaven. It's payback time for decades of humiliation by Victorian mercantilists.

On April Fools' Day, stock indexes fall again, extending the losses from March. The emergency lockdowns on both sides of the Atlantic push the global economy into the sharpest downturn since the Great Depression.

Bill Gates says this is a new world war, but this time with all of humanity on the same side. Suddenly, war is a medical emergency and not a political act.

I focus on the bright side. The coronavirus crisis is bad, but the climate crisis could be a lot worse.

33. Waging global war

On Easter Sunday, Boris Johnson rises from his hospital bed. He's spent three nights in intensive care, under an oxygen mask, on the brink of death. But now he's risen, thanks to the National Health Service. He records a short video to acknowledge his NHS care team: 'I can't thank them enough. I owe them my life.'

Johnson's recovery changes him. He understands the stakes in the coronavirus war. He knows both the cost of defeat and the joy of victory over death, and he's determined to steer the ship of state toward that victory. But he's still the same old clown.

A Downing Street propaganda person says: 'Our response has ensured that the NHS has been given all the support it needs … The prime minister has been … providing leadership during this hugely challenging period for the whole nation.'

I know better. Johnson's government missed the chance to push early and hard on mass testing. And successive governments since 2010 have failed to stockpile enough PPE for health and care workers. NHS managers are facing their worst nightmare in stark reality. They weren't prepared for a pandemic.

The British death toll from the coronavirus is soon the highest in Europe. By the end of May, the body count has risen to more than that inflicted by the Luftwaffe during the Blitz. British exceptionalism has never been so humiliating.

France, Spain, and Italy all suffer badly too in the pandemic. But Germany comes out relatively well. Despite its larger population, it logs less than a quarter of the death toll in Britain. The German healthcare system was impressively well prepared, with far more intensive-care beds, an effective testing and tracing capability, enough front-line workers, and solid political support for an early and effective lockdown.

Johnson can't claim victory in this war. His government has let down its citizens. Churchill made mistakes too, but not like this.

Johnson isn't the only let-down. In America, President Trump puts US funding of the WHO on hold 'to assess the World Health Organisation's role in severely mismanaging and covering up the spread of the coronavirus' – in a doomed attempt to cover up his own incompetence.

The WHO is the spearhead of efforts to coordinate national responses to the pandemic into a coherent global strategy. The Trump administration is weakening those efforts at the worst possible time, just when the carnage is peaking in Europe and North America and when it's looming as a dire threat everywhere else.

That's the medical news in the corona war. The economic news threatens to be even worse.

The International Monetary Fund predicts that global economic output per head will contract by four percent in 2020. Even if the rest of the year turns out well, the IMF forecasts a three percent global contraction. All of humanity is in this war together.

But Britain is taking it on the chin. It faces a 35 percent dip in economic output in the second quarter if the lockdown continues for three months. And government borrowing will erase the gain from a decade of austerity.

The damage to human civilisation is only just beginning. The crisis is revealing fault lines that have been growing for decades. Economic inequalities, ecological destruction, and political corruption are combining explosively to risk social collapse.

I recall a political concept called the Overton window. This is the range of policies that people find politically acceptable at a given time. During normal times, only a narrow range of ideas is in view. But in a crisis, people begin to look at fringe ideas.

The triumph of neoliberalism has let huge global corporations put a stranglehold on the global economy. Their relentless pursuit of profit and growth has pushed the planetary environment to breakdown and caused a climate crisis. Even if humans can restore the natural order, continued growth will bring further existential threats.

On the bright side, the pandemic has done more to slow down climate breakdown and ecological collapse than all other impulses combined. The emergency response across the world has shown what people can do in a crisis. Politics as usual is gone, economics is toast, and it's time for a philosopher to weigh in.

The new fascism exposes a deep contradiction. The neoliberal era was based on the myth of the selfish individual as the foundation of all values. Yet humans have prosocial impulses that prompt them to identify with something larger, if only their fascist leader. I say a new generation of leaders should plot a new course by extending fairness and compassion to all human and nonhuman life on Earth. The years of stoking and exploiting tribal divisions must end, on pain of human extinction in a hothouse apocalypse.

That message is my calling card. But I find it hard to focus on the big picture while the pandemic crisis goes unchecked. With the prime minister in bed, UK government policy is drifting behind the screensaver message that ministers are following the science.

I should have stayed in Germany. There, a one-month lockdown has brought the epidemic under control. German diagnostic labs responded rapidly, and in April they're testing enough people to trace coronavirus carriers effectively, with results that look like the best in Europe.

On Monday 20 April, in an ironic reminder that the pandemic is working wonders for the climate by shutting down movement, leaving streets nearly empty and skies a flawless blue, the US benchmark price for oil sinks to below zero. Peak oil at last?

I don't think so. The manifest destiny of Trump America is still to go out in a blaze of dirty glory.

The United States is playing the bad actor in the global fight against the coronavirus. Trump is posing as a wartime president leading a national struggle, but his America has already lost. By the end of May, Americans have paid for electing him with more deaths to Covid than in the Korean and Vietnam wars combined. Also, forty million workers are unemployed, and many of their jobs are gone forever. America has become a failed state.

The UK hasn't sunk that far, but it's still showing the world how not to manage a pandemic. Its government chose not to take part in the EU joint procurement scheme for ventilators and PPE. British officials attended the meetings but expressed no interest.

I've lost hope of reason prevailing on Brexit. The faster the post-Brexit trade talks break down, the sooner a backlash can begin, but this means months of patience.

EU chief negotiator Michel Barnier reports: 'The objective that we had for tangible progress … has only been partially achieved. The United Kingdom did not want to engage seriously on a certain number of fundamental issues.'

The UK has been quietly sabotaging the sessions. The talks are suspended. No deal by the end of the year means WTO rules with high tariffs and customs barriers. Yet Johnson is holding fast to the deadline. He's determined not to let his Great Britain remain in the purgatory of vassalage any longer.

Downing Street officials issue a statement from their bunker: 'We will not ask to extend and, if the EU asks, we will say no.'

Sir Ivan Rogers nails the impact of the refusal: 'Her Majesty's government is in reality forcing firms which are facing an existential crisis over Covid-19 right now and for the next several months to prepare simultaneously for a no-deal exit at year end.'

Johnson returns to work in Downing Street on Monday 27 April and delivers a little speech in front of Number 10 to prove his fitness. Two days later, his fiancée Carrie delivers a healthy son.

Then Boris goes back to more downtime at home.

On Thursday, Johnson appears again to front the daily government pandemic press briefing alongside the scientists. He looks tired and often out of breath as he says Britain is 'past the peak' of its epidemic and on the 'downward slope' of the statistical graphs. Maybe he's past his peak and on the way down.

Brexit negotiators remain without a lead. The Brexit turd is still stinking, and Johnson is past his peak as the party champion. I say Britain would do well to buck the downside, dump the turd, flush the loo, and wash its collective hands of the whole BoJo bandwagon while singing *Happy Birthday* twice.

———

On 4 May, thanks to the miracle of technology, I enjoy a Zoom meeting with Rachel. Given the lockdown, meeting in the flesh is no longer an option, but we agree a video call might be fun.

I've prepared for Zoom calls by turning my desk to point the webcam at my bookcases. This is a visual cliché, I know, but it has the merit of distracting attention from my pixelated mugshot. I've buzz-cut my hair down to stubble and not shaved my chin for a while, so I look like a Russian convict on camera.

For Rachel's benefit, I decide not to dress up. Any suggestion of elaborate preparation is a bad way to telegraph the casual confidence a philosopher should project in the contingencies of his corporeal presence. I wear an old denim shirt and sweatpants.

Rachel appears to be in an upstairs room with angled creamy white walls sloping up to a ceiling ridge. Her camera tilts slightly upward, suggesting a laptop screen pushed back. She looks as ever from the neck up, but below it she's wrapped in a loose silk or satin kimono-style gown in a dark blue tone.

'Great to see you again.' I begin, 'How are you?'

'Good, thanks. I see you're relaxing in lockdown.'

I stroke my chin. 'Concentrating on essentials. I'm blogging all this for the benefit of future historians. They won't care about my hair or my chin. But how's life in London? I hear things are worse there.'

'Yes, you have life easy down in Bournemouth. We're having to really take care, especially with public transport. I'm trying to isolate and work from home, but sometimes I have to go out, for food and so on.'

'Can you do all your work from home?'

She pulls her wrap together to cover her chest more fully. 'For now, yes, but I don't know how long we can go on like this.'

'None of us do. It's the new normal.'

'I hope this never becomes normal. Anyway, let me get to the point. I wanted to ask you a few questions if you don't mind.'

'Fire away.' I sit up straighter in my chair.

'Actually, I'm interested in why you joined the Conservative party and why you left.'

'Is this part of your job now?'

'Yes, in a way, but I'm also genuinely interested. If I can relate to your reasons for leaving, I might think about my own membership.'

'Okay, fair enough. I joined, as I think I told you years ago, because I was inspired by the coalition Cameron and Clegg formed. I thought that was a promising way forward, to bring British politics more in line with the style I'd seen working well in Germany for years. Also, I'd never really been on board with the left-wing politics I'd encountered as a student. And my mother and her consort had been party members, so I understood the style and so on of local Conservatives. Oh, and when I came back from Germany it was a great way to get an instant social life. That's why I joined.'

'Yes, that makes sense. I understand all that. But why didn't you get involved before you went to Germany? Why not even before that, when you were a student?'

'Remember I was a student in the early Seventies. We were far too into rock music – sex and drugs and rock and roll, as we used to say. All that was much more interesting – much more *real* – than the old-fogey nonsense the student Conservatives were peddling. They just wanted to be president of the Oxford Union and go into careers in law or banking. Desperately boring people. I was into radical chic: "Turn on, tune in, drop out," as Timothy Leary, the acid guru, used to say.'

Rachel looks attentive, even agog, if that's possible in a Zoom image. 'Really? A hippy, studying – what was it? – physics and PPE?'

'Just the style. Urban cowboy, easy rider, like in the movies and music. We were all doing it. I hung out with the English crowd, the artists, the writers. I thought maybe I'd become a writer too, or at least a cultural guru of some sort, like a philosopher.'

'Didn't you get involved in student politics, party politics?'

I shake my head as if the sheer idea were mad. 'Student politics for me meant radical causes. Remember my girlfriend Judy was a Marxist. We were all into Ban the Bomb, make love not war, and of course feminism, and anti-racism, anti-colonialism, anti-capitalism. British party politics at the parliamentary level just seemed impossibly dull and boring. It looked like Monty Python self-parody.'

Rachel blinks at all these ideas. 'Feminism I can relate to as well, and anti-racism and so on, but self-parody? Really?'

'I may be exaggerating slightly, but not much. There was a huge cultural divide. British politics was completely uncool, like a whole generation behind the times.'

'And now? How can you take parliamentary politics seriously after all that?'

'Good question. In short, with difficulty. I understand the practical imperatives. We can only work with what we've got. When the national resources at the disposal of politicians are as meagre as they've been in Britain during my formative years, you see the need

ALBION   353

to cast the net wider. In my case, the wider field was obvious. Europe was up for grabs.'

'Okay, good.' She perks up suddenly. 'I wanted to ask you about Europe. Why was that where you looked – and not, say, America?'

'We looked at America too, believe me. Our dream was to go and start a new life in California – Hollywood and life on the road. But we had to be realistic. After the Second World War, it was obvious that we had to sort out Europe and keep out the Soviets and so on.'

'Right, but how did fighting the Soviet occupation in Europe relate to your left-wing politics?'

'Easy – the Soviets were the ultimate baddies, betraying all our radical ideals with what Judy used to call their state capitalism. Do you recall the French existentialist philosopher Jean-Paul Sartre? Well, he was on our side at first – I read some of his novels and really enjoyed them – but then he joined the Communist party and sided with Mao Zedong, so we had to leave him behind.'

'Sartre – wasn't he with Simone de Beauvoir, the feminist?'

'Yes. They were a couple for decades, not married but as good as. Judy loved her book *The Second Sex*.'

'I see,' she says slowly. 'This is all beginning to make sense. You were never really a Conservative at all.'

'Take care. My reasons were all sound. As one gathers experience, one matures and becomes more practical. I learned that big ideas are all very well, but there's always a point where the rubber hits the road, so to speak. Parliament was still the bottleneck through which all our ideas had to be funnelled – unless we were serious about revolution, of course.'

'Well, weren't you?'

'Not if it meant blood on the streets. Judy used to say the best way forward was the Long March through the institutions.'

'And that's what she did – as an MP, I mean.'

'Exactly. And it's what I could do, as a philosopher in the Conservative party. Toning up the debate and jazzing up the ideas and so on.'

Rachel hitches up her gaping kimono again. 'And that's what you tried with Sir Robert in Poole.'

'In my own tiny way, yes. Until the whole Brexit issue blew up and I realised I'd rather see revolution in the streets than accept the sort of nationalist government the Brexiteers now have in mind.'

'Okay, I think I've got it. One last question – why don't you like Boris Johnson? If Brexit weren't an issue, would you support him?'

'No, I still wouldn't vote for him. I remember his type from Oxford. Callous, arrogant rogues, with no ideas at all beyond self-promotion. Boris was just in love with the idea of posing as the great orator at the dispatch box. He chose to back Vote Leave for no better reason than that he could exploit the disruption it caused to get himself into power.'

'But Boris was friends with David Cameron, and you supported him.'

'Exactly, Boris betrayed him! If he'd stayed on Dave's side in the referendum, it's quite likely Remain would have won and we'd have been spared all this agony. Dave could still be prime minister, nudging the the party to stop bashing the EU. And he'd probably have managed to avoid the horrible bodge Boris has made of his response to the coronavirus crisis.'

'Okay, apart from his being a callous, arrogant rogue, betraying Dave, backing Brexit, and bodging the coronavirus crisis, can you imagine ever voting for Boris?' She grins suddenly, as if she's just got the joke.

I smile too and remain silent.

She sighs quietly and sits back. 'Okay, enough said. Thanks for that, Andy. The interrogation is over. You've given me a lot of food for thought. Thank you for your patience.'

'You're welcome. Is that all you wanted?'

She raises her arms to push her hair back behind her shoulders. This causes her kimono to gape further, exposing more bare skin. She looks down and closes it with a smile. 'That was it. Apart from just touching base, of course.'

'Of course. I guess that concludes the day's business.'

A young man with a naked torso walks into view behind her. He puts his hands onto her shoulders, bends down, and speaks quietly into her ear. She looks down and nods, then glances back at her webcam. 'I have to go now, Andy. Thanks again for the call.'

'You're welcome.' Before I can say more, the session ends abruptly, leaving me facing a blank screen.

I sit back and frown. Does she really think I might rejoin the Conservative party while Brexit is still in play? Is she now back in a relationship that makes my presence in the margins of her life no more than a nuisance? Should I move on?

The answers are easy. I shall never rejoin a Tory party that spurns my EU citizenship. I need to accept that for me Rachel is like a former student. I must move on.

That sorted, I go out for my daily exercise session. I combine it with a shopping expedition by hiking along the beach to a remote supermarket, with my sandals in my rucksack, and hiking back along the street with a few days' food in the sack. This is a feature of life under lockdown I could learn to like – it hits a deep resonance with an ancient hunter-gatherer past that modern civilisation has otherwise all but erased.

Later that day, I discover that Conor Burns has resigned as a trade minister after being found to have abused his position as MP to intimidate a member of the public. A Commons committee says he broke the rules, and he admits his guilt.

I smile – Rachel bailed out just in time.

———

Back to Brexit. Johnson seems to fear that any concessions in the Brussels trade talks might involve the UK in helping to prop up the EU economy after the pandemic. EU officials suspect he's planning to hide the damage from a hard Brexit within the wider damage wrought by the coronavirus. I'm sure he is.

A new crisis pops up. On the day after the UK-wide lockdown came into force in March, Dominic Cummings drove to Durham with his wife and their son. Because he had Covid-19, he said, they were in a hurry to arrange childcare. Two weeks later, he drove to a beauty spot some miles from Durham before returning to London. All this was in breach of the lockdown rules.

On Sunday 24 May, in a doomed attempt to calm the crisis, Johnson claims at a press conference in Downing Street that Cummings had simply 'followed the instincts of every father' by driving to Durham. Then, on Monday, in a master class of damage control (not), Cummings tells a cock-and-bull story to defend his actions.

The public reacts with fury, contempt, and anguish. A BBC anchor complains: 'He made those who struggled to keep to the rules feel like fools and has allowed many more to feel like they can flout them.'

Boris backs Dom but ruins the credibility of his government.

During the entire month of May, the warm and sunny weather breaks all British records. Globally, 2020 looks set to be the hottest year since climate measurements began.

This is the human predicament. Brexit is done, the coronavirus is rampant, and the climate is on the boil. Yet I feel fine. I know where I stand.

34. The darkest hour

Like millions of other people, I spend weeks marooned in isolation. Unlike millions of others, as a philosopher I'm used to living this way and find it entirely natural and even quite pleasant. The simple chores of everyday life, like going shopping for food, become survivalist adventures, and the simple pleasures, like jogging along the beach, feel more intense when the few people around me are socially distanced. It's like living in a post-apocalypse movie.

Out on the seafront one warm and brilliantly sunny morning, leaning on a weathered wooden rail bordering a ridge of dune beside a long open stretch of sand, wearing little shorts and a light tee, with my perforated rubber running shoes by my side, I look out over the empty vista and find my soul becalmed in a vast inner peace. The sky is a deep, clear blue, with not even a wisp of vapour to veil its endless volume. The sea is smooth and calm out to the horizon, with nothing but a few small yellow floats to dot its shimmering surface. The whole wide beach is as empty as a desert shoreline.

Poole Bay beach, stretching in an unbroken golden ribbon for miles to the left of me, has been slowly transformed over the years as ever more public furniture is installed along the prom that runs along it. Serried ranks of unlovely beach huts stand beside it, with handrails and lampposts, with bench seats and litter bins and notice-boards and flagpoles and beach shops and restaurants – all that clutter now idle, quietly decomposing, like the ruins of an ancient civilisation. When the people are gone, the serenity of nature freezes the entire scene in a magic spell. It hints at primal memories of a prehistoric past. Contact with such eternity is balm to my soul.

On one bright day in late May, I drive around Poole Harbour toward Swanage and then head north to Studland, where I park near the wild beach I know so well.

On this sunny day, I revel in a springtime English paradise of fresh greenery. As I walk along the coastal path, beside rows of old and unoccupied beach huts, past little stands of trees and clumps of weeds and nettles, past hillocks of sand and a coastline strewn with boulders and seaweed, I feel mute solidarity with the scattering of socially distanced fellow spring breakers who are also slaking their thirst for nature before returning to the lockdown.

Once that's done, I drive back briskly. I'm a few miles from home when my car's engine cuts out. I coast to a halt, call out an emergency service to confirm a breakdown, call a truck to ferry the car to my dealer, pack the rucksack in the boot, and walk home.

Days later, I find that my trusty German lifeboat is *kaput*. Its fuel pump has disintegrated and damaged its injectors, expensively. With great sadness, I sell it – as well as the headlights and speedometer stored in my garage – to a local scrap dealer. Another link with my life in Germany is gone.

———

It's June, and President Trump, with four US flags behind him, threatens to send in the military against 'Antifa' protesters supporting the Black Lives Matter movement.

Democratic senator Ron Wyden says: 'The fascist speech Donald Trump just delivered verged on a declaration of war against American citizens.'

Following his rant, Trump crosses the road to pose for a photo outside a historic church while holding up a Bible. He's preceded by armed police and mounted national guardsmen firing teargas and rubber bullets to chase away protesters.

Watching the live action on television, Ben Harley, a biker in Florida, says: 'My mother just shouted out, "God give him strength! He's doing a Jericho walk!" – and then she started speaking in tongues.'

Harley changes his social media profile photo to an image of

Trump outside the church, with added rays of light emanating from the Bible, and says: 'I believe this is a president who wears the full armour of God.'

On Tuesday night, military Black Hawk helicopters circle low above Washington to intimidate protesters and looters. National guardsmen in combat gear stand in front of the Lincoln Memorial. Days later, a new fence around the White House separates the president from the people.

Donald Trump is a classic fascist. He uses military force to demand submission, then despises as weaklings those who submit. The only role he offers Boris Johnson is as shambling sidekick. Any trade deal with Trump will bear a heavy price.

As red lines in trade talks, Johnson's government pledged not to relent on British environmental protection, animal welfare, or food standards. Now it proposes to import US foods produced using dangerous, cruel, and disgusting means, and to let US pharma giants make big profits selling drugs to the NHS.

British voters are furious. Their government is trampling over all their cherished principles.

The Black Lives Matter protests spread to Britain. In Bristol, a crowd topples a statue of Edward Colston, a city benefactor and slave trader. Other monuments are at risk. Activists in London even deface statues of Winston Churchill and Queen Victoria.

In my local patch, the BCP council considers removing the statue of Lord Baden-Powell from the Poole quayside following threats by opponents of his homophobia, racism, and support for Hitler. I'm dismayed to find that when Baden-Powell read *Mein Kampf* in 1939, he called it a wonderful book.

The statue of Baden-Powell has been there since 2008. I posed beside it with my council running mates Buzz and Ali in 2015. Five years on, council leader Vikki Slade has it boarded up and allows local scout fans to guard it.

Amid all this turmoil, trade talks between the UK and the EU are not going well. EU leaders warn the UK government to expect no deal unless it accepts a level playing field. Team Johnson rejects this demand, as well as a demand to let EU fishermen retain rights to fish in UK territorial waters, and rebuffs EU attempts to give the European Court of Justice a role in adjudicating disputes.

On Monday 22 June, I buy a small Volkswagen to replace my scrapped car. I'm too addicted to the joy of driving a German car to go cold turkey. I'll tough out the green guilt so long as my carbon footprint is otherwise blameless.

A car is both a big investment for a poor boy and an admission of defeat on a big question. In the remaining six months before the national drawbridge is pulled up, there's no real chance that I can wrap up my affairs in the UK and emigrate to Germany. As a man in the autumn of my years, I feel my options closing in fast.

On Wednesday, when it's too hot to stay indoors, I risk a bus ride to Studland. I sit on a socially distanced seat behind a facemask while the double-decker negotiates a narrow heathland road with cars parked nose to tail on either side, then I glare out in stoic silence for a full half an hour while the diesel monster does a back-and-forth, inch-by-inch elephant dance with an ambulance, blue lights flashing, urgently trying to pass in the opposite direction. Hours later, rather than risk the bus again, I walk back to home base.

On Thursday, I take delivery of my new ride. It's a great relief to be able to tool around the neighbourhood in cool comfort again. When my workroom gets too hot on a summer afternoon, I can go for a spin and turn up the air conditioning, safe in my social bubble. The new toy soothes the sting of losing my right to escape to Germany as I hunker down for the Brexit ordeal.

Boris Johnson has other things on his mind. He decides that Covid put him in intensive care because he was overweight. Now he wants to slim down. But even party loyalists are wondering whether the Johnson they voted for has gone for good. He's made a horrible mess of his first six months in office. He says he's proud of what he's achieved, but no one else is.

Britain's performance fighting the virus has been dismal, leaving it at the bottom of the league of comparable European states. Nor has the UK fared well economically. In the first half of 2020, it's suffered its largest fall in output in recorded history. Insiders say Johnson's leadership has been shambolic.

As the days of June run out, Johnson rules out an extension of the Brexit transition period. He says he'd wanted Brexit so badly, he stamped his feet and got it for Christmas. He'd eyed it as a fine vehicle to launch global Britain into a new golden age. But now it's *kaput*, going nowhere, and he's reduced to sitting in a static driving seat going: 'Poop-poop!'

On Independence Day, at Mount Rushmore, President Trump says what he thinks of the BLM protests: 'Our nation is witnessing a merciless campaign to wipe out our history … Angry mobs are trying to tear down statues … and unleash a wave of violent crime in our cities.'

He refuses to take a knee: 'We stand tall, we stand proud, and we only kneel before almighty God.'

Back in blighted Britain, chancellor Rishi Sunak pumps more billions into the economy. Soon Brits will face a hefty tax hike.

In Europe, tax justice is a priority for the German presidency of the European Council in the second half of 2020. The Germans want to set minimum tax levels in the EU to prevent a race to the bottom on corporate tax rates. This will only spur the Brexiteer tax dodgers to go for no deal.

Team Johnson has narrowed the scope of talks with the EU to trade. Boris has swept all the other issues off the table. Unfortunately for his image as a feisty sovereign leader, he's now stuck, because his trade policy is dictated by Donald Trump.

In another rash move, Boris nominates his Tory chum Chris Grayling – 'Failing Grayling' – to chair the UK intelligence and security committee. This is a powerful committee with an important role, and it's powerful enough to elect a better qualified MP as its new chair. Boris has bungled again.

On Wednesday 15 July, as usual at prime minister's questions, Boris is unable to cope. Opposition leader Keir Starmer cites a major new medical report and asks what assurance Boris can give that the UK test-and-trace capacity will be fit for purpose in time for the next winter season.

Boris responds with bluster: 'Our test and trace system is as good as, or better than, any other system anywhere in the world.'

Starmer asks him if he's read the report.

Has he hell: 'I am of course aware of the report.'

Starmer suggests Boris is in denial about the weakness of the UK response and wonders what he might like to say to the families of those who died due to his negligence.

Boris can't resist a schoolboy joke. Accusing Starmer of raising too many topics at once, he says it looks like he has 'more briefs than Calvin Klein' – *ta-dah!*

It's pitiful.

———

On Monday 20 July, EU leaders strike a deal on their coronavirus recovery package. They agree on a rescue fund of three-quarters of a trillion euros and sign off on the next seven-year EU budget of just over a trillion euros. It's a big day for Europe, but it's also a big enough bill to nail down the lid on any chance that Johnson will relent in his determination to tear the UK free of the EU and all its expensive safety nets. The lid boxes in the Remainers and leaves Leavers to feed the vultures in the money markets.

On that day too, the latest anniversary of the day Apollo astronauts first stepped onto the Moon, I drive to the remote village of

Deadbury. The two-hour trip each way is a fine proving run for my new car. Once there, I spend an hour sightseeing and taking photos of old pubs and so on while keeping my distance from the villagers. That's already enough before I head off home again.

Why Deadbury? I guess it was Rachel who triggered the trip. I don't want to get too florid with my metaphors, but she expelled the demons in my dreamscape and prompted me to clear out the skeletons in my closet and put my psychic house in order. Deadbury is ground zero for a former succubus.

Here my narrative arc requires that I tell a deep, dark story. I'll do my best to keep it light and fun.

Cast your mind back to 1974, to the Ealing student commune, just weeks before Judy and I set off for Berlin.

A key flash of insight for my dialectical logic came to me while I was injecting loud music via headphones. I had what I hoped were the right records playing as I read pages of handwritten notes. For my cryptic lines on Hegel's philosophy, I channelled Beethoven's music, including the sublime *Ode to Joy* that became the EU anthem. For my pages of set theory formulas, I rattled my brainwaves with David Bowie's apocalyptic new album *Diamond Dogs*. The resulting fusion of ideas powered my summer of big dreams.

Our planning for the months in Berlin was minimal. A friend of the commune called Vicks would be visiting her friends in the city and assured us we'd find a ready welcome there. She was an exotic creature, blonde and beautiful but also vague and absent-minded, who had studied maths but then drowned in the counter-culture. Once, in a day alone in the house with me, she told me she dreamed of writing a phenomenology of fucking, and I said she'd be hard put to improve on the novel *Fear of Flying* by Erica Jong or on *The Dialectic of Sex* by Shulamith Firestone. Vicks liked to walk around naked, piss in the garden, and generally freak out boring people. We were taking a chance in trusting her.

Judy and I took the train through East Germany to West Berlin. Emerging at Bahnhof Zoo (immortalised a few years later in the movie *Wir Kinder vom Bahnhof Zoo* starring David Bowie), we let Vicks put us in a local student commune much like the Ealing one, which was fine for a few days, until she moved us to a radical and probably illegal squat near the Wall. She then departed, leaving us to cope there as best we could for the rest of the summer.

The Berlin squat was in an abandoned factory next to the Wall in Kreuzberg. Its members did jobs for local biker gangs, hosted a rock band, helped to detox drug addicts, and organised street theatre for left-wing causes. A dining hall featured a beggar's banquet table permanently laden with loaves of bread, joints of meat, bowls of fruit, and bottles of beer. A communal bathroom featured multiple unscreened loos and a bathtub big enough for three. The rooftop looked over bleak miles of watchtowers and minefields and tank traps and armed guards in the 'death strip' along the East Berlin side of the Wall. All this made us feel like the innocent couple in the musical *The Rocky Horror Show* – which we'd seen with communal friends in London a year earlier.

The experience gave me great brain food for my dreams. Judy found work teaching English to university researchers, while I made a few marks by teaching Turkish kids in Kreuzberg. But I spent most of my time reading Hegel, in English and German in parallel, in the American Memorial Library a few U-Bahn stops away.

The Berlin summer was a defining experience for me. I began to sense that my ulterior destiny was to explore the abysmal depths of the German tragedy. That still-murky sense made me begin to pull free of my innocent coupling with the beautiful fellow PPE student from a comfortable middle-class background. For all her radicalism, Judy was gradually easing me into a blameless life of British normalcy.

I didn't know it at the time, but the Berlin trip reset the clock.

Like a zombie, I'd been recruited on a mission that plumbed the depth of my inner constitution. I feared that nothing in British academic orthodoxy would be ugly enough to take on the demons that lurked behind the primal evil Germans unleashed during the Third Reich. But I had to give it a go. Back in Oxford, I buckled down to studying set theory at the Mathematical Institute.

An American sage once wrote that anyone who would become great must make a primal sacrifice. My sacrifice was my prospect of a normal life with Judy. I sacrificed it with Dostoyevskian folly by indulging a secret passion for a mutual friend called Karen.

I first met Karen at about the same time I met Judy. We were all undergraduates together and had overlapping circles of friends. Karen struck up a relationship with my college friend Jeff.

On her later visits to visit Jeff in the Ealing commune, Karen always took care not to join in the sexual libertarianism. My concern for her fragile modesty was part of what drew me to her. I wanted to encourage her to be more confident.

Karen became a journalist. She cut a slim and unassuming figure and looked quite cute and sexy to me, but she was tougher than she seemed when I began to let my sensual gaze dwell on her. I nursed intentions of angelic purity, but beneath them I sensed a murkier current of carnal lust.

Consider, please, that the decade of the Seventies was when the age of sexual outreach peaked, when swingers and wife-swappers were rampant, when all the novelists started saying 'fuck' and even thinkers like me began to think more freely.

My sensual ambitions revved up in April 1975 when I visited Karen. She was sharing a farmhouse commune in Wales with other Oxford arts graduates. I limbered up for the visit with tracks by the glam rock band Roxy Music. I was excited to see her again.

After we went shopping together, she invited me to her bedroom to help her adjust the hems of a new pair of jeans. Once I'd knelt beside her to pin them up, I sat on her bed watching as she pulled off the jeans to expose a bottom trimmed with little red lace panties. I guided her gently onto my lap and kissed her on the lips, in a tentative, exploratory manner.

She pulled back, embarrassed, face distorted in close-up like a Picasso painting, eyes big with trepidation, and said, quietly: 'That was out of character.'

So, in true British style, we went meekly downstairs and had a nice cup of tea beside the fire. I returned to Oxford – just in time to watch the last Americans in Vietnam evacuate from Saigon.

Our sex games had a political backdrop. The UK entered the European Communities (as the union was then known) in January 1973 under Edward Heath's Conservative government. He was a committed European, but his premiership was soon in trouble.

A general election in February 1974 – for which Judy and I campaigned in Ealing – led to a hung parliament and a minority Labour government under Harold Wilson. He won a majority in a second election in October. To placate Labour Eurosceptics, he pledged to renegotiate the terms of British membership in the EC and then to hold a yes/no referendum on whether to stay.

The EC heads of government granted a revised deal in March 1975. MPs voted overwhelmingly to accept the deal in April. New Conservative leader Margaret Thatcher was clear: 'The paramount case for being in is the political case for peace and security.'

The referendum was scheduled for June, and when I visited Karen the government campaign for Yes was in full swing.

Back in Oxford, I voted Yes. The nation agreed with me. In a national turnout of over sixty percent, a two-thirds majority of voters said Yes. Brits had opted decisively for Europe.

I wrote the first volume of my trilogy that summer. Working in my tiny Oxford bedsit, I first drafted it by hand, then typed it up, then added handwritten symbols, then had the pages photocopied and bound under the title *Dialectical Logic*. The book began with a quotation from Lenin on dialectics and ended by quoting Chairman Mao on contradictions. Between those endstops, it developed its logical dialectic as a mathematical Big Bang from a null start.

Just as I took possession of the bound volumes, Karen visited me at my new student commune in south Oxford. I led her up to my bedroom to wait as I got ready. Standing beside my bed, she put down her coat and took off her blouse. This left her upper body naked. She let me watch as she slowly slipped on a pullover.

I stood and watched, but all I said was: 'I'm feeling dirty. I'm off to take a bath.'

This was in character. I didn't get too excited by such scenes. Judy looked so good naked she was happy to let people see her, and Karen did no more than reassure me she was trying to comply with the exhibitionist *Zeitgeist*.

Judy and I hardly met that summer (she worked in London), but on the day of Karen's visit she was due to arrive soon. Also, Karen's boyfriend Jeff was due to arrive, so there was really no time for sex games. Let's move on.

In the last quarter of 1975, reader reactions to *Dialectical Logic* – based probably on reading the preface and the challenging quotes fore and aft – were dismissive, so I redeveloped the core idea as an Oxford graduate thesis with the title *Truth and Provability*, which won me a distinction in 1976. I then spent a hot summer, a summer with a record heatwave, mostly alone. I didn't see Judy or Karen. Instead, I got a temporary job as a road-repair labourer in the grounds of Blenheim Palace and read a stack of delicious novels by the former St Anne's fellow Iris Murdoch about unrequited love.

I wrote the second volume of *Dialectical Logic* over the summer of 1977. This tract was forbiddingly mathematical and very hard to read. Along the way, I relaxed by reading a controversial new book by the right-wing historian David Irving, *Hitler's War*, as a kind of preparation for a new career in the Ministry of Defence, where I started two days after finishing my mathematical typescript.

While I was serving time in the ministry, I enjoyed a couple of strangely awkward lunchtime pub dates with Karen, who was based just a few streets away as a reporter on a national newspaper. I submitted my typescript to the Oxford examination board as a doctoral thesis, and in June 1978, two examiners – one of them my later friend Dan Isaacson – grilled me in an oral exam. I stumbled on several forgotten details and had my effort rejected.

Days later, I went and reported the outcome to Karen. By then, she was sharing another London commune with Judy, who by then had joined the Communist Party of Great Britain (CPGB). As I sat alone with Karen in the kitchen, in a scene that later reminded me of the wartime teashop scene between Briony and Robbie in the 2007 movie *Atonement* (with a Dunkirk drama and based on a 2001 novel by Ian McEwan), I tried to explain my tortured feelings for her. She responded by saying she didn't want to see me again.

I resigned from the ministry. After serving out my notice, on a snowy day in January, I signed on as unemployed. At the depth of the British winter of discontent, I watched Judy on the TV news call dustmen and gravediggers out on a nationwide strike. I felt feverish and restless and went on long walks. I repeated a mantra: 'One God, world without end.'

I endured days of what doctors called 'hypomania' that put me in a psychiatric ward. My brain resumed normal service in time to watch Margaret Thatcher take over as prime minister in May.

I did odd jobs for months, until in late 1979 I wrote a third volume with the title *Dialectical Logic*, seeking to present the key ideas informally. Coincidentally, the last time I saw Karen was at a party on Leap Day 1980, when she refused to dance with me – and instead danced to Abba music with a new chap she later married. My third volume was a rushed job and it didn't work as I'd intended. A fresh pair of university examiners politely awarded it a dummy degree in late 1980. A few months later, hypomania hit again.

Once I'd recovered from all that in sunny Poole, I landed a job in Japan. After a charming, delightful, wonderful year there, the prospect of returning to Blighty gave me another brain fever.

That was it, my trio of torments. I finally found peace teaching physics and mathematics in the home counties, before moving to Germany. I soon found my unholy past was just what I needed to triangulate the abyss that lurked in Germany's past.

I tried later, from Germany, to rescue a veneer of peace with Karen, but without success. She married, had kids, and settled in Deadbury. Decades passed, and I worked for salvation.

Back in Britain again, working with the Conservatives, I picked at my old scars cautiously. You may recall that I printed out a pixelated image of my painful succubus in October 2015. Well, in July 2020, now that I've abandoned the Conservatives and faced down the looming risk of viral death in the pandemic, I tear up the printout.

My sense of relief is enormous and exhilarating. I check and find that my views on philosophy and Germany are in good shape. My lively interest in Rachel has cut the final knot. Deadbury is just another village for me. *Free, free, free at last!*

For good or ill, that marathon drama defines my life. Against its lurid backdrop, the whole Brexit saga looks like a formalistic diplomatic minuet, the coronavirus crisis like little more than a metaphor for a world gone sour. I'm a new man, a soul forged in a mighty furnace, a diamond in a world of dross.

It didn't seem funny at the time, but now I see the comic side. Diamond? Who's kidding whom?

———

Deliverance from the pandemic may be at hand. A team at the University of Oxford says it now has a Covid-19 vaccine that looks promising in early trials. HM government has already ordered a hundred million doses, both as an encouragement to the team and as a bid for first place in the global pricking order for jabs.

Boris Johnson will no doubt try to claim the credit.

—

The UK parliament's intelligence and security committee finally publishes the Russia report that Johnson was suppressing. It says Russian cyber capability poses a threat to British national security, yet the government chose not to investigate evidence of Russian state interference in UK democracy.

The committee reveals how the UK in the Putin era has welcomed the influx of Russian oligarchs into London and not asked where their wealth came from. British lawyers and accountants found devious ways to recycle the dirty money through the London laundromat, while the new elite used its laundered loot to extend its patronage and influence across the British establishment.

The committee concludes that Russian influence in the UK is the new normal. Numerous Russians with very close links to Putin are well integrated and accepted in London, and a large private industry has developed in the UK to service their every need.

The UK intelligence agencies made no attempt to investigate how Russia disrupted the 2016 Brexit referendum. The Russian elite used its clout to influence the outcome, and the British elite of Tory old boys welcomed its laundry-fresh meddling.

I read in a book by Luke Harding that Alexander Yakovenko, the ambassador of the Russian Federation to the UK from 2011 to 2019, returned to Russia in 2019 for Vladimir Putin to award him the Order of Alexander Nevsky and appoint him as president of the diplomatic academy. Yakovenko explained to his colleagues that the state was rewarding him for smashing the Brits to the ground: 'It will be a long time before they rise again.'

In parliament this week, Keir Starmer asks the prime minister about the Russia report. He goads Johnson to say all this stuff about the report is just sour grapes over the 2016 referendum result.

This is a Freudian slip. The only reason for Johnson to mention the referendum is that he feels guilt over suppressing the Russia report. He then burbles into a lame gag about 'more flip-flops than Bournemouth beach' before segueing on to say: 'We are delivering as the people's government.'

As Winston Churchill might have said, recalling his famous speech before Congress in December 1941: 'Some delivery, some government.'

The British ship of state is marooned, shipwrecked, stuck in the weeds, up the creek without a paddle. My diamond incarnation, forged in mortal extremity, has kicked its timbers, put the boot in, measured the result, and found a boatload of rot. Before going to work on repairing the planks, a wise man takes the time to record his last will and testament.

35. Solving the problem

I plan to leave a sobering moral legacy. Cast into a reflective mood by memories of my darkest hour and my gloomy ride to Deadbury, I sit and contemplate my philosophical pilgrimage toward the essays of 2013 and 2019 that we've already reviewed. Confronting the truth about oneself is hard, but nothing less will do as moral ballast to stabilise my account of the Brexit saga.

Fazit One: My dialectical philosophy was doomed to meet a cold reception in Seventies Oxford. My readers feared any warming to Hegel's insights would invite Marxist mayhem.

Fazit Two: My attempts to woo Karen into more spontaneous and friendly relations were doomed to disappointment. Once you start to get a fear response, you need to stop.

Looking down from 2020, I guess I should have known the primal evil I chose to tackle would leave some nasty scars.

But my career path turned up in the Eighties. By late 1980, I was having fun teaching A-level physics in London. I met a perfect Chinese girl, Xi, who was gentle, modest, intelligent, and serious, and we enjoyed being together. Also, over that winter, I watched a BBC series dramatising Douglas Adams' charming comic fantasy, *Hitch Hiker's Guide to the Galaxy*. But London was depressing me, so I got a job teaching English in Japan.

As luck would have it, my flight to Japan took off the morning after the royal wedding of Charles and Diana, so I was there on the street to see them ride past the site of what was later Portcullis House. I enjoyed this experience in the company of my new friend Xi, whose gentle Singapore English sweetened the day.

I had a great time in Japan. Teaching English wasn't too taxing, and I spent my spare time reading Richard Feynman's lectures on physics (all three volumes of them). I returned to England a year later and found a job teaching physics and maths at a college in the home counties. I met up with Xi again, and we began a relationship touched by the mood of David Bowie's song *China girl*.

In that year, 1983, I became a fan of Mahatma Gandhi, inspired by the new blockbuster biopic *Gandhi* directed and produced by Richard Attenborough. Gandhi advocated elective celibacy as a road to spiritual clarity, which he promoted with the metaphor that people who took this path were diamonds among the softer stones of humanity. As I pursued my close but chaste relationship with Xi, I found this claim convincing – especially as it echoed the claims made for millennia by Buddhist and Christian monks.

Gandhi's doctrine of non-violence was an attractive philosophy for a troubled war nut like me. I wasn't convinced by his claim that it would have worked against Hitler, but I was impressed by what he said in 1946 after affirming that the Holocaust was a crime: 'But the Jews should have offered themselves to the butcher's knife. … It would have aroused the world and the people of Germany.'

I still had to crack the German nut. After years of teaching the same old A-level physics, I applied for a publishing job in Germany in 1987. While I brushed up my German in preparation, I read Martin Gilbert's big book *The Holocaust* with horror: The deaths really were a sacrificial offering. When I then saw Elem Klimov's movie *Come and See* depicting German genocide in Byelorussia, I despaired about taking the job.

To my great relief, on my first Sunday in Heidelberg, I encountered, by chance, up close and in person, German chancellor Helmut Kohl and Israeli prime minister Shimon Peres, surrounded by an official entourage, walking side by side into the Church of the Holy Spirit. I found that chance encounter both auspicious and reassuring.

My quarter-century in Germany was happy and productive. After a decade of immersion in the world of research-level science, in 1997 I read a new book, *The Conscious Mind*, by a promising young Australian philosopher called David Chalmers. The book attracted a cult following and led to a series of conferences aimed at working toward a science of consciousness. I went to many of them. I also wrote a series of papers, all reprinted in my 2009 book *Mindworlds*. That book marks the high point of my philosophical career.

About then, I discovered the works of an English mystic called Andrew Harvey. I loved Harvey's book *The Way of Passion* on the Sufi poet Rumi. Here was a pair – mystic and poet – who understood what I'd gone through to reach the clarity of my diamond years. Harvey had been a brilliant young fellow at Oxford (while I was there) until he suffered a series of what were blandly called nervous breakdowns and embarked on a mystic path. Eventually, after meeting with religious mystics from all faiths worldwide, he starred in a BBC video documentary before retreating into a more secluded life.

I pursued a more worldly philosophy. After *Mindworlds*, I wrote a book on the emerging global organism, Globorg, and befriended the Schwetzingen pastor Matthias, whom we met earlier in this story. Matthias introduced me to a new text for German pastors called *Gott 9.0* that presents a Hegelian philosophy of divinity by means of a colour-coded series of dialectical levels. These levels are historical stages in the sophistication of thoughts about God, and they culminate in an emerging paradigm that's now in use as a pastoral aid among the evangelical community in Germany.

I was fascinated by the colour-coded dialectic. Over the next few months, I wove it into my next book, on world history, which I published shortly before my return to England.

There you have it – my trip down memory lane, mellowed by the years into a tale I can now recall with a wistful smile instead of pangs of remorse. We're getting closer to that magic moment when we experience the new dawn.

First, the German nut: Is a European Fourth Reich looming or is the wreckage of the Third the seedbed for something better in the world of political forms? This is the cloudbank before the splendour. My exile among the Tory faithful on the southern shores of the Brexit Isles has given me a seaside wilderness from which to glimpse the face of the almighty in swirling cloudscapes over the windswept sea.

German evangelists present their 'spiral dynamics' in a baffling fog. They say level one is security and survival, level two *we* versus *you*, level three ego, level four duty and order, level five achievement and status, level six personality and equal rights, level seven sense and wholeness, and level eight global consciousness.

I see things more concretely. Recalling that God here is just a symbol for the greatest good or the supreme end of all our mortal striving, God One is food and shelter, God Two a spooky afterlife, God Three a warrior hero, God Four the heavenly father of the patriarchal monotheists, God Five the divinity of the Protestant Enlightenment, God Six the multicultural totem of anthropological humanism, God Seven the identity fetish of existentialists and racists, and God Eight the globalist ideal of techno-modernists and internet gurus.

On this reckoning, if we ignore the boring details, God Nine is Gaia, the planetary organism of eco-warriors and Friends of the Earth. But I see more in the ninth paradigm.

Human beings are evolutionary latecomers hosted in an animal species. The apes that embody them are better than cows and pigs mainly by virtue of the finely woven neuronets they grew within their skulls. If the tapestries the humans weave are too random or flawed, the presumption is all too easy that their ape hosts are devalued and ready for recycling.

I know this is a hard and stoic doctrine. It's our duty to weave a worthwhile offering to God, as it were, from the silken threads in our heads. Failure puts us in the company of cows and pigs. Our human speciesism is the problem here: We really need to start being kinder to all the other animals on Earth.

What is a human being anyway? An animal with a soul on top. Theologians might say the soul is the nexus of a reflexive miracle blessed with insight about what it's like to be a person. As an amateur neuroscientist, I say the soul is a Platonic shadow cast by the information processed in an electrical field pulsing rhythmically over the cerebral neuronet. The reflexive logic of its insight is what my dialectical logic was all about.

In other words, I say, human personality is a cultural construct. Its modern iteration is a product – perhaps the key product that made all the rest possible – of liberal humanism, which is itself a recent spinoff from the Judaeo-Christian tradition.

During the Third Reich, Germans disenchanted with Christianity flirted with old pagan ideas because they were fed up with glorifying the spark of soul in every passing human bag of meat. Their disenchantment arose from a paranoid fear that Jews were quietly waiting for Christianity to domesticate the blond beast. This was the fear Friedrich Nietzsche was bold enough to express. For my part, I see the spark of soul as a knot of reflexive logic.

Transhumanism is my thing. Personal identities, in the sense that counts for liberal humanism, are dissolving in the brave new world of social media and cloud computing. When people begin to augment their human forms with bionic limbs, ultrasonic ears, infrared eyes, chips in the brain, and robot bodies of all kinds, the personal identity that matters will be a legal identity recognised within a stable social order. This order must be valid for all human beings, throughout Gaia.

The ninth paradigm, boiled down to a slogan, is: *Beat the meat!* Overcome your meat body and open your meat brain to the truth!

Then the god in Gaia may grant you salvation when Extinction Rebellion leads the charge against the polluters and the consumers who defy their Earth mother in lives of wanton selfishness. This is the kind of wild warning I'm tempted to preach.

The politicians still embracing the ideas of levels one through eight are behind the curve, peddling a business model that's no longer valid. Nationalism is obsolete. Science and technology have globalised everything.

In my fanciful imagination, the Europe of the ever-closer union is the seedbed for this transhuman paradigm shift. The new order will change everything. This is my diamond epiphany.

———

The clouds have cleared. A shaft of light has appeared on the horizon. Lo, a figure is discernible in the dawning landscape.

Zaross has brought down tablets from his Olympian retreat. The tablets bear inscriptions carved with a diamond stylus:

- We humans on Planet Earth must learn to think and act as one.
- Our human embodiment is fragile and needs institutional support.
- Our planetary home is fragile and needs our care and protection.

This is the ninth revelation.

Thus spoke Zaross.

———

Nietzsche's prophet Zarathustra was his fictional stand-in for the ancient Persian prophet we know as Zoroaster. The Zoroastrian faith lives on today in a minority global diaspora – the Queen singer Freddie Mercury came from a Zoroastrian family.

My acquaintance with Nietzsche's Zarathustra dates back at least to my days in the Ealing commune. My fellow communard Maggie let me handle her old leather-bound copy of Nietzsche's fiction and admire the original German text set in angular *Fraktur* script. She could read it for pleasure, but I couldn't, and that was a challenge.

Years later, I find I'm so taken by the whimsy of writing a book of modern prophecy through the voice of an ancient hero that I've inserted my ninth revelation into a Nietzschean meme. It looks fun to me – better than my usual solemn stuff, anyway.

Let's not be fooled by the preposterously overwrought style. Think about what I'm really saying. We need to love God Nine, be gentle and tolerant with each other, and take care of the planet. Big deal – what else is new? This looks like a rather lame result for a lifetime of philosophy.

Let's try and unpack what I really mean. Let's unspool the story in the anecdotal style that's worked so far.

My fate is tied to global politics. As an exile on the Brexit Isles, Andy the prophet, seer, and revelator isn't immune to the plague germs in the waters swirling around him as he emerges still damp from the spin cycle of his Rachel years. Even as a human diamond, he can still weep and bleed.

With that in mind, leaving the mountaintop revelations aside for the moment, we can start by getting solemn again.

Whatever else happens, the economic fallout from the coronavirus pandemic will distract the postmodern world for a generation. In the longer term, it will accelerate the rise to dominance of the biomedical sciences in their gathering ascendancy over bare physics. I know the strength of molecular biology is down to its foundation in physics, where mathematics keeps things steady. But the change of focus, from particles and forces to the evolution of complex systems based on carbon chemistry, heralds a new era.

I see a rise in the importance of medical resources and services as pillars of state power. The previous age was dominated by military power resting on the physics of explosions and so on. Soon the doctors will inherit the Earth and turn swords into scalpels. Already the frontline fighters in the corona war are the medics.

I believe in the dialectical interdependence of machines and morals. People like the young Winston Churchill and his German counterparts saw war as a glorious thing, apt to bring out the best in fighting men. Only after the Second World War, with its carpet bombing and its industrial genocide and its nuclear finale, did the idea finally sink in that war is hideous, obscene, and atrocious. The moral judgement mirrors the facts on the ground.

As machines are refined to the nanoscale and spread so far that their presence transforms the intimate lives of everyone on Earth, so human morals change. Previously taboo subjects like sexuality, madness, and death have become routine topics of public debate. Today, we see that this exposes the moral barriers surrounding those topics to some big changes. As I see it, this forces a shift from martial to medical ways of bringing out the best in us.

I see signs of a transition from physics to biology in responses to climate change. Persuading people to mobilise will take time, but when action does finally come, policies based on bare physics will give way to approaches based on bioengineering. We can run cars on fuel milked from bionic bugs that live on carbon dioxide and water, we can suck greenhouse gases from the atmosphere with a trillion designer trees, and we can live like our tribal ancestors in a bionic paradise with tech embedded all around.

My drift from everyday politics to the Zaross revelation is all too natural. The human experiment on Planet Earth has not been kind to the formerly beautiful surface of the six-zettaton ball of rock we humans call home. The accelerating pace of human industry on Earth, as we buzz back and forth on our various errands, has run up a massive debt to the natural environment. The biosphere has spawned a human race that needs to be humbled.

A climate crisis could easily extinguish a species that so wilfully and wantonly wrecks and poisons its planetary home in its childish quests for wealth, power, and luxury. We might well think like me of identifying with Gaia. Selfish human thinking has led to the crisis, and only selfless thinking – or rather thinking with the self of Gaia at heart – can lead us out of it. This much seems valid.

The way out of the climate emergency need not be a return to the past. New technology is the gift that keeps on giving. Life on Earth meets every new challenge by evolving ever more refined forms and tricky tweaks to continue its progress. Like the nanotech of carbon-based biosystems, the nanotech of silicon-based info-systems is just more of the stuff of life.

I recall a meme from the world of philosophy. The view from nowhere is the perspective we adopt when doing science. It aspires to maximum universality – we dream above and beyond our station in the here and now to see the bigger picture, and we don't stop until we can't go on.

We live most vividly, most truly, in our most exalted imagin-ation. And we live with our tools and our gadgets. If my smart phone or my car is essential to what I do, it's part of me. I'm not just a little spark of current raising electrical storms across my cerebral cortex. My ego isn't that small. And it isn't just big, either. It's beyond big. It's in a zone where size is no longer defined. It's everywhere and nowhere.

Opening my mind to planetary dimensions is child's play for me. Our lives will go global. We humans will sink with a sigh into the welcoming embrace of the global group mind of social media. Cloud nine will body forth as a planet with a mind of its own.

I got this big idea in a small town in Germany. Some personal background to its inception may help.

I lived the last five years of my stay in Germany in Schwet-zingen, in the first-floor apartment of a postwar detached house set in a neat patch of garden. My street ended in a jogging trail that led past the palace gardens into an infinite expanse of forest. I was near the town centre, where in a hall above a quad an evangelical congregation met on Sundays. With the Rhine and the forests nearby and a superb local road system, Schwetzingen was a place I could happily have grown old and died in.

Thanks to all my philosophy, I was no fan of organised religion. In fact, I followed the rise of the New Atheists in the decade after 9/11 with enthusiasm and read all their books. I posted a torrent of comments in threads appended to a series of web posts by Sam Harris, the young atheist who later became a moralising neuroscientist. I collected my comments in a draft book I called *Godblogs*, and I put teasing extracts from this script into an autobiography I wrote in 2011.

One teaser goes like this: 'Goof, the God of our fathers, exists and is real, and is a potential object of scientific analysis. Goof is the attractor behind genetic determinism, the proof that natural selection acts first at the level of genes, not of individuals or groups. Goof is the phenomenal manifestation of human genocentricity.'

Another goes thus: 'The fact that we are, as Richard Dawkins puts it, lumbering robots dedicated to the replication of our genes, so apparently subversive of religion, finds its most vivid expression precisely in the religion he excoriates. Good ole Dawkins fundamentalism: Goof is great, and Dawkins is his prophet!'

Dawkins fundamentalism is a reduction to biology of Goof, God Four. But its biological twist folds nicely into God Nine. Back in the Naughties, I squeezed the Dawkins meme into God Eight, Globorg.

Since 2016, the guiding light of Globorg has been obscured in the fog of war by the fans of Putinesque populism. Also, the biologically rooted narrative of Gaia and the environmentalists has grown stronger. A new meme, a Gaian fiction, will soon be coined to fill the god-shaped hole in the attractor behind human evolution.

God Nine is born.

Zaross says God is not a presence out there, or in here, or anywhere specific. The word denotes a primal state of being that precedes all concepts. Before consciousness dawns in an embodied
brain, a primal being reflects a world, buds off from it, and buds
again until a mind emerges from the mire. The primal dialectic unfolds into an ice-cream cone universe. A mind dawns on a world.

God is a pet name for the mushroom cloud that hangs over us.
We grow toward God as we build our towers of worlds. We realise
ourselves in a stack of determinate beings. My tower is topped and
tailed in mystery, in God.

The universal 'I' is the alpha and the omega of the rising path.
I feel the rhythmic opening and closing of the universal loop as the
breath of life, an act of love. Zaross has a hard shell, but this is his
homage to Jesus and Rumi.

My *Godblogs* draft was done when I moved to Schwetzingen.
There I met Clara. She was the estranged wife of a middle manager
somewhere who lived with her young teen daughter in the ground-
floor apartment below mine. Clara struck me as intensely attractive
when she ventured out in the garden in summer. Her facial features
were clear and well proportioned, and her face was framed by brown
hair cut in a style I recalled from the Swinging Sixties. Her daughter
was blooming, and they set up a trampoline in the back garden to
have fun on while they kept their bodies in shape. I'd lounge on my
balcony and watch them bouncing joyfully up and down.

Like me, Clara kept up a routine of running and swimming.
When it was hot, she would attend to the garden slowly, barefoot,
in tank top and little skirt, while I lurked butt-naked in the shade.
Living as neighbours on such terms helped us learn to trust each
other. Clara was a dutiful soul who believed in God, and she invited
me to come with her to the Sunday meetings her pastor Matthias
led downtown.

I soon struck up a debate and then a friendship with Matthias. Clara's kind invitation had borne nourishing fruit. The exercise of reconciling my New Atheist reading with the Christian rites I faced pushed me into a marathon of reading and reflection that flowered forth as a polemical draft for a little book on Jesus.

When, on a weekend retreat with Clara and others in the flock, I introduced Matthias to the American mystic philosopher and 'integral thinker' Ken Wilber, and Matthias introduced me to the dialectical business of Gods One through Nine, I was primed and ready. The spirit moved me to expand my little draft on Jesus into a book on the place of religion in history. Weeks later, the thinker Rowan Williams, who at the time was the Archbishop of Canterbury, kindly called the book 'a lively, provoking and hugely original essay' for its back cover. Matthias was impressed, and he read the book carefully.

Clara soon moved off to a new job in another town, but I took it with aplomb. I'd got what I needed, and it was good.

———

You may be asking how all this philosophy and theology relate to the crisis in my life triggered by Brexit and the coronavirus. Well, the great German philosophers are link figures here.

Hold tight now. Immanuel Kant took the big step of reducing God Five – the Enlightenment ideal – to rational psychology. Hegel took the next step with his dialectical or anthropological story for God Six.

Following this dialectic, Nietzsche grew up with God Six in Bismarck's Reich and became a prophet for the racist triumphalism of God Seven. And Heidegger was a champion in Hitler's Reich for God Seven who lived to see its demise in the globalised world of God Eight.

Scrolling on to the new millennium, the world as it existed in 2016 – including the United Nations, the World Bank, the World

Wide Web, and the European Union – was the expression in hard fact of a collective thrall to God Eight.

I see the brutal impulses behind the twin crises of Brexit and the Trump era as assaults by people stuck in God Six or Seven to overthrow the pious hypocrisies of God Eight. But I also see them as labour pains for the birth of God Nine among us.

The climate crisis will not be solved by rational statespersons around an eighth-paradigm table. The Gaians and the Extinction Rebels who usher in the ninth configuration can only do so on the back of massive disruption. Zaross predicts that the six-pack and seventh-heaven fantasies of the populist movements behind Brexit and the Trump presidency will be used by the cloud-nine rebels to force cracks in the eightfold-way consensus.

Those who like harmony in history will always be dismayed by new developments. Brexit was the shock that forced Brits to see themselves less proudly and forced other Europeans to see their shiny new union more critically. In both cases, their pride in crude economic measures of success and progress need to be torn down and replaced by something more sustainable.

When future Brits seek to make something worthwhile of their bleak island home, they'll go green. When mainland Europeans seek to revamp their union, they'll go green too. They'll do so because the rest of the world will no longer let them export their problems. Nine or nothing; Gaia or the abyss.

Zaross revelates all this in an original conception born in the sin of his willed immersion in the German tragedy. He's unmoved by Andy's outrage at Brexiteer vandalism. As a true philosopher, he rises above the fray to *solve the problem*.

36. Dream date, silent scream

The thirteenth Bournemouth air show, once scheduled for August 2020, doesn't happen. Or rather, it's restyled as a virtual event, cobbled together from edited video clips of previous shows. I'm happy to forget it – I really don't want to see the Battle of Britain Memorial Flight yet again, even just virtually.

But I have a good way of marking the Sunday of the restyled event. I've arranged to meet with Helen and David for tea on the terrace at the same hotel we visited seven years ago, when I was fresh back from Germany and found my ears assailed by the 'sound of victory' in the garden. This is our first extended physical meeting since the lockdown began months ago.

The hotel is handling the lockdown as well as it can, given that it hosts mostly elderly guests who are unlikely to change their ways. The staff wear masks and have put hand sanitiser stations at all the outside doors, but they make no effort to badger the guests into wearing masks or social distancing beyond the quiet reminders of spaced tables and place settings for diners. I'm cool with that – the guests are old and rich enough to choose their own fates.

Helen and David wear cowboy bandanas for masks, like bank robbers, but soon let them slip down to their necks. I take off my disposable mask once I'm out on the terrace.

The weather this Sunday is intermittently sunny and cloudy, but we're sheltered by our table's parasol from both the solar glare and a brief shower of rain. The nearest occupied table is a metre away, and the occupants there aren't fussed, so all's well on the contagion front. The seascape to our south, visible over the clifftop, is flat and calm, broken only by a pair of big cruise liners berthed at anchor a mile offshore, languishing in idleness for the duration of the pandemic. They're easier on the eye than warships.

We've dressed as normally as pandemic sloth allows. I'm airing my familiar linen suit with perforated shoes. David has a tan suit with a blue shirt, going for the old Bush-and-Blair Iraq War vibe, and Helen opts for a baggy dark cardigan that disguises those extra lockdown pounds. After weeks of sitting at home alone in lounge-wear, even this boring attire seems theatrical.

I complain: 'I thought the hotel was going to put a big TV screen out here so we could watch the virtual air show.'

'I don't care about that,' says Helen. 'For me, this is just a chance to meet and catch up after so many months at home.'

I smile. 'Me too, actually. It's good to see just clouds in the sky and enjoy the peace. If I want to watch aircraft videos, I can find them on YouTube.'

A waiter brings a tray bearing coffee, cut sandwiches, sweet cakes, and hot scones with jam and cream.

We set to on the scones while they're still warm, delighting once more in the simple pleasure of this English tradition.

Then, over coffee, Helen begins on a favourite line of conversation, namely the ritual denunciation of Donald Trump's latest idiocies. This prompts us to embark on an animated discussion of the upcoming US presidential election and the prospects of victory for Joe Biden and Kamala Harris, given Trump's obvious intention to cheat in every way possible to hinder that victory.

I recall a question I asked myself seven years ago: Europe or America?

The answer is now obvious – linguistic nativism wins out. English is trumps, even for Brits who speak a second language.

But what do I really know of America? Like anyone else, I've read the comic books and seen the action movies, which already make it feel like home. I've played with American war toys and danced to American music. And Judy and I befriended plenty of Americans during our years together.

My year in Japan revived my fascination with America. Once I was settled back in Blighty, I applied for jobs at colleges all over California from my base in the home counties. I was even offered a financed place on a doctoral program at Stanford – just after I'd accepted a job in Germany. The hand of fate.

My first trip to America was from Germany, over the Christmas season of 1988, when I visited New York for two weeks. I spent the time minding a penthouse apartment on the lower East Side for a Jewish lady who was off visiting her family in New Jersey. I luxuriated in this fine home alone with the help of such props as a recent paperback by Donald Trump, *The Art of the Deal*, which impressed me (yes, but it was ghost-written) with its zest.

While in Manhattan, I visited the Flatiron building and said hi to Springer colleagues I'd met on their visits to the Springer palace in Heidelberg. One young editor there showed me her city apartment, which left me thinking I was better off in Heidelberg.

Back in my German palace, I boasted in *Who's Who in the World* that I was a member of the American Mathematical Society, the American Physical Society, the New York Academy of Sciences, the Planetary Society, and the GeoSphere Society.

The last two of these memberships were key for my 1991 article in *The Visual Computer* proposing an electronic globe I called the Globall. This proposal raised interest in Microsoft and prompted Al Gore, who was then serving as vice-president for President Bill Clinton, to write to me in solidarity. I was still angling for a US job offer.

My next visit to America was in the spring of the year 2000, when I flew to Tucson, Arizona, for a conference on the emerging science of consciousness organised by the dynamic young professor David Chalmers. Dave was quite a rock star with his long hair and stage presence, and he led a group rendition of his own rock classic, *The Zombie Blues*, to animate revellers at the 'End of Consciousness' party he held at his spread in the hills west of the city, where some of us jumped into his pool.

I went to Tucson again in 2002 for the same reason. This time I presented a poster, as they say in the trade, on my own philosophy of consciousness. Dave was amused that I carried the slide show for this poster stored on a flash drive hung on a cord around my neck. In a happy encounter, a lovely blonde German girl called Anne presented her own poster on a panel near mine. She was based at a university near Mannheim, and we promised to keep in touch.

A few months later, at the Mount Sinai School of Medicine in New York, I met Anne again, this time for a conference on new work in neuroscience. But she seemed attached to another woman, so I swallowed my disappointment and went home alone.

My next trip to the new world was organised by SAP, my new employer. This was a conference on metadata, held in Seattle, where Starbucks did the catering, with plenty of strong coffee to keep us all buzzing. We enjoyed a guided tour of the nearby Boeing production line as well as a nerd banquet at Microsoft, where I felt truly at home with the campus vibe.

After that, in 2004, I taught a technical SAP class in Atlanta, Georgia, and drove my German colleagues around the city in a rented Ford Lincoln. I came back from the trip with baseball caps from Coca-Cola and CNN, both based in Atlanta, and memories from the airport of passing long lines of US troops in desert camo about to fly to Iraq.

Months later, again thanks to SAP, I was back in New York for a conference on the World Wide Web. I talked with Tim Berners-Lee and watched the glamorous babes, back from the Daytime Emmy awards at Radio City a few blocks away, drink champagne and pose on pink carpet at my hotel before I flew back to Frankfurt.

In short, I'm as infatuated by America as any Brit can be, but I don't love it more than Germany – or even Japan.

On the Bournemouth hotel terrace, Helen and David have their own reason for loving America after a vacation on the West Coast where they drove down from Canada to California. But they seem to love Canada more. As a Canadian wag once put it, living on the northern border of the United States is like living next door to a biker gang.

Brexiteers often feel the same. Those who fear an American apocalypse might wreck their Nylon dream of untaxed riches find a second source of hope in CANZUK.

Canada, Australia, and New Zealand – the 'white' dominions in the British Empire – form a club with the UK that's even more exclusive than the Five Eyes union led by Trump America. Since the combined populations and economies of the three former dominions only just balance the UK, Brexiteers breezily imagine they can rule the school from London and ignore Ottawa, Canberra, and Wellington.

CANZUK is what Brexiteers really mean by Global Britain, plus the Crown territories and dependencies where they can hide their plunder. They say anyone who doesn't like it is free to leave the country. But they've closed the door on Europe. Bastards.

———

On the same weekend as our hotel meeting, senior Conservatives are demanding that Boris Johnson smarten up his act. He's on holiday in a remote part of Scotland with his girlfriend Carrie and isn't bowing to their pressure to sack his education secretary Gavin Williamson, who's let a disastrous fiasco blow up regarding the summer's A-level exam results. MPs are furious.

On Monday, the Cabinet Office EU transition taskforce briefs government ministers and officials with a classified dossier laying out 'reasonable worst-case scenario planning assumptions' for the end of the transition period. It warns that a hard exit could cause a major economic crisis. I find it scary.

Later in the week, Johnson emerges after his holiday not to tackle the exam crisis but to joke with its victims: 'I'm afraid your grades were almost derailed by a mutant algorithm.'

Ministers were warned that the algorithm revises A-level results downward to avoid grade inflation, but they shrugged. Another 'mutant' algorithm to steer housing policy follows the market but recommends building over miles of Tory countryside.

In the following week, Boris Johnson also faces a showdown with furious MPs over his government's chaotic handling of the coronavirus crisis. They're angry that they're being ignored by the cabal around Dominic Cummings in Downing Street.

In short, the government is looking thoroughly incompetent at everything it touches. A new public opinion poll shows Labour level with the Tories for the first time since Johnson took over as leader of the party.

At prime minister's question time on Wednesday 2 September, the parliamentary transcript *Hansard* records a telling exchange.

Keir Starmer asks Johnson about the exam fiasco: 'When did the prime minister first know that there was a problem with the algorithm?'

Johnson replies with a riff on the pandemic: 'All summer long, he has been going around undermining confidence … the parents, pupils, and teachers in this country are … going back to school in record numbers, in spite of all the gloom and dubitation …'

Starmer accuses Johnson of 'playing games' and quotes a Tory MP: 'It's mess after mess, U-turn after U-turn … It's a fundamental issue of competence. God knows what is going on. There's no grip.'

Johnson ducks the issue again: 'This is a leader of the opposition who backed remaining in the EU and now is totally silent on the subject. … This is a leader of the opposition who supported an IRA-condoning politician who wanted to get out of NATO and now says absolutely nothing about it.'

Starmer is angered: 'I worked in Northern Ireland for five years with the police service of Northern Ireland, bringing peace … I ask the prime minister to have the decency to withdraw that comment.'

Johnson instead changes tack again: 'We are getting people back to work. What he wants to do is extend the furlough scheme.'

Starmer despairs: 'I asked him to do the decent thing … This has been a wasted summer. The government … have lurched from crisis to crisis … the only conclusion is serial incompetence.'

Watching all this on television, I can only agree.

The UK chief Brexit negotiator David Frost writes in a Sunday paper that 'we' want to be able to control our own laws and do things our way, 'we' are not going to be a client state, 'we' are not going to compromise on having control over our own laws, 'we' are not going to accept level playing field provisions that lock us in to the way the EU do things, 'we' are not going to let 'them' control our money or the way 'we' organise things, and 'we' want to take back control of our borders.

Frost claims to speak for the UK, but I stand back warily from the toxic 'we' the curmudgeonly baron is splashing around.

Lord Frost studied medieval history at Oxford and says it's a fine training for his new job. I think a medieval punishment may be the best cure for Frost damage.

———

I drive to Deadbury again in September. Soon after my visit in July, I wrote to Karen and apologised for all the distress I caused her 42 years ago. I proposed that if she felt so disposed, we might meet up again in Deadbury to negotiate peace terms that can round off our relations more amicably. Amazingly, she agrees to meet for a pub lunch on Monday 7 September, at the Lord Snooty.

I'm there well before one, in my linen suit over a black T-shirt and black rubber shoes. The shirt has a slogan on the front to out me as a bookworm, and my chin glitters with silver stubble.

The pub is set on a main road through the village, beside a central crossroads. Trucks and tractors trundle loudly past. Directly opposite the pub is an ancient stone building supported by pillars over what must have been the village marketplace long ago.

I sit on a slatted wooden chair on the covered forecourt of the premises with an air of lordly disdain, casually reading *The Spectator*. Pedestrians hurry back and forth before me, hoping to complete their errands before the clouds above the village shower gentle rain upon us all. Beside my chair, a framed notice reminds guests to wear masks in all the hotel's public spaces.

Karen walks up without ceremony, before the rain begins, with just the careworn presence I've studied in her recent images on social media. She carries an umbrella and is clad in an olive-green country jacket with lots of pockets, made of waxed cotton and cut in the style of the motorcycle jackets of half a century ago, along with faded blue jeans and brown hiking boots. Her straight grey hair, once a soft shade of brown, is cut in a bob around her head, and her face, though set into lines drawn by years of strain, is still animated by an intelligence I recall from her student days.

I stand dreamily and press my hands in prayer: 'Namaste.'

'Namaste,' she replies quietly as she looks down at the table, decides not to put her rolled umbrella on it, and watches a truck rumble by. 'Shall we go indoors? It's going to be rather noisy out here.'

'Yes,' I reply as I pocket my magazine. I see that her manner is brisk and practical, and she makes no attempt to register my new presence four decades on. No doubt she's already learned more than enough by checking my blog.

At the door, we're asked to fill out forms in case we need to be contacted for a coronavirus warning, and then we take a table for two beside the window onto the forecourt. The guests at other tables are distant enough and wear no masks, so I try to relax.

'So,' says Karen as we study the menu, 'What made you decide to contact me now, after so many years?'

'The coronavirus, I think. If one of us were to die now, there'd be no more contact, so it seemed like now or never.'

'I suppose so,' she muses. 'Still, I think it's an invasion of privacy. I was going to ignore your letter, but then I thought you might persist, and I decided to cut it off before you even thought about it.'

'Well, that's clear, then. Message received and understood. Apart from that, how are you?'

She glances into my eyes and snorts with what seems to be impatience. 'As you see, fine. I suppose you know I'm still teaching yoga, but you may not know I'm a widow now. Douglas died in April, from the coronavirus.'

'I'm very sorry to hear it,' I say quietly. 'I only met him once, back in 1980, so I can't say more. Were you infected?'

She frowns. 'No, I wasn't there. We separated last year.'

'I see. How have your kids taken it?'

'Oh, well enough. They live away now.' She shrugs off her jacket to reveal a deep-red kaftan top with Indian embroidery on it. Her interest in India began with a trip there shortly before we lost touch in 1980, and it continued with the yoga connection I followed to trace her again on the web.

'Yoga has kept you in good shape,' I venture.

She frowns again. 'I hope you're not carrying the virus.'

'Not much chance. I live alone, and my neighbours are old people who are shielding.'

'Well, don't breathe in my direction.'

The Indian connection intrigues me. At Oxford, I recall, Karen was acquainted with our fellow student Andrew Harvey, who was born in India and later wrote mystic words on the poet Rumi, so perhaps she likes Rumi too. I ask her.

She loves Rumi. It seems to break the ice.

Well, you can imagine the rest as well as I can. Two old lags with a troubled past catch up on things, cautiously, but cordially enough not to break the spell. A pleasant hour later, we depart with vague farewells.

I drive back to Poole in peace. Nothing but the demons of Brexit stand in the way of a new chapter in my life story. I feel liberated from the heavy shackles of bad old karma.

The rural English landscape around me resembles a painted theatre backdrop of stage greenery. The grey sky above me is a luminous swirl of fine raindrops and solar photons, veiling the deeper infinity of space.

That space is my true home. This planet is my settlement, my base, my smallholding, and the space around it is my play garden. All the rest, the great beyond, is mind set free, a silent tomb for all the thoughts and dreams anyone ever had.

In space no one can hear you scream.

———

My inner space is calm now, but not my outer space. Brexit looms, Trump rules, and the virus is untamed.

Chaos looms again the next day. In the Commons, during a debate on the UK internal markets bill, Northern Ireland secretary Brandon Lewis admits under questioning: 'Yes, this does break international law in a very specific and limited way. We're taking the powers to disapply the EU law.'

The law is stated in the withdrawal agreement the government signed with the EU only months ago. This new gambit suggests the signing was in bad faith. Any hint that the Brexiteers see their legal commitments as optional is a dealbreaker.

EU officials demand that Johnson's government abandon its mad idea of turning the UK into an outlaw state by the end of the month or face legal action.

Former Conservative party leader Michael Howard joins former Tory prime ministers John Major and Theresa May in accusing the government of tarnishing Britain's international reputation.

On Saturday, former prime ministers John Major and Tony Blair publish a joint op-ed in *The Times*: 'Last October, the UK concluded an international treaty with the EU for the terms of Brexit. ... Last week, with ... the Brexit negotiations in disarray, the UK government published a bill that it openly admits is a violation of that treaty. ... If parliament passes this bill, the UK will end up before the European Court of Justice.'

Johnson is deliberately trashing Britain's international standing. He looks like a captive of Michael Gove and Dominic Cummings. They propelled him to Downing Street and let him act the part of prime minister so long as he let them run the show.

They're planning to force a no-deal Brexit. Johnson hasn't lost control – he never had it. His government is a disaster. History will damn him as one of Britain's worst prime ministers.

I feel betrayed. How low can they go?

37. Sex, death, and paradise

When the House of Commons debates the UK internal markets bill, Boris Johnson says the EU isn't negotiating in good faith. He says it's even trying to 'blockade' clotted cream imports to Northern Ireland from Devon.

Former Labour leader Ed Miliband speaks for the opposition. He demolishes the government's case and declares: 'The prime minister should be focusing on securing a Brexit deal, not breaking international law and risking no deal. He is cavalier on international law and cavalier on our traditions. This is not the serious leadership we need.'

Boris has no reply. Yet thanks to the merciless application of his party whips, he still wins the division by 77 votes.

Days later, in prime minister's question time, Keir Starmer says the Conservatives are 'reopening old wounds on Brexit' with their bill and says the government should focus on the pandemic.

I see only useless feuding. Johnson should remember Churchill and form a government of national unity.

In her State of the European Union address, Ursula von der Leyen rises above the British mess: 'This is the moment for Europe to lead the way toward a new vitality. … This is our opportunity to make change happen by design.'

But she can't ignore it: 'Negotiations with the UK have not progressed as we would have wished. The withdrawal agreement took three years to negotiate, and we worked relentlessly on it. The result guarantees our citizens' rights, financial interests, the integrity of the single market, and the Good Friday agreement. The agreement has been ratified by both parliaments and cannot be unilaterally changed, disregarded, or disapplied. This a matter of law, trust, and good faith.'

Even US Democratic presidential candidate Joe Biden, who's proud of his Irish ancestry, weighs in: 'Any trade deal between the US and UK must be contingent upon respect for the agreement and preventing the return of a hard border. Period.'

I've lost hope for the Britshow. Johnson is Britain's old-school version of Donald Trump.

The pandemic is still bad news. Scientists fear a second Covid wave is coming. More than eleven million people in England will soon be living under enhanced lockdown measures. Critics say the test-and-trace system is failing.

But Johnson's mind is elsewhere. He's drawing too much fire for his two-fingered salute to international law. It's already offended a US presidential candidate, the European Commission president, five former UK prime ministers, and his party's former leader.

To add to his troubles, Boris is losing weight. And he feels he's underpaid. As prime minister, his income has dropped to less than half of what it was when he was a backbencher in receipt of fat emoluments for his weekly column in the *Telegraph*. Like any hired help, the prime minister is expected to pay taxes and buy his own food, and he still supports four of his children.

Donald Trump is looking worse. Bob Woodward's book *Fear* about Trump's first year or so in office painted a portrait of him that ended with the ringing quote: 'You're a fucking liar.'

Trump chooses to dictate his own version of history to Bob in a series of interviews for the second volume. *Rage* duly opens with a coronavirus briefing in January, where US national security adviser Robert O'Brien tells Trump: 'This will be the biggest national security threat you face in your presidency.'

Trump tells Bob in February that the coronavirus is 'more deadly than even your strenuous flus' and yet: 'I wanted to always play it down. … I don't want to create a panic.'

Months later, Trump hasn't budged: 'I'm comfortable,' he says when Bob asks him about the virus. 'It's gonna go. It's gonna leave. It's gonna be gone. It's gonna be eradicated.'

Woodward ends *Rage* with this clear conclusion: 'Trump is the wrong man for the job.'

Trump has his own take on Bob: 'I love this guy, even though he writes shit about me. That's okay.'

On 24 September, Trump holds a White House press conference where he spouts nonsense about the virus and hints at how he'll subvert American democracy in the presidential election.

The first question goes to *Playboy* reporter Brian Karem: 'Will you commit to make sure there's a peaceful transferral of power after the election?'

'We're going to have to see what happens,' says Trump. 'I've been complaining very strongly about the ballots, and the ballots are a disaster.'

Karem persists: 'Do you commit to make sure that there's a peaceful transferral of power?'

Trump blows it: 'Get rid of the ballots and you'll have a very peaceful – there won't be a transfer, frankly. There will be a continuation. The ballots are out of control. You know it.'

Karem later says he's met killers with more empathy.

On the next day, Trump makes a speech at the United Nations General Assembly to say he's spent trillions boosting US military strength and to boast that the United States is 'by far' the world's most powerful nation.

He then sums up his 'America First' philosophy: 'If you want freedom, take pride in your country. If you want democracy, hold on to your sovereignty. And if you want peace, love your nation. Wise leaders always put the good of their own people and their own country first.'

Days later, *The New York Times* reveals that Trump paid just fifteen hundred dollars in federal income taxes for the years 2016 and 2017 combined. He paid no income taxes at all in ten of the previous fifteen years. He faces hundreds of millions of dollars in debt coming due and faces a long audit battle with the Internal Revenue Service. He's busted.

I admire China. President Xi Jinping delivers a speech to the UN General Assembly on the same day as Trump. Xi is more statesmanlike. He makes three main points.

On Covid, he says: 'We should follow the guidance of science, give full play to the leading role of the WHO, and launch a joint international response to beat this pandemic.'

On the political issue of national sovereignty, he says: 'We should stay true to multilateralism and safeguard the international system with the UN at its core ... we should respect a country's independent choice of development path and model.'

On climate change, he stresses the urgency of the issue and the need for effective global action. He calls on all countries to pursue innovative, coordinated, green, and open development, and he declares that China aims to achieve carbon neutrality by 2060.

I know all this is political boilerplate. But it's also much more. It's performative language, the sort that acts and commits to action simply by virtue of having been spoken. Trump never really grasped that basic political mechanism, with the result that the rubbish he speaks leads to failed and incoherent government action.

The first American presidential debate of 2020 is an ugly farce. Trump repeatedly interrupts Joe Biden, declines to condemn white supremacist groups, and suggests he might not accept the results of the election. CNN correspondent Dana Bash calls it a shitshow.

At one point, Biden responds to a typical Trump tantrum with this cracker: 'Folks, do you have any idea what this clown is doing?'

Trump reserves the right to call the election for himself: 'This is going to be fraud like you've never seen. We might not know for months because these ballots are going to be all over.'

Biden delivers a ringing verdict: 'You are the worst president that America has ever had.'

Then, shortly after midnight on Friday 2 October, Trump tweets that he and Melania have tested positive for Covid-19.

On Saturday, Donald Trump, 74 years old and clinically obese, wakes up in the presidential suite at the Walter Reed medical centre in Bethesda, Maryland.

On Sunday evening, Trump, still sick, rides in an armoured limousine outside the hospital and waves to supporters.

On Monday, he flies back to the White House, climbs to the balcony, raises both his thumbs, peels off his mask, and, breathing heavily, stages a Mussolini moment of boastful rhetoric. Then he unleashes a Blitzkrieg of manic tweets.

On Tuesday, he tweets a video of his sunset return with heroic music: 'We're going back to work. We're gonna be out front. As your leader I had to do that. I knew there's danger to it, but I had to do it … I stood out front. I led.'

On Wednesday, he claims his infection was 'a blessing from God' and gives an interview on the Fox Business channel: 'I'm feeling good, really good, I think perfect.'

I sigh. It's back to the Trump of yore.

———

The 2020 Nobel prize for physics is awarded to three people for their work on black holes. Sir Roger Penrose, Rouse Ball professor emeritus of mathematics at the University of Oxford, is one of them.

I'm delighted for Sir Roger, who seems the very model of a brilliant but absent-minded professor. He wrote a row of books on my shelves, but I feel unable to revisit them until I've escaped the pull of the black hole in Anglo-American politics.

Boris Johnson speaks up at the Conservative party conference: 'I've read a lot of nonsense recently about how my own bout of

Covid has somehow robbed me of my mojo. This is self-evident drivel, the kind of seditious propaganda you would expect from people who don't want this government to succeed.'

Johnson is spoiling for years of rhetorical warfare with the EU. His ministers no longer care whether the UK negotiates a trade deal or defaults to WTO rules, because the economic red ink will be lost in the Covid bloodbath and swirl away unseen in a supermassive fiscal black hole. Johnson will go down the hole too, but not before spouting off a lot more gas about Brussels.

Thoughtful Germans are increasingly inclined to dismiss the Brexit project. It's an attempt to create a state-subsidised chumocracy, not a secret plan for world domination. Boris is spoiling for a punch-up with Europe merely to please English Tory bulldogs.

At the EU summit in Brussels in mid-October, Angela Merkel airs impatience: 'We want an agreement, but of course not at any cost. It has to be a fair agreement from which both sides can profit.'

A Downing Street spokesman fires back: 'The trade talks are over. The EU have effectively ended them yesterday when they said they did not want to change their negotiating position.'

Johnson tries to gloss over his failure: 'They are not willing, unless there's some fundamental change of approach, to offer this country the same terms as Canada. I concluded that we should get ready for the first of January with arrangements that are more like Australia's.'

His reference to Australia here is a euphemism – as all keen students of Foreign Office Newspeak memos recall – for a no-deal Brexit, the worst possible outcome, the Armageddon scenario, where government officials retreat to the nuclear bunker beneath Whitehall to steer the nation through an almighty hammering.

———

October is wet and windy in Dorset. I take time out from my desk to walk on the exposed grassland that runs along the clifftops of the

Jurassic Coast, where a vast seascape stretches southward beside the coastal path. Such communion with the elements is balm to the soul of a seer marooned on an island fortress run by madmen.

Imagine the scene. A lumpy expanse of green sward, dotted with shrubbery and low trees, stretches invitingly westward for miles, from Durlston Castle to the town of Weymouth and beyond. The eastern end was once a training ground and firing range for tanks from Bovington, a few miles inland, but the furrows and craters they left are now reclaimed by grass and shrubs. This is a bleak ersatz for the endless forest paradise I enjoyed so much in Germany, where I could run barefoot for miles and bathe naked in secluded lakes, but it's a lot better than nothing.

For these walks, I park my Volkswagen in Swanage and set off kitted out for a serious hike. My rucksack is a black Berghaus bag, my hat has a wide brim and a chin-cord held with a spring-loaded woggle, my shirt is a red tartan Berghaus design worn over olive cargo shorts, and my all-terrain sandals are made in China.

I first wore a woggle when I was a boy scout back in the days of President John Kennedy. Then it was the little leather loop that fastened the scout neckerchief. That woggle was emblazoned with a gilt fleur-de-lys. I later learned that Lord Baden-Powell wanted a swastika until he was talked out of it.

On one day out striding, I'm transfixed by the sight below me on the sea of a Royal Navy minehunter steaming around on man-oeuvres, looking as cute as the tabletop models I deployed as a boy. It's liaising with inflatable boats containing Special Boat Service commandos from their base in Poole. I see the boats speed alongside a few innocent-looking small craft as if to check them for illegal immigrants trying to sneak into England. It looks like a diorama for the fortress mentality I recall from the movie *Dunkirk* in the scene where the tired and homesick troops in their rescue boat cruise past the white cliffs of Dorset.

Days after this transfixing encounter, the BBC television news is dominated by breathless accounts of how SBS commandos from Poole used their boats plus four navy helicopters to storm the oil tanker *Nave Andromeda* off the Isle of Wight. Nigerian stowaways on board had frightened the crew into hiding in a safe room on the tanker, which was due to arrive at Southampton that morning. But the SBS men boarded the vessel and apprehended the stowaways. I smile to see the Commons defence committee chairman Tobias Ellwood explain that no one was hurt in the operation.

The narrative of an island fortress fighting off foreigners who seek to exploit its generous asylum provisions, its bountiful welfare benefits, its lucrative employment opportunities, its world-beating culture as a soft power superpower, and its brilliantly successful political system is irresistible to a native population beaten down by the real story.

The real story gets worse by the day. On Halloween, Johnson announces a belated second lockdown of England that will last into December. This move leaves businesses already struggling to get ready for the end of the Brexit transition in December with no time at all to prepare for new trading conditions in January – which anyway haven't yet been agreed with Brussels even in principle. It's looking horribly like a self-made Dunkirk catastrophe.

——

In the run-up to the US presidential election, Donald Trump is campaigning furiously in a final burst of manic energy and packing in the crowds at his superspreader events around the country. By contrast, Joe Biden is campaigning in a much duller mode and hardly appearing in public at all. Against all the odds, Trump could win.

Trump seems confident that the 'silent majority' of Americans who voted him to victory in 2016 will rise again, in defiance of the pollsters, and give him another term. I'm eager to hear that silent majority say loud and clear: 'You're fired.'

Voting day comes and goes. Days of uncertainty follow.

Then, early on the morning of Saturday 7 November, Trump tweets that there will be a 'big press conference' at the Four Seasons in Philadelphia.

An hour later, the Four Seasons Hotel Philadelphia tweets: 'To clarify, President Trump's press conference will NOT be held at Four Seasons Hotel Philadelphia. It will be held at Four Seasons Total Landscaping – no relation with the hotel.'

Shortly before ten, Trump amends his tweet to announce the event at Four Seasons Total Landscaping that morning.

It's a magical location. Four Seasons Total Landscaping is on a street in the northeast outskirts of the city, between train tracks and an expressway, that runs up to a correctional centre and down to the docks. The business is next to an adult bookstore selling dildos and across the road from a crematorium.

There, between porn shop and crematorium, the gardening centre hosts a historic press conference. The triad of sex, death, and the promise of a landscaped paradise is only Tennessee Williams away from an older New Orleans where heroine Blanche was told to take a streetcar named Desire, transfer at Cemeteries, and get off at Elysian Fields. The location is made for eternity.

At about midday, on the Four Seasons parking lot, with its broken concrete paving and roller garage doors, President Trump's lawyer, the former New York City mayor and pop-up star of the 2020 *Borat* movie, Rudy Giuliani, holds his press conference in front of a garage door hastily plastered with Trump–Pence signs.

Giuliani is holding the meeting to support Trump's allegations of massive voter fraud in the presidential election. He speaks for Trump: 'He's not going to concede when at least six hundred thousand ballots are in question.'

A reporter says Joe Biden has just been declared the winner.

Giuliani sputters: 'Don't be ridiculous.'

The reporter cites 'the call' on the big TV networks.

Giuliani looks confused: 'The call? Who was it called by?'

The reporter says 'all the networks' have reported the award of Pennsylvania's twenty electoral college votes to Biden.

Giuliani quickly rallies and mocks: 'Oh, my goodness! All the networks.'

Reporters ask him whether he can change the result.

He looks confident: 'Of course!'

The event is the poop end of Trump's presidency. The contrast between the Donald's demiurgic entry into the 2016 campaign, gliding down on a gilded escalator from the heights of Trump Tower in New York, and this farcical meltdown of his 2020 effort is a divinely ordained object lesson in bad karma.

The comic finale causes legions of young Americans to hoot with glee at the ending of a sick joke that's kept them in thrall for four years.

Jersey City boy Kevin says: 'We didn't think it was real. But we realised, oh my God, this isn't a joke … I think this will provide eternal happiness for me when I think about it.'

38. 'The war is over'

Alexander Boris de Pfeffel Johnson loves women. The American tech entrepreneur Jennifer Arcuri had an affair with him from 2012 to 2016, while he was married to Marina Wheeler, his second wife and mother of four of his kids.

Arcuri is more than twenty years younger than the man she called Alexander the Great. She says they first had sex in her London flat just before the 2012 London Paralympics and then met often: 'Boris wanted to drink wine, have sex, and be totally involved in politics.'

It ended badly. She was angered when he failed to defend her going with him at public expense on overseas trade trips. Looking back, she says: 'A great leader is charismatic, courageous and brave. None of these words I would use to describe Boris Johnson.'

A new biography of Johnson by Tom Bower says Boris endured a miserable childhood in a broken home. He says his father Stanley was a feckless, self-obsessed, violent, miserly, alcoholic, wife-beating adulterer. He says his mother Charlotte, Stanley's wife, had a nervous breakdown in 1974 and was admitted to a psychiatric hospital. Boris, then ten years old, was deeply traumatised.

Like Charlotte, Boris Johnson's wife Marina endured much. Boris had earlier enjoyed four years of rumpy pumpy with a female colleague of his on *The Spectator* in a liaison that led to an abortion and a miscarriage. He was thrown out of the shadow cabinet for lying about it. Marina finally filed for divorce after Boris took Carrie Symonds as his mistress.

As with Donald Trump, the damage inflicted by a bad father may help explain the bad behaviour of the son.

I see nothing to admire in the sexual vagrancy of Johnson the son. Winston Churchill remained faithful to his one and only wife for many decades and yet managed to live a full life. My own younger self was a fan of casual sex, to my later embarrassment, until the hard brilliance of a diamond life put me right. I know the temptation and the moral lapse there. Much like the serial sleaze of Trump's pursuit of pussy, the sad mess of Johnson's trail of shags is bad for the state that employs him as leader.

To suggest why, I cite a story from *The New York Times*. Trump's most ardent supporters include young white US males who like guns and form militias, some as Proud Boys. The Proud Boys have a code of honour that includes a ban on masturbation. Proud Boy Aaron from Cleveland says the ban 'does wonders for your determination, energy levels, and productivity' but doesn't make you a misogynist.

I'll just say any sexual activity burns energy and productivity. Johnson and Trump were both goofing off instead of working well. Yet voters seem to relish the juicy spills. They love the rude vitality of their bad-boy leaders.

———

Americans face a reckoning with China, and their coronavirus calamity makes them uneasy about how it might end. But they misunderstand Chinese priorities. The sage Kong Fuzi (Confucius) said three things are needed for government: weapons, food, and trust. A leader should give up weapons first, food next, and trust last. In a world of fake news and truth decay, Johnson and Trump seem to have the opposite priorities.

Johnson's cardinal failure in government is to sacrifice trust. Negotiations with the EU depend on building enough trust to talk in a spirit of fair exchange, but Johnson gives no heed to that.

To underscore the missing ingredient, the young German MEP Theresa Reintke addresses the European parliament in late October with these words: 'Boris Johnson has been lying to the people in the UK. … These lies have to stop.'

She urges him to tell the truth: 'First, Brexit is a mess, second, finding a solution to this mess is not going to be easy for either side, but thirdly, … there are many different levels to how difficult this can become. So, prime minister, stop blaming others for your own actions.'

I'm on her side. No one can trust a liar.

Brexiteers are losing it. Clear proof comes when British trade negotiators announce their very first big post-Brexit trade deal. The glorious deal is with the canny negotiators of Japan.

The deal largely replicates the previous and still extant EU–Japan deal, but it differs in detail, as the Japanese foreign minister explains for his home audience back in Japan: 'We have maintained Japan's high level of access to UK markets … and for some products … we realised improved access.'

Johnson and his underlings are hopeless at negotiating. Their incompetence in the EU trade talks is causing disbelief among business leaders. Johnson is failing them.

The cheerleaders for Brexit Britain have lost the plot. Some of them are pushing the virtues of a notion they call the Microsoft model for the UK in the global market. This means selling British values as an all-in deal with endless ways to upgrade. Buy into the UK and you get a champion of world order plus legal and education services and fintech expertise thrown in – a bargain!

The Brexiteers forget that the moral contortions needed to ram Brexit through wreck any trust a potential customer may have in Britain or its hollowed-out economy. Their buccaneering optimism is as doomed to disappointment as hopes for the climate on Planet Earth if Trump wins a second term.

Microsoft co-founder Bill Gates has just written a book about climate change. After more than a decade studying the topic and investing in the innovations 'we' will need to address it, he proposes a plan for what 'we' will need to do to cut back greenhouse gas emissions. I like his use of the majestic plural for us Earthlings.

By contrast, the Bozza is playing to his home crowd. They're the bullseye for the territorial 'we' he sprinkles in his orations from the dispatch box. But his government is losing goodwill fast. His lazy and careless approach to the job is plain to see.

Sir Ivan Rogers says Johnson is stalling in talks with Europe so that he can opt for no deal if Trump beats Biden in the November election. With a Trump win, Johnson would then make a quick and dirty US trade deal. By contrast, a Biden administration would be a problem, because Biden's advisers see Johnson as scum thrown up by the same populist wave that brought Trump to power.

Then comes good news. Joe Biden is the winner.

Boris is caught off guard. His message of congratulation to Biden is a bodged overwrite of an unused message to Trump. A official tries to explain away the gaffe: 'As you'd expect, two statements were prepared in advance for the outcome of this closely contested election. A technical error meant that parts of the alternative message were embedded in the background of the graphic.'

Biden won't be surprised.

Another good news story offers light at the end of the pandemic tunnel. The pharmaceuticals giant Pfizer in collaboration with a German start-up called BioNTech – founded by a married pair of researchers of Turkish ethnicity – come up with a Covid vaccine based on new mRNA technology that shows ninety percent efficacy in early trials. A mass rollout can start in the new year.

Next, British national politics perks up again.

In late summer, Boris Johnson and his partner Carrie dined at Chequers with a journalist called Allegra Stratton, and Boris urged her to apply for the new job of Downing Street press secretary. Boris then defies the appointment team to get her: 'Forget the process. I'm giving the job to Allegra. I've got to do this because if I don't, Carrie will go fucking crackers about it.'

But the Downing Street director of communications, Lee Cain, is a working-class northerner who doesn't want a posh southerner in his team. He finds Stratton impossible and threatens to resign.

Carrie has Boris by the balls. She's a former head of Conservative party communications in CCHQ and holds strong views of her own. Boris knows appointing Allegra will look like cronyism.

A former cabinet minister puts it politely: 'The prime minister's girlfriend is deciding senior non-ministerial appointments, which I think is without precedent.'

Carrie's influence is unhealthy. One day back in March, when the pandemic was looking scary, she even tried to stop Boris hosting a Covid crisis meeting so that he could help her nix a report in *The Times* claiming she wanted to get rid of their dog.

Dom Cummings told officials to block her calls about the dog. Carrie asked Lee for help, but he was busy. She tried to get the meeting rescheduled, but Dom told Boris to ignore her.

'Carrie fucked the … office up for a whole day,' said an official. 'All over something trivial about her dog. She went bananas.'

On Halloween Saturday, plans for a second national lockdown are leaked to the media before Johnson has even decided on it. He's forced to hastily arrange a televised press briefing that evening to announce the lockdown before the leak becomes a big scandal.

An official says: 'Boris was apocalyptically incandescent.'

Boris suspects his office boys Cain and Cummings are behind the leak. He decides to clean up the office.

On Wednesday, over lunch with Carrie and Allegra, he floats the idea of appointing Cain as chief of staff. They nix it because Cain indulges macho sexism in the office.

A week later, Johnson decides to grill both Cain and Cummings on the leak and to confront them with hostile texts by Vote Leavers, where they call Carrie 'Princess Nut Nut' behind her back.

Boris goes nuts and fires both office boys. Dom holds out until late on Friday the thirteenth, then packs up his things in a cardboard box and strides out of the iconic black front door of Number 10, just in time to be caught on camera for the evening news.

That evening, hours after Dom's big exit, Downing Street staff hear the happy sounds of a victory party from the upstairs flat where Carrie lives with Boris.

The victorious women have a new agenda. Carrie is a green campaigner for the environment, Allegra is a posh girl with a social conscience, and the director of the Number 10 policy unit, Munira Mirza, is a former member of the Revolutionary Communist Party. All three are united against the Vote Leave diehards.

Boris still hasn't doggy-bagged the Brexit turd. He hopes to pivot away from the mess and turn things around before the next election in 2024. He doesn't dare imagine the meltdown he'd get from the coronavirus and a hard Brexit together. He's still peddling cod-Churchillian dreams of sunlit uplands.

Sir John Major airs his disgust at the mess in a speech to lawyers at the Middle Temple on a special day:

'On this day in 1923, Hitler failed to seize power in Germany. In 1938, it marked Kristallnacht and the Nazi assault on Jews. And in 1989, the Berlin Wall fell.'

Warming to his theme, he asserts: 'We are no longer a great power. We will never be so again. … Suddenly, we are no longer an irreplaceable bridge between Europe and America. We are now less relevant to them both.'

He bemoans Brexit in detail: 'There is no consensus on Brexit, and never has been. It was a bitterly divisive policy and uncorked a populism that may be difficult to quell.'

He damns it: 'Emotion overcame reality. And, in the search for hearts and minds and votes, fiction defeated fact and fostered a belief in a past that never was, whilst boosting enthusiasm for a future that may never be. If that mode of politics takes root, it will kill all respect in our system of government.'

His verdict is crushing: 'Brexit is the worst foreign policy decision in my lifetime. I have seen the EU from the inside and know its frustrations. But have no doubt we were better off in than we will be out.'

He begins a litany of betrayals thus: 'Brexit was sold to the nation as a win-win situation. It is not. We were promised we would stay in the single market. We have not. We were told trade with the EU would be frictionless. It will not be.'

Fatal facts. Knockout blows.

On Friday 4 December, the chief negotiators Michel Barnier and David Frost conclude that the conditions for a post-Brexit trade deal have not been met and pause the talks. In their joint statement, they say 'significant divergences' remain.

On Saturday, Ursula von der Leyen and Boris Johnson agree over the phone that their negotiators should risk a 'final throw of the dice' to try to salvage a deal. They issue a joint statement: 'We agreed that the conditions for finalising an agreement are not there due to the remaining significant differences on three critical issues: level playing field, governance and fisheries.'

On Tuesday, the UK government drops its plan to break the law for Brexit. But France is still aggrieved about fishing access and threatens to veto any deal until it's sorted. An EU diplomat explains: 'A bad deal poses fundamental risks to the EU in ten years' time. We are all with the French on this.'

On Wednesday, ahead of an EU summit on Thursday, Merkel tells German parliamentarians that the chief remaining issue for her is that the UK and the EU legal systems will soon diverge.

On Wednesday evening, Johnson dines with Dr von der Leyen at the Berlaymont building in Brussels. Over a fish menu, alongside Frost and Barnier, they have what Ursula later calls 'a lively and interesting discussion' on the state of play. Downing Street calls it 'a frank discussion' and adds that 'very large gaps' remain.

A former MEP with contacts in the Brussels secretariat offers more insight. Boris went in hard during a pre-dinner chat with Ursula, urging her to sideline Barnier, whom he dismissed as an obstacle to a deal, joking that Brits and Germans knew how difficult the French could be. Ursula said Barnier's mandate was solid. She asked Boris if he had any fresh proposals, but no, he had none. After that, the dinner went downhill fast as Boris cracked more jokes. He didn't seem to realise how serious the situation had become.

Perhaps it dawned on him later. He tried to call Merkel and Macron, but they both declined, saying he should talk to President von der Leyen. His divide-and-conquer trickery had failed.

By Sunday, Boris has pledged with Ursula to 'go the extra mile' and extend the talks, but then adds: 'I'm afraid we're still very far apart on some key things … The UK certainly won't be walking away from the talks … But what we can't do is compromise on that fundamental nature of what Brexit is all about.'

On Thursday night, he asks Ursula to drop key demands and complains about the EU pandemic recovery fund. His Downing Street minions say the UK will end all talks after a no-deal exit and go for trade on WTO terms.

Meanwhile, in the European parliament, German Green MEP Theresa Reintke repeats the plain truth: 'The best deal the UK can get, and it will stay that way, is to be part of the European Union, to sit here around the table in Brussels and take decisions together. No matter what happens in the next days, weeks, months, years ahead, our interdependence will always be stronger than Brexit.'

Then, on Saturday 19 December, during a televised Downing Street news conference, Johnson begins to shake his head and stumble over his words: 'It is with a very heavy heart that I must tell you we cannot continue with Christmas as planned.'

He announces tougher coronavirus restrictions to contain a more infectious mutant strain of the virus spreading in southeast

England. Just days ago, in PMQ, he said 'cancellation' of Christmas
was 'inhuman' and mocked Keir Starmer for suggesting it.

The Winter Solstice is a bleak day. The UK goes into inter-
national quarantine to contain the mutant virus. The border with
France is closed and Channel Tunnel services are suspended. Most
European countries announce bans on travellers from Britain.

Health secretary Matt Hancock is candid in a televised interview: 'The new variant is out of control.'

Yet Downing Street remains adamant with its Brexit hard line.
The transition period will end as planned. Even the most loyal Tory
press organs express incredulity at the way things are going.

The Sun is blunt: 'Boris Johnson has made a pig's ear of things
recently.'

Brits face a mutant virus that raises their peril as shockingly as
in a disaster movie. The UK has racked up a thousand deaths from
Covid per million of the population. By contrast, Japan has scored
eighteen deaths per million.

Johnson's government created the conditions for the mutant
strain to appear by mismanaging the pandemic. An earlier lockdown
could have halved the death rate. After its belated lockdown, the
government again failed to do the right thing in time. Brits are now
in quarantine. I'm exiled on Plague Island.

To illustrate Johnson's failure, *The New York Times* reveals how,
when the pandemic took off in March, British officials scrambled to
procure supplies and hurriedly selected companies for thousands of
government contracts. Billions were paid out to companies run by
cronies of Tory politicians or to obviously poor choices.

The government cobbled together its procurement system in
March and appointed the Tory grandee Lord Deighton as its head.
He handed big contracts to companies where he had financial
interests or personal connections. His team abandoned competitive
bidding and hid the details from public view.

In all, the government's pandemic record is disastrous.

But back to the other disaster, the Brexit trade talks. On the evening of the Winter Solstice, Johnson tells the European Commission president that he won't sign the Brexit trade deal.

'I cannot sign this treaty, Ursula,' he says. 'I can't do something that is not in my country's interests.'

Boris cites 'the hammer' that lets Brussels retaliate anywhere if he restricts EU fishing access to British waters.

He explains: 'We can't have this Monty Python situation, where we're trapped in the car with a giant hammer outside the gates to clobber us every time we drive out.'

Ursula pauses and says calmly: 'Okay, thank you, Boris.'

On Wednesday, she calls him to withhold the hammer.

On Wednesday evening, Johnson updates the cabinet. Michael Gove, whose task it is to oversee the no-deal preparations from a Whitehall war room, responds with huge relief: 'Rejoice!'

Early on Christmas Eve, Boris calls Ursula: 'We really need to get this over the line now. We've got to get Frosty and his team home for Christmas.'

Boris then calls Frosty and says: 'Go and close it out.'

Twenty minutes later, Boris calls Ursula: 'Do we have a deal?'

'Yes, we do,' she replies.

The deal is finally secured at lunch time on Christmas Eve.

Minutes later, President von der Leyen announces: 'We have finally found an agreement. … We can finally put Brexit behind us. Europe will be able to move on.'

She adds: 'At the end of successful negotiations I normally feel joy. But today I only feel quiet satisfaction and, frankly speaking, relief. … And to our friends in the United Kingdom, I want to say, parting is such sweet sorrow.'

I do feel sorrow, but it's far from sweet.

She concludes: 'It is time to leave Brexit behind.'

Then Boris Johnson sounds off: 'I am very pleased that this afternoon we have completed the biggest trade deal yet, worth 660 billion pounds – a comprehensive Canada-style free trade deal between the UK and the EU.'

He touts his red lines: 'We have taken back control of our laws and our destiny. We have taken back control of every jot and tittle of our regulation, in a way that is complete and unfettered. … British laws will be made solely by the British parliament, interpreted by UK judges sitting in UK courts, and the jurisdiction of the European Court of Justice will come to an end.'

Senior Conservatives all over the land puff out a sigh of relief when their nemesis Nigel Farage tweets: 'The war is over.'

The prime minister records a Christmas Day video to announce his 'glad tidings of great joy' to TV viewers nationwide before they settle down to hear the Queen's traditional Christmas message.

I'm relieved. I open my *Lord of the Rings* box set and watch its three movies over the three days of Christmas. I've upheld my own festive tradition.

My relief lasts only until I read the pundits in the press the next day. Someone writes: 'This deal is going to hurt. We have lost a continent to gain an empty husk of sovereignty.'

On Monday, EU ambassadors gather to approve the new deal. On Wednesday morning, Ursula signs it. On Wednesday evening, after votes in both houses, Boris signs it. On Thursday morning, less than a day before it's due to come into effect, the Queen gives it her royal assent as the European Union (Future Relationship) Act, 2020.

EUFRA 2020 seals the Tory victory over UKIP.

39. Perfidious Albion

Brexit is done, but its aftermath dominates British life in 2021.

The member of parliament for Poole, Sir Robert Syms, has concerns about the economy. He's pensioned off his Mercedes and now drives an old Volkswagen.

He likes the new EU trade deal: 'This is good news. Many local businesses will be happy … It will be win-win for the UK.'

The Tory member for Bournemouth West, Conor Burns, who resigned as minister in disgrace last year, spent Christmas serving food to the hungry and helping the homeless.

On the trade deal he's bullish: 'This is a personal triumph for the prime minister … It has delivered what we wanted.'

His former assistant Rachel – peace and blessings be upon her – is moving up the party hierarchy. With her irresistible charm, she could go far. I'm forever grateful to her.

Now for the bad news.

The average cost of shipping a lorryload of goods across the Channel rises so much that many hauliers just say no. Euro share trading leaves London and relocates to Amsterdam. Scottish fishermen stop exporting fish to the EU because the new rules hold up their fish for too long to stay fresh.

Exporters across Britain say the new customs systems don't work. Companies need to fill out millions of complicated forms. They'll burn billions of pounds a year on red tape.

The Confederation of British Industry responds to the scenes of devastation with two words: 'Absolute carnage!'

Britain's virus agony is literal carnage. On the eve of Holocaust Memorial Day, a shamefaced Boris Johnson addresses the nation to lament Britain's passing the grim milestone of a hundred thousand officially confirmed Covid deaths.

The year also starts badly in America. On 6 January, President Donald Trump incites a violent mob to storm the Capitol building in Washington. A week later, he's impeached again.

When Joe Biden takes over the presidency, Americans have suffered four times the British Covid death toll, the worst year for lost jobs since World War Two, and the biggest stress test of their democracy since the civil war. It's a disaster zone.

—

I mark the end the Year of the Rat by reading a new book by the political journalist Peter Oborne. He documents 'the new moral barbarism' in British politics.

He says: 'I have never encountered a senior British politician who lies and fabricates so regularly, so shamelessly and so system-atically as Boris Johnson. … Conservative party lies and distortions in the 2019 election were cynical, systematic and prepared in advance. Johnson's Conservatives deliberately set out to lie and cheat their way to victory.'

He sees more: 'At the heart of the new politics is the nightmare assumption that emotion is more important than thought.'

I begin the Year of the Ox by reading the new book by Bill Gates on how to avoid a climate disaster. The six years from 2015 to 2020 were the hottest six on record. The level of carbon dioxide in the atmosphere has reached a record high.

Gates says humans add over fifty billion tons of greenhouse gases to the atmosphere every year, but we need to make that zero: 'If we … make serious plans to achieve that goal, we can avoid a disaster … and preserve the planet for generations to come.'

—

Johnson says Britain has won the jab race with Europe. The EU member nations were slower to vaccinate EU citizens.

The victory is largely thanks to the University of Oxford, where scientists came up with a cheap and robust vaccine in record time.

With German elections in September, the fact that the EU has let the UK win is explosive. German finance minister Olaf Scholz says the EU vaccination strategy is a 'total shitshow' and blames Dr von der Leyen.

Former top Eurocrat Jean-Claude Juncker weighs in: 'Britain took the decision to have an emergency decision-based approach whereas the European Union, the commission and the member states, were more budget conscious … We were too cautious.'

The quick win is catnip for the Brexiteers. Britain has suffered badly in the pandemic, with by far the highest Covid death toll in Europe and the fourth highest death rate per capita in the world. But in the end, they say, going it alone paid off.

Boris Johnson hails the Oxford win as a vindication of Brexit and the bold spirit behind it. I know better.

———

Brits love their royal family. When Prince Philip dies peacefully just months short of his hundredth birthday, the news gets blanket TV coverage for hours and newspaper headlines for days.

Prince Philip came from the Danish royal family and began life in exile in Paris. After an English prep school, he went to a school in Germany, then to the Scottish boarding school Gordonstoun. Prince Charles went to Gordonstoun too and called it Colditz with kilts. But Philip toughed it out. He went through naval college, adopted the surname Mountbatten, and married Elizabeth. Sir John Wheeler-Bennett says he was 'a German Junker' at heart.

British royalty's German connection is as strong as the British aristocracy's deep French connection from the Norman Conquest. If English populists had their way, they'd all be out.

The Queen is worshipped as a totem of God Six. Press barons push her cult to distract the public from the venal working of Her Majesty's government. With a sovereign Queen as top cover, Boris and his gang can get away with murder, or Brexit.

At the European parliament, MEPs ratify the Brexit trade and cooperation agreement. They also pass a resolution calling Brexit a 'historic mistake' by a big majority.

———

Boris Johnson says he'll deliver 'jabs, jabs, jabs and jobs, jobs, jobs' as he hails a Conservative by-election win in Hartlepool. The Tory easily wins a seat that was Labour for over fifty years.

Johnson connects to the man in the street. On his victory lap of Hartlepool, he's greeted by a giant inflatable version of himself. He strides toward it and asks: 'Who's that fat bloke over there?'

Brits love it. His feisty shtick has destroyed the pious preaching of the liberal intelligentsia.

In regional and local elections, Labour wins Wales, Conservatives make big council gains in England, and the SNP wins big in Scotland. Tories do better in the more deprived areas and Labour do well in the more prosperous ones.

Maybe the only way to rescue Britain from the populists is to build a green-goddess socialist intelligentsia.

Brexiteers are doubling down on their folly. Home secretary Priti Patel is hitting EU citizens with a 'hostile environment' policy. Those who visit the UK to secure job offers before going home to apply for a work visa are being stopped, locked up, and expelled. A witless Johnson tells his MPs to 'stick with Pritt'.

Dominic Cummings blogs that Johnson tried in 2020 to stop a leak inquiry because it implicated a friend of Carrie, he tried to get party donors to fund expensive renovations to his Downing Street flat, his dithering led to tens of thousands of excess deaths during the second wave of the pandemic, and his government was far too slow to shut the borders when the pandemic began.

In oral evidence to a Commons select committee, Cummings adds his opinion that Johnson is unfit to be prime minister.

Cummings says he told Johnson: 'This whole system is chaos

… You're more frightened of me having the power to stop the chaos than you are of the chaos.'

He says Johnson replied: 'You're right, I am more frightened of you having the power to stop the chaos. Chaos isn't that bad; chaos means that everyone has to look to me to see who's in charge.'

Boris upstages the media fuss by marrying Carrie in a small ceremony at Westminster Cathedral. Carrie cheers the paparazzi by running around barefoot in an expensively hired boho dress at the garden reception in Downing Street.

———

Days before a big Group of Seven meeting in Cornwall in June, President Biden issues the UK with a formal diplomatic reprimand for imperilling the Northern Ireland peace process.

At the G7, Johnson airs dreams of glory: 'We will relaunch the G7 … We will be joined by our friends, the leaders of India, South Korea, Australia, and South Africa – a Democratic Eleven with the UK a competitive and creative player in the centre of the field.'

He adopts a Churchillian pose: 'President Biden and I will sign a charter that underscores our joint commitment to NATO.'

This is his empty tribute to the Atlantic Charter that Churchill signed with Franklin Roosevelt in August 1941.

But he's derailed at the conference by bruising encounters with Emmanuel Macron, Angela Merkel, and the two EU presidents. Lord Frost, wearing union jack socks, chilled all three meetings.

———

Scientists say July was the hottest month ever recorded.

The Intergovernmental Panel on Climate Change says human activity is heating the biosphere. The temperature rise will exceed two degrees this century unless we make deep reductions in greenhouse gas emissions. The IPCC says our current trajectory will lead to a rise of about three degrees by 2100.

Three degrees means heat no human has yet experienced, with

collapse of the west Antarctic ice sheet, higher sea levels, shrinking rainforest, and thawing permafrost. As white ice melts, solar heating will accelerate. Over a billion people will need air conditioning to survive.

Greta Thunberg adds her gloss in Scandinavian *Vogue*: 'Our relationship with nature is broken. But relationships can change. When we protect nature, we are nature protecting itself.'

———

President Biden decides to end the US presence in Afghanistan by the end of July. The war has cost more than two thousand US lives and more than two trillion dollars.

Weeks before the deadline, the Taliban takes effective control of Afghanistan. Panic spreads, US citizens evacuate, and thousands of Afghans struggle to get places on the last flights out.

In London, shocked MPs in emergency session debate what they can do, aghast that we're surrendering to Islamists.

Johnson admits Britain can't fight on without US support. His Atlantic charter is worthless. His furious MPs see Britain impotent and friendless in a frightening world.

———

British woes ramp up in September. Pubs have no beer, farmers have no workers to pick their fruit, and there's a shortage of lorry drivers to get goods to the shops. All this is down to Brexit, because in his haste to outdo his chum Dave, Boris ended free movement of labour with the continent.

Staff shortages look set to be disastrous for a struggling NHS. The Covid body count worldwide passed ten million in May, and a virulent new delta strain is circulating worldwide.

In her State of the European Union address, Ursula von der Leyen says more than seventy percent of adults in the EU are now fully vaccinated against the coronavirus. She says the EU is sharing half of its vaccine production by giving more than 700 million doses to the rest of the world. Hinting at the jab race, she adds that the pandemic is a marathon, not a sprint.

But Boris is focused on posing as leader of Global Britain. He and President Biden announce a trilateral security partnership with Australia to deploy a new fleet of nuclear-powered submarines in the Indo-Pacific region. They call it AUKUS.

Australians had agreed to buy twelve cheaper subs from France in 2016. But then they decided they wanted something punchier. They put out feelers, and Aussie prime minister Scott Morrison negotiated AUKUS secretly with Biden and Johnson behind closed doors at the G7 summit in June.

France is informed just hours before the pact is announced to the world. The French foreign minister calls it a stab in the back. Others condemn the British opportunism in stealing business from France without regard for grand strategy.

Brexit labour troubles worsen in October. Drivers wait in long lines at petrol stations, fights break out as pumps run dry, soldiers are called out to drive tanker lorries, and food crops rot in the fields, all for lack of workers from the EU.

Inflation is rising fast as well. Energy is more expensive than anywhere else in Europe. Three million households in Britain live in fuel poverty. Yet the government still cuts welfare payments and pushes half a million more people into poverty.

At the Tory party conference, Boris Johnson revels in his pride and joy, 'that vaccine, a UK phenomenon, the magic potion,' then says: 'We are embarking now on a change of direction … We are not going back to the same old broken model, with low wages, low growth, low skills, and low productivity, all of it enabled and assisted by uncontrolled immigration.'

CBI director general Tony Danker responds sourly: 'Ambition on wages without action on investment and productivity is ultimately just a pathway for higher prices.'

ANDY ROSS

Germany is the most successful exporting democracy in the world. Its high wages come from businesses with high productivity, not the other way around.

But Germans no longer trust the British government. They say dealing with Johnson is worse than dealing with Trump.

The new German chancellor, Olaf Scholz, a Social Democrat, plans to revitalise Germany under his 'traffic light' coalition with the Greens and the Free Democrats. He's moving on.

Meanwhile, journalists leak millions of files recording the secret offshore affairs of many hundreds of billionaires, national leaders, and public officials worldwide. The records reveal London as the money laundering capital of the world.

In Westminster, two Commons select committees confirm that the Johnson government's early response to the pandemic was one of the worst public health failures in British history.

A spat with France over Britain's miserly allocation of fishing rights to French trawlers then flares up. The war of words threatens to widen into a cross-channel trade war.

Lord Ricketts, the former UK ambassador to France, says: 'It's a case of total collapse of confidence, after so many cases where the British government hasn't respected its word. The prospect now is of real economic damage and a spiral downwards.'

When dozens of migrants drown in the Channel, Johnson writes a letter to President Macron to air some wild demands for easing the crisis, but then tweets the demands to the world before the letter arrives in Paris. Macron is furious and tells his officials Johnson is a clown and a knucklehead.

—

When Britain hosts the United Nations climate conference COP26 in Glasgow, world leaders share hot air – 'blah, blah, blah' – and endorse only vague commitments. The event leaves our Earth on track for an intolerable 2.4 degrees of warming by century's end.

———

On my birthday, I lunch with my sister Helen. Her husband David died on All Saints Day. At the funeral, as David wished, I deliver a brief lecture on thermodynamics and the conservation of information. At the following reception, held in a clubhouse bar beside a golf course swathed in darkness, I talk with Deb, the beautiful girlfriend from my teenage years, and her husband Colin.

Deb is ageing well and still has a brightly animated spirit. She winds me up to muse at length on the perils and promise of writing books. She loves the idea I might earn millions.

I tell her I'm now a director of a multimillion local company and she responds more warmly. She's a material girl, so I don't tell her I'm an unpaid director. Why spoil it?

At one point, after discussing marriage and relationships, I say: 'I'm used to living alone now. I can endure it.'

'Perhaps you won't need to,' she says, her eyes shining.

As we leave, saying our goodbyes to Helen, Deb leans into me with her head almost on my shoulder. I put a protective arm around her and exult in our togetherness.

It lifts my mood.

———

Back in the Darwinian swamp of Westminster, Boris Johnson bogs himself down in a sleaze scandal that puts his premiership in danger. Polls show the Conservatives running well behind Labour and historic low ratings for Johnson. Another poll shows a big majority of Brits would vote to rejoin the EU.

The next scandal is over government Christmas parties held in 2020 in breach of the lockdown rules. This topic is easy for voters who don't care about politics to understand. It has cut-through, as pundits helpfully explain.

Responding to the virulent omicron strain of the coronavirus, Johnson announces a new package of social restrictions. But his attempt to introduce Covid passes prompts a Commons rebellion by a hundred Tory MPs. His new rules are voted through only with Labour support.

During the last prime minister's questions of the year, a rattled PM goes ape. With his wild mop of hair quivering, his red-rimmed piggy-eyes staring out balefully, and an outthrust finger jabbing and thrusting aggressively, the wounded Boris shouts childish rhyming slogans in response to Sir Keir's coolly lawyerly attacks.

Friday brings a killer blow: A by-election in North Shropshire hands victory to the Lib Dem candidate. The result turns a former massive Tory majority into a solid Lib Dem majority.

It's a resounding thumbs-down on years of Tory misrule.

On Saturday, Lord Frost resigns in disgust.

———

The political circus is too dispiriting. In the dark winter evenings, I find refuge in a series conceived and presented by the charismatic young physics professor Brian Cox. He and the BBC have created an engaging introduction to the physical universe and its evolution from hot Big Bang to a dark and lingering death. Cox even touches the deeper mysteries that make the life of a philosopher worthwhile. My takeaways:

The arrow of time enacts a cosmic Holocaust.

Only logic is eternal.

40. The greased piglet

The New Year break is the calm before the storm. Boris and Carrie Johnson nurse their new baby girl, but there's no sign of relief for the king of Downing Street.

To kick off the first prime minister's question time of the year, the prime minister says: 'I want to apologise … there were things we simply did not get right, and I must take responsibility.'

Sir Keir Starmer replies: 'After months of deceit and deception … Is he now going to do the decent thing and resign?'

Johnson tries to look downcast: 'I accept that we should have done things differently on that evening.'

The evening in question was on 20 May 2020, when England was in full lockdown. Johnson's principal private secretary Martin Reynolds had sent an email to a hundred staff: 'After what has been an incredibly busy period, we thought it would be nice to make the most of the lovely weather and have some socially distanced drinks in the Number 10 garden this evening.'

Tables were set up in the garden for the drinks, and about forty staff members came along. Many of them took up the invitation to 'BYOB' – bring your own booze.

Boris and Carrie were there, enjoying the cheese and wine. An official even joked about being photographed by drones.

Senior civil servant Sue Gray is investigating the events of that evening and other alleged parties and is writing a report. Johnson refuses to say more until he sees it.

Bournemouth East MP Tobias Ellwood is not amused. He says Johnson must 'lead or step aside' and 'show some contrition' to get a grip on the situation.

Bournemouth West MP Conor Burns is undismayed. He says: 'I have absolute confidence and belief in Boris Johnson.'

Poole MP Sir Robert Syms says nothing.

New poll results are revealing. Almost seven out of ten voters think Boris Johnson's apology was insincere. Keir Starmer now has a huge poll lead over Johnson: More than half say Starmer is more trustworthy, and only about one in six say Johnson is. Starmer also has a ten-point lead on who would make the better prime minister. More than six in ten voters say Johnson should resign.

A cabinet minister remarks: 'Number 10 is a fucking mess ... it's a fucking disgrace. Heads have to roll.'

Johnson decides to blame his staff. He dubs the effort to do so Operation Save Big Dog. He calls his plan for a series of distracting policy announcements Operation Red Meat.

An MP says sardonically: 'Boris is preparing to lay down the lives of his staff to save his own.'

Brexiteer Tory MP Andrew Bridgen has decided: 'I don't need to see what Sue Gray says to know that for me Boris Johnson has lost the moral authority to lead the country.'

Then, in a new embarrassment, Number 10 apologises to the Queen for two staff parties held on 16 April 2021, the night before Prince Philip's funeral. They involved about thirty people and later converged in the garden at Downing Street, where they continued past midnight, thanks to a suitcase filled with bottles of wine.

At the time, England was under Covid restrictions that said people could only socialise indoors with those from their household or support bubble. They could only socialise outdoors in groups of up to six people or two households.

Lib Dem leader Sir Ed Davey hits out at the drinker-in-chief: 'While he was enjoying an illegal garden party, others were attending socially distanced funerals. ... The Queen sitting alone, mourning the loss of her husband, was the defining image of lockdown. Now it unites us all in disgust at Boris Johnson and the rotten government he leads.'

Seeing his moment, Dominic Cummings offers his memories. He says he discussed the drinks party on 20 May with Johnson and told him: 'You've got to get a grip on this madhouse.'

When Johnson waved him aside, Cummings told Reynolds the event was in breach of the rules, and Reynolds said he'd check with the prime minister. Dom pronounces his verdict: 'The PM lied to parliament about parties.'

MPs say their inboxes are 'off the scale' with angry complaints from their voters. Constituency activists hope he'll be gone before local elections in May. Members of local party associations find his lax approach to rules indefensible, and councillors who hope to be re-elected are getting anxious.

Poole Conservative Association chair and former mayor Ann Stribley, JP, MBE, laments: 'If he doesn't go soon, we'll lose all the local elections that are coming up, or very many of them, and do immense damage to the party. We've had a number of members saying they can't continue to be members while Boris is there.'

The prime minister's question time on 19 January opens with Conservative red-wall MP Christian Wakeford changing sides to sit with Labour. The whole wall is now at risk.

Sir Keir Starmer accuses the prime minister of 'defending the indefensible' while Labour is working on a plan to help people deal with rising energy prices. He accuses Tory ministers of being 'too distracted by their own chaos' to make a plan.

The session climaxes when former Brexit minister David Davis stands up and calls for Johnson to resign. He gives a cogent reason: 'I expect my leaders to shoulder the responsibility for the actions they take.'

Quoting words originally spoken by Oliver Cromwell, he adds: 'You have sat there too long for all the good you have done. In the name of God, go.'

—

On 25 January, Metropolitan police commissioner Dame Cressida Dick makes a big announcement: 'As a result of the information provided by the Cabinet Office … the Met is now investigating a number of events that took place at Downing Street and Whitehall in the last two years.'

One of the parties was held for Boris Johnson. At an event in Downing Street for his 56th birthday on 19 June 2020, when social gatherings indoors were banned, he was given a cake while about thirty of his staff sang a chorus of *Happy Birthday*. This was minutes before he chaired a Covid strategy meeting.

Another blow comes right away. The counter-fraud minister Lord Agnew of Oulton quits at the dispatch box in the House of Lords, citing the government's 'desperately inadequate' efforts to stop public money being stolen. He cites 'schoolboy errors' such as giving Covid loans to companies that weren't even trading during the pandemic.

He says the Treasury appears to have 'no knowledge or interest in the consequences of fraud to our economy or society' and was 'almost impregnable' to his 'endless exhortations'.

He estimates the total cost of fraud to the taxpayer is 29 billion pounds a year. The Treasury has already written off more than four billion of the almost six billion pounds stolen from its emergency Covid schemes – billions upon billions wasted.

Another blow comes when former transport minister Nusrat Ghani accuses Boris Johnson of not taking her complaints seriously after she told him a whip had told her she was sacked because of her 'Muslimness'. The whip in question swiftly denies the allegation, but Johnson is forced to promise an investigation and denounce Islamophobia on camera.

All this turmoil bothers Sir Robert, who finally comes off the fence to stand against Johnson when he tells a reporter: 'I think the prime minister really ought to consider his position.'

He explains: 'We're going to get paralysis in government for some weeks and months and that's not good for the country. ... Most of us want to just move on and get back to normal politics. We can't do that with him in place.'

It's the birthday party that bothers Conor Burns, who tries to defend his hero: 'It was not a premeditated, organised party. He was, in a sense, ambushed with a cake. They came to his office with a cake, they sang *Happy Birthday*, he was there for ten minutes.'

In a wild bid to rescue his image, Johnson comes out fighting for question time on 26 January. He storms into the chamber and shouts crude abuse at the Labour front bench, backed by a howling chorus of tribal bloodlust from the Tory back benches. This animal house continues for half an hour, with no sign of cool debate. It's primal scream therapy, not politics.

Understandably, many Tory MPs are deeply unhappy at all this. The PM has lost faith in his chief whip, so he sets up three former whips along with his pooper scooper Conor Burns to run a shadow whipping operation.

Behind the scenes, Johnson is in emotional torment, his mood fluctuating wildly. He veers between complacent confidence and a determination to fight on. He fears his magic is gone. A friend says: 'A lot of his trains of thought didn't make a lot of sense. He's quite up and down. He doesn't trust any of his team.'

Johnson telephones his cabinet ministers to complain about his staff. This lifts his mood in time to address a meeting of Tory peers. One of them reports: 'He turned up and was quite dismissive about the inquiry, talking about when all this stuff has blown over. He seemed to think the report would be fine.'

It won't be. Sue Gray is said to be stunned at the chaos and dysfunction she's uncovered.

The muddle begins at the top. Colleagues say Johnson begins his workdays at Number 10 with a meeting in the cabinet room, where he and others discuss the morning newspapers and stories that interest him, but he often lets the sessions lose their focus. He clearly dislikes working through his daily red box of urgent papers and actively resists being managed in meetings.

Conservative local councillors fear the local elections in May will be a catastrophe. Yet most Tory MPs don't share their fear. The next general election is two years away, so if local councillors are mowed down in May the party still has time to topple its tainted king. Anyway, none of the likely replacements as prime minister has a strong enough base in the party yet.

Boris aims to survive by pushing his operations Big Dog and Red Meat. A friend says he'll fight on because he can't bear the thought that his old Etonian rival could boast a longer premiership: 'The prime minister ... wants to outlast Dave.'

Operation Red Meat looks desperate. It starts with a stream of rushed and contentious policy announcements, such as a wild plan to scrap the BBC licence fee in revenge on BBC lefties and a mad scheme to send asylum seekers to Ghana – a suggestion met with a swift rebuttal from Accra.

All this may be too late. A senior Tory says: 'He's a lame duck. It's a question of days and weeks now, not months.'

The Conservative party has lost its soul. There was a time when no Conservative would have dreamed of partying in a government building on the eve of a royal funeral or of passing a death sentence on that quintessentially British institution, the BBC.

Brexit has turned the Tories into revolutionaries. The Brexiteers believed the shock 2016 referendum result made them the anointed instruments of the will of the people. Brexit was a viral meme, and Boris was a superspreader.

Sir Tony Blair – now a Knight of the Garter – wisely says the real problem posed for the nation by Johnson's premiership is the lack of a coherent plan for Britain's future.

No plan, no future. I should have stayed in Germany.

—

Just as Sue Gray is about to publish her report, Scotland Yard asks her not to publish the best bits. She's faced with a choice of either publishing a heavily redacted version with the key details excised or delaying publication until after the police work is done, which may take months.

Former supreme court justice Lord Sumption says the police have no legal right to demand a delay. Others agree. The only legal reason the Met can have for their request is that her report could contaminate witnesses or jurors in a trial. But lockdown breaches result only in fixed penalty notices, which makes them legally about as routine as speeding tickets.

A cabinet minister points out the main outcome of the police request. Johnson is now out of the danger zone and unlikely to face a confidence vote or a leadership contest until the Mets are done. No wonder he suddenly looks cheerier.

David Cameron once likened Boris to a 'greased piglet' for his extraordinary ability to wriggle out of tight scrapes. Well, the piglet is doing it again.

Angry MPs accuse Dame Cressida Dick, Britain's most senior police officer, of playing into Johnson's hands. Dick is married to Helen Ball, who as her assistant commissioner for professionalism is leading the Partygate inquiry. An observer disposed to paranoia might suspect that Dick and Ball have become dupes in a stealth operation to save the PM.

Sir Ed Davey senses the risk: 'A stitch-up between the Met leadership and Number 10 will damage our politics for generations, and it looks like it is happening right in front of our eyes.'

SNP Westminster leader Ian Blackford agrees: 'This does look as if it's a stitch-up, and the only person that benefits from that is Boris Johnson.'

Sue Gray distributes a twelve-page 'update' on her report on Monday morning. Its key findings are simple but damning.

It lists sixteen parties and says Downing Street is under criminal investigation for twelve of them. Gray finds some of the behaviour at these gatherings 'difficult to justify' and notes 'a serious failure to observe ... the high standards expected' that reflects 'failures of leadership and judgment'. She states: 'A number of these gatherings should not have been allowed to take place or to develop in the way that they did.'

The parliamentary transcript *Hansard* records heated words in the Commons on Monday afternoon.

Johnson opens with a statement: 'I am sorry for the things we simply did not get right and sorry for the way this matter has been handled. ... I of course accept Sue Gray's general findings in full ... I get it and I will fix it.'

Keir Starmer responds: 'The prime minister repeatedly assured the House that the guidance was followed ... Now he has finally fallen back on his usual excuse: it's everybody's fault but his.'

Johnson overeggs his response: 'This leader of the opposition, a former director of public prosecutions – although he spent most of his time prosecuting journalists and failing to prosecute Jimmy Savile, as far as I can make out – chose to use this moment continually to prejudge a police inquiry.'

This is an unwise smear. Jimmy Savile was a notorious paedophile, a convicted sex offender who exploited his fame and celebrity to commit numerous loathsome crimes against minors before his death in 2011. As the director of public prosecutions at the time, Starmer was ultimately responsible for the decision not to prosecute Savile, but the full extent of the offending was revealed only four years later. Anyway, the key decision on the case was taken before Starmer was in post. Disgracefully, the PM knows all this.

The Commons session continues.

Ian Blackford fulminates with righteous scorn for the PM: 'He has wilfully misled parliament.'

The Speaker objects to the word 'wilfully' and asks him to withdraw the comment.

Blackford tries again: 'He misled the House.'

The Speaker asks him to withdraw the word 'misled'.

'Mr Speaker, the prime minister has misled the House.'

The Speaker expels Blackford from the House.

Wrong man – he should have expelled Johnson for the Savile smear and for his lies and obfuscations.

When the PM arrives in his Commons office on Wednesday, he pumps his fist in victory and says: 'Come on! Good noise from the colleagues.'

At PMQ that morning, he's boisterous and defiant as he calls Sir Keir Starmer 'a lawyer, not a leader'.

Labour MPs later hit back on Twitter, calling Johnson 'a liar, not a leader' – language banned in the House of Commons.

All this plays out as Russian forces mass on the Ukraine border in apparent preparation for an invasion. US officials say they may be unable to impose effective sanctions on President Putin if he goes ahead because for years the British government has tolerated Russian money laundering in London. State department officials express 'dismay and frustration' at the failure to act.

In late January, to mark the second anniversary of what for me was a tragic event, Her Majesty's government issues a hundred-page document titled *The Benefits of Brexit*.

Johnson says in his foreword: 'Brexit was not an end in itself but the means by which our country will achieve great things. And so that historic night two years ago marked not the final page of the story, but the start of a whole new chapter for our country, our economy and our people.'

After too many mind-numbing details, the conclusion hints at what it all means: 'Looking ahead, we are setting out a clear agenda for changing how we regulate and drive our economy forward … We now have the freedom to be the best regulated economy in the world and to make policy choices that are designed for the UK.'

Taken as a whole, the report misrepresents the consequences of Brexit and inflates the claimed future benefits. It fails to separate changes enabled by Brexit from changes the UK could have made within the EU. It presents as benefits changes that carry costs, such as the return of trade barriers that EU membership had left behind. And it fails to engage with the serious challenges confronting any push for regulatory freedom.

The whole tone of the text is breezily optimistic and fatuously uncritical. It fails to show how the new freedom will deliver any net benefits at all.

Nearly six years on, Her Majesty's government is still echoing the Vote Leave rhetoric of 2016.

On that sad note, the Year of the Ox comes to an end.

———

The Year of the Tiger begins with Dominic Cummings saying that removing Johnson from power is 'an unpleasant but necessary job' and recalling why: 'He sees his job as just to babble to the media every day … He said to me, "I'm the fucking king around here and I'm going to do what I want." That's not okay.'

Johnson's Downing Street policy chief Munira Mirza has been one of his closest colleagues for over ten years. He trusts her and relies on her. She now quits over his ugly attempt to smear Starmer. She writes: 'This was not the usual cut and thrust of politics; it was an inappropriate and partisan reference to a horrendous case of child sex abuse.'

Minutes after she quits, two Downing Street staffers quit too. Hours later, chancellor Rishi Sunak distances himself from Johnson over the smear: 'Being honest, I wouldn't have said it.'

On Friday, health secretary Sajid Javid says he thinks Starmer did a 'good job as director of public prosecutions' and deserves 'absolute respect' for his work in the post.

The cabinet descends into rancour that night. Numerous Tory MPs have now called on Johnson to resign. Once 54 of them hand their letters to the 1922 Committee chair Sir Graham Brady, he's required to call a vote of confidence in the prime minister.

Tobias Ellwood is getting impatient with the chaos: 'This is all going only one way and will invariably slide towards a very ugly place. I believe it's time for the prime minister to … resolve this so the party can get back to governing.'

Ellwood hands his letter to Sir Graham and says: 'I felt it was the right thing to do. Trying to justify the current style of government was untenable. … This is overshadowing and distracting from everything else … The trajectory only heads one way.'

On Johnson, he says: 'His set piece response to the Sue Gray report was to bring up Jimmy Savile, which has gone exactly the wrong way … This is the wrong thing to say at the wrong time.'

He's scathing about Johnson's ability to tackle big international issues. He was aghast when on Monday the PM postponed a call with Putin to give a statement about Partygate: 'You don't put off a phone call with Putin. That's the priority.'

In other news, the queue of trucks waiting for clearance to pass through Dover to France is now longer than the Channel Tunnel. The holdups are due to the extra time British border officials need to check the new paperwork. At the start of January, HM Revenue and Customs launched a new computer system to manage goods moving into or out of UK, but it's glitchy.

In Northern Ireland, a DUP representative in Stormont orders a halt to Brexit checks on food and farm products coming into the province from Great Britain. This will likely trigger a legal conflict with the EU and risk a hardening of the border with the republic.

In consequence, the Northern Ireland first minister and his deputy resign. Northern Ireland now automatically reverts to direct rule from Westminster. All this reawakens the dread spectre of a return to sectarian violence in Ireland.

Yet Johnson is upbeat. On Friday morning, he holds a meeting in the cabinet room for his staffers. Quoting Rafiki, the shaman mandrill in *The Lion King*, he says change is 'good and necessary' even when it's difficult. He gives a pep talk like a rugby captain and urges them to get back on the pitch.

Details of the parties are still coming in. Johnson may have attended six of them, and there may be pictures of him to prove it. If the Mets hit Johnson with a fine, he must face a vote of no confidence.

Even if he survives, the vote will be damaging. After smearing Starmer in parliament, Johnson has put himself on borrowed time, and surviving a vote will give him exactly one year to restore his fortunes. Most observers say he's doomed.

He knew the smear was grossly misleading. But he felt smeared by the party scandal and wanted to hit back, so he said it anyway. When beset by scandal, he says, the best defence is more scandal. Keep on throwing out ever more disgusting poop and let the press report it. Soon everyone will forget how it all began.

The move was classic Trump. And like Trump, he's determined to cling on to power. Number 10 is his last-ditch bunker. A senior adviser reports: 'He's making very clear that they'll have to send a Panzer division to get him out of there.'

But the resignation of Munira Mirza was a big loss for him, as a minister explains: 'If he's lost her, he really is screwed. There really isn't anyone left. It's a bit like losing Carrie.'

Even Carrie may be thinking he should quit. A source explains: 'She was saying she'd had enough a couple of weeks ago. She was telling friends the pressure on her was too much.'

Another source recalls the history here: 'For Boris, Carrie was a fling. He never expected to be with her long term. He was shocked when Marina said she was divorcing him.'

Yet another tries to explain the upshot: 'Boris is trapped in an emotionally disruptive relationship. I think he's definitely scared of her, and I think she dominates him.'

Johnson loyalist Sir Charles Walker, a former vice-chair of the 1922 Committee, offers a more distanced view: 'It's an inevitable tragedy. He's a student of Greek and Roman tragedy. It's going to end in him going.'

———

Boris Johnson has inflicted deep and lasting damage on Britain: Inflation is soaring, the tax burden is rising, fuel prices are surging, the waiting list for NHS operations in England is more than six million, the backlog of criminal court cases exceeds sixty thousand, the social care system is close to collapse, the civil service is broken and demoralised, the union with Scotland is in jeopardy, relations with France and Europe are dire, the pensions system is no longer fit for purpose – it's a shameful rap sheet.

Ever since his student days, Boris has been fascinated by the fall of the Roman Empire: 'When things start to go wrong, they can go wrong at extraordinary speed.'

I smile to read the political obituary that *FT* columnist Simon Kuper writes for the king of Downing Street: 'Johnson's premiership has been largely spent sabotaging his own Brexit agreement with the EU and mismanaging Covid-19.'

The original sin behind all the chaos and failure of the last six years is Brexit. Europhiles like me still recall a judgement made by the former deputy prime minister under Margaret Thatcher and now Conservative grandee Lord Heseltine: 'Without Boris Johnson, David Cameron would have won the referendum.'

———

I take refuge from the winter storm in the parliamentary teacup by reading a good book. Bill Gates has recommended it, and I savour it and enjoy it.

The book is *The Codebreaker* by Walter Isaacson, and it tells the story of Jennifer Doudna, who in 2020 won the Nobel Prize in Chemistry with her former collaborator Emmanuelle Charpentier for their work in developing the CRISPR technique for cutting and pasting genes. The technique is based on a molecular trick evolved by bacteria to fight off viral infections.

The secretary general of the Royal Swedish Academy put it thus: 'This year's prize is about rewriting the code of life. These genetic scissors have taken the life sciences into a new epoch.'

This is what gets me going, not politics. As I've argued already, we're about to see not bare physics but the new life sciences driving human progress in this century. The task of politicians is to smooth our ride by getting out of the way.

Science is our salvation. As Isaacson put it: 'Scientists … say that their main motivation is not money, or even glory, but the chance to unlock the mysteries of nature and use those discoveries to make the world a better place.'

I wish more politicians saw their vocation that way.

I said logic is eternal. Logic is the scaffolding of life. It's life that matters and life that's eternal. Life is a mystery, but its main parts – organisms – are love machines.

This would have been a good place to end.

—

On 24 February, the Russian fascist leader Vladimir Putin launches an all-out military invasion of Ukraine. Within hours, it's clear that this is the worst unprovoked military assault in Europe since the Barbarossa Blitzkrieg of 1941.

The world looks on in horror. A new chapter in world history has begun. People are talking of a third world war.

But the world has changed since 1941. Within days, the global media spotlight on tank attacks and stiff Ukrainian resistance has united world opinion so clearly against Putin that even his Chinese whisperers choose to keep a cautious distance from their erstwhile partner.

His appalling adventure will lead to the ignominious end of the Kremlin kleptocrat. Economic sanctions will effectively cripple his criminal regime. His only escape is to rattle his nukes.

Europe is advancing toward freedom from end to end. But for the rebel regime in London, with its murky Russian connections, the writing is on the wall – or in this book.

The answer

I launched this odyssey with a big question divided into four parts. Let's answer them one by one.

———

What deeper forces led to Brexit?

Some stories for Brexit start with nostalgia for empire and go on to explore the venal workings of an inbred British establishment plotting to avoid new EU tax regulations and turn the UK economy into a tax-haven casino for crooks and chancers worldwide.

Other stories praise Brexit as escape from the belly of the beast. They cast the EU as a new USSR determined to enslave its citizens in a bureaucratic dinosaur.

I suspect the root of the whole Brexit drama is a British fear of being overwhelmed by Germany in a Fourth Reich. Transfixed by empire, fans of Global Britain see one even where it doesn't exist. I say modern Europe has outlived its imperial past.

The British fear is partly a national post-traumatic response to having fought two wars with Germany in the twentieth century. But it's also a fear of having old ways of life and lazy habits of work and thought exposed to the rude forces of a modernising continental culture that threatens change.

Young Brits don't fear such change. I don't either.

———

What horrors has Brexit exposed?

On the European stage, the Brits are now cast as the baddies. This is a tough cookie for Brexiteers to swallow, not least because it cuts across the heroic and self-regarding narrative that lies behind their feelings of patriotism and cultural self-worth. But no plausible narrative for the Brexit adventure that I've encountered casts it in anything but an unforgiving light.

Globalisation is stuttering as political nativism and pandemic lockdowns together disrupt global supply chains and the free movement of people. But the globalisation of science and technology has brought with it new trends in popular cultures and lifestyles that no political upstarts or medical authorities can undo. Planet Earth now hosts a single cultural ecosystem with regional variants.

Within the region of Europe, the Brexit revolution dooms its children to disaster. It overestimates the autonomy and majesty of British life in comparison with that of Europe's shared civilisation. Even the English language is a European mongrel.

German nationalists learned their lesson the hard way. Alongside Russians and Americans, Brits put them right. Now it's the turn of EU citizens to put Brits right.

Let's hope the political revolution we need to restore sanity on the British Isles is less bloody.

———

How can Britain and Europe move on from the mess?

On my reading, Brexit was all about the ring of power. Like the wretch Gollum in *Lord of the Rings*, Brexiteers didn't want to share it. They drew their ring around the British Isles.

I say to them: Loosen the noose and breathe free! Break out of the nationalist straitjacket and smell the wind of change that circles our globe in the age of space tourism and the climate crisis.

Political populism is a scam, a racket for insiders.

———

By what right do I presume to pass judgement on all this?

Well, my work in science and philosophy is my pride and joy, but you can see from this story that – much as I hate to admit it – I'm also a political animal. If this book does what I hope it might, its political impact could help us start a revolution. In this respect, might is right.

———

ANDY ROSS

In the end, this has been a personal story. Europe was the stage for the tortured psychodrama I've narrated with comic grandiosity. I've learned a lot from my ordeal.

Our true home is the surface of our planet, Earth. Europe is a part of the surface distinguished by a strangely blessed culture that hosted Christianity and the rise of science. Within Europe, Britain and Germany have been the twin poles of my zigzag path through our bountifully endowed Garden of Eden.

I've seen the rise and fall of one disfigurement, the Berlin Wall, in my binational life. Now I've watched the growth of another zit, the Brexit pustulence. I hope to live long to enough to witness the erasure of this monstrous carbuncle from the face of Europe.

As for my personal baggage in love and logic, I hope you found it light enough to contemplate with charity.

Thanks

Thank you for reading my story.

The facts in it are reported as reliably and correctly as I can manage. But adding detailed notes and references would make this book too bulky and forbidding. To check an apparent point of fact, you can use Google or follow the notes and links on the blog page for this book:

www.andyross.net/albion.htm

The dialogue scenes are based on conversations in which the exact words went unrecorded, so I've reimagined those exchanges. Also, a few names are fictional, to veil actors who value privacy.

In the interests of full disclosure, the scene set in August 2018, where I told you I met Rachel, miraculously, in Bournemouth and talked about Islam, was fiction. The whole series of Rachel miracles from then on is fictional. And the Karen meeting in Deadbury was fantasy. All that stuff was fake news.

Reading a book on politics and philosophy is hard work. And my tangled tale is at best an elegy for a virtual world. A thread of fiction and fantasy makes the medicine go down. But in the end, truth is stronger than fiction.

I thank Rachel's muse for being such a star. And I thank all the people whose various contributions made up the story. I beg anyone who feels slighted to forgive my impertinence.

Andy Ross
February 2022

Printed in Great Britain
by Amazon

77585180R00254